SURVIVAL I V

1970s Britain
& the television series

edited by Rodney Marshall

© Copyright 2023 Rodney Marshall, *Out There Publications*
© Cover artwork Jaz Wiseman 2023
(Essays are individually owned by specific writers as indicated in the text)

ACKNOWLEDGEMENTS

In 2021 I put together a collaborative book about British television in the 1960s, exploring how TV was both reflecting society and – at times – helping to shape or influence popular culture. I chose to limit *Swinging TV* to a single genre, the contemporary 'action-adventure' series. Pre-dating the 007 franchise, *Danger Man* had inspired a decade of exciting espionage entertainment and escapism; the genre seemed the perfect match for the decade itself. Individual writers explored series through a particular angle or theme: The Establishment, cars, set design, music, fashion, gender, technology & science, the Cold War, etc.

The overriding aim of this new book, *Survival TV*, is similar in the sense of wanting to place television series within their cultural context. The main difference to its 'predecessor' is that here I offered each contributor a wide field in terms of genre: sci-fi, cop shows, political drama, sitcoms, period drama, anthology series, action-adventure, children's drama, even US imports. Some have chosen to explore a single series, or the impact of a specific writer, while others have assembled more general essays, or compared and contrasted two shows. In each case, 70s British culture and society is the contextual glue.

My sincere thanks go to every one of the writers who has contributed: JZ Ferguson, Michael Herbert, Trevor Knight, Mike Pegler, Andrew Roberts, Al Samujh, Stu Sterling, Darren Flower, and Cailin Thomas. I hope that by the time you have finished reading *Survival TV* you will agree that there is some fascinating material here. In addition, the book is a celebration of the 1970s televisual world, a genuine 'Golden Age' in which colour came to an increasing number of households and the three TV channels offered up an impressive range of iconic series which millions of people shared, in what was, in most other respects, a deeply divisive decade.

Finally, a thank you to Jaz Wiseman, who created the striking cover. In his own words: 'The background is a 70s test card - the broken tv set sums up the 70s depression, the circle design is synonymous with underground 70s punk, the *Survival TV* font is like the TV series'.

Rodney Marshall
Suffolk, UK, January 2023

PREFACE: DESPAIR AND HOPE

'It was the best of times, it was the worst of times, it was the age of wisdom, it was the age of foolishness, it was the epoch of belief, it was the epoch of incredulity, it was the season of light, it was the season of darkness, it was the spring of hope, it was the winter of despair.' (*A Tale of Two Cities*)

As any social historian is keen to observe, we tend to reconstruct and make sense of the past by dividing it up into artificial chunks, be it centuries or decades. Those decades then become synonymous with an overriding 'feel'. Britain in the 1950s, for example, is often seen as an austere post-war grey world in which cities were slowly being rebuilt and where rationing was still part of daily life until mid-1954. Mention the 1960s, and one immediately thinks of economic boom and a thriving popular culture – of music, fashion, photography, television action-adventure – which attracted global interest. Naturally, the social picture of both decades is far more complicated and nuanced than that. Nor does a decade exist in isolation from what came before or what immediately follows. Nothing radical happened at midnight on the 31st December 1969, for example. As Dominic Sandbrook notes, 'In many ways this habit of giving decades different historical personalities is a bit of a gimmick, a quirk of the calendar, that distorts the way we remember the recent past.' [1] Yet, Britain in the 1970s conjures up a grim, bleak picture for so many. Admittedly, this is hardly surprising. In many respects it is remembered for economic decline, unemployment, financial crises, strikes which led to a succession of State of Emergency situations. Some of those strikes left people literally in the dark, resulted in rubbish building up on the streets, panic buying in the shops, commercial television off-air for nearly three months, *The Times* newspaper disappearing for almost a year, even bodies left unburied. Until a deal was done with the IMF, the nation was on the point of a bankruptcy which the rest of the developed world frequently commented upon.

On the streets of Belfast, it was a decade of almost unimaginable violence and chaos, while Mainland bombings and assassinations brought fear, panic, and politically motivated murder to London and elsewhere. The Notting Hill carnival riots highlighted issues of integration, immigration and inherent racism. The 1970s saw a student killed at a demonstration, another murdered in a football ground. If the newspapers were to be believed, a knife-wielding skinhead, football hooligan or mugger could be lurking around any street corner. In 1971, Home Office figures indicated that violent crime was, indeed, increasing by an alarming rate.

Edward Heath's vision of 'One Nation' seems ironic given the crisis of identity in Britain in the 1970s. The subject of national identity was frequently discussed as Britain joined the Common Market, both Wales and Scotland had referendums about devolution and the British Government constantly debated what to do about Northern Ireland as civil war in Belfast became a distinct possibility. Extremism seemed to be the order of the day, from Enoch Powell and the National Front through to the revelation that Communists were seeking to infiltrate the Labour Party, just as they had the trade unions.

However, just as the 1960s are often seen through rose-tinted glasses, the 1970s are frequently viewed through depressingly dark ones. In many respects, it was a decade which brought positive cultural change. The large numbers of people who turned out for the 'Rock Against Racism' march and concert in April 1978 reflected the fact that increasing numbers of people welcomed social change and diversity. It was the 1970s – not the 1960s – which saw huge advances in both the Feminist and Gay Liberation movements. On one level, this took the form of ground-breaking publications such as *Spare Rib*, *Gay News* and the founding of the Virago Press. In more practical terms, legislation began to tackle both equal pay and domestic violence, the first Women's Aid refuges and Rape Crisis Centres were established, while the 'Reclaim the Nights' marches demonstrated the public's demand for radical change, including the police's (perceived) attitude. The much-publicised infiltration of the

Miss World contest by feminists and GLF members was a visible reminder that, increasingly, marginalised people were willing to demonstrate for their rights. The relative failure of extremist political groups to capture the public's imagination suggests that most people did not share either the skinhead mantra that 'there's no black in the Union Jack' or Mary Whitehouse's belief that homosexuality was a sin. The 1970s was also an important decade for the ecology movement, from the founding of the Ecology Party itself, to a more general interest in nature, the environment and green issues, reflected in both adult and children's television drama.

One of the dangers of breaking social history up into neat decade-long chunks is that we can easily forget how the past impinges on the present day. With the benefit of hindsight, we can say that many of the 1970s social issues highlighted by commentators were a result of mistakes made in the late-1950s and 1960s. For example, by 1970, 1.5 million Brits were stuck in post-war tower blocks, many of them shoddily-built in isolated locations far from amenities. While initially some people understandably greeted these 'streets in the sky' as a radical improvement, the buildings were often poorly maintained and rapidly deteriorated. The result was frequently what Dominic Sandbrook calls a 'brutal concrete reality' [2] which often brought with it intimidation, violence, vandalism, litter, graffiti, and social isolation. The high-rise 'utopian' vision of architects could rapidly become a grim real-life dystopia.

The 1970s is often considered to represent the 'Golden Age' of British television, from chat shows, hard-hitting police procedurals, children's series, dystopian science fiction, through to the wide variety of sitcoms. These shows were not created in cultural vacuums. They both reflected and engaged with the 70s zeitgeist. In terms of the sitcom, despite the simplistic dismissal of the genre as reflecting middle-class suburbia, many of the series explored genuine concerns. Wendy Craig's housewife, Ria Parkinson, in *Butterflies* (1978-83), for example, takes us far beyond the traditional, comforting limitations of the family sitcom in a series which explores the frustrations of domesticity, midlife crises, drugs, and teenage pregnancy amongst other subjects. Series as different as *Whatever Happened to the Likely Lads?* (1973-74) and *Fawlty Towers* (1975 & 1979) both explore class conflict in a changing world.

The variety of series offered in the ever-expanding 'children's TV' slot – itself a controversial subject – provided older ones with a rich menu of fantasy, sci-fi, dystopia and social realism which increasingly refused to talk down to its viewers, from the atmospheric and sinister *Changes* (1975) and *Children of the Stones* (1977) to the hard-hitting *Grange Hill* (1978-). In the case of *Blake's 7* (1978-81) one could argue that it blurred the boundaries between teenage and adult television.

The 70s was a memorable decade for the historical costume drama, with LWT's *Upstairs, Downstairs* (1971-72), *The Onedin Line* (1971-80) and *Colditz* (1972-74) all leaving a lasting impression. The fact that the BBC had been willing to join forces with Universal Studios to make the highly acclaimed *Colditz* suggests that 'Auntie' was modernising its approach or attitude to television drama.

Several adult series explored topics such as environmental disasters and state surveillance in chillingly realistic fashion. The semi-fantastic action-adventure series, as a broad generalisation, reached its endgame with *The Persuaders!* (1971-72) and *Jason King* (1971-72), even if both *The New Avengers* (1976-77) and *Return of the Saint* (1978-79) tried to revive and update the two most successful 60s versions. (In the case of *The New Avengers*, which features heavily in this book, perhaps it should be re-evaluated in its own right, as a mid-1970s show, rather than as a postscript to a 60s series.) While several earlier police procedurals (including *Z-Cars* and *Gideon's Way*) had, arguably, taken us far beyond the cosy world of *Dixon of Dock Green*, the popular genre was about to be rudely gate-crashed. *The Sweeney* (1974-78) is, arguably, the television drama series most closely associated with the 1970s, both in terms of the methods used to shoot it and its daring mix of violence, strong language, and humour. It provided the 'shock of the new'. Its viewing figures, which peaked at almost twenty million, demonstrate the pull which television drama could have in an age where almost every household had a television, increasing numbers were 'investing' in a colour set, while the era of the VCR, or videocassette recorder – still in its infancy – would soon have a dramatic effect on TV culture. Times were changing in the television world, as in the real one. [3]

© Rodney Marshall

1. Dominic Sandbrook, 'Why does the 1970s get painted as such a bad decade?' BBC online, 16/04, 2012
2. Dominic Sandbrook, 'The Green Death', *State of Emergency*, p. 189. In fairness, as the *Guardian*'s 2015 article about Glasgow's now demolished Red Road flats illustrates, for some residents the high-rise housing did, initially, offer a far better alternative to the overcrowded, squalid slums that they had been living in, in places like the Gorbals. It was, arguably, the buildings themselves and their locations which were deeply flawed, rather than the initial concept.
3. The genuine sense of television in the 1970s as a shared national experience is clearly badly eroded today, with so many choices, in terms of both the channels available and a multitude of ways for viewing any show. Arguably it has been partly replaced by a sense of a global audience/market. Even the television/cinema polarity has been partly undermined, with many new films immediately available on streaming platforms.

'Britain is an armchair nation. Nine out of ten of us watch television as our main leisure pursuit.'
(***The Guardian***, April 6th, 1976)

'More than other institutions, it was the BBC and ITV that defined and disseminated the national experience in the 1970s.'
(**Dominic Sandbrook**, 'A Better Tomorrow', *State of Emergency*, p. 46)

Sir Timothy Hobson: But we *are* living in a transitional period.
Sir Michael Dace: Of course, but aren't all periods transitional between one thing and another?
(*This is Quarmby*, The Guardians, 1971)

'The 1970s are almost universally regarded as the high point of British television'
(**Dominic Sandbrook**, 'A Better Tomorrow', *State of Emergency*, pp. 46-47)

Mr. Hamilton: What the hell's wrong with this country? You can't get a drink after three, you can't eat after nine, is the war still on? (*Waldorf Salad*, *Fawlty Towers*)

Philip Carter: I want us out of this Dark Age.
(*Whatever Happened to Cardinal Wolsey?, 1990*)

'You could watch certain television shows in the knowledge that almost half the nation was sharing the same experience, at the same moment. In the case of something like the *Morecambe & Wise Show*, it provided social 'glue' at a time of deep division.'
(Rodney Marshall)

1970s TIMELINE

1970 *The Six Wives of Henry VIII* plays begin transmission (Jan 1st)
1970 *Spearhead from Space* (*Doctor Who*) begins (January 3rd)
1970 *The Silurians* (*Doctor Who*) begins (January 31st)
1970 *Doomwatch* first broadcast (February 9th)
1970 *Catweazle* first broadcast (February 15th)
1970 First National Women's Conference held (February)
1970 *Ambassadors of Death* (*Doctor Who*) begins (March 21st)
1970 Plans unveiled for Milton Keynes, a 'city of the future' (March)
1970 Skinhead attacks on Asian residents in Brick Lane (April)
1970 *Inferno* (*Doctor Who*) begins (May 9th)
1970 Equal Pay Act (May 29th)
1970 The Kinks' *Lola* is released (June 12th)
1970 *In the Summertime* reaches Number 1 (June 13th)
1970 *Shadows of Fear* pilot is broadcast (June 17th)
1970 Edward Heath becomes UK Prime Minister (June 19th)
1970 PM tells House of Commons Britain will become 'one nation'
1970 Two-day curfew begins on Falls Road, Belfast (July 3rd)
1970 Environmental journal *The Ecologist* first published (July)
1970 *The Wonder of You* reaches Number 1 (August 1st)
1970 *UFO* series first broadcast (September 16th)
1970 Science fiction series *Timeslip* starts (September 28th)
1970 First meeting of UK Gay Liberation Front at LSE (October 13th)
1970 *The Female Eunuch* is published (October)
1970 Protestors interrupt Miss World contest, Albert Hall (Nov 20th)
1970 Council workers' strike (October and November)
1970 Power strike leads to electricity cuts (December)
1970 State of Emergency declared (December 12th)
1970 *The Railway Children* film released in UK (December 21st)
1970 *The Doomsday Book: Can the World Survive*? published
1970 1st part of post-apocalyptic *Sword of the Spirits* published
1970 Budget introduces admission charges for museums & galleries
1970 Eric Morecambe & Ernie Wise win their first BAFTA TV awards

1970 Cambridge Science Park is founded
1970 FPA instructs clinics to make the Pill available to single women
1970 *World in Action* investigates Drug Squad corruption
1971 Child Poverty Action Group: 1m children living in poverty
1971 *Terror of the Autons* (*Doctor Who*) begins (January 2nd)
1971 66 die in Ibrox stadium stairway crush (January 2nd)
1971 *Six Dates with Barker* begins broadcast (January 8th)
1971 *Look-in* magazine first published (January 9th)
1971 *The Mind of Evil* (*Doctor Who*) begins (January 30th)
1971 First students enrolled at the Open University (January)
1971 Lord Wilberforce hands power workers c. 15% pay increase
1971 *Bless This House* first broadcast (February 2nd)
1971 Rolls Royce calls in receivers (February 4th)
1971 First British soldier killed in Northern Ireland (February 6th)
1971 Decimal Day (February 15th)
1971 *Mr Benn* first broadcast (February 25th)
1971 Report highlights housing discrimination re. immigrants (Feb)
1971 3 Royal Highland Fusiliers murdered in Belfast (March 10th)
1971 *Get Carter* first released in the UK (March 10th)
1971 *The Claws of Axos* (*Doctor Who*) begins (March 13th)
1971 Third reading of the Industrial Relations Act (March 24th)
1971 First International Women's Day rally in London (March)
1971 Unemployment rises to 800,000 (April)
1971 Ford hands workers 33% deal after two-month strike (April)
1971 *The Two Ronnies* comedy sketch show first aired (April 10th)
1971 Sex education film *Growing Up* causes controversy (April 16th)
1971 UCS Clydeside shipbuilders march on Downing Street (June)
1971 *Sunday, Bloody Sunday* released (July 1st)
1971 *The Guardians* first broadcast (July 10th)
1971 *The Devils* released (July 16th)
1971 T. Rex's *Get It On* reaches Number 1 (July 24th)
1971 Internment of terrorist suspects introduced in NI (August)
1971 Unemployment rises to 900,000 (August)
1971 Nationwide Festival of Light interrupted by GLF (September)
1971 *Jason King* first broadcast (September 15th)
1971 *The Persuaders!* first broadcast (September 17th)

1971 *The Rivals of Sherlock Holmes* debuts (September 20th)
1971 Fleet Street pay disputes see newspapers fail to appear (Sept)
1971 *The Generation Game* first broadcast (October 2nd)
1971 *Upstairs, Downstairs* first broadcast (October 10th)
1971 *The Onedin Line* first broadcast (October 15th)
1971 *Sunday Times* investigates torture of internees in NI (Oct 17th)
1971 Immigration Act passed to end mass immigration (October)
1971 *Straw Dogs* released (November)
1971 20,000 London march; unemployment approaches 1m (Nov)
1971 Two police officers sentenced for assaulting an immigrant
1971 *Carry On at Your Convenience* released (December 10th)
1971 *Ernie* reaches Number 1 (December 11th)
1971 *A Clockwork Orange* released in the US (December 19th)
1971 Erin Pizzey founds Chiswick Women's Aid refuge
1971 4 million foreign holidays taken; it will be 13m a decade later
1971 Home Office statistic: 62% rise in violent crime in past 4 years
1971 London Feminist Groups rise from 7 to 56 in 2 years
1971 Delia Smith publishes *How to Cheat at Cooking*
1971 47% of married women in work
1971 42 British soldiers shot dead by IRA snipers in calendar year
1972 1.5 million colour TV sets in the UK
1972 *Day of the Daleks* (*Doctor Who*) begins (January 1st)
1972 Sci-fi serial *Mandog* debuts (January 3rd)
1972 BBC1 broadcasts *The Question of Ulster* debate (January 5th)
1972 NUM strike (January 8th)
1972 BBC *The British Empire* series offers a critical view (Jan 11th)
1972 Unemployment tops 1m mark; PM's Questions suspended
1972 Ziggy Stardust Tour commences, in Aylesbury (January 29th)
1972 *The Curse of Peladon* (*Doctor Who*) begins (January 29th)
1972 Bloody Sunday, 26 unarmed civilians killed by soldiers (Jan)
1972 British Embassy, Dublin, burnt to ground by protestors (Feb)
1972 Power cuts and strikes; warning that 'Full Blackout' looms
1972 British Government give in to NUM demands (February 19th)
1972 Car bomb at Aldershot barracks kills seven staff (Feb 22nd)
1972 Wings single *Give Ireland Back to the Irish* (February 25th)
1972 *The Sea Devils* (*Doctor Who*) begins (February 26th)

1972 Deposit of Poisonous Waste Act
1972 *The Brothers* first broadcast (March 10th)
1972 British Government imposes direct rule In NI (March 24th)
1972 The Limits to Growth report published (March)
1972 *The Mutants* (*Doctor Who*) begins (April 8th)
1972 *Love Thy Neighbour* first broadcast (April 13th)
1972 *The Time Monster* (*Doctor Who*) begins (May 20th)
1972 Lennon/Ono *Sunday Bloody Sunday* released in US (June 12th)
1972 *Frenzy* released (June 21st)
1972 Feminist magazine *Spare Rib* first published (June)
1972 Bloody Friday sees 22 bombs set off in Belfast (June 21st)
1972 *Gay News* first published (June)
1972 Poulson fraud/bribery reveal redevelopment corruption (July)
1972 State of Emergency declared amidst dock strike (July)
1972 *The Harder They Come* helps introduce reggae to UK
1972 Idi Amin (Uganda) expels 60,000 Asians with UK passports
1972 First out-of-town hypermarket in the UK opens (September)
1972 *Colditz* first broadcast (October 19th)
1972 M15 warn Harold Wilson about friends' KGB connections (Oct)
1972 Brutalist Stock Exchange Tower officially opened (Nov 8th)
1972 *Watership Down* is published (November)
1972 *Carry On Abroad* released (December 15th)
1972 Publication of Paul Ferris' *The New Militants*
1972 Publication of *The Joy of Sex: A Gourmet Guide to Love Making*
1972 Tutankhamun exhibition, British Museum attracts 1.7 million
1972 Local Government Act 'modernises' old counties system
1972 Conservationist John Betjeman appointed Poet Laureate
1972 Enoch Powell voted 'Man of the Year', twice, in BBC poll
1972 58 black and Asian police officers out of 110,000
1972 64 British soldiers shot dead by IRA snipers in calendar year
1972 Rugby Union's Five Nations abandoned due to fears about IRA
1973 Britain's formal accession to European Economic Community
1973 SNP 'It's Scotland's Oil' slogan (January)
1973 *Whatever Happened to the Likely Lads?* broadcast (Jan 9th)
1973 'Fanfare for Europe' festival held in UK (January)
1973 Folk-rock band Strawbs reach No. 2, *Part of the Union* (Feb)

1973 *The Wombles* first broadcast (February 5th)
1973 *Frontier in Space* (*Doctor Who*) begins (February 24th)
1973 Betjeman's *Metro-Land* documentary broadcast (Feb 26th)
1973 *The Dark Side of the Moon* released (March 1st)
1973 Rioting on a Belfast estate sees British troops sent in (March)
1973 Government announces plan to build Channel Tunnel (March)
1973 Old Bailey and Ministry of Agriculture bombings (March 8th)
1973 *Seven of One* begins broadcast (March 25th)
1973 Stock Exchange elects first women members (March)
1973 The pilot episode of *Porridge* is broadcast (April 1st)
1973 Bob Marley's *Catch A Fire* released (April 13th)
1973 *Thriller* series begins broadcast (April 14th)
1973 *The Tomorrow People* first broadcast (April 30th)
1973 *The Green Death* (*Doctor Who*) begins (May 19th)
1973 *Tubular Bells* album released (May 25th)
1973 *O Lucky Man!* released (June 20th)
1973 *A Touch of Class* released (June 20th)
1973 *Man About The House* first broadcast (August 15th)
1973 Science fiction *Moonbase 3* debuts (September 9th)
1973 Kings Cross and Euston station bombings (September 10th)
1973 *Eye Level* reaches Number 1 (September 29th)
1973 Big Biba Kensington department store opens (September)
1973 *Don't Look Now* released (October 16th)
1973 *Carry on Girls* released (November 9th)
1973 Government announce 5th State of Emergency (Nov 13th)
1973 Banking crisis in the UK (November 31s)
1973 *The Time Warrior* introduces Sarah Jane Smith (Dec 15th)
1973 *The Party* opens at the National Theatre (December)
1973 Oil crisis as OPEC raise prices from $2.40 to $11.65 a barrel
1973 D of E highlights health problems of living in tower blocks
1973 Publication of anti-modernist *Small is Beautiful* essays
1973 Property prices rise 70% in two years
1973 *The Norman Conquests* trilogy opens in Scarborough
1973 *Carrie's War* published
1973 Virago founded, to publish new & out-of-print women's books
1973 Unemployment drops from 1m to 500,000 in 18 months

1973 250 new companies in Aberdeen ('Tartan Texas')
1974 In UK, there are still twice as many b/w TV sets as colour ones
1974 Three-Day Week introduced to conserve energy (January 1st)
1974 ITV launch *Wish You Were Here* (January 7th)
1974 *Invasion of the Dinosaurs* (*Doctor Who*) begins (January 12th)
1974 *The Pallisers* first broadcast (January 19th)
1974 *Tiger Feet* by Mud reaches Number 1 (January 26th)
1974 Edward Heath calls a General Election (February 7th)
1974 *Bagpuss* first broadcast (February 12th)
1974 Turkish Airlines flight to London crash, killing all 346 (Mar 3rd)
1974 Harold Wilson becomes PM for a second time (March 4th)
1974 Abba win Eurovision, Brighton Dome with *Waterloo* (April 6th)
1974 *Mirror* publishes 'League of Violence' of football hooliganism
1974 *Happy Ever After* (May 7th)
1974 UVF bombings in Dublin kill 26 civilians (May 17th)
1974 Student killed at anti-National Front demonstration (June 15th)
1974 House of Commons bombing (June 17th)
1974 *Tinker Tailor Soldier Spy* published (June)
1974 Tower of London bombing (July 17th)
1974 *Peace News* publishes GB75 private army plans (August)
1974 Far-right group Civil Assistance claim 100,000 members (Aug)
1974 US President Nixon resigns after Watergate scandal (Aug 9th)
1974 First murder at an English football match (August 24th)
1974 Police close Free Festival in Windsor, arresting 220 (Aug)
1974 *Rising Damp* first broadcast (September 2nd)
1974 Guildford pub bombings (October 5th)
1974 Harold Wilson wins 'snap election'
1974 *Times* reports on 'sorry state' of London's West End (Oct 16th)
1974 *Confessions of a Window Cleaner* is released (November 8th)
1974 McDonalds opens its first UK 'restaurant' (November 13th)
1974 Birmingham pub bombings (November 21st)
1974 Peter Hall's *Akenfield* film is released
1974 James Herbert's *The Rats* published
1974 Publication of dystopian *Concrete Island*
1974 Publication of *Scream Quietly or the Neighbours Will Hear*
1974 Publication of *Housewife* and *The Sociology of Housework*

1974 *Memoirs of a Survivor* published
1974 'Bubblegum pop' Wombles most successful band of year
1975 *The Sweeney* first broadcast (January 2nd)
1975 *The Changes* first broadcast (January 6th)
1975 Margaret Thatcher becomes Leader of Opposition (Feb 11th)
1975 Moorgate Tube crash kills 43 people (February 28th)
1975 Rollermania as *Bye Bye Baby* reaches Number 1 (March 22nd)
1975 *Sky* first broadcast (April 7th)
1975 *The Good Life* begins (April 4th)
1975 *Survivors* first broadcast (April 16th)
1975 European Community (Common Market) Referendum (June)
1975 *Jaws* first released in the US (June 20th)
1975 *Times* reports Elton John had sold 75m records (June 21st)
1975 Report shows 41% of sales in UK are foreign cars (August 14th)
1975 *Teeth 'n' Smiles* opens at the Royal Court (September 2nd)
1975 *Shadows* is first broadcast (September 3rd)
1975 *The Machine Gunners* published (September 18th)
1975 *Fawlty Towers* first broadcast (September 19th)
1975 *Time* magazine hails North Sea oil as 'national survival' (Sept)
1975 *Space Oddity* reaches Number 1 (November 8th)
1975 Ross McWhirter politically assassinated (November 27th)
1975 *Bohemian Rhapsody* reaches Number 1 (November 29th)
1975 *The Naked Civil Servant* broadcast (December 17th)
1975 UK population falls for first recorded time as 269,000 emigrate
1975 James Herbert's *The Fog* published
1975 Publication of dystopian novel *High-Rise*
1975 Publication of *Blott on the Landscape*
1975 Underhill Report: Militant aims to infiltrate Labour Party
1975 *The History Man* is published
1975 National Trust membership tops 500,000
1975 Ecology Party formed, forerunners of Green Party
1975 Monthly readership of UK's leading porn magazines tops 5m
1975 Unemployment among immigrants twice the national average
1976 Historical fantasy *The Georgian House* debuts (January 2nd)
1976 *Bouquet of Barbed Wire* first broadcast (January 9th)
1976 *The Seeds of Doom* (*Doctor Who*) begins (January 31st)

1976 James Callaghan becomes PM after Wilson retires (April 5th)
1976 Long-running *Dixon of Dock Green* ends (May 1st)
1976 *Logan's Run* released in the US (June 23rd)
1976 *Weapons of Happiness* opens at National Theatre (July 14th)
1976 Riots at the Notting Hill Carnival (August)
1976 *The Duchess of Duke Street* first broadcast (September 4th)
1976 *George and Mildred* first broadcast (September 6th)
1976 *The Fall and Rise of Reginald Perrin* first broadcast (Sept 8th)
1976 *Dancing Queen* reaches Number 1 (September 4th)
1976 *Gangsters* first broadcast (September 9th)
1976 *Pressure* released, 1st feature-length Black British film (Oct)
1976 *The New Avengers* first broadcast (October 22nd)
1976 Domestic Violence Act (October 26th)
1976 *Rocky* released in the US (November 21st)
1976 Sex Pistols release first single, *Anarchy in the UK* (Nov 26th)
1976 Sex Pistols swearing on live TV show makes headlines (Dec 1st)
1976 Government unveil IMF deal (December 15th)
1976 Apocalyptic novels *Deluge* and *The Fifth Horseman* published
1976 Number of Chinese takeaways overtakes fish & chip shops
1976 London's first Rape Crisis Centre opens
1976 *Jackie* magazine selling 600,000 copies per week
1976 National Theatre building on the South Bank opens
1977 *Children of the Stones* first broadcast (January 10th)
1977 *Robin's Nest* first broadcast (January 11th)
1977 *Sweeney!* film released in the UK (January)
1977 Queen's Silver Jubilee (February 6th)
1977 *The Turbulent Term of Tyke Tyler* published (February 7th)
1977 The Clash release their first single, *White Riot* (March 18th)
1977 *Citizen Smith* first broadcast (April 12th)
1977 *Abigail's Party* opens at Hampstead Theatre (April)
1977 *King of the Castle* first broadcast (May 8th)
1977 *Star Wars* first released in the US (May 25th)
1977 Rock band Queen at Earls Court; 19m UK records sold (June)
1977 1 million line London streets for Jubilee procession (June 7th)
1977 *Alternative 3* broadcast (June 20th)
1977 'Battle of Lewisham' between SWP and NF (August)

1977 *Target* first broadcast (September 9th)
1977 Dystopian political drama *1990* first broadcast (Sept 18th)
1977 *2-4-6-8 Motorway* is released (October 7th)
1977 *Coronation Street* tackles the subject of rape (October 19th)
1977 Fire Brigade Union strike; soldiers take over duties (Nov)
1977 First *Reclaim the Night* march in Leeds (November 12th)
1977 *The Sun Makers* (*Doctor Who*) first broadcast (November 26th)
1977 *Mull of Kintyre* reaches Number 1 (December 3rd)
1977 *Saturday Night Fever* released (December 16th)
1977 *Star Wars* opens in London (December 26th)
1977 *The Professionals* first broadcast (December 30th)
1977 *The Ice Age* is published
1977 JRR Tolkien's *The Silmarillion* published
1977 The Morecambe and Wise Christmas Special attracts 20+m
1978 The number of colour TV sets in the UK rises above 11 million
1978 *Blake's 7* first broadcast (January 2nd)
1978 Thatcher, *World in Action*: immigrants could 'swamp' UK (Jan)
1978 Radio 1 does not broadcast *Glad to Be Gay* in its Top 40 show
1978 *Grange Hill* first broadcast (February 8th)
1978 *Pennies From Heaven* first broadcast (March 7th)
1978 *Wuthering Heights* reaches Number 1 (March 11th)
1978 Sci-fi series *The Doombolt Chase* first broadcast (March 12th)
1978 *The Hitchhiker's Guide to the Galaxy*, BBC Radio (March 8th)
1978 *Law & Order* first broadcast (April 6th)
1978 *Night Fever* reaches Number 1 (April 29th)
1978 Rock Against Racism march & concert attracts 80,000 (April)
1978 *Sweeney 2* first released in the UK (April)
1978 Only 52 attend national conference of Communist Party (Apr)
1978 *Rivers of Babylon* reaches Number 1 (May 13th)
1978 *An Englishman's Castle* first broadcast (June 5th)
1978 *Grease* released (June 16th)
1978 *Black and White Minstrel Show* is cancelled (July)
1978 Jeremy Thorpe charged with conspiracy to murder (Aug 3rd)
1978 *SS-GB* published (August 24th)
1978 Industrial dispute; *Times* out of circulation for almost a year
1978 Saatchi and Saatchi 'Labour Isn't Working' poster (October)

1978 BBC off air for two days due to strike (December 20th)
1978 Union membership rises from 44% to 56% in a decade
1978 'Television violence & adolescent boy' report by WA Belson
1978 136,000 video recorders sold
1978 *The Cement Garden* published
1979 'Winter of Discontent': strikes and freezing weather
1979 *YMCA* reaches Number 1 (January 6th)
1979 *Heart of Glass* reaches Number 1 (February 3rd)
1979 Scotland/Wales referendums see 63%/59% turnouts (Mar 1st)
1979 MP Airey Neave assassinated by IRA car bomb March 30th)
1979 *Bright Eyes* reaches Number 1 (April 14th)
1979 Margaret Thatcher Britain's first female PM (May 4th)
1979 The Comedy Store in London opens (May 19th)
1979 Official UK unemployment 1.1m (May)
1979 *Rocky II* released in the US (June 15th)
1979 *The Omega Factor* first broadcast (June 15th)
1979 Jeremy Thorpe cleared in murder conspiracy trial (June 22nd)
1979 *Are 'Friends' Electric?* reaches Number 1 (June 30th)
1979 Strike sees ITV off the air for eleven weeks (August 6th)
1979 Assassination of Louis Mountbatten (August 27th)
1979 *Message in a Bottle* reaches Number 1 (September 29th)
1979 *Not the Nine O'Clock News* sketch show debuts (Oct 16th)
1979 Marks & Spencer launch their Chicken Kiev 'ready meal' (Oct)
1979 *Monty Python's Life of Brian* released in UK (November 8th)
1979 *Another Brick in the Wall Part II* reaches Number 1 (Dec 15th)
1979 *To the Manor Born* 23.95m, highest 70s non-live audience
1979 The Members' *Sound of the Suburbs* reaches Number 12
1979 *Poverty in the United Kingdom* is published

CONTENTS

Preface: Despair and Hope: Rodney Marshall (Pages 4-8)

1970s Timeline (16-25)

Introduction: A Window to the Past – the Landscape of 1970s Television Trevor Knight (28-48)

The British Nightmare versus The American Dream: Mike Pegler (49-71)

The Party's Over: The Last Hurrah of the Action-Adventure Heroes Al Samujh (72-81)

'England Soon?' Surveillance States & Tyrannical Regimes: Rodney Marshall (82-107)

Nation's Apocalyptic Visions: Gender in *Survivors* and *Blake's 7*: Stu Sterling (108-125)

'What You Don't Know, You Don't Know': Malcolm Hulke's 1970s work on *Doctor Who*: Michael Herbert (126-161)

Adventures on Earth, in Space and Time: Trevor Knight (162-190)

Children's Dystopia: Darren Flower (191-231)

"Shut it!": A Brief Overview of *The Sweeney*: Cailin Thomas (232-235)

Roger and Out: A Personal View of *The Sweeney*: Rodney Marshall (236-245)

Avengerland in the 1970s: **A Brave New World** JZ Ferguson (246-316)

Opening Pandora's Box: *Shadows of Fear* **and** *Thriller*: Rodney Marshall (317-349)

Zodiac: **Lessons from the Stars:** JZ Ferguson (350-393)

Two Visions of Suburbia: *The Fall and Rise of Reginald Perrin* **and** *Terry and June*: Andrew Roberts (394-409)

Trapped in A Doll's House: *Butterflies*: Rodney Marshall (410-420)

Contributors (421-423)
Select Bibliography (424-428)

A WINDOW TO THE PAST – THE LANDSCAPE OF 1970s TELEVISION

If television is a window to the world, it can also be a window to the past, reflecting the trends, issues, and concerns of the time. For viewers of a certain age, we might look through a round, square or arch window but like any window the view can depend on one's own perspective - in this case influenced by factors such as age, memory, personal preferences, and the extent to which the view is tinged with nostalgia.

My perspective is as a child of the 1960s, so whilst my earliest TV memories are of that decade, those of the 1970s are stronger and more vibrant. Stronger in part, of course, because I was older. I began the 1970s as a 7-year-old, so this was the decade I grew from child to teenager and to the cusp of adulthood. Consequently, my television viewing broadened and developed during that period. In the 1960s my television diet comprised *Play School, Watch with Mother,* the worlds of Hanna-Barbera, Gordon Murray (*Camberwick Green, Trumpton, Chigley*) and Gerry Anderson (*Stingray, Thunderbirds, Captain Scarlet*) along with some ITC action-adventure series and a few *Doctor Who* stories (though I was so traumatised by one Patrick Troughton episode that I stopped watching for a while). The start of the 1970s began with much the same – though by now I had become a *Doctor Who* devotee. By the end of the decade, I was glued to programmes such as *The Professionals, Tinker Tailor Soldier Spy, Minder, Blake's 7* and *Sapphire and Steel*. My viewing journey between the beginning and end of the 1970s was a rollercoaster ride of diverse and sometimes great television, some of which will be explored in depth throughout this book.

Vibrant in part because of colour! Although colour television began in the UK in 1969, it would be the 1970s before most of us could experience this, either because colour television broadcasting had not reached our television region or because most families still had black-and-white sets and would do so for some time. My family's first 'colour' television was orange! A Murphy's push button black-and-white set in an orange casing. It felt so modern. The future was indeed here today. Little did we realise that it wasn't and whilst designs from previous decades stood the test of time, colour cased television sets, along with our soda syphons, hostess trolleys and electric carving knives would become retro objects in museums of popular culture. My parents' first proper colour television arrived a few years into the decade, in 1974. A Philips colour television set rented from the Co-op. It was housed in a teak cabinet and had six pre-set station buttons at the top right of the set under which was a satisfyingly firm, square, push button on-off switch. Even now I vividly recall seeing colour television in my own house for the first time. I had been called in from the garden to see our new television in action and saw a scene from ITV's *General Hospital* featuring Carmen Munro (Sister Frances Washington) and Tony Adams (Dr Neville Bywater). It was amazing and exciting. It felt like this window to the world in our living room had suddenly become real. Colour had arrived. Channels still broadcast some black-and-white programmes and movies for years to come but, even so, the magic box in the corner of the room had changed forever.

The television landscape of the 1970s was very different from today and this influenced both the programmes made and how we watched them. Television was very much a shared experience. Whereas now we 'consume' television whenever, wherever, and however we like - with people viewing different content on different devices - in those days households normally had one television which we collectively gathered around together to sit and watch. There was no catch up, DVDs or streaming services so if you missed a programme – that was it; it was unlikely you'd have the chance to see it, save for some very occasional repeats. Although video cassette recorders (VCRs) were available by the mid to late 1970s they were extremely expensive machines, so only a small percentage of homes had one. It wasn't until the 1980s that the VCR boom hit the UK.

There may have been arguments about the household choice of viewing, but this was minimised because there were only three network channels: BBC1, BBC2 and ITV. Furthermore, at the beginning of the 1970s, broadcasting was restricted largely to peak hours in the day and evening. The BBC closed around 11pm with the national anthem. This was followed either by a test card and high-pitched tone (memorably satirised by a pyjama wearing Rowan Atkinson rubbing the top of a wine glass in a sketch from *Not the Nine O'clock News*) or on some nights Open University programmes where beige-suited kipper tie wearing bearded men would lecture sleep-deprived students on various subjects to the early hours.

I mentioned that our Philips television set had six pre-set buttons. Two buttons were labelled BBC1, one was labelled BBC2, another VCR (anticipating the growing demand for video recorders) and the final two were labelled ITV. The second ITV button was in preparation for a potential ITV2 channel which had been proposed by the Independent Television Authority (ITA) and had been discussed for some time. A fourth national television network would not become a reality until the 1980s, but whilst there were only three networks available in the 1970s, it wasn't strictly true there were only three channels. Regional television was prominent in the 1970s, both in the BBC but particularly the ITV regions. Independent Television had been established in 1955 as a network of separate regional companies which operated as both broadcasters and programme makers with their own distinct identities. ITV regional companies came and went over the years through successive franchise licence reviews but there was stability throughout the 1970s, largely because the 1974 franchise review saw minimal changes as companies were given time to recoup the significant costs of switching to colour television broadcasting.

Outside peak viewing hours, ITV television schedules were quite different across the regions, with some programmes only available in certain ITV areas. This meant that, if you were lucky enough to be able to receive signals from more than one region through your aerial, you had a wider choice of viewing. I remember the excitement when my parents had a new TV aerial installed and, in addition to ATV (ITV1), we now also received HTV and (best of all) Granada, which really appealed to me as it frequently repeated favourite programmes from the 1960s and early 70s.

The ITV regions were powerhouses for TV production. The 'big five' regional franchises were ATV (which covered the Midlands), Granada (Northwest), Yorkshire TV, plus Thames and London Weekend Television which shared the London/Southeast region, and they produced some of the biggest programmes for the ITV network. Other regions developed their own distinctive and popular brands, however. Harlech Television, better known as HTV, served Wales and the West of England and specialised in historical, fantastic, or supernatural adventures series aimed at children and family audiences, including *Arthur of the Britons, The Clifton House Mystery, Sky, Pretenders, The Georgian House, King of the Castle* and, perhaps most memorably, the haunting and brilliantly disturbing *Children of the Stones.* Southern Television, serving the South of England, produced hugely popular children's television across the decade including *How, The Flockton Flyer, Freewheelers, The Famous Five* and *Worzel Gummidge* starring Jon Pertwee, but also produced drama series such as *Dick Barton* and *Spearhead* about the lives and stories of a group of soldiers in a fictional army regiment. Many may recall the 'Anglia Knight' trophy which featured as the symbol for Anglia Television, based in Norwich, who produced popular programmes such as the "quiz of the week" *Sale of the Century, Survival and Tales of the Unexpected.*

Although BBC regional television variations were not as significant, regional television was still an important feature of the BBC's charter. There was no internet and so 1970s households relied heavily on regional television news alongside BBC local radio –

where available – and local newspapers for knowing what was happening in their part of the UK. My family used the second BBC button on our television set to watch either BBC Northwest or BBC Wales just for a glimpse of what was happening in other regions which, in those days, seemed so far away! The BBC promoted and celebrated the UK's regions notably through the immensely popular news and current affairs programme *Nationwide* (1969-83) which followed the early evening news on BBC1.

Nationwide was, in many respects, a descendant of the popular *Tonight* programme hosted by Cliff Mitchelmore which ran from 1957 to 1965. Although *Nationwide* began in September 1969, originally just on Tuesday and Thursday evenings, it became almost a national institution in the 1970s having switched to five days a week in 1972. The magazine format programme covered major stories of the day presented by one of its main hosts who included Michael Barratt, Frank Bough, Sue Lawley, and Bob Wellings, but much of the programme was devoted to sharing often light-hearted stories from across the regions. These were often introduced by regional TV presenters who therefore gained a prominent national spotlight.

The 1970s was the decade when the television became cemented as an essential feature of the UK household. In January 1960, just under 67.5% of households had a television set. By January 1970 this had become almost 91.2% of households and figures grew throughout the decade so that by January 1979 over 97.5% of households had a television. [1] With only three national television channels, choice was limited but the box in the corner had never been so popular. Consequently, viewing figures for programmes were huge. BARB (the Broadcasters' Audience Research Board) did not commence reporting television viewing figures until 1981 and so there is no definitive source of statistics. Nonetheless, reported viewing figures of around 20 million were common whilst much higher viewing figures are reported for programmes such as *Miss World* in November 1970 (23.76 million), *To the Manor Born* in November 1979 (23.95 million) and the *Mike Yarwood* and

Morecambe and Wise Christmas shows in December 1977 (21.4 and 21.3 million respectively). [2] Broadcasters can only dream of such viewing figures today where programmes with audiences of over 4 million are considered extremely successful.

In 1972, the then Minister of Posts and Telecommunications, Chris Chataway, the former high-profile broadcaster, international athlete, and pacesetter for Roger Bannister's breaking of the four-minute mile, announced that there would be no allocation of a fourth television network at that time. This was a disappointment to many, including the Independent Television Authority which had submitted a strong case for an ITV2. As compensation, Chataway removed the current restrictions on the number of hours of television and radio that could be broadcast each day, although broadcasters still had to meet obligations to minimum hours for education and Welsh language programmes and a maximum quota of 14% airtime devoted to US television programmes and old movies.

ITV was quick to take advantage of this change and introduced a wide range of popular and successful daytime television programmes during the 1970s, including drama programmes such as *Crown Court, Emmerdale Farm* and *The Cedar Tree*; creative programmes such as *Paint Along with Nancy, Houseparty* and *Farmhouse Kitchen*; quiz shows and panel games such as *Mr & Mrs, Jokers' Wild* and *Quick on the Draw*; and factual programmes such as *Out of Town, Money-Go-Round* and *Good Afternoon*. In addition, ITV used the afternoon slots to repeat popular UK and US drama programmes. Throughout the decade BBC1's afternoon output continued to focus on children's television and schools' programmes except for certain sports events and the hugely popular *Pebble Mill at One* magazine programme, broadcast live each weekday from Birmingham's (then) Pebble Middle studios which later spawned the late-night spin-off *Saturday Night at the Mill*.

Whilst the quota of airtime for US television programmes remained the same, the 1970s saw a further increase in popularity for US imported television programmes, many of which were shown at peak times. This may have been due to the expansion of colour television and high-quality production values of these programmes (most of which were on film and – of course – in colour), the fact that many programmes featured movie star leads, or because the style and format of many of these programmes contrasted to that of much of the UK television output. This was not completely new of course. US television imports had been popular in previous decades, but in the 1970s as UK television moved away from the upbeat, glamorous action-adventure series of the previous decade there was an increasing appeal of the US counterparts even if – in many cases – they too were more downbeat than their 1960s predecessors.

TV Westerns remained a staple of UK television with programmes in the early 70s such as *Bonanza, The Virginian, Gunsmoke, The High Chaparral* (with its memorable theme tune, a reworking of Telstar by The Tornados – which I bet you're whistling now) all of which had been running since the 1960s, plus the series *Alias Smith and Jones*. The latter was a light-hearted Western series about the adventures of a pair of buddy-buddy ex-outlaws who go straight. The characters and their relationship were heavily influenced by the successful 1969 movie *Butch Cassidy and The Sundance Kid*. Co-lead Ben Murphy went on to star in another fondly remembered but short-lived TV Western series, *Barbary Coast* in 1975, co-starring with William Shatner – a show which was similar to the very successful *Wild Wild West* series in the previous decade. Never let a good idea go to waste. Another successful mid-70s TV Western import *How the West was Won* shown on ITV was loosely based on the 1962 Hollywood film and starred James Arness (of *Gunsmoke* fame), Eve-Marie Saint, Fionnula Flanagan and Bruce Boxleitner and was a more serious drama set in in frontier America at the time of the Civil War.

Another long running drama about a western frontier family hit UK screens in 1974 – but continued into the 80s. *The Little House on the Prairie*, based on the 'Little House books' by Laura Ingalls Wilder, told the largely fictionalised tales of the Ingalls family, their neighbours and community as they established a new life in Minnesota. Whilst by no means to everyone's taste, the wholesome, family-oriented drama proved very popular with simultaneously comforting but often emotional stories – not dissimilar to another popular 1970s series *The Waltons* which, though set between the two world wars, was very akin to a TV family Western. The more soap opera style of these programmes reflected the continuing appeal of such glossy, expensive character-driven US dramas along with programmes such as *Rich Man Poor Man, Marcus Welby MD* and, most successfully, the global juggernaut that was *Dallas*. These shows contrasted with the often grittier, studio bound, video shot UK drama series of the time.

Although many US comedy programmes compared unfavourably with homegrown programmes in what is regarded as a peak period for UK TV comedy, selected US comedies and comedy dramas also proved successful with UK audiences such as *Happy Days, Mork and Mindy, The Mary Tyler Moore Show, Rhoda* (a spin-off series) and *The Love Boat*. It's notable that there was a shift in tone of imported US comedy series throughout the decade which seemed to echo a wider shift in society and audience tastes and expectations. Thus, wholesome family comedies such as *The Partridge Family* which ran from 1970 to 1974 gave way to sharper, edgier comedy series such as *Soap, Taxi and WRKP in Cincinnati* towards the end of the decade. It is tempting to suggest a similar development in one of the greatest comedy/dramas ever made, *M*A*S*H*, which began its run in 1972 with awkwardly stitched on laughter tracks but by the end in 1983 was regularly serving us storylines with a powerful emotional punch. In truth, however, the programme had always done this – using the vehicle of comedy packed with likeable if crazy characters and ostensibly about the Korean War – to present audiences with moving drama and thinly veiled attacks on the Vietnam war and the folly and terrible consequences of war in general.

Of all US television imports in the 70s, the US television detective programmes were and have remained the most successful and many of these and their lead characters have become icons for the era. These shows tended to be well written with strong, entertaining, but sometimes tough storylines; they had high production values, top quality direction and great use of locations which provided a backdrop to the stories. They also featured wonderful actors and supporting actors giving often career high performances. *Columbo* (Peter Falk), *Kojak* (Telly Savalas), *Starsky and Hutch* (Paul Michael Glaser and David Soul), *Ironside* (Raymond Burr), *The Rockford Files* (James Garner), *Cannon* (Willian Conrad), *McCloud* (Dennis Weaver), *McMillan and Wife* (Rock Hudson and Susan Saint James) *Hawaii Five-O* (Jack Lord), *Police Woman* (Angie Dickinson), *The Streets of San Francisco* (Karl Malden and Michael Douglas). Many of the lead characters had a particular and distinctive hook or trait. Columbo's crumpled raincoat, Mike Stone's (*The Streets of San Francisco*) trilby fedora hat, McCloud's Stetson hat, Kojak's lollipops, Ironside's wheelchair, Dave Starsky's baggy cardigans and distinctive red and white Ford Grand Torino car, Frank Cannon's weight. These were not cheap tricks but clever devices which served as identifiable and defining elements of their characters.

The popularity of these characters spilled into other mediums including tie-in books, comic strips, annuals, and music. Building on their fame, David Soul and Telly Savalas released number 1 hit records whilst British impersonator Bill (Billy) Howard achieved a number 6 UK hit with *King of the Cops*, a comedy version of *King of the Road* featuring Howard's spot-on impressions of McCloud, Columbo, Steve McGarrett, Cannon, Ironside and Kojak. Music was often central to the appeal of the programmes too, as many featured memorable theme tunes which instantly drew the viewers into the living room but also underlined the style and tone of the programmes themselves.

In contrast to many US imports, British television contemporary drama adopted an increasingly 'un-glossy' and downbeat approach as the decade wore on. One reason was that, as ever, television reflected the political and social landscape of the day. After the emergence of post-war austerity in the 1950s when Prime Minister Harold MacMillan proclaimed, "You've never had it so good", followed by the swinging 60s and the optimism forged in the 'White Heat of Technology', the 70s felt a much more pessimistic decade. This was not immediately the case. The early 70s were something of an overspill of the late 60s with a colour, vibrancy and brightness reflected in design, fashion, music, and television – from glam rock to Lord Brett Sinclair's wardrobe in *The Persuaders!*

As the decade progressed, however, it seemed that Britain had lost its confidence and optimism. The bright colours of the early 70s were replaced by various shades of brown in the latter part of the decade as the nation struggled with a series of economic and social upheavals including three-day weeks, power cuts, strikes, high unemployment, a collapse in sterling and an IMF loan, swingeing public expenditure cuts and high inflation. This was reflected in the shifting tone of British television drama which became increasingly dark and edgy as the decade progressed, often focusing on a seedier side of society, and featuring flawed or anti-heroes and unsettling themes. Violence, nudity and swearing became more commonplace as writers and directors deliberately pushed boundaries to produce provocative and unflinching drama which reflected a harsher and more critical image of the nation. This, in turn, attracted the ire of critics, including Mary Whitehouse the conservative campaigner and leader of the self-appointed National Viewers' and Listeners Association. She became a prominent figure in the decade, railing against the permissive society and how this was reflected on television. Whitehouse's views attracted both ridicule and praise and arguably influenced broadcasters both to self-censor some viewing but also to push boundaries even further.

Another factor for the tonal change in British drama was that by the mid to late-70s Lord Lew Grade's ITC company had switched emphasis from making high quality, glossy and mostly filmed British television series aimed at the US and international market, to movie production, with considerable initial success. Lew Grade and ITC's contribution to British television was immense and responsible for many classic programmes of the late-1950s and 1960s including most of the defining series from the action-adventure genre. ITC continued to produce a number of hugely popular and high-quality programmes in the 70s, beginning with one of its greatest and most glamorous action-adventure series, *The Persuaders* starring Tony Curtis and Roger Moore, a perfect duo of male leads. Other classic adventure and fantasy series followed: *UFO, Space 1999, Jason King, The Protectors, The Zoo Gang* and *The Return of the Saint*. Nevertheless, ITC's television output increasingly focused on mini-series, such as *Moses the Lawgiver, Jesus of Nazareth, The Shillingbury Tales, Will Shakespeare* or entertainment shows, including the glorious and hugely successful *The Muppet Show.*

Therefore, in contrast to US imports, much of the UK television drama output of the 70s was aimed at the domestic market and most programmes were produced on video rather than film other than for occasional outside location shooting. This gave them a more studio bound, slightly grittier feel with the mix of colour video and studio lighting creating a starker contrast of light and shade and a deliberately bleak, sometimes claustrophobic tone. This suited the mood of the decade very well but, unfortunately, does mean that through our window to the past, many of these programmes look more dated compared to those shot on film. Nonetheless, British 70s television drama featured excellent writing, great casts and star making performances. With a few notable exceptions, there was a transformation in tone of British television drama away from escapism, glamour, and heroic figures to more grounded and downbeat themes with characters who could be very ordinary or conversely edgier, anti-heroic figures.

Many UK police and detective series focused on everyday British life and storylines. Long running series *Z Cars* and *Dixon of Dock Green* remained very popular although, by now, George Dixon was well past retirement age. *Softly Softly Task Force*, a spin-off of *Softly Softly*, itself a spinoff from *Z-Cars*, was a new procedural police drama series for the colour age. ITV's *Hunter's Walk,* devised by Ted Willis, the creator of *Dixon of Dock Green*, ran from 1973 to 1976 and featured the everyday lives and cases a small provincial police force in the fictional Midlands town of Broadstone. In contrast *New Scotland Yard* which ran from 1972 to 1974 was a more hard-hitting police series focusing on the capital city's high-profile crimes investigated by two senior officers of the CID's Central Office.

The first two series of *Special Branch*, starring Derren Nesbitt (1969-1970), and *Van Der Valk,* (1972 and 1973), starring Barry Foster as the eponymous Dutch detective, were other examples of tough ITV police series mainly video filmed studio productions in the early seventies. However, both were subsequently revived and reinvented by Euston Films, a subsidiary of Thames Television formed at the start of the decade by Thames Executives Lloyd Shirley, George Taylor, and Brian Tesler. Euston Films pioneered shooting dramas on 16mm film on location with rapid turnaround times. This gave programmes a grittier and edgier tone and provided viewers with a visually seamless transition of interior and exterior scenes compared to studio-based dramas, where there was a more jarring tonal distinction between interior scenes on video and exterior scenes on film. Euston Films' influence on television production in the 70s and 80s was considerable.

The revived *Special Branch* (1973-74), starring George Sewell, was Euston Film's first filmed production and paved the way for further, successful action crime dramas in the latter part of the decade including *Out* (1978) starring Tom Bell as released criminal, Frank Ross, the revived *Van Der Valk* (1977) and most memorably, *The Sweeney*, starting John Thaw and Dennis Waterman as Jack Regan and George Carter of the Flying Squad. This massively successful series ran from 1975-1978 and spawned two movies. It was an unflinchingly uncompromising, edgy, and violent crime series where the moral and legal boundaries between right and wrong were sometimes blurred. Regan and Carter were tough, sweary, hard drinking policemen. They took risks, cut corners, and didn't always respect authority but they got the job done and (almost) always succeeded in bringing villains to justice. The BBC's response to *The Sweeney*'s success was *Target*, a filmed series which ran from 1977 to 1978 and starred Patrick Mower as Det. Supt Hackett and Brendan Price as Det. Sgt Bonney of a regional crime squad in Southampton. Whilst moderately successful, the show seemed a pale imitation of *The Sweeney* but with less interesting lead characters, whilst the programme also attracted criticism for its levels of 'excessive' violence.

Other British crime fiction featured more quirky or enigmatic plots and characters. These included private detectives such as cockney wise cracking Marlowesque *Hazell* played by Nicholas Ball, down at heel Frank Marker in *Public Eye*, superbly played by Alfred Burke, and dishevelled misfit Eddie Shoestring the computer expert turned 'private ear' for Radio West, played by Trevor Eve. Surely 'private ear' was an affectionate nod to *Public Eye*? *The Rivals of Sherlock Homes* which ran from 1971 to 1973 featured cases investigated by assorted fictional Victorian and Edwardian detectives. Each stand-alone episode featured outstanding actors in the lead role such as John Neville, Peter Vaughan, Ronald Hines, Donald Pleasance and Derek Jacobi. *Zodiac* was a light-hearted escapist thriller series from 1974 starring Anton Rodgers and Anouska Hempel as a detective inspector and astrologist who form an unlikely partnership to solve crimes. *Strangers* which ran for four series starting in 1978 featured a North of England detective team, called Unit 23, who went undercover to catch criminals.

This team was led by the gravel voiced, woollen glove wearing DS Bulman, played by Don Henderson, a character who first appeared in a nastier form, in the 1976-77 thriller series *The XYY Man*, which starred Stephen Yardley as a criminal recruited to work for British Intelligence. This was one of several 70s television programmes which reflected a more realistic and murkier world of spies and espionage such as *The Sandbaggers*, starring Roy Marsden as Neil Burnside, Head of Special Intelligence Force and *Callan* a tough and thoroughly believable assassin working for British intelligence superbly played by Edward Woodward. Though *Callan* first appeared on British screens in 1967, with a pilot and two monochrome series, it switched to colour in 1970 for two further memorable series.

Fear of Russian infiltration of British Intelligence resonated in the 70s where the Cold War conflict between East and West was all too real. Unsurprisingly, therefore, it featured in various television dramas. Ian Curteis' 1977 TV movie *Philby, Burgess and Maclean* starring Anthony Bate, Derek Jacobi and Michael Culver in the self-titled roles dramatized the infamous Russian spy ring that infiltrated British Intelligence, whilst Dennis Potter's 1971 play, *Traitor*, in the *Play for Today* anthology series featured a wonderful lead performance from John Le Mesurier as a fictional character inspired by Kim Philby. Most successfully, the superb *Tinker Tailor Soldier Spy* 1979 mini-series featured an all-star cast brilliantly lead by Alec Guinness who didn't just play but inhabited the role of George Smiley.

The TV spy and secret agent genre was by no means all grim fare, however. *Spyder's Web* which ran for one series in 1972 was a much more light-hearted, offbeat espionage series created by Roy Clarke of *Last of the Summer Wine* fame. *The Adventurer* was a frankly ridiculous series of 25-minute stories starring Gene Barry as a fictionalised version of himself - part time movie star, part time US espionage agent. Much more enjoyably, *The New Avengers* brought back bowler-hatted agent John Steed (Patrick Macnee) this time accompanied by Mike Gambit (Gareth Hunt) and Purdey (Joanna Lumley) for two series of brilliant and stylish escapist adventures in the mid-70s where the trio took on a series of mad scientists, power-crazed villains, international spies, sleeper agents and even Nazi monks trying to resuscitate Hitler. Another Brian Clemens and Albert Fennell series, *The Professionals*, which began in 1978, was equally action packed but much tougher and more violent. Lewis Collins and Martin Shaw played Bodie and Doyle, close but sometimes combative pair of agents for CI5, headed by the no-nonsense Cowley played by Gordon Jackson. CI5 protected the country against domestic and international agents, terrorism, and organised crime in a 'give as good as you get' way. The series captured a mood of the time and became one of Britain's biggest, most successful programmes of the 70s and 80s.

Russian infiltration, terrorism, espionage, and crime were just a few of many fears prevalent in the UK during the 70s and reflected in television and popular culture. Several series prayed on familiar themes of fear of the unknown. Gerry Anderson's *UFO* (1970-72) featured threats of invading aliens harvesting human organs for survival. Threats from mysterious or primeval forces were reflected in the classic series *Children of the Stones* (1977) and Nigel Kneale's anthology series *Beasts* (1976). Kneale's play *The Stone Tapes* reflected our continual fascination with ghosts and the supernatural as did BBC's glorious series of classic *Ghost Stories for Christmas* and which ran between 1971 and 1978 and, much more light-heartedly, the children's series *The Ghosts of Motley Hall* (1976) and *Rentaghost* which began in 1975. Meanwhile *Sapphire and Steel*, which began in 1979, dealt with threats from time itself.

The optimistic promise of science and technology seen in the 60s, culminating in the 1969 Moon landings, was replaced by a bleaker, pessimistic fear of the catastrophes these could cause. In *Doctor Who* many of the earthbound Third Doctor stories featured consequences of when science went wrong whilst this was the very premise of the Sci-Fact series *Doomwatch* (1970-72) where the scenarios of many stories seemed chillingly prophetic. Terry Nation's *Survivors* (1975-77) was set in a post-apocalyptic world following a laboratory accident with a man-made virus which caused a pandemic which wiped out most of the human species. Gerry Anderson's *Space 1999* (1975-78) envisaged the disastrous consequences of the Moon being used to store massive supplies of nuclear waste due to Earth's reliance on nuclear power. A massive explosion at these waste dumps flings the Moon and the crew of Moonbase Alpha out of Earth's orbit towards a series of adventures in deep space.

Nuclear waste was a feature of the 1977 series *Raven* starring Phil Daniels as an ex-borstal youth under the care of Michael Aldridge as a professor of archaeology. They combine to fight government plans to bury nuclear waste in manmade caverns near an ancient stone circle which the Professor believes are strongly connected to the Arthurian Lore. The Professor and youth adopt a Merlin and young Arthur like relationship and the series drew on both current fears but also contemporary fascinations with the Arthurian legend, mysticism and the spirit of the 'new age' which offered an antidote to the threats of the modern age. A similar theme was explored in *The Changes* (1975) where a mysterious phenomenon created by the Necromancer, a living stone from the time of Merlin, causes people to destroy the technology of the modern age and revert to a pre-civilised society.

The theme of modern society breaking down and the intervention of unknown primeval or alien phenomena was also covered in Euston Films' *Quatermass* (1979) starring John Mills as a retired and world-weary version of the character. This bleak view of a tyrannical or dystopian future was at the heart of several extremely varied series from the decade. Terry Nation's *Blake's 7* (1978 -81) focused on an unlikely team of flawed freedom fighters battling against the totalitarian Federation. Featuring memorable characters and strong stories, in many ways the series was an intergalactic version of Robin Hood, with Blake, Avon and their team pursued by versions of Guy of Gisborne and the Sheriff of Nottingham in the form of Travis and Servalan. The US series *Logan's Run* (1977-78) inspired by the film of the same name, was set in a post holocaust 23rd century where population control was exercised through euthanasia as the population enthusiastically submit to the Carousel ceremonies when reaching thirty years old. Closer to home, *1990* (1977-78) envisaged a near future British police state and starred Edward Woodward as journalist Jim Kyle working with a resistance movement.

The 1977 'mockumentary', *Alternative 3*, claimed that, for some time, scientists had realised the Earth would soon be unable to support life due to pollution and the impact on climate change. The third alternative solution (after a drastic reduction in population or construction of underground shelters to accommodate officials and scientists) was a secret mission organised by scientists and the military to colonise Mars of which the US and Russian space missions of the 60s had supposedly been steppingstones. Originally intended to be broadcast on 1 April, the programme was clearly fiction, featuring several well-known actors as supposedly real-life interviewees, and it even had a cast list in the closing credits. Nevertheless, because it reflected genuine fears of the time, the programme attracted both considerable controversy and conspiracy theories suggesting that it had been made with actors to divert viewers from the fact that it was all true.

As contemporary drama focused on increasingly bleak themes, audiences of the 70s looked to the past for escapism, with numerous historical dramas throughout the decade, some of which proved immensely popular in Britain but also in the United States and other countries too. Many of these were lavishly produced miniseries with stellar casts that portrayed fictionalised stories of historical figures. These were not romanticised reflections of the past, however, but focused as much on the flaws and struggles of these individuals as much as their achievements. Unsurprisingly, royalty was a particularly popular theme such as the BBC's *The Six Wives of Henry XIII* in 1970 starring Keith Michell followed by *Elizabeth R* in 1971 starring Glenda Jackson. Both attracted very large audiences and spawned feature films. ITV focused on 19th and 20th century royalty with a trio of series. Arguably the best was *Edward the Seventh* (1975) which starred Timothy West as Edward and Annette Crosbie as his mother Queen Victoria. Edward's life was again covered – albeit as a supporting character – in *Lillie* (1978) which starred Francesca Annis as Lillie Langtry, actress, influential woman of society and courtesan of Edward VII amongst others. Finally, *Edward & Mrs Simpson* (1978) starred Edward Fox and Cynthia Harris in the title roles and told the story of the events leading to the dramatic 1936 abdication of Edward VIII.

The Fall of Eagles, made by the BBC in 1974, covered the decline and fall of three imperial houses in central and Eastern Europe – the Romanovs of Russia, the Hohenzollern Kaisers of Germany, and the Hapsburg Emperors of Austria & Hungary. The series comprised thirteen separate plays written by prominent writers of the period and featured a star-studded cast. In some ways this was a precedent for one of the BBC's most popular historical dramas of this or any other decade. *I Claudius* (1976) adapted two Robert Graves novels to portray the turmoil of the Roman empire from 24 BC to AD 54. After initially attracting a negative reception, the series became enormously popular but also controversial for its reflection of themes of betrayal and depravity through its graphic portrayal of sex, nudity, violence, rape, and incest in scenes which would not have been permitted on television in the previous decades.

Other popular period dramas focused on the lives and loves of a variety of prominent individuals in history. These included *Jennie: Lady Randolph Churchill* (1974), starring Lee Remick in the title role; *Dickens of London* (1976) with Roy Dotrice as the great novelist; *The Strauss Family* (1972) with Stuart Wilson as Johann Strauss Jr; *Disraeli – Portrait of a Romantic* (1978) starring Ian McShane as the statesman and author and *Napoleon and Love* (1974) with Ian Holm in the title role – a figure he seemed almost born to play. Many other highly successful historical dramas of the decade featured fictional characters. Some were created specifically for television such as *The Onedin Line* (1971-1980) about ambitious seaman and businessman James Onedin, *Upstairs Downstairs* (1971-75) covering the saga of the Bellamy family and their servants who resided in 165 Eaton Place, Belgravia from the turn of the century to 1930, and *The Duchess of Duke Street* (1976-77), created by *Upstairs Downstairs* producer John Hawkesworth, about Louise Trotter who progressed from kitchen assistant to mistress of the Prince of Wales and then owner of the exclusive Bentick Hotel. Others were adaptations of classic books or book series such as William Makepeace Thackeray's *Vanity Fair* (1972), Anthony Trollope's *The*

Pallisers (1974-75), Winston Graham's *Poldark* (1975-77) Arnold Bennett's *Clayhanger* (1976), HE Bates' *Love for Lydia* (1977) and Leo Tolstoy's *Anna Karenina* (1977).

Escapism was also provided through television light entertainment. Many look back on the 70s as a golden age and whilst many eras may stake a claim to the crown, this was certainly the decade of television variety superstars such *as Morecambe & Wise, The Two Ronnies, Benny Hill, Stanley Baxter, Dick Emery, Mike Yarwood*, and a host of light entertainment programmes which commanded peak viewing times and big audiences. Numerous famous singers of the day had their own successful variety shows such as *Val Doonican, Des O'Connor, Nana Maskouri, Roger Whittaker, Lulu, Cilla Black and Cliff Richard. Opportunity Knocks* with Hughie Green and a clapometer had been a popular talent show since the 1950s but was now joined by *New Faces*, very much a forerunner of *Britain's Got Talent* with Tony Hatch in the Simon Cowell Mr Nasty role. Quiz and game shows were massively popular such as *Bruce Forsyth's Generation Game, Celebrity Squares, Winner Takes, Blankety Blank, Sale of the Century* to the more intellectually challenging *Ask the Family*. Whilst in 1972 contestants first sat in the famous *Mastermind* black chair.

Unlike today, situation comedies were a staple part of most evening's television viewing during the 70s. Some focused on a changing British society – in particular, the impact of immigration but with decidedly varied results. *The Fosters* was a conventional comedy revolving around a family and their relationships, but importantly was one of the first British television programmes to feature an entirely black cast. *Mixed Blessings* rather unsubtly dealt with the subject of interracial marriage whilst *Mind Your Language* drew its comedy through the interplay between a host of lazy racial stereotype characters in an English language class. Perhaps most controversially *Love they Neighbour* focused on the uneasy relationship and racial tensions between a socialist white chauvinist and his neighbour, a Conservative voting West Indian immigrant.

Although the programme tried to use comedy to reflect an important and challenging subject matter, it was done with little sensitivity and with frequent use of racist language meaning that it would be an uncomfortable watch today.

In contrast, some situation comedies from the 70s remain timeless beloved classics of the genre and still attract sizeable audiences through repeats such as *Dad's Army* (which began in 1968) *Whatever Happened to the Likely Lads, Porridge, Fawlty Towers, The Good Life, The Fall & Rise of Reginald Perrin, Rising Damp, Some Mothers Do 'Ave 'Em,* and *Sykes*. Several surreal and zany comedy series were popular then, but also went on to influence comedy through future generations, such as *Monty Python's Flying Circus, The Goodies, Ripping Yarns, Rutland Weekend Television and Spike Milligan's QI*. Other comedy series, though immensely successful, are perhaps seen as more 'of their time', such as *Are You Being Served?, Bless this House, It Ain't Half Hot Mum* and *Man About the House*.

Looking through our window to television in the 1970s, we can see something for everyone. It is no wonder that, for many, the 70s is their favourite television decade because it served viewers a smorgasbord of contrasting styles, themes, and genres. Legendary comedy and entertainment, lush and extravagant historical fiction, socially grounded plays, gritty contemporary thrillers, exciting action and adventure. Boundary pushing adult dramas sitting side by side with classic children's television and other safe, comforting, family-friendly and familiar series. Storylines that were traditional or modern, mystical, quirky, and humorous, or serious, hard-hitting, and thought-provoking. This was the era of the dour and the dazzling, the ordinary and the extraordinary, the frightening and the fantastic, the light and the dark. Saints and sinners, heroes and anti-heroes, togas and tiaras. Essential escapist viewing and Survival TV.

© Trevor Knight

1. Figures from Closer. The home of longitudinal research. www.closer.sc.uk/data/television-ownership-in-domestic-households
2. From 1970s Television Introduction – Nostalgia Central. nostalgiacentral.com/television/tv-by-decade/tv-shows-1970s/1970s-television-introduction

THE BRITISH NIGHTMARE VERSUS THE AMERICAN DREAM

'*All* that we see or seem/Is but a dream within a dream.' Edgar Allan Poe (*A Dream within a Dream*)

'You may say I'm a dreamer/But I'm not the only one.' John Lennon (*Imagine*)

'Paul is quitting The Beatles', the headline said on the front page of *The Daily Mirror* on 10th April 1970. It had to happen I suppose, but somehow the notion of the group most symbolic of the 1960s zeitgeist being finished was hard to take in.

'The dream is over...what can I say?' Lennon famously sang in his solo song *God*, on an LP jammed full of shocking, dream-busting pronouncements. This idea of the 'dream' would become, ironically, recurrent and strangely applicable throughout the coming decade...and while Lennon's bluntly-presented obsession with 'reality' was part of his personal therapy, that collective 60s 'dream' was arguably about to turn into a living 70s nightmare...

So, The Beatles split up and despite Lennon's own comment that '...it's nothing important', the truth is, it was. It was and is important because it very neatly bookends the era which provided us with so much musically and in a wider sense, creatively. In September that same year, superstar guitarist Jimi Hendrix died, followed less than a month later by Janis Joplin, both aged 27. Less than a year later, Jim Morrison would also be gone, at the same age. It felt distinctly like the end of something special. The sands were shifting as the new decade took shape and everything was affected. Television was no exception. Most of the action-adventure which had entertained us and pushed the envelope in the previous decade would now be forever consigned to it.

The Avengers, The Saint, Danger Man, Man in a Suitcase, The Prisoner, The Human Jungle, Strange Report and *Randall And Hopkirk (Deceased)* were all now finished. Each of these groundbreaking shows and many more had taken us to places hitherto unthought of for TV, with my personal favourite, *The Prisoner*, pushing the limits of the medium arguably further than any of them and establishing the high watermark for the years to come. With the television portfolio of 1960s so strong, what could the 1970s possibly offer? Was the golden age of television over?

If you had asked me that question thirty years ago, I probably would have answered instantly, "Yes" because for much of my life I had always considered the 1960s to be the superior decade, both musically and in terms of television. And, to an extent, I still believe that to be the case. More recently though, I have come to realise that what we got in the 1970s, while maybe less sensational, was at the very least beginning to become more representative of the society which was producing it. One could argue that much of the groundwork for this progression was laid in the previous decade. One could also argue that while social issues were more prominent in 70s action-adventure and sitcoms, they were by no means explored in any great depth or with the sensitivity they demanded. There was still a long, long way to go. Comedy, in retrospect, seems to have explored and exploited what these days would be considered particularly unsavoury aspects of British life in the decade, with sexism, racism, class and religious prejudice parading their ugly heads frequently.

I suppose there are two ways of looking at this. Art imitating life is, in general, a desirable thing, where one's creation has some social significance. But when the life being imitated is tainted by grossly unenlightened attitudes on a range of subjects, does the art itself become tainted? I think it probably does – unless it is saying something intelligent. I think that a certain strain of television output from the 1970s is indefensible, much of it presented as comedy, though some does creep into other types of show. Some of the hideously dated 'comedy' from this era is frankly unwatchable now, devoid of artistic merit and grossly offensive. An absolute 'bloody' nightmare, in fact.

In a more general sense though, the thematic landscape of 70s action-adventure on the television seems to have polarised, with British TV taking us on an apocalyptic journey into hell, while in the US, the impression that the sun was shining and was going to stay that way right into the 1980s had to be maintained. This is, as I say, a generalisation but one which can be supported and sustained in several ways. As anyone who has ever looked into the concept of the American Dream knows, there is much more going on under the surface and the nightmare is never really very far away. So, what I'm suggesting is that with British TV in the 1970s, the anxieties and fears are frequently in full view, whereas in the US they are glossed over, but the stylish veneer is only skin deep. Paranoia and division are still there, it is just being presented figuratively. Curious that in mentioning John Lennon earlier, he too had decided (quite literally) to bear all, before moving to the US and commit himself 100% to the American way of life. New York, he said, was 'the greatest place on Earth.' Furthermore, it is notable that Patrick McGoohan, one of the most dynamic and enigmatic faces on British television in the 1960s, also decided to relocate to the US (the West Coast in his case) having arguably unleashed his own equivalent of the Lennon/Ono avant-garde sound collage LPs in the form of the final episode of *The Prisoner* – a nervous breakdown on 35mm film – on the British public before trotting off to the States permanently. [1]

And so, in the UK in 1970 we had a new government – a Tory government – leading us through an era of high inflation, strikes and an energy crisis. Times were about to get tough and so too, it seems, were TV's action heroes. One series which notably rolled over into the 1970s and into colour, was *Callan*. A lone insider-outsider operating in a violent, humdrum and hopeless world, where everyone is a potential enemy, there is little room for love and certainly never any escape from the system. This, in many ways, almost sets the tone for 1970s TV in Britain... it's going to be bleak and unforgiving and the line distinguishing hero from villain is going to become very, very blurry. Edward Woodward's intense turn as Callan would come to an end (in series form at least) in 1972, finishing in a similar way to the climax of *Dirty Harry*, which had stirred up controversy the year before in cinemas, with its unapologetic depiction of violent criminality and police brutality in San Francisco. I mention the Clint Eastwood characterisation from the big screen because, throughout the 1970s, there is a tangible link between what is happening in cinemas and what we see flickering into our living rooms. Harry Callaghan is another one of these 'misfit' heroes, existing in his own, ring-fenced world, where no real relationships are possible, except with his .44 magnum. Callaghan operates under the blanket of 'the law', just about, so we're not in any doubt as to what 'side' we are rooting for, it is more about the methods used. I would contend that the sequel to *Dirty Harry*, 1973's *Magnum Force*, actually poses a lot more interesting questions about the real identity of the antagonist. Is it the reprehensible criminal being depicted, is it the vigilante outfit responding, or is it the system itself that's the problem? "I hate the goddam system. But until someone comes along with some changes that make sense, I'll stick with it" says Callaghan. So, we ride with it. Good versus evil? Or evil disguised as good, versus evil? Or something else? And don't get me started on *Death Wish*... There's something rotten at the heart of American society everybody and we're going to milk it.

In the UK, Mike Hodges gives us *Get Carter* – a film so 'unswinging' it's not even funny. No attempt at all is made to provide the audience with any particularly 'likeable' characters, maybe one or two deserve our pity, but basically this defining gangster film, a direct descendant of 1947's *Brighton Rock* in terms of tone, takes 'bleak', magnifies it by a factor of 100 and shoves it in your face saying, "take this post-60s Britain". It features Michael Caine in arguably his most memorable film role, even though he doesn't really have to do much except act like a bastard throughout, with one small moment of tender emotion on show. It's the old 'avenging angel' plot again – except this time it's more of an 'avenging devil' situation. A nice guy is murdered by some particularly nasty gangsters and so it falls to his even nastier brother to ride into town and kill everyone. It's a plot which will be familiar to any cinema-goer. But at the centre of the drama is this recurrent theme of hopelessness, despair and the living nightmare.

The same year, Stanley Kubrick gave us *A Clockwork Orange*, a film which would become so mired in controversy that the director himself withdrew it from circulation, even though the source material, the book, had been written a decade earlier. Whereas Jack Carter was an avenging devil, with a purpose, albeit resulting in a series of violent acts, the central character in Kubrick's film is a delinquent psychopath, with no redeeming qualities at all. Yet again though, despite the reign of terror meted out by Alex and his Droogs, our sympathies and sensibilities are manipulated in this film, where we are asked to consider the responsibility of 'the government' for what goes on. Either way, both films present us with that grim view of the world around us which we would come to understand as dystopia. Interesting also that the criminal activity in *Dirty Harry* was based on real events, whereas *A Clockwork Orange* was withdrawn by Kubrick because it had allegedly *inspired* real events. So, art imitating life is fine, so long as it does not flip the other way around?

One of the first major new action series out of the blocks in the 1970s was *The Persuaders!* Essentially a new vehicle for Roger Moore after the end of *The Saint*, he was joined by Tony Curtis as a 'transatlantic crime fighting duo'. Another of Lew Grade's ventures into selling action to the Americans, this time around something felt different. The show, while undoubtedly entertaining, failed to make a major impact in the US and, while it faired reasonably well in the UK, was not the resounding success all involved had hoped for. While the onscreen dynamic between the two leads is good – for they were both top professionals – somehow the jet-setting lifestyles of millionaire adventurers drafted in to help fight international criminals just doesn't chime with the gloomy complexion of the early 1970s, certainly in Britain at any rate. Audiences were beginning to seek the sugar-highs of light entertainment shows and sitcoms – a good deal of which were (arguably) trashy – and seemed less willing to invest time in action and adventure. Robert Vaughn's new show, *The Protectors*, although harking back to the era of the 25-minute short, would go the same way, as would another relatively short-lived series, *The Adventurer*, also a half-hour presentation. And as for the *Department S* spin-off *Jason King*...opinion is divided about this series. Personally, it's never been one of my favourites and laid itself open to parody even at the time with *The Two Ronnies* lampooning it.

'Discontent' is a word one could apply to both American and British society in the 1970s and so it is no surprise that this should filter into entertainment, be it cinematic, on the small screen, or musically. The situation in Northern Ireland had been deteriorating for years, but by the early 70s it was now in sharp focus. Incidents including shootings, bombings, murders and acts of terrorism were now becoming commonplace, with plenty of innocent people being caught up in conflict which would stretch way beyond the decade. Two titans of popular culture from the 1960s, John Lennon and future knight of the realm Paul McCartney, both released their musical statements on the issue, Lennon's *The Luck Of The Irish* lashing out at historical atrocities perpetrated by the "British brigands" and McCartney's *Give Ireland Back To The Irish* leaving the listener in no doubt as to what he was thinking. In the meantime, miners were striking, energy was in short supply, and three-day weeks were just around the corner. Little wonder that Slade were on the telly singing *Mama, Weer All Crazee Now* in 1972 and David Bowie, having spotted and exploited the gap in the pop market left by the abdicating Fabs, was taking his fans into a fantasy world of alter-ego and escapism. The success of Pink Floyd's *The Dark Side Of The Moon* on both sides of the Atlantic was due, in part, to heavy promotion, but also because the themes explored on the record struck a chord with both societies. Angst, anxiety, paranoia, the 'us and them' perception and feeling of being left rudderless, lonely and on the cusp of mental breakdown were just the tonic for the Americans, as they limped away from Vietnam. As the decade drew on, the unrest would not relent, but simply morph into other culturally shocking embodiments of rebellion.

The Vietnam War and the antics of Richard Nixon were both highly symbolic of the duality at the heart of American society, which exists to this very day. The 'dream' famously promoted by Martin Luther King in the 1960s sounded and still sounds so good, but the dreamer himself had been brutally assassinated for expressing it. How many people have to get trampled on to make the American Dream work for one person or as a kind of collective delusion? Nixon himself would come to be the public face of the 'dark side' of the Dream. The line of dialogue often cited from Oliver Stone's biopic released in 1995, when the president, portrayed by Anthony Hopkins, looks at a portrait of JFK and says, "When they look at you, they see who they want to be. When they look at me, they see who they really are" neatly sums up this delusion. This is a man who had to go on television and publicly declare, "I'm not a crook" for heaven's sake. The American people are constantly looking for a superhero, only to be saddled with a flawed alternative. So, what happens? These 'superheroes' emerge instead on film and TV screens. It's almost as if those creating entertainment in the US acknowledge that society is blighted with problems of an economic, racial and domestic nature, but they create infallible fictional protagonists to rise above it all. The most obvious example, I suppose, would be Superman, 'fighting for truth and justice and the American way.' No surprise then that one of the biggest films of the 1970s would be *Superman*...but I'm getting ahead of myself. While in the UK, film and television was beginning to be used to expose social problems, in the US it was almost being used to begrudgingly admit to them, before neatly dealing with them in a fantastic way.

On the television in America, possibly the most 'iconic' example of this 'flawless superhero' was Marshal Matt Dillon in *Gunsmoke*. One of the longest-running shows in US history, the series went on into the middle of the 1970s, having started back in the mid-50s. Towards the end of its run, the superhero idea was taken to an almost absurd degree, with the main character literally being used as a resolution to whatever drama had unfolded, usually turning up in the final act and shooting someone. As the 1970s moved on, audience figures were showing signs that the Western was a genre they were moving away from...at least the romanticised versions they had been offered for decades. However, there is a school of thought that says America 'needs an enemy' to justify itself... perhaps a charge which could be levelled equally at any society; just look at the events unfolding across the globe today. As far as the US is concerned though, the concept of collectively 'fighting an evil' is something which would burst spectacularly onto the big screen later in the decade and change the face of western entertainment forever...

In the meantime, US TV drama and its superheroes...One of the very best creations from the US in the 1970s is *Columbo*. The character, often referred to as a dishevelled detective, brought to life by Peter Falk, initially in 1968 in a pilot, would become one of the most celebrated in TV history after a run of highly successful 'howcatchem' features which would turn the 'whodunnit' formula on its head. In this series, we know who the antagonist is from the start...the fun comes from watching Falk's character determine this too and then hound them into submission. Columbo is a genius. He catches his suspects unawares. They assume him to be a harmless idiot and therefore allow their guard to drop, at which point he unnerves them with a volley of razor-sharp observations and deductions, often tying them up in logic. Each show is a masterclass in mind games, during which our (super) hero eventually always triumphs. Crucially though, Columbo's world is almost always set in glitzy Los Angeles. The villains (and victims) often live in enormous houses, wealthy people, winners in the race to achieve the

American Dream, entitled sociopaths, committing murder as a means of solving a problem. In *Columbo*, we are essentially presented with a veneer of American society...everyone is successful but there's a few bad eggs in there that need extracting by our genius (male) superhero. It's as if the message is, "Yeah, we have murderers, but they all have loads of money and big cars, so... what the hell?" The less well-off are represented occasionally (one could argue, *continually* in the person of Columbo himself) but the murderers are almost always those who have made a success of themselves but turn out to be rotten to the core. The American Dream is concealing a nightmare – right there, in every instalment of *Columbo*. A great example of this is the episode *Candidate For Crime*, in which Jackie Cooper's political slimeball Nelson Hayward is running for the Senate, but also murders his campaign manager, has an extra-marital affair and actively deceives the authorities. Patrick McGoohan turns up in *Columbo* several times, sometimes even directing, once again staying true to his tendency to have to get completely involved in a project. Typically, it is he who is largely responsible for what is considered to be the weirdest episode of the entire series, where he deliberately plays with the formula and the tone of the show, presenting a very 'dream-like' set of sequences indeed involving non sequiturs and odd behaviour.

"Where is the entertainment value in depicting the downfall of ordinary people?" I hear you cry. This is a valid point and I concede that the added element of untouchability contributes to the sensationalism of the stories. However, it doesn't seem to be so much of an issue in UK drama of the time. In the 1960s, *Man in a Suitcase*, for example, featured a hero with arguably as many flaws as strengths and *The Prisoner* basically ended on a downer each week. British drama, one way or the other, was definitely more willing to explore the idea of a hero who doesn't necessarily win.

M*A*S*H, a US comedy drama and latterly drama comedy, set in the Korean War, is another great example of thinly veiled political commentary which, unsurprisingly, was a massive hit both in the States and in the UK. When it started in 1972, the Vietnam War was still ongoing and so parallels with that were inevitable but could never be explicitly expressed as this would have led to it being pulled from the schedule. What the writers were able to do though, under the auspices of comedy, was make more statements than perhaps they could in a drama. Criticism of foreign policy or undermining the military is never easy while a war is being waged, even an unpopular one. Comedy had been given a military setting before in the US, with *The Phil Silvers Show* brilliantly lampooning the institution. Now though, with hundreds of casualties each week, a balance had to be struck to avoid creating the impression that war was in some way a subject for humour, whilst at the same time dealing with the issue through the licentious power of comedy. The episode known as *Dreams* dispenses with the comedy format and delivers some powerful content through the medium of dreams, during which the main characters fail to receive any respite, despite being asleep. This episode was broadcast several years after the Vietnam War had ended and probably would not have been put out earlier in the 70s. The final episode of the show drew one of the highest audiences ever in television history and was broadcast in 1983.

By the time *The Sweeney* hit the small screen in 1975 (having been 'piloted', if you want to call it that, the previous year), the UK was halfway through a turbulent decade which had seen the demise of the hippy dream and the harsh reality of division and unrest simmer and boil over for the next generation. With the cosy, now irrelevant format of *Dixon of Dock Green* about to fizzle out, the stage was set for something far more uncompromising and brutal to shift the paradigm. In many ways the elements which *The Sweeney* became so well-known for – the drinking, the violence, the political incorrectness, the...*realism*, would also make it vulnerable to parody as it almost became the stereotypical new standard for TV cop shows. Many copied the format, but none matched it. John Thaw's Jack Regan is perhaps one of the most inscrutable TV detectives ever. It is stated and shown explicitly more than once that he is a violent man. So much so in fact that he is sometimes indistinguishable from the villains. George Carter, played memorably by Dennis Waterman, and occasionally the victim of Regan's iconic "shut it!", takes a more measured approach and is generally written as a more sympathetic character, but when it comes down to it, he gets completely stuck in when there's a fight and is sucked into Jack Regan's debauched world after the death of his wife. The two leads then are depicted as drinking, smoking, womanising and beating the hell out of villains. A world away from *Columbo*...(yes, ok, he likes a cigar, but that's where it ends). Personally, the character I find most fascinating in *The Sweeney* is Regan's boss Haskins, who is well aware of the shortcomings of his Inspector but is usually happy to 'turn a blind eye' to all of it in the name of results. It's a superb piece of character acting from Garfield Morgan. Furthermore, the stories do not always end in resounding victory for the squad. Social and domestic issues of the day are frequently woven into either the plotlines or characterisation, with The Troubles in Northern Ireland being one such example. The bombastic theme tune which runs over the opening titles is played at the end at a slower, more reflective pace, inviting the viewer to consider what they have just seen rather than simply to get up and walk away feeling smug that everything turned out well. Society in *The Sweeney* is grubby, unsavoury, dangerous, corrupt and unfair, populated with vicious criminals. Looking back at *The Sweeney* now, it's easy to dismiss it as a 'time capsule' and kid ourselves that we have moved on from a lot of the shenanigans depicted in the show. The reality however is probably very different. Whatever your take on *The Sweeney*, one thing is for sure: it pushed audiences out of their comfort zone and British police drama would never be the same again. As with all things, the series ran its course and 'jumped the shark'; when Morecambe and Wise made a guest appearance, that was surely a sign that Regan and Carter had been absorbed by the sanitation police.

So, here we are in the middle of the 1970s, with British drama getting gritty and realistic and American action moving a little in that direction, but still preferring to remain romanticised. *Kojak*, which first aired in 1973, was a big success like *Columbo* on the UK shores. Another cop drama, this time set in New York, with Telly Savalas in the lead, memorably dishing out one-liners as often as lollipops, this was a series which showed us more grime than *Columbo* and a hero who was more trigger-happy (Columbo didn't even carry a gun). There is more to *Kojak* than simply Wild-West style shoot outs though. Some of the stories deal with psychological issues and social problems like drug addiction and racial tension. It is undeniably an era-defining masterpiece, which gets the balance right between entertainment and social commentary (for its time), with, of course, the killer theme tune. It is also obviously a vehicle for Savalas, himself a larger-than-life personality, who made his way to the top of the UK pop charts mostly off the back of the success of *Kojak* in 1975 with the (in)famous song, *If*. There is genuine suspense in some episodes and the New York backdrop is a great precursor to later shows like *The Equalizer* (in the next decade). On the other side of the country, yet another detective show was building up steam in the form of *The Rockford Files* and this time I wonder how much notice its creators had been taking of British shows of the same ilk. [2]

Jim Rockford is most definitely a flawed character, played perfectly by James Garner. However, his shortcomings are largely explained away as the series develops and we learn to love the character as a bit of a rogue, rather than an ambiguous law-breaker. He has served time, we hear, but that turns out to have been a miscarriage of justice and he has since been pardoned. However, this adventure has enabled him to foster a great many interesting associations with somewhat seedy or dangerous characters. His relationship with his dubious friend Angel is reminiscent of the Callan-Lonely dynamic, but Rockford is far less ruthless. His down-at-heel gumshoe characterisation with a history of prison time has echoes of Frank Marker from *Public Eye*, but despite all the everyman attributes – not least, living in a trailer on the beach in Malibu – he is still *on a beach in*...Malibu. And many of his cases bring him into contact with, again, the very wealthy. So, Jim Rockford is a lovable rogue operating in an exotic location, rubbing shoulders with the rich...once more, a more sanitised approach from America. No marks deducted for action though. Virtually every episode features a car chase and a good punch up, sometimes a shoot-out and usually some romantic intrigue. It's pretty wholesome American stuff to be honest and completely addictive. The tone is almost comedy-drama. That's why it was so successful. Audiences in the UK, dealing with blackouts, unemployment, terrorist atrocities and grey, winter weather could tune in to *Columbo*, *Kojak*, *The Rockford Files* or *Hawaii Five-O* and lose themselves in another world of fast cars, fancy locations and formulaic comfort stories where the hero always wins...or they could watch *The Sweeney*.

I mention *Hawaii Five-O* and I need to flesh that out a bit. The cop show, which started in the 1960s, was a mainstay of American and British television all through the 1970s. Set in Hawaii, it predates the later *Magnum PI* series, which took up the location mantle, by two decades and delivers, certainly in the earlier years, some fine compelling police drama. It's pretty much pure escapism and highly recommended. The scenery is stunning, the theme tune is one of the most iconic in TV history. Sure, crime happens in Hawaii, a lot of crime over the years, but the sun always shines, and the criminals are always caught. Police Chief Steve McGarrett is another superhero.

Another very significant event in the middle of the decade as far as big-screen entertainment is concerned was a certain film about a killer fish. When Steven Spielberg released *Jaws* into the cinematic arena, the summer blockbuster was born and audiences were, once again, captivated by film over television. The symbolism of 'something sinister lurking below the surface' was not lost on American audiences and played into the feelings of paranoia which were endemic across society. What did the shark represent? Communism? Something closer to home? Later in the decade the idea of evil in the heart of the community would be explored more vividly with the advent of the slasher movie, exemplified by *Halloween* and exploited by numerous other imitations. The release of *The Exorcist* in 1973 and its subsequent notoriety had perhaps been a warning sign that America's obsession with horror and the supernatural was heading for a peak in this decade. It was a way for the public to look into its own heart of darkness and almost partake in mass catharsis, the downside being that once you have been scared or offended, where do you go then? How extreme does the film have to become before people simply become desensitised? At what point does an intelligent statement about the contradictions in America tip over into gratuitous exploitation? In all honesty, cinema – and American cinema at that – had been doing a lot of heavy lifting in this decade. *The Godfather* had set the bar high enough in 1972, beginning as it does with the famous line of dialogue, "I believe in America" and then going on to explore themes of love and loss, power and money, immigration and prejudice, family and betrayal, violence and corruption on an epic scale, all a metaphor for the American Dream. Barnstorming performances from actors like Pacino, DeNiro and, of course, Brando, were the talk of film-lovers everywhere. What Spielberg did though was to make sensational – or blockbuster – films accessible to a wider audience again. Kids, in other words. But nothing could have prepared the younger audience for what was about to happen next...

Science fiction had enjoyed a reasonably successful run as a genre both in cinema and on the television, on both sides of the Atlantic. In a sense, in Britain, it was the perfect genre with which to explore dystopia. Stories could be set way off in the future or just a few years hence and be presented as science fiction, or with elements to it, and appeal to younger audiences as well as adults. Rod Serling had made use of the form (and many others) as a way to impart his excellent parables or intelligent social commentary to audiences. *Star Trek* depicted a future where humans had overcome their problems and set about exploring space, again acknowledging problems but presenting them as being other planets' ones. In the UK, *Doctor Who* had survived the 1960s, thanks in part to the genius concept of having the main character regenerate every few years and be played by a different actor. The 1970s kicked off with *Doctor Who* in colour for the first time (obviously only any good if you had a colour set), with Jon Pertwee taking on the role, later handing the baton over to Tom Baker, who would take the show into the next decade. The 1970s proved to be arguably the best era for the show in terms of quality of stories and memorable performances. Pertwee's production team enjoyed exploring political and religious allegory as well as environmental concerns and pushing it as far as they could without the BBC realising, while the early Tom Baker stories went in hard with the gothic horror, earning the ire of Mary Whitehouse and producing some classic highlights of 1970s television.

Terry Nation had created the Daleks in the 1960s, and he was fascinated with the idea of dystopia. Many of his Dalek stories deal with the idea of a world gone wrong, with warfare destroying society and issues of morality in the face of absolute power explored. Most famously, in the Tom Baker serial *Genesis Of The Daleks*, broadcast in 1975, the Doctor and his companions are thrust into a society which has become the ultimate dystopia, ravaged by war and policed by fascists driven by one goal: total annihilation of the other side. Out of this, the Daleks, the doomsday machines, are created by the brilliant but unhinged scientist Davros. His character is contrasted strongly with Tom Baker's Doctor, who when given the opportunity to avert the development of the Daleks, famously asks the question, "Have I that right?" All the while, Davros has earlier confirmed that if he had the power to destroy all life everywhere, he would do it, because it would "set him up among the gods". The serial is frequently voted among the best ever by fans, largely because of the fundamental themes it explores and the sensitive way it does so. However, Terry Nation didn't stop with *Doctor Who*... oh no, he wanted more dystopian drama, so he gave us *Survivors* and *Blake's 7* as food for thought.

Survivors seems particularly relevant in 2022 as it deals with a society which has been virtually wiped out by a pandemic. Other details are strangely similar too, but the essential point is that we are post-apocalyptic as well (another of Nation's obsessions). *Blake's 7*, initially touted as 'The Dirty Dozen in space', soon becomes a dramatic exploration of interpersonal dynamics. It is a show which has one of my favourite endings...after losing the eponymous Blake and then finding him again, he is shot and the implication is that everyone dies at the end...so, not exactly a 'happy ending', more traditionally associated with US drama, as we have seen. This is the ultimate downer, but the reason I like it is that it has the boldness to *be* a downer. Admittedly, all this happens at the end of the show, which technically was shown in the 1980s, but it's primarily thought of as a 70s production. It was the correct way to end the series, so full marks to the BBC for allowing it to happen.

The success of science fiction shows in the latter part of the 1970s is primarily down to the appetite generated for them by one factor and one factor alone...*Star Wars* changed everything. One can debate its merits as a film forever, with the accolades for the 'greatest science fiction picture ever' probably better bestowed on *2001: A Space Odyssey* or *Planet Of The Apes*, but the impact of *Star Wars* was so profound that it is still being felt today. Not only did it launch numerous copycat films and shows, it also helped revitalise others, like *Star Trek* and alter the direction of established franchises like James Bond, whilst at the same time throwing into stark relief the contrast between the dazzlingly brilliant special effects in the film compared with the low-budget efforts of British TV. Suddenly, films were being judged by their effects, rather than their cinematography or symbolic depth. Cinema and by extension, television, would never be the same again. Everything and everybody had to go into space. As mentioned, the producers of Bond gave us *Moonraker*, judged by some to be the most absurd outing ever for the secret agent (although that is debatable). But beyond the impact the film had in terms of boosting science fiction into the mainstream and resetting audience expectations, it also did something else. It provided a new 'canvas' if you like, for the old school Western format to be played out on, turbo-charging the 'good versus evil' scenario once again, which British drama had spent the decade edging away from. Ironic then that a film which set the bar so high technically also had the effect of dumbing-down the complexities at the heart of the drama.

Two other major events occurred in 1977 which had huge cultural ramifications. The first was the death of Elvis Presley. While musically, the man they called the 'King of Rock and Roll' had not released anything new which could be considered of note for several years, his demise was enormously symbolic. There simply had never been any single recording artist comparable to Elvis and although the decline in his physical health had been noticeable for a while, I don't think the world was quite prepared for him actually to die so soon. The man who, in many ways, embodied the American Dream was no more. Only nine years previously, he had appeared on national television singing *If I Can Dream*...while two years later he famously posed for photographs with Richard Nixon at the White House, having written a rambling letter to the president about the 'war on illegal drugs'...you see where I am going with this? Appearances versus reality. While Elvis' own relationship with drugs was perhaps 'the prescription kind' and therefore not 'illegal' and the extent to which they were responsible for his decline will be debated forever, the entire episode is still dripping with irony at the very least. And this from the man who shied away from commenting on Vietnam, saying he was 'just an entertainer'. Whatever your views on the man and his contradictions, the lasting legacy of his music is indelible. No Elvis, no Beatles and therefore... who knows? The second important milestone in 1977 was the explosion of punk into the mainstream, with much attention being given to The Sex Pistols in the UK. Their album *Never Mind The Bollocks, Here's The Sex Pistols* coupled with controversial singles *Anarchy In The UK* (released at the end of the previous year) and *God Save The Queen* – which of course features the lyric 'There is no future in England's dreaming' released to coincide with the monarch's Silver Jubilee – was more than enough to send the establishment and the media into meltdown. Their notorious expletive-laden Bill Grundy interview from December 1976 had set them up with a good deal of publicity, exploited by their manager and remains one of the most shocking TV moments in history. Punk did not happen overnight and had in fact been developing over time in the US before it exploded in Britain, but The Pistols are seen by some as the very essence of that nihilistic spirit which resulted from years of stagnation following the promise and optimism at the end of the 1960s. It's a simplistic view, because the music of the Sex Pistols, while undoubtedly angry and loud, does bear up under close inspection. The construction of the songs is simple and technically sound, with Steve Jones' guitar work holding together well and John Lydon's words, while sneered and irreverent, are certainly not deranged or meaningless. They had something to say, and they said it and then, just like that...they were gone. The following year, the eccentric drummer Keith Moon of The Who would leave us at the age of 32, having pushed his wild lifestyle one step too far, another link to the previous decade wiped out far too soon. Only four years earlier, Mama Cass had also died at the same age in the same flat.

Like all impactful cultural moments, The Pistols opened the door for this fresh angry sound and a new generation of acts followed, counterbalancing the disco craze of the late 70s, while the old stalwarts from the previous decade were still holding their own... McCartney scoring a massive success with the grossly out-of-kilter yet monster-selling single *Mull Of Kintyre* at the end of 1977, while *God Save The Queen* had been somewhat appropriately kept off the official top spot (so they say) by Rod Stewart's *I Don't Want To Talk About It*. And cue the return of Edward Woodward (himself not averse to a bit of singing) in the BBC's latest foray into dystopia, *1990*. With Orwellian themes by the bucketload, the show explores a scenario where martial law has led to a completely new bureaucracy taking over, bringing with it all the trappings of a moribund society. It is a stark prediction for a year only just over a decade hence, which fortunately did not materialise...at least for the UK. In the US around this time, the science fiction green light handed to every studio by *Star Wars* was also producing some memorable material, but nothing like the explicit dystopian shows being aired across the pond. The US had *The Incredible Hulk*, which as well as being classic television, is also a show with great depth and layers of meaning, disguised as a children's fantasy. Bill Bixby's David Banner is stuck in his own personal hell, while life outside goes on and the raging demon which dwells within him and cannot be controlled can certainly be interpreted as a metaphor for America. The show does caveat the Hulk's rages by insisting that he will not kill, because Banner will not kill, but the overall duality at the heart of the show's character is plainly reflective of the country in which it is set. Themes of loneliness and desperation are here again, but partially overshadowed by the fantastical elements. Again, it's as if America wants to examine its complicated construction, but cannot bring itself to do so openly, so it resorts to superheroes/heroines once more, with *The Bionic Woman* picking up on the success of *The Six Million Dollar Man* and running with it, providing us with another fantasy protagonist, in a similar style to Wonder Woman. One thing American action-adventure did achieve in the 1970s was placing female characters in the spotlight, with *Charlie's Angels* being a prime example, although there is considerable justifiable criticism levied at the shows for exploiting the perceived 'sex appeal' of the leads and placing a considerable emphasis on it to sell the product. In the case of *Charlie's Angels*, even the show's title could be viewed as patronising.

In the UK, *The Avengers* was resurrected as *The New Avengers*, featuring Joanna Lumley as the female lead, a role which propelled her forward into further work of a similar nature, notably *Sapphire & Steel* at the very end of the decade, continuing a thread of strong female characters first established in the original *Avengers* series in the 60s. *The New Avengers* itself was a fun concept, but ultimately it proved to be less successful than its predecessor and wrapped after two series. [3] It is fascinating that as the 70s moved on, there was a minor resurgence for action-adventure in its more familiar shape from the 1960s. *The Sweeney* had ended but *The*

Professionals became almost like a slightly more comic book version of it. Lewis Collins and Martin Shaw are the elite CI5 operatives, working under the guidance of the incorruptible George Cowley, played to perfection by Gordon Jackson, in a show which draws on the success of the 'buddy cop' genre in the States, exemplified by *Starsky & Hutch* and which still had a long way to run as a concept and gives it a UK spin. Some of the action sequences are a little over-the-top, but in general *The Professionals*, though once again politically incorrect by today's standards, is a strong end-of-the-decade entry for UK action-adventure, helped mainly by decent writing and the charisma of the protagonists. Lewis Collins is definitely someone who could have played Bond, but I suspect his brooding, dangerous physicality probably was a little ahead of its time...*for the time*. Interestingly though, as if to offset the sensational world of CI5, we also have *The Sandbaggers*, which is a real gem in the UK espionage collection. A series notable for its lack of 'action' in the traditional sense, but still ready to shock audiences by dispensing with central characters without a moment's notice. It is daring stylistic advances like this that I find interesting, unpredictable twists that keep an audience on its toes.

US television was about to enter another golden era of sorts, not with action-adventure or comedy but with...soap opera. Who could possibly have known that *Dallas* would end up being as popular as it did? The most interesting thing about *Dallas* is that it, perhaps more than any other show in US history, exposes the real contradiction at the heart of the American Dream. There's even a sort of 'sub metaphor' for it in the juxtaposition of Bobby and JR Ewing. The show was originally intended to focus on the marriage of Bobby Ewing (played by Patrick Duffy, who had recently been part of the sci-fi craze himself, portraying the protagonist in *Man From Atlantis*) and be primarily a 'families at war', 'star crossed-lovers' story (and that's a plot that dates back centuries), but slowly the public began to take to Larry Hagman's portrayal of the sly, scheming, thoroughly amoral oil baron JR Ewing. He is one of the most compelling anti-heroes in the history of television and it really says something not just about the American Dream, but about humanity itself that, as an audience, for the most part, you want JR to succeed in his villainy. The joy comes from watching him screw people over, time and time again. Sometimes, Bobby, his more sympathetic brother, will step in and neutralise his machinations and that's fine because it creates an interesting dynamic between the two. Just about every theme known to humanity is explored in *Dallas* over its long run out of the 1970s, all through the 1980s and into the 1990s. It hit its absolute peak fairly early on when the episode revealing 'who shot JR' was broadcast, attracting one of the highest audience numbers ever seen for television. The misadventures of the most dysfunctional family in TV history even include an entire season's worth of events being literally written off as a 'dream' as a way of explaining Bobby Ewing's demise and resurrection. Now that is some insane writing. As the series progressed, the plots became more and more absurd, seriously pushing the limits of plausibility and even ending (the series at any rate) on a supernatural note. Love it or hate it, *Dallas* is one of the most influential and successful TV shows ever and went some way in finally enabling American TV drama to explore some of the most unsavoury aspects of American life in their full, dirty glory. It's very clever because it requires you, the viewer, to buy into the sleaze and relish it...and for that reason, despite its garish sensationalism, especially in the later seasons, it provides a great social document. Yes, these are the super-rich once again taking centre stage, but that's what America was and is doing all the time on a global level and the Ewings, with all their peccadillos and faults, show us both the dream life and the nightmare that comes with being wealthy. In a way, they exist in their own private dystopia, driven by malice and greed, which would become so resonant and characteristic of the 1980s. For UK audiences, the glamour and opulence being offered by *Dallas* and later *Dynasty*, proved to be an overwhelming temptation and tonic for the political problems at home. The 'Winter of Discontent' as it became known in 1979, when the then Labour government (having taken over from Edward Heath's Conservatives) had tied itself up in knots and internal battles, with industrial action grinding many services in the country to a halt, had taken its toll and once again people wanted pure escapism. The US stood ready to provide it. By the end of the decade, the golden age of British television was over; we had all been seduced by the lore of the American Dream.

While the 1960s had given us heroes and heroines, the 1970s, for the most part, provided us with the unceremonious removal of much of the optimism, trampling all over our naivety with little sensitivity. Times had 'a-changed' once more and Bob Dylan, after experiencing a decade of highs and lows commercially, producing some of his best-ever work (*Blood On The Tracks*) alongside some of his least inspired, ended the decade by finding God. Urban legend says that during a concert in Arizona, when an audience member demanded 'rock'n'roll' from Bob, he responded by saying "If you want rock'n'roll you can see *Kiss* and rock'n'roll all the way to the pit (hell)." Extraordinary words from the man who wrote *Like A Rolling Stone* and propelled rock'n'roll into the 21st century virtually single-handed. In 1979, Blondie told us that 'dreaming is free' and while that is certainly true, if you spend too much time dreaming you find that time has flown by. On the 8th December 1980, John Lennon was shot dead outside his apartment building in New York City by a man intent on becoming famous. The 1970s had begun with the end of The Beatles and the 1980s had begun with the end of the possibility that they could ever reunite. The dream was well and truly over.

© Mike Pegler

1. Editor: We could add Patrick Macnee to this list of exiles. It's hard to think of a character who had come to represent a certain type of 'Englishness' more than John Steed. Macnee had moved to the US in 1969, initially to Malibu, and then to Palm Springs.
2. Editor: It has been suggested by some critics that *Man in a Suitcase* was a possible source of inspiration for *The Rockford Files*.

3. Editor: It should be noted that this had more to do with a lack of finances rather than disinterest from UK TV audiences. The fact that the series had been financed first by French and then Canadian sources probably speaks volumes for the 'state of the nation' in the mid-70s.

THE PARTY'S OVER: THE LAST HURRAH OF THE ACTION-ADVENTURE HEROES

The 1970s is remembered as a time when reality finally caught up with the television detective series. The cosy 'Bobby on every corner' scenario of *Dixon of Dock Green* was overshadowed by the arrival of the hard-hitting 'Flying Squad' in *The Sweeney*. Little Johnny would never again be warned off petty pilfering in the local sweet shop; Jack Regan and his crew went after real villains – and they went in hard, with an eye-opening amount of violence for many viewers of the time.

However, just before the unabashed, hard-nosed, 'Flying Squad' team hit UK TV screens, the last of the ITC action-adventure heroes ushered in the new decade with a splash of colour and glamour before the 1970s became identified as an era of industrial strife, economic stagnation and decline. At the height of the 1971 television season Lew Grade's ITC Television presented *The Persuaders!* This had been one of the most talked about TV series even before it hit the screen; the reason being that it promised viewers the pairing of two of the biggest stars on either side of the Atlantic.

In arguably his second greatest coup of the decade (well he did televise the life of Jesus!) Grade managed to secure the services of Hollywood legend Tony Curtis for this new series. Couple this with the talents of the similarly globally admired Roger Moore and TV viewers everywhere would be waiting for the outcome with bated breath. The results didn't disappoint; *The Persuaders!* arguably became the zenith of the ITC action-adventure canon. Grade knew he couldn't pull his punches after casting such a strong leading pair so, fortunately, the production budget stayed in step with the casting pay bill. Add to that supporting actors and crews who ensured that all of that investment was reflected up on the screen and you had all the makings of a sure-fire classic.

The Persuaders! was quite literally the ITC peak, building on the performance and experience of the many series that had gone before, much loved shows such as *Randall and Hopkirk (Deceased), Department S* and *Strange Report* to name but a few. Even as times were changing Lew Grade could still read his audience pretty well, in terms of providing entertainment and escapism. Escapism was certainly needed at a time when the news was underpinned by violence in Northern Ireland and mainland bombings. Not long after the initial run of *The Persuaders!* were the beginnings of the energy crisis, which would eventually lead to the three-day week and national power and petrol shortages, so a little glitz and glamour (even via repeats) was more than welcome.

Like *The Avengers* before it, *The Persuaders!* sat in a world generally unknown to the majority of its viewers, although this wasn't a picture book, deserted fantasy world like the former series. However, neither was it a world that reflected the realities which Britain was facing, as a new decade dawned and its industrial competitors would eclipse the UK's heady days of world leading performance of the 1960s. *The Persuaders!* was rigidly bound in a world of strict class structures and privilege. Lord Brett Sinclair (Roger Moore) was a typical 'silver spooned' upper-class adventurer, enjoying deference from both his employees and the 'lower orders' by way of his simply being born into a title. Danny Wilde (Tony Curtis) on the other hand was a self-made man, pulling himself up out of New York's Bronx by his bootstraps, but nevertheless enjoying the style and luxury that his millions of dollars could buy. Whilst his roots are occasionally touched on within the series, they are only fully reflected in the episode *Angie, Angie...*in which Danny comes across a face from his New York past in a story which has deadly consequences.

Lord Brett's privileged ancestry is constantly referred to within the series, mostly exploited for humour as he 'entertains' Daniel with numerous 'shaggy dog' stories about his distant kith and kin. This peaks in the episode *A Death in the Family* in which we see (in the style of the classic Ealing film *Kind Hearts and Coronets*) Roger Moore displaying his acting range as several members of Brett's family, who are under threat from a psychotic killer. In *Greensleeves* we learn that a fellow Old Harrovian chum of Sinclair's went on to become the President of an African republic; his Lordship has clearly always moved within the circles of 'movers and shakers', even in his schooldays.

Learning from a past that saw rubber palm trees being dotted around Elstree Studios' backlot to convince the monochrome era viewing public that they really were in the Bahamas (or some other highly exotic locale) the producers – fully aware from earlier ITC shows that colour exposes artifice – finally whisked their stars into the real world of glamour and adventure. As a series *The Persuaders!* is split between exotic adventures filmed in the south of France, and Home Counties tales set a stone's throw from their production base at Pinewood Studios in Buckinghamshire. Out on the Continent our heroes truly are in 'Martini-land', a place where the sun shines so brightly you can almost feel it emanating from your television screen. Here 'the jet set' enjoys a degree of exclusivity, which will shrink and fade with the growth of the package holiday and explosion of tourism that will come in the decade ahead. Clearly for the moment, however, 'the in crowd' to which our playboy sleuths belong denies itself nothing. All of this is on display in *The Persuaders!*: the finest designer wardrobe; the very best in food and drink; exclusive suites in even more exclusive hotels; fast, expensive cars; sculpted, chisel-jawed boys and bronzed, voluptuous girls. Carrying over a motif from 'the swinging sixties', *The Persuaders!* is, in the wider view, clearly out of step with the particular trend that will gain impetus in the early years of the 1970s. With the occasional exceptions, such as Joan Collins' strongly independent character Sidonie in *Five Miles to Midnight* or

Hannah Gordon's undercover policewoman in *A Home of One's Own*, female guest stars are (for the most part) cast as much for their looks as for their acting abilities, as the series fails to chime with the growing feminist movement.

Another burgeoning crisis that lies outside the world of Brett and Danny is the 70s coming problems with fuel and energy. This is clearly evidenced in the types of personal transport our heroes choose to exploit. In Lord Brett Sinclair's case he parks a stunning Bahama Yellow 1970 Aston Martin DBS outside his wonderfully appointed Queen Anne's Gate 'pied-a-terre' in the heart of London. With a 6-cylinder engine that barely nudges 25 miles per gallon in fuel consumption it is clear to see that after his televised adventures, Lord Brett is going to spend a lot of time queuing at petrol filling stations as fuel shortages begin to bite in 1973/4. Similarly, Danny Wilde drives a beautiful and exclusive Ferrari Dino 246GT, which has around the same mpg as the DBS.

As entertainment *The Persuaders!* was obviously as far away from the day-to-day world of the 1970s as you could get, and the lavish application of style and glamour meant that it was one of the most watched television series of the year. The stories were tight and well-paced, the direction was sharp, and the clean-cut good guys invariably won out over the broadly drawn (sometimes comic book) villains. True, it didn't reflect the era in which it arrived but that is to be expected because it was produced before the new decade had found its feet. In every changing decade there is a period of 'cultural drag', as a new era is ushered in; politics, economics and style all hang over from the days gone before. In this way it could be argued that *The Persuaders!* is not just the climax of ITC action-adventure, but the pinnacle 1960s series, as so much of its colourful flamboyance would not have been out of place in the era of 'flower power'. It certainly held true to the morals and mores of that time.

As with any peak, on the other side there is always a way down, and *The Persuaders!* was not, as it might have been, a triumphal swansong for ITC's action heroes. The series travelled in tandem with *Jason King*, a show which debuted in the very same week on ITV. A spin-off of the 60s series *Department S* it saw Peter Wyngarde's eponymous hero going solo and trotting the globe in almost the same circles of glamour and luxury as Danny and Brett; but not quite. In the 70s the law of diminishing returns had begun to catch up with ITC. As a result, something that would become very familiar as the decade progressed was imposed upon Wyngarde's new show: budgetary restraint. Now the show's producer, the legendary cost-cutter Monty Berman, was not unused to cutting corners or costs, as he ploughed out product such as *The Champions* in the 1960s, but this time the cuts were deep. Unlike his former production partner Bob Baker, Berman was unable to dodge the bullet. Thus, whilst Baker's *The Persuaders!* had been filmed in the glossy style viewers had come to expect from ITC, on 35mm film, Jason King's potential was literally cut in half, as Grade's organisation ordered that it be made on cheaper 16mm film. In terms of the visual look of the product this meant that the output would be far less sharp and even at times a little murky.

Whilst *The Persuaders!* enjoyed the luxury of almost unfettered Continental travel for half their stories *Jason King* was very much pulled down to earth. Based in Monty Berman's familiar territory, EMI-MGM Studios Borehamwood – something of a poor relation when compared to the stylishly appointed manor house studios at Pinewood – *Jason King* was pretty much grounded within the studios, or on the highways and byways of the surrounding Hertfordshire countryside. The restricted budget only allowed for the tiniest amount of overseas location shooting. Even then these were strictly limited scenes shot around a few locations in Europe. To keep a tight lid on costs, scenes were shot, almost guerrilla style, with the smallest possible crew, usually only with Wyngarde himself, in a very concentrated period – no prolonged and costly stays. These limited shots of the hero wandering round in 'mute' footage were then sliced down and squeezed into various episodes to give an impression of a similar globetrotting style to *The Persuaders!*

Also similar to the earlier show was Jason King's penchant for indulging himself, again all the best hotels, finest of foods and driving a swish Bentley as his chosen wheels. However, two of the greatest indulgences were *Jason King's* portrayal of women, and the central character himself. If *The Persuaders!* was rather out of step with the emerging feminist movement, then *Jason King* was light years away from it! In King's world, women were (in the vast majority of episodes) simply playthings and decoration; to illuminate the manliness of the titular hero, he was often surrounded by young and attractive women. In the second aspect Wyngarde himself was later to comment that he really was overindulged in being given his own series. Slightly ruefully he reflected that the series did not work as well as it might have, simply because he had stripped out that core relationship with his co-stars from *Department S*. As such he had no-one to bounce off and the series, enjoyable as it might have been, was considerably weaker by comparison. The final outcome being that Jason King the character created a memorable icon that would resonate down the years, but that *Department S* is (rightly) better and more fondly remembered than *Jason King* the series.

Fast forward 12 months to the height of the televisual year; in the Autumn season of 1972 viewers are invited to join the latest ITC hero in a series entitled *The Adventurer* starring Hollywood actor Gene Barry, supported by Barry Morse, who had found fame across the Atlantic as Lt. Gerard in hit series *The Fugitive*. Once again produced by Monty Berman, if *The Persuaders!* was the zenith of ITC action-adventure, then *The Adventurer* easily wins a one-horse race to be the nadir of the house style. Style is not a word that rests easily upon *The Adventurer* wherein its diminutive star (with an ego some 20 or 30 times his height!) is often dressed in the most appalling 'Rupert Bear' checked trousers. The worst of 1970s fashion is only the beginning of the ills of *The Adventurer*. Again shot on 16mm, and (mercifully?) shrunk to a half-hour format, the show looks to be the cheapest of cheapjack productions that was ever put on screen by Berman and his team. This despite the fact that the series benefited from far more continental filming than *Jason King* did; possibly Lew Grade indulging his problematic star's desire to see Europe whilst he was here? The scripts are mostly dodgy, and saddled with an imported lead who has all the charm, style and acting ability of something that (wholly in keeping with the early 70s) would at any time fall foul of the era's Dutch Elm Disease! Even the spirited character playing of Barry Morse fails to save the show; in this author's opinion it is definitely for ITC completists only. It speaks volumes about the quality of the end product that the series is best remembered for its titles sequence, which is accompanied by a fantastic theme tune by *007* and *The Persuaders!* composer John Barry. By the end of the series the coffin lid was halfway closed for ITC action-adventure.

Following something of an ITC tradition, the 1972 autumn season also introduced more output in the shape of Gerry Anderson's *The Protectors*. It was something of a sign of the times, and the waning fortunes of ITC, that this production was out of step with the Andersons oeuvre, in that it was not initiated as a concept by the husband-and-wife team. In their 'gap years' between *UFO* and *Space:1999* Gerry Anderson had been presented with a simplistic brief for the show by Sir Lew Grade. The show was to be about an international group of private detectives who were successful because they worked outside the law. That was it, the rest of the production was Gerry and Sylvia's to flesh out. Another shift for ITC was that the series was to be financed by the Faberge company, whom Lew had previously tried to interest in *The Adventurer*. The series also gained an unusual credit for a company called Ferdporqui Productions, which was in fact the organisation representing the show's star, Robert Vaughan. The principal cast also included Nyree Dawn Porter and Tony Anholt, making this ITC's final three-leads series. Relationships did not bloom, however, and news filtered back from the set that all was not well between the lead and his co-stars, a problem that was allegedly exacerbated by the presence of Sherwood Price, the screen-credited executive of Ferdporqui. Again shot on 16mm film, like *The Adventurer* the show also suffered from the retrograde step of cutting back to a half hour time-slot, which meant that in reality writers had under 25 minutes of screen time to build plots and develop characters. This somewhat explains why the background of why the wider background of *The Protectors* Organisation is hinted at, but never clearly developed, rather represented in the closing credits by the silhouetted appearance of the mysterious 'fourth Protector'. Despite these shortcomings the show made enough impact to have a second series, although a third series' development ended abruptly when Faberge pulled the plug on funding. Like the other 16mm ITC productions of the early 1970s, scripting was uneven on *The Protectors*, and it is renowned for the fact that Lew Grade called the Robert Vaughan directed episode, *It Could be Practically Anywhere on the Island*, the worst episode he had ever seen of anything. It was wholly uncharacteristic of Lew to belittle anything he had produced, but when the central premise of this (utterly self-indulgent) broad comedy episode is trying to find microfilm plans of an atomic plant, which have been swallowed, then passed, by a starlet's pet poodle, you can understand his angst!

Both Lew and ITC were taking new directions in the early 1970s. After the success of *Moses the Lawgiver* in 1974 and Grade's ennoblement to the peerage in 1976, Lew sought the blessing of another Lord by making the epic television series *Jesus of Nazareth*. All eyes were on prestige as the televisual landscape began to change, and Lew was also turning towards the film industry. After the production of *Space:1999* and the global success of *The Muppet Show*, Grade's organisation took one last look at the action-adventure hero, at the same time looking back towards the former glories of ITC by reviving a much-loved character from the company's heyday, Simon Templar. Unlike his 1960s incarnation, this new Saint, thankfully titled *The Return of The Saint* and not Son of The Saint, would not be confined to the studios' backlot and the

Elstree country lanes. This time Simon Templar was allowed to roam the Continent in search of action, adventure, glamour and beautiful women. As with *Space:1999* co-production and co-funding were the order of the day, with Grade's U.S. associates being hands-on in production, and the massive budget being part funded by Italian television's RAI, which accounted for certain decisions on locations and casting. The show was warmly received, making a star of Ian Ogilvy, but looking at it from the remove of the 21st century it is clear that the time of the action hero had passed. The lavish, indulgent adventurer was out of step in an era of punk rock, in which television had come to reflect the more realistic expectations of its viewers. The bubble had burst: Great Britain was no longer the 'happening' cultural hub it had once been; economic power had been stripped away as businesses failed to move with the times. We were on the doorstep of a sea-change politically, which would have far-reaching effects upon the whole country for many decades ahead. The time had passed. [1]

The much beloved and lavish action-adventure hero was dead. He would return, occasionally, by way of parody or affection pastiche as those who had grown up with these familiar characters moved into the entertainment industry themselves, and nodded to their heroes in series such as *The Comic Strip Presents...* A (sort of) revival would come by way of the advent of home video, when the ITC back catalogue was exploited and enabled many fans to relive those glory days once again. Interest arose to the point where *The Saint* had yet another (independent) television revival and even a Hollywood film. [2] The ITC shows, however, were clearly things of their time and remakes or re-imaginings have never truly captured the spirit of that age, simply for the fact that they (and we) are beyond it.

© Al Samujh

1. Editor: I might throw in a brief mention for *The Zoo Gang* (1974), the six-part mini-series made on 35mm and with

lavish location shooting on the French Riviera. While it has been (somewhat unfairly) referred to as the geriatrics' *Persuaders!*, it was an action-adventure with a difference, in using older, 'classic' film actors in the lead parts. John Mills and Lilli Palmer are impressive in their roles, there are some delightful locations, and it has a restrained charm arguably lacking in some of those other ITC shows of the mid-70s. Nevertheless, as Al Samujh observes, *The Persuaders!* represented the spectacular (tongue-in-cheek) swansong. The age of the swinging action-adventure was well and truly over.

2. Editor: The same applies to the Hollywood version of *The Avengers*. Unsurprisingly, neither the makers of the Val Kilmer film (1997) nor the Ralph Fiennes movie (1998) recaptured the spirit of 1960s action-adventure.

'ENGLAND SOON?' SURVEILLANCE STATES & TYRANNICAL REGIMES

"We'll cure that troubled mind of yours."
(Dr. Mark Thorn, *Appearances*, *The Guardians*)

As the 1960s made way for a new decade, producer Rex Firkin and writer Vincent Tilsley – who had been working together on the World War 2 drama *Manhunt* (1969-70) for LWT – put forward an idea to the same network franchise holder for a new drama, *The Guardians* (1971). Tilsley had been a prolific script writer since the mid-1950s, often adapting classic novels into period television serials, in addition to working briefly on two significant 1960s ITC adventure series, *Man in a Suitcase* and *The Prisoner*, including penning the iconic episode *The Chimes of Big Ben*. *The Guardians* is a left-field drama which is hard to label or categorise. Set in the near future – the 1980s – we might call it a dystopian political thriller, yet it combines elements of spy-fi, sci-fi and social satire. In many ways, just as the BBC's *Doomwatch* (1970-72) prefigures the eco sci-fi of *The Green Death* (1973) and Terry Nation's *Survivors* (1975-77), *The Guardians* paved the way for a decade of dark, dystopian political drama, including Edward Woodward's *1990* – which I will come to later – and Nation's *Blake's 7*, whose faceless Federation men recall The Guardians of the Realm themselves.

The opening of the first episode plunges us directly into angry exchanges between Guardian troops and demonstrators, with the protestors employing firebombs, and the troops responding with smoke flares and water cannons, the violent clashes caught on camera by the EBC. Director Robert Tronson's effective use of handheld camera helps to convey the general sense of chaos and panic. This initial scene allows us a snapshot or flavour of the 'state of the nation', before we are gradually offered a contextual back story and rule book, two requirements for any futuristic dystopia. *The Guardians* is no exception, and we can draw up a short list of some of its basic ingredients before examining the series in detail:

- A coalition government has recently made way for a puppet PM and cabinet, concealing a dictatorship
- The traditional police force has been superseded by a military-style armed security force, the 'Guardians of the Realm'
- 'Subversive' demonstrations and strikes are suppressed by the Guardians and by new legislation respectively
- The Queen has gone into self-exile until democracy is restored
- Identity cards are obligatory and read by machines
- There are increasing restrictions for television and the press, including a ban on showing images of 'civil disorder'
- A Communications Committee decides what news should be released publicly
- Capital punishment has been reinstated
- A sterilisation programme is in place for people deemed unsuitable for procreation
- 'Rehabilitation centres' contain and confine political dissidents
- The Communist Party is now illegal and both government spies and paid informers are on the lookout for its members
- Citizens are actively encouraged to inform on each other: "Tell us: Keep England Safe"
- Prisoners are routinely drugged, interrogated and tortured, sometimes leading to their deaths
- The current dictatorial regime is seen as a 'transitional' measure, with free elections to be restored at some point in the future, at which time the Guardians will be disbanded

This is by no means an exhaustive list, but it gives a flavour of the 'State of England', the playful title of the opening, introductory episode. That first instalment is cleverly constructed by Tilsley. The frantic search for an armed assassin in a multi-storey car park at the very end allows him to bookend the episode with action, while every scene in between is dialogue driven, as we constantly flit between a cabinet meeting, an interview at a Guardians HQ and an appointment at a psychiatrist. Both the Guardian captain, Tom Weston (John Collin) and the government psychiatrist, Dr. Benedict (David Burke), will eventually be revealed to be dissidents. However, even without this knowledge, the opening episode leaves us with a clear impression of people hiding behind masks and playing deadly games with poker faces, while reluctant Prime Minister, Sir Timothy Hobson (Cyril Luckham), is seemingly powerless and all at sea, not even aware of where the Guardians have rehoused England's nuclear armoury.

The fact that the second episode, *Pursuit*, picks up at the exact moment where *State of England* left off, is an early warning that *The Guardians* is both a serial and a series. Having already seen the shady First Secretary, Dennis Norman (Derek Smith), in charge of cabinet meetings, we now hear his voice interrogating the captured hitman. It is, perhaps, the first hint that Norman – rather than simply being the spokesman for what the PM will later call "a concealed dictatorship" – is possibly the spider at the centre of the political web. The PM himself hints as much; when Norman describes himself as the government's 'stage manager', Hobson replies: "Well, it's the stage manager who brings down the curtain; perhaps he's the most powerful member of the troupe." Hugh Whitemore's story effectively cuts between the 'civilised' conversation of the PM with the head of EBC, in the exclusive, anachronistic surroundings of a gentleman's club, and almost psychedelic flashbacks to the earlier brutal torture of the (now dead) revolutionary. This allows us to reflect on the contrast between the veneer of respectable society and its disturbingly dark underbelly.

LWT's *The Guardians* clearly bases the EBC on the BBC, even down to its logo. The state-financed channel is seen offering its viewers both soporific content and didactic, patronising news bulletins. It appears to be already under state control, even before the PM's dinner with the EBC's Francis Wainwright (Richard Hurndall) where Hobson reminds him that the television network's charter requires "impartiality", and the Head of EBC argues that this does not override the "need to tell the truth". Hurndall provides a polished performance, and his eloquent, quietly passionate character enables us to gain an insight into the PM's past, a time when he was "compassionate", "politically honourable" and "ideological". The meeting of the two men provides a fascinating, brilliantly scripted debate about censorship but also leaves us with a puzzle which we are still trying to solve at the very end of the series: whether the PM is simply weak-willed and ineffectual, naïve, delusional, out of touch, or whether he has, to an extent, sold his soul. The ambiguous depiction of Sir Timothy is at the heart of *The Guardians*. While it has been observed that the series lacks the traditional protagonist seen on a weekly basis – no actor appears in all thirteen episodes – Hobson is, arguably, the closest we come to a main character. Much of his time is spent trying to justify the government's tyrannical regime in terms which might seem reasonable:

"People often resist what is good for them at first. Later on, they see the good, and accept it."

We frequently see him attempting to reassure people that 'benevolent' dictatorship is for the 'greater good', in public broadcasts, meetings, private dinner parties, even in conversations with his own son. One of the problems is that it is unclear whether he genuinely believes in the system himself. Openly opposed to the menacing presence of The Guardians, he veers between carefully worded speeches, often ghost-written for him, and genuinely heartfelt comments. He is mentally trapped in a nostalgia for an England long past, if indeed it ever existed. At times it comes across as an elegy to lost youth, and a fear of old age beckoning; he even refers to "the skull beneath the skin". One moment he readily reminds colleagues that "all opposition is illegal", while in the next he confesses to "a seed of doubt" about both the lack of an alternative voice and the regime's ethics. As viewers we are left to decide whether the writers have created a fascinatingly enigmatic character who does not fully understand his own motivations, or an unlikely figure whose mood/opinion swings are unbelievable. One might argue that his internal conflict mirrors the series' thematic concern with moderate and extreme factions on both the inside/outside of power. (Is there even an implication that within many of us there are moderate and extreme elements in conflict with each other?) For me, Sir Timothy is a similar character to the increasingly frail monarch, King Berenger, in Ionesco's Theatre of the Absurd play *Le Roi se Meurt* (*Exit the King*), unwilling or unable to face grim reality.

Nor is Sir Timothy the only central character who remains elusive and enigmatic. This particularly applies to the mint-popping government First Secretary. Brilliantly portrayed by Derek Smith, Dennis Norman, on one level, is a disturbingly distorted precursor for Nigel Hawthorne's Sir Humphrey Appleby's *Yes, Minister* character, particularly in his cynical advice to the PM. Despite his public persona as an eloquent, chillingly cold, demonic figure, we have seen his nephew/lover murdered in the opening episode and, at times, he comes across as a tortured individual. Politically driven to prevent a return to what is referred to as the "permissive" society of England in the 1960s, his private life is that of a closeted homosexual. It is left unclear whether this public/private conflict is meant to make him more human, or simply add an extra layer of hypocrisy. Like so many aspects of *The Guardians*, Norman is impossible to 'read'. Indeed, as the series' ironically upbeat Wilfred Josephs theme tune warns us, we cannot take anything at face value. In several episodes, we see Norman tackling jigsaw puzzles and this, in a sense, reflects the challenge for the viewer as we struggle to piece together the complex narrative threads.

Even some of the rules or laws I listed earlier are less than transparent. Several of these change as the series progresses, while one major question – "Who is the real Head of State?" – is voiced, yet the answer remains unclear. With the Queen in self-imposed exile, a PM who is sometimes a puppet figure, sometimes (seemingly) free to run the government, a First Secretary initially answering to 'The General', but later apparently in charge himself, it is impossible to tie anything or anyone down in this murky dystopian world. It is equally unclear who the main dissident voice belongs to, as a succession of anti-government characters – some carrying the code name Quarmby – appear at various points in the overarching plot. What is transparent is that the current regime is a fascist one, justifying itself with the argument that the general public does not know what is best for it and that "efficiency" is more important than liberty. The PM famously comments that "democracy is a form of group suicide". *The Guardians* is a series which continually blurs the lines. Nor is there a simplistic good/bad polarity. Many of those dissidents we encounter appear to be as amoral as the institutions they wish to interrupt, sabotage or usurp. Certainly, they are just as willing to spill blood. As Clare Weston (Gwyneth Powell) observes, they have "no sentiment, no love".

This brings me on to the Guardians themselves. The title of the series points towards the symbolic importance of the so-called 'Guardians of the Realm'. Their collective name has an old-fashioned, romantic, chivalric sound to it, and their slogan is equally ironic: the three Ps of 'Peace, Prosperity, Protection'. In reality, they are an aggressive military police force, offering disturbing echoes of Nazi SS troops, from the Swastika-style logo on their uniforms to their Big Brother posters. They offer us a constant visual reminder that – for all the carefully crafted soundbites put out by the government – this is an Orwellian military dictatorship run partly on a constant fear factor. The fascist regime is justified from within by several conflicting arguments: this is a period of transition, requiring radical measures which can be lifted once things have settled down; the previously mentioned "democracy is a form of group suicide"; the suggestion that a lack of individual liberty is the collective price to be paid for a new stability. In what is, essentially, a speech-driven series, the example I gave earlier of the PM/EBC moral debate about censorship is echoed on several occasions as the writers explore the ethics of dictatorship, censorship, sterilisation and capital punishment. Ironically, this can be seen as both a strength and a weakness of the series.

Despite the series privileging dialogue over action, when the latter breaks out it tends to be deeply disturbing. Both *Appearances* and *This is Quarmby* provide the viewer with chilling images of the Guardians' ruthless action when hunting down 'freedom fighters', regardless of whether they are (equally ruthless) terrorists, or simply civilians speaking out. A terrorist attack in *Appearances* leads to a high-speed car chase – backed by a very 70s score – resulting in the bombers clinically dispatched in a shoot-out, blood splattering a 'Peace-Prosperity-Protection' poster. In *This is Quarmby*, the rogue interruptions to radio and television – calling out the government and demanding a return to democratic elections – sees the unarmed pirate broadcasters eventually machine-gunned to death, the chilling soundscape captured on state radio before the censors can override it. It is, arguably, the most powerful episode in the series, one which sees ex-Head of Intelligence Sir Michael – brilliantly portrayed by Richard Vernon – asking the PM questions he should have already asked himself. Why should these peaceful Quarmby broadcasts be stopped? Shouldn't this form of democratic protest be allowed? Not for the only time in the show, Hobson privately admits that he shares some of the people's concerns. Sir Michael's other question – "Who will guard [i.e. monitor] the Guardians?" – is one which Sir Timothy never answers or resolves, despite his own misgivings. *The Guardians* constantly muddies the proverbial waters, however. Anti-government individuals regularly display a willingness not only to kill establishment figures but to also cold-bloodedly murder innocent people caught in the middle. 'The end justifies the means' appears to be their battle cry, which, in one sense, makes them no different from the government itself.

Earlier, I used the term Orwellian and, in a sense, all dystopian television dramas – including *The Prisoner*, *The Guardians*, *1990*, *Blake's 7* and *Edge of Darkness* – pay tribute to *1984*. Here we have a state of identity cards, surveillance, drugged interrogation, 'happy pills', demonic medics, and the reintroduction of capital punishment, in a Britain which has chosen to distance itself ideologically and politically from other nations. As is often the case in both spy-fi and dystopian drama, much of the dramatic tension is created by both a collective paranoia and the presence of 'insider outsiders' and 'outsider insiders'.

Nevertheless, *The Guardians* was not created in a cultural vacuum. It is very much 'of its time'. Produced soon after the beginning of the decade, unlike the creators of *1990* the writers of *The Guardians* had not experienced a substantial slice of the politically, economically and socially unstable 1970s to draw upon as context for their scripts. (The 'Troubles' in Northern Ireland *are* referenced, and the series was not broadcast on Ulster Television). Instead, it is the 1960s counterculture which is blamed by Hobson's government for the current situation. Both Carnaby Street and the Beatles are referenced as examples of a Swinging 60s malaise – an era seen as creating moral, political and social confusion – which led to "national breakdown". Unlike in *1990* where the unions will be seen as being an integral part of the powerful regime, here they have been singled out as the chief subversive faction, their right to strike slowly undermined, while the Communist Party has been outlawed, its followers considered to be suffering from both "neurosis" and "paranoia", and in need of having their "troubled minds" cured by psychiatrists, as Dr. Mark Thorn, played with evil relish by Dinsdale Landen, is happy to tell one of his incarcerated patients, Tom Weston.

Unlike *1990*, stylistically and structurally *The Guardians* pushes the envelope. The writers are happy to drop in both characters and plot threads which then disappear, only to re-emerge in later episodes. They are equally willing to combine gritty realism with almost

'Theatre of the Absurd' scenes and characters, while also offering us Pinteresque dialogue where we are challenged to root out the subtext beneath the seemingly banal or mundane. As Harold Pinter once said of the dialogue in his own plays: underneath what is being said, something else is being 'said'.

A daring example of the Pinteresque occurs at the beginning of *The Logical Approach* where a seemingly kind and friendly prison guard chats away about the delights of apple crumble while a teenage prisoner is eating what turns out to be drugged food. Having been sedated, he is given a dose of lethal cyanide moments later. It is a scene which offers us chillingly banal dialogue, followed by the disturbing sight of someone being 'put down' by a doctor amidst the argument that this method of execution is 'humane'. There is a genuine, constant desire to shock us as viewers. *The Guardians* happily veers between brutal murders, often captured on camera – such as the previously mentioned machine-gunning Guardians killing unarmed dissidents on a train, a man stabbed to death by a tramp wielding a sharpened umbrella, or a psychiatrist strangling a man in drag on his couch – and a stagey, theatrical approach. One episode, *The Killing Trade*, is a virtual two-hander set in an apartment, as Clare Weston and Eleanor Benedict (Lynn Farleigh) swap life stories. The social and political satire covers class, gender and sex.

On the subject of irony, *The Guardians* makes great use of euphemistically titled organisations, including the 'rehabilitation' treatment which would be redeployed in *1990*:

Hobson: Did you know that we have a rehabilitation centre in Britain? Not a prison, you know; it's for political offences.
Chris: A concentration camp?
Hobson: We call it a 'rehabilitation centre'.
Chris: And who do you 'rehabilitate'?

The PM's son, Christopher (Edward Petherbridge), is just one of several characters in *The Guardians* who embarrass him by either requesting to be saved from one of his 'autocue' speeches or asking a straightforward question to cut through the bureaucratic, linguistic propaganda, a 'no bullshit' method which will be regularly employed by Edward Woodward's Jim Kyle in *1990*. The fact that Hobson comes across most of the time as a decent human being makes the political regime even more disturbing, in a strange sense. The constant use of propaganda speeches, however, is a labyrinth which we as viewers are trapped inside, like a hamster in its wheel, reflecting the fate of the innocent victims of both the regime and opposition groups.

In summing up, *The Guardians* draws upon familiar Orwellian ideas, but in daring ways. First, there is a distinctly playful structure, including characters, plot threads or scenes left hanging and picked up again in later episodes. Second, we have some utterly bizarre characters one might not expect in any TV drama, never mind a 1971 political thriller, such as a sexually voracious female assassin who carries suicide pills in her pearl earrings, a useless private detective who simply changes his hats as 'camouflage' and willingly submits to being strangled to death, and a dirty tramp who transforms himself into a deadly action man. Third, there is the tendency for the static, speech-driven drama to be interrupted by shocking content, such as violent murders, suicide and euthanasia, even a black immigrant setting fire to herself on the instructions of a cult-like church. All of this makes *The Guardians* a disturbing, fascinating, if flawed drama, quite unlike any other. I will explore some of those potential flaws in the brief final section of this chapter.

I have deliberately avoided giving away the dramatic twist in the final episode, *End in Dust*. Suffice it to say that its darkly humorous – arguably deliciously absurd – conclusion is in keeping with what comes before. If you have yet to discover *The Guardians*, I can promise that a most unusual, unique series awaits you.

*

"I'm bound by miles and miles of steel chains that they made out of what used to be red tape."
(Jim Kyle, *Whatever Happened to Cardinal Wolsey?*, *1990*)

Television audiences would have come to *1990* (1977-78) with Edward Woodward's previous series, *Callan* (1967-72), still relatively fresh in their minds. No doubt his memorable performance in the central role as a damaged secret service agent, David Callan, played a part in the decision to cast him as journalist Jim Kyle in the later series. The two shows do share connective tissue. While *Callan* is often labelled as both spy-fi and an action series, it has a distinctly dystopian feel to it, as Mike Pegler observed in his chapter. 'The Section' almost operates outside the law and its colour-coded filing system sees some people placed under surveillance simply for joining the 'wrong' party, not so different from the state's decision that "idealism can be [medically] treated" in *1990*. While there is no suggestion that British society in *Callan* involves similar widespread censorship and controls to those that we see in *1990*, it is, nevertheless, a bleak world. While both Callan and Kyle possess positive qualities, neither represents a hero. In addition, each is troubled by self-doubt, often questioning their professional roles and actions. Callan's espionage work identifies him as part of the Establishment, even if he rails against it. While Kyle's newspaper may be anti-Establishment, his job makes him a relatively privileged citizen, arguably on the same power/powerless side as the PCD. However, as to the insider/outsider polarity, the boundaries are somewhat blurred, as Callan uses his associate 'Lonely' to enable him to gain access to the 'other' London of the criminal underworld, while in *1990* he has another contact, 'Nameless', to feed him information from the law enforcers. (Shady import/export agent Dave Brett – played with typical roguish charm by Tony Doyle – provides Kyle with another secret sharer, particularly when it comes to the action-adventure plot strands, in addition to providing access to that 'other' world operating inside/

outside the law.) Kyle's odd relationship with the fascinatingly enigmatic female Deputy Controller of the PCD adds a morally grey area to his supposedly anti-state positioning. In *1990*, both the rules and the legal process itself appear to be a moveable feast which can be circumvented or bent by those in power.

William Greatorex's dystopian political drama was broadcast in two mini-series on the BBC, September-October 1977 and February-April 1978. Like *The Guardians*, it is something of a forgotten show, perhaps partly because it was tucked away on BBC2 and never repeated. While set in the near future, in theory, like most effective dystopias it also offers us a distorted portrait of the troubled times people were living through in the real world. Among the many features of his imagined future, which are gradually drip-fed to us as the series develops, are a mixture of realities and fears which concerned both the media and the general public in mid-1970s Britain: escalating inflation and national bankruptcy, the 'brain-drain', all-powerful trade unions, a curtailed working week, print union interference with press freedom, bugging and state surveillance, political corruption, and escalating violent crime were all factors at a historical time in which a State of Emergency had already been declared five times since the decade commenced. In addition, far right and far left extremism were genuine concerns, while a complete shutdown of services and even a military coup were both seen as distinct possibilities. Labelled '1984 + Six' by its creator, we might suggest that *1990* also represented 'Reality + Six', rather than a far-fetched piece of tele-fantasy.

The clichéd saying about fact being stranger than fiction rings true when one reads about some of the events which took place in Britain during the early to mid-1970s. A selective list might include the killing of unarmed civilians by British soldiers, curfews amidst fears of civil war in Northern Ireland, KGB connections to major political figures, the M15 bugging of 10 Downing Street [1], a political assassination in Suburban London, bombs detonated at the Tower of London and House of Commons, record numbers of people emigrating from the UK, media reports of the West End crumbling into urban decay...all dystopian *facts*. The so-called 'Battle of Lewisham' had taken place just before the first series of *1990* was broadcast. None of this is meant to imply that Britain in the mid-1970s was either a surveillance state or a tyrannical regime; however, as I have indicated, many of the pieces of Greatorex's fictional jigsaw were based on the strange times being played out in the real world. This fascinating, sadly neglected, television series took a country in an almost permanent State of Emergency and added a dark Orwellian twist. It would be fair to say that, as a generalisation, the first series (and cast) of *1990* is far, far stronger and that its second run is less innovative, becoming more of a vehicle for Woodward as a dissident 'action' man. [2] For the purpose of this second section of my chapter, I will be exploring the initial series. We might start by drawing up a list or timeline of some of the (fictional) events and changes which have taken place in *1990*'s grey new world, just as I did with *The Guardians*:

- The nation became officially bankrupt
- Elections took place but only 20% of the population voted
- The new government is supported by a PCD (Public Control Department)
- Sterling has been replaced by the weak 'Anglo-dollar'
- Housing, goods and services are limited and supplied on the basis of an individual's (constantly reviewed) 'Life Score'
- ARCs (Adult Rehabilitation Centres) are being opened for 'social misfits'
- Ombudsman's court decisions are government controlled
- The Government circumvents European humanitarian conventions
- There has been a failed military coup
- A three-day working week is often in operation
- There is widespread bugging and state surveillance
- The state controls most industry, press and media
- The state uses mind-control 'happiness' and 'misery' pills

- Civil servants and union leaders comprise the Alphas
- Import/export agents exist outside normal state controls
- On-going 'brain drain' despite PCD monitoring points of exit
- The 'skilled' sign P17s binding them to UK work for 10 years
- Pubs replaced by 'leisure centres'; drinkers are 'graded'
- People can be reduced to 'non-citizens', nameless numbers
- There is an increasing number of dissident groups

This list is by no means exhaustive – and some aspects change during the course of the series – but it offers a taste of the dystopian world in which Jim Kyle operates as both an investigative journalist for *The Star*, one of the few remaining genuine newspapers, and as a latter-day Scarlet Pimpernel. As one can see from the list, many of the aspects of the regime are elements found earlier in the decade in *The Guardians*, a reminder that dystopian television dramas tend to draw upon familiar, shared, Orwellian ideas.

The two-part 'pilot' or introductory episodes, *Creed of Slaves* and *When Did You Last See Your Father?* were broadcast on successive nights. From the very start of *Creed of Slaves*, post-titles, [3] one could almost be fooled into thinking that *1990* had been filmed in monochrome. The soulless and rundown housing estate we see is a sea of grey concrete, looking out on to wasteland, with colour virtually drained away. There is an immediate sense of monitoring and surveillance. A doctor's arrival on the estate is logged by two PCD men; a cynical Kyle listens in to a House of Commons speech being made by the Home Secretary Dan Mellor (John Savident); Kyle and his secretary Marly's conversations are being tracked by a government spy in one of a vast number of PCD listening booths. There is an effective contrast between the shabby and instantly recognisable newspaper offices, the almost sci-fi PCD monitoring set and both the Commander's decadent headquarters and his female deputy's opulent Regent Street apartment with their expensive artworks. With Kyle aware that his office is bugged, there is a sense of a cat-and-mouse game of espionage chess being played out. He is immediately established as 'old school', unwilling to rely on modern technology such as the 'voice impetus' machine which "makes far too many mistakes", while Marly (Honor Shepherd) playfully suggests that he is not "up with the times". Greatorex's script allows the dialogue to casually drop in information about the state of the nation, such as Kyle's comment that anyone capable of fixing the voice impetus machine has long since emigrated to the US. It is a society which is breaking down, where things do not work as well as they are purported to, itself a running leitmotif.

We have been plunged into a UK which has the feel of an Eastern Bloc country, with its grim cityscape of rundown tower blocks, urban wastelands, misty docks, muted colours and the suppression of both democracy and free movement. It appears to be a world of disinformation, rather than simply misinformation. Kyle's editor, 'Tiny' Greaves (George Murcell), cheerfully warns him that if he maintains the high standard of his investigative pieces the government "will be sending you to the coal mines", a nice twist on the proverbial Siberian salt ones. Or to a new, euphemistically labelled Adult Rehabilitation Centre, outside one of which a photo-journalist has already had his camera smashed and been taken inside "for interrogation". (Intriguingly, Jim Kyle's articles seem to fluctuate between those which support the regime and others which undermine it.) Much of the dry humour is delivered by Woodward as his character takes satirical swipes at the status quo, describing – for example – the ombudsman's court judges as:

"Ventriloquists. When they say 'no' you can see the Home Secretary's lips move."

The opening part of the story introduces topics which subsequent episodes in the initial run will pick up on and explore in depth, such as the ARCs, the control of the printed word, the corrupt judicial system. Having established this strange yet eerily familiar world,

Creed of Slaves weaves a web of seemingly separate plotlines. First, there is Dr. Vickers (Donald Gee) and his family. In contrast to Jim Kyle, who has, after all, actively encouraged PCD surveillance through his professional job, Vickers is depicted as a victim of the system, selflessly supporting helpless outcasts, but also desperate to take his bronchial-asthmatic daughter to live in a warmer climate, yet whose exit visa application and subsequent appeal have both been rejected. We see PCD men forcing their way into his home – "we have right of entry" – before ransacking it while searching for bogus evidence that he has criminal connections to do with smuggling people out of Britain. Once Greatorex has revealed that Jim Kyle leads a double life – helping people escape – we have a sense of plotlines crisscrossing and characters who will, inevitably, connect.

Already, in *1990*'s opening episode, we have a disconcerting mental image of a giant web, with both the PCD and the Home Secretary at its centre, and individuals like Vickers potential flies to be trapped. In addition, with the mysterious 'Faceless' (Paul Hardwick) offering Kyle Top Secret information from within the PCD, and a government mole hidden within *The Star*'s staff, there is further blurring of the boundaries, adding to the general sense of distrust bordering on paranoia, illustrated by the Controller's reference to the presence of a "Judas" amongst his staff. Even one of the Deputy Controllers of PCD, Delly Lomas (Barbara Kellerman), is openly cynical about both the Home Secretary himself and some of the state's operations, describing two of the doctors who have been placed in charge of the new ARCs as "freaks", "monsters", "Mr. Hyde and Mr. Hyde", while seemingly accepting the necessity to open these "correction" houses. As in *The Guardians*, the doctors working in these institutions are depicted as unethical sadists.

There is a *frisson* of sexual attraction between the fiercely ambitious Lomas and the married Kyle in the midst of their mutual suspicion, almost a fore-echo of Avon and Servalan's fascinatingly strange rapport in *Blake's 7*. Frustratingly, with Lomas/Kellerman departing after the initial run, we never discover how much of a human heart she possesses under her ice-cold exterior, something which is hinted at as she protects Kyle from time to time. This is part of a more general blurring of lines, something which, as one reviewer of *1990* has observed, is key to its success:

'The banality of evil runs throughout the series. On the one hand, Skardon, Lomas and Tasker are simply bureaucrats doing a job (in their minds they no doubt see themselves on the side of law and order). It's this blurring between "good" and "evil" which is so compelling – the PCD may be oppressive, but their public face can appear to be reasonable. This is key – if you can keep the nastiness buried then maybe you stand a chance of fooling most of the people.' [4]

This acute observation – which could equally apply to *The Guardians* – connects with the quotation which inspired the title of the first episode, a fragment taken from a famous, insightful comment of William Pitt the Younger:

'Necessity is the plea for every impingement of human freedom. It is the argument of tyrants; it is the creed of slaves.'

Many of the methods employed by the government's PCD are justified as necessary in a state facing financial problems, limited resources, a 'brain drain', and so-called anti-social behaviour. Almost total control of individual freedom – be it in the form of public ownership of commerce and industry; job opportunities and restrictions; the state benefits system; television and the press; the use of "mind-bending" doctors, electric-shock treatment and drugging of 'dissidents'; exit visas; the rejection of some as 'non-citizens'; even surveillance – is explained away either through misreporting, silence or the age-old argument that it is all for 'the greater good', the clichéd notion that draconian legislation and institutions like the ARCs are a 'necessary evil'. No doubt PCD's leadership triumvirate would consider themselves to be 'apprehensive patriots', the very phrase used by the real-life Colonel Stirling when proposals for his GB75 organisation were leaked in the mid-70s. [5]

The union-dominated nature of the government in *1990* reflects the fact that Greatorex's series is very much a product of the times. This was, after all, a period of political crisis where the power of the unions seemed to be almost absolute, able to shut down newspapers, television networks, public transport, energy supplies ...even dictating the working hours on the filming of George Lucas' *Star Wars*. Given the fact that the unions had forced successive Conservative and Labour governments to their knees, threatening to bring the country to a stand-still, there is a pointed, satirical irony to the fact that they are depicted as power sharers and Alpha citizens in *1990*. I have seen it observed in several reviews of the series that the fictional government is a 'socialist' one. Nevertheless, in one sense it does not matter whether it is seen as left or right-wing. *1990* is about extreme state control, and – as history tells us – this can be either fascist or a distorted version of socialism.

There is a running leitmotif in the series of a brain drain and people in general seeking to escape Britain. In *When Did You Last See Your Father?* PCD's high command is discussing and lamenting the success people have had in illegally leaving the country and the irony behind this:

Tasker: When I was a kid, they were all trying to get *into* this country: Africans, Asians –
Lomas: Now even some of *their* kids are trying to get out.

This theme plugged into a mid-1970s concern. As Dominic Sandbrook's essay 'A Third World Country' observes, it was a frequent topic in newspapers and for social commentators, 'with long queues outside the various Commonwealth High Commissions' and a staggering 269,000 leaving the UK in 1975 alone, looking for a fresh start overseas. [6] It was Margaret Thatcher who commented in 1975:

'We are in danger of a brain drain such as we have never seen before. Our best and most creative people…will not stay here to be harried and abused.' [7]

Her remarks could be straight out of a *1990* script. Of course, there is one major difference between fact and fiction in this context. In real-life 1970s Britain, people were free to leave; in Greatorex's imagined world – where exit visas are almost automatically denied to anyone working in key professions – 'people smuggling' has become big business. As Jim Kyle remarks, they are "making a fortune out of human misery", a comment which seems depressingly familiar to us now, forty-five years on. It is a nice meta touch from the creator of *1990* that artists and writers are welcome to leave Britain whenever they like, presumably partly because of an 'anti-culture' philosophy and also because they are deemed to be potentially dissident, simply by choosing those professions. (The impression that the state mistrusts The Arts is, of course, not limited to fictional dystopias.)

It is only in the third episode, ironically titled *Health Farm*, that we gain visual insight into some of the most sinister aspects of state control. When union leader Charles Wainwright (Ray Smith) reveals the "anti-freedom" truth of the UK in a speech in the US we see how quickly the Home Secretary and PCD can muddy his name through falsified evidence and then – in a genuinely dystopian twist – we see him undergoing electro-convulsive treatment to 'cure' his idealism. It is a landmark moment in the series which has, up until now, talked up a dystopian regime but here finally delivers it, visually. In some respects, it makes it even more chilling that this barbarism takes places in supposedly nurturing settings. The doctor in charge proudly tells Kyle: "No barbed wire, no straitjackets, no padded cells. After all, this is 1990."

As Delly Lomas drily observes, the ARCs have a genteel veneer:

"Manicured lawns, velvet glove service and daily prayers to inner cleanliness."

As my earlier list indicated, *1990*'s landscape contains many typical dystopian features. However, some of the social changes which have taken place are, on the surface, trivial ones, such as the disappearance of traditional pubs and their replacement by soulless, "antiseptic" 'leisure centres' which Kyle laments in *Health Farm*:

Kyle: I used to like pubs. Especially the old ones. Sawdust on the floor, people laughing, there was always some hammer-fingered pianist playing Lily of Laguna.
Lomas: Obsolete. I prefer these centres, where citizens are graded according to their importance to society, and drink accordingly.
Kyle: Spirits for shop stewards and civil servants only, wine for local authority form pushers and beer for essential prols. And the undeserving poor, without status cards, can queue all night outside state pharmacies, guinea pigs for 'happy pills'.
Lomas: Recreation should be directed, as well as work.

Lomas' 'status apartheid' comments ensure that we cannot dismiss Kyle's reminiscing as simply rose-tinted nostalgia. Those status cards and continually reviewed 'Life Scores' – a precursor of the ratings system seen in *Black Mirror*'s social media satire *Nosedive* – feel particularly prescient.

Kyle's double identity – as investigative reporter and modern-day Scarlet Pimpernel – brings with it two goals: to help desperate people escape and to scrape away the veneer of 'respectability and banality', to quote the blogger from earlier; whether it is the corrupt court judges, the ARCs, leisure clubs, or a state-controlled press. In *Decoy* he describes the *British Gazette* in withering terms to a young female journalist who has recently joined the newspaper:

"A state-run propaganda rag...Well, go on printing the handouts and believing that Pulitzer is a breed of dog and you'll be alright."

Kyle's cutting comment is a perfect example of the witty, biting cynicism and barbed comments and exchanges in *1990*. He is a professional man of words and part of the viewer's enjoyment revolves around his savage repartee and desire to 'call a spade a spade' in a society which prefers platitudes, euphemisms and toned-down vocabulary, where 'riots' are called 'social disturbances', 'ghettos' are 're-settlements'. It is a language drained of any subversive or emotive elements, an equivalent of Orwell's 'Newspeak'. It is no surprise that writers and artists have been encouraged to leave a country devoid of colour and colourful language. In a Fleet Street "of journalistic junkies, living on their fix of state handouts", who better than an articulate and cynical reporter to ride roughshod over it all? Particularly when, like Baroness Orczy's Sir Percy Blakeney, Kyle leads a secret double life during a new Reign of Terror. [8] Ultimately, he and the other individuals who are brave enough to stick their heads above the proverbial parapet continually face the same problem: how can one person make a difference, never mind defeat the system? As rebel judge Philip Carter observes: "One puff does not tilt a windmill". Part of the downbeat nature of the first *1990* series is witnessing the human cost when individuals do protest: a dissident writer jailed, a Trade Union leader reduced to a zombie, a pregnant court judge's wife left traumatized by PCD thugs, his own (neglected) family's home raided and ripped apart...and Jim Kyle left to reflect on each occasion that he has played a part in the seemingly inevitable events and personal tragedies. This sense of inevitability also refers to the final episode in the initial *1990* series, with Kyle stripped of all privileges. As the PCD Commander gloatingly observes:

"Without these documents, you no longer exist. You are now a non-citizen."

With Kyle officially reduced to a number – shades of *The Prisoner* – we gain our first images of that 'other' London, a Blitz-like cityscape of crumbling arches and rubble, a far cry from the opulence of PCD headquarters or the exclusive, 'fine dining' restaurant which the House of Lords has been converted into. This is a dangerous, menacing world populated by the 80,000 city vagrants who exist on the outside of society in a new Dark Age. The ultimate irony is that it is also a place which the likes of Jim Kyle – for all his qualities – has never thought of investigating, until circumstances force him into living in it. In many respects, *Non Citizen* is the most powerful *1990* episode as we focus on Jim Kyle himself, seeing how quickly his cheeky swagger can be replaced by the body language of a broken man. It also takes Edward Woodward out of his comfort zone, bringing a sublime, emotive performance out of him, a reminder of the benefits of having a highly talented 'star lead'.

*

The common dystopian ground between *The Guardians* and *1990* is there for all to see. Many of the ingredients in their tyrannical regimes are shared ones. The role of The Guardians and the PCD is, thematically and culturally speaking, unsurprisingly similar. It is the creative methods used to deliver those fictional worlds to the viewer which are in stark contrast. *1990* privileges realism, action and dialogue-driven plots. The tendency in *The Guardians* is for characters to deliver long, theatrical speeches. As the *Cult TV Lounge* review suggests, at times this can lead to 'unbelievably clumsy...speechifying...excessive talkiness'. [9] The main drawback to this approach is that some of the scenes – even one of the episodes – could have worked equally well as radio drama. Television is a visual medium, after all, reminding me of director Nicholas Ray's comment that, 'If it's all in the script why make a film?' Initially, any dystopia series faces the challenge of introducing the viewer to an unfamiliar, alien world where the changes require explanations, something which inevitably leads to a limiting 'tell, not show' approach, with 'plot' almost written across the actors' foreheads. Less forgivable is the tendency to provide us with stagey, lengthy moral debates. The LWT series privileges duologues, monologues, and even inner thoughts, which, however well-written and orally powerful, can be visually barren or come across as didactic speech making. [10]

Where *The Guardians* excels is in its radical, playful approach to characterisation, dark humour and plot structure. Graham Crowden's dirty tramp, for example, is a startlingly inventive *Godot*-type character whose presence in a dystopian drama could easily have been ridiculous yet works brilliantly. The narratives are experimental in the way that overarching plot threads and dramatic scenes are sometimes put on hold, only to be re-released later in the series. The ultimate example of the series' gallows humour – pun fully intended – is when an underground group carry out the cold-blooded assassination of the 'public hangman' Tom Henryson, (Norman Bird), in *I Want You to Understand Me*. The senselessness of the 'symbolic' killing is that he was simply a puppet, a work of fiction dreamed up by the regime, a timid, peaceful, out-of-work actor who had never executed anyone. Disinformation is drip-fed by a tyrannical regime and readily swallowed by amoral terrorists.

In many ways *The Guardians* and *1990* offer us intriguingly contrasting approaches to similar subject matter. The earlier series is more ambitious, cerebral, daring, inventive and shocking. It is also more theatrical and static. *1990* combines dystopian themes and a flawed 'hero' fighting 'the system' within a more conventional 'action-adventure' framework. It has a vibrancy arguably lacking in *The Guardians*, even if, ultimately, both series offer an almost unremittingly bleak, nihilistic vision. Rather than suggest that one is better than the other, they make fascinating dramas to compare.

One weakness which these two dystopian dramas arguably share concerns an issue or challenge faced by any series attempting to set its story in the *near* future, as opposed to the past, present or distant future. In terms of costume, technology and environment – both sets and location-based street scenes – the worlds of *The Guardians* and *1990* often appear instantly recognisable. There are attempts by the design teams to make some familiar objects look faintly futuristic: a chess set, telephones, surveillance equipment... [11] Nevertheless, most of the clothes, cars, music and the language employed scream '1970s!' Limited budgets at both LWT and the BBC may partly explain this. However, in fairness, there is also a major dilemma. The creators of both series wanted familiarity as well as a futuristic hint. On one level, they were offering contemporary social critiques. As the subtitle of *The Guardians* playfully asks: 'England soon?' In a sense, this represents the underlying theme or subtext in both dramas.

That rhetorical question – 'England soon?' – leads me to a final, positive note. Part of the fun of 70s dystopian television – particularly when viewed with hindsight – is sifting through the mix, and trying to decide for ourselves which elements or ingredients are pure science fiction, which constitute warnings of what might easily become realities in the near future, which aspects are distorted mirrors of the 1970s and, finally, whether there are examples of a 70s fiction become 2020s fact. The widespread use of CCTV surveillance, a Britain which has cut itself adrift from its European neighbours, the spread of fake news, a public television network which seems increasingly wary of criticising its government ...some viewers today will inevitably draw connections. That is up to the individual to interpret, a fundamental right in any democratic society, yet a deafening absence or luxury in both *The Guardians* and *1990*. [12]

© Rodney Marshall

1. During the Profumo scandal, Harold Macmillan requested that M15 bugged the Cabinet Room, a waiting room and the Prime Minister's study, as revealed in 2010 when the official history of M15 was published (The *Guardian*, April 18th 2010), cited by Dominic Sandbrook, 'King Rat', *Seasons in the Sun*, p. 74.
2. Barbara Kellerman (Lomas), George Murcell (Greaves) and John Savident (Mellor) all left *1990* after the initial run. Lisa Harrow, Clive Swift and Yvonne Mitchell are, in effect, their replacements. The previous PCD's office set is updated to make it more futuristic. However, there is a sense that the initial series of *1990* had completed a natural, narrative cycle and it is almost universally agreed that the second run lacks some of the initial series' innovative edge. One of the more interesting conflicts in the second series is the tension between Kyle and his friend Dave Brett, with the journalist arguing that the Pentagon dissident groups should maintain peaceful action – 'the pen is mightier than the sword' – while Brett argues that terrorist-style attacks are both required and justifiable. The ending is satisfactorily unclear, with a Thatcher-like Home Secretary reassuring the dissidents that democracy will be restored, reminding me of Sir Timothy Hobson's frequent (private) reassurances in *The Guardians* that the Guardians themselves will soon be disbanded and free elections brought back.
3. Even the intriguing main titles sequence offers us a colourless spectacle as figures are trapped within the high walls of an ever-decreasing white box.
4. www.archivetvmusings.blog, March 16th 2017.
5. Cited by Dominic Sandbrook, 'Could It Happen Here?', *Seasons in the Sun*, p. 139.
6. Dominic Sandbrook, 'A Third World Country', *Seasons in the Sun*, p. 99.
7. Margaret Thatcher, from a speech at Alnwick Castle, July 30th 1975.

8. Jim Kyle is not a superhero in the manner of the Scarlet Pimpernel, Zorro, Superman, or Batman. Nevertheless, he shares their duality and some of their daring qualities.
9. *Cult TV Lounge*, 16/07/2018.
10. As Kevin Lyons observes in his 2018 balanced review of the series: 'Philosophical debates do not good drama make', The EOFFTV Review, 20/09/2018.
11. In one episode of *The Guardians*, we see that the motorway signs are in kilometres rather than miles, which is an effective, simple touch.
12. As Dr Benedict tells 'The Dirtiest Man' in *The Guardians*, he has to both conform and be labelled: "Administratively speaking, there is no way of dealing with individuals." It is, arguably, a weak point in the system, and one which offers hope.

NATION'S APOCALYPTIC VISIONS: GENDER IN *SURVIVORS* AND *BLAKE'S 7*

Terry Nation was first and foremost a storyteller. Today his work for television carries a 'cult' following reserved only for those writers that genuinely left their mark on viewers' collective consciousness. His writing had all the ingredients that keeps audiences hooked – well plotted, pacey story lines with action, excitement and cliff-hanger suspense. However, as with any ingredients, success in their use is always down to the way in which they are blended. This was where Terry Nation was a master. This chapter looks at Nation's apocalyptic visions of the 1970s: in particular the initial series of *Survivors* (1975), predominantly written by him; and the first series of *Blake's 7*, broadcast in 1978 and exclusively penned by its creator. It delves into Nation's writing to conclude that it had more going on than was immediately obvious. It begins by looking at his influences and where his post-apocalyptic ideas may have originated. Then, using *Survivors* and *Blake's 7*, it shows how in discreet but definite ways his writing was ahead of his time. Nation's wonderful use of his staple ingredients for a good story – action, countdowns and cliff-hangers – was blended with more subtle flavours that pointed to social inequality and captured the political direction of the future. This was most notable in the area of gender where writing female leads and placing them on an equal footing with their male counterparts was a theme in Nation's 1970s television writing. His blended narrative of action-centred stories with believable female leads resulted in large audiences being influenced subconsciously. Looking through this lens hopefully prompts a radical reconsideration of Nation's work, and how it prefigures some of the ways in which 'progressive' gender ideas are delivered on television to us today.

Terry Nation was born in 1930 and grew up immersed in the exciting and action-filled worlds inhabited by Bulldog Drummond, Richard Hannay and those created by Edgar Wallace, Raymond Chandler and others. The excitement of a pacey but atmospheric story would influence young writers of the future and we can see shadows of writers like John Buchan and Sapper (H.C. McNeile) in Nation's work. The 1930s and 1940s would also leave an indelible mark on the lives of all those that lived through them for other, darker reasons. Nation was no different. It was during this period, sitting in the air raid shelter, that he began making up stories to entertain himself and no doubt keep his mind away from the reality of what was happening at the time [1]. His father, Bert, was overseas fighting the Nazis, which influenced Nation to shape his best known and most evil creation on them, the Daleks, or 'intergalactic Nazis' as he called them [2]. He also saw his mother Sue playing a strong and leading role during the threat of bombing raids as an air raid warden (ARP) [3] when women were doing what had previously been seen as male roles and had not been encouraged or allowed to pursue in peacetime [4]. His mother would likely later influence his writing when placing strong female characters in leading roles.

The influence of the 1970s also looms large over the scripts of *Survivors* and *Blake's 7*. Decades provide a false banding of a time or period, in that there are no substantive lines that society and its people consciously cross when moving from one to another. However, in historical terms a character is often attributed to a decade and the 1970s character was quite distinctive. An adult living through the 70s would recognise descriptions of them being grim, bleak and with high unemployment. A time of economic decline and strikes which prompted a series of emergency situations and left people 'literally' in the dark. Newsreels from that time show an almost real-life dystopia with stark pictures of rubbish building up in the streets, bodies being left unburied and panic buying in the shops. Twentieth century historian Dominic Sandbrook describes Terry Nation's 1970s televised depictions of the future as 'almost unremittingly depressing', with *Blake's 7* presenting an 'even grimmer version of the future than *Survivors*' [5]. *The Daily Mail* at the time reported that 'the really depressing thing about *Blake's 7* was that the future was much the same as the present only, Lord help us – much worse'. [6] Television in the 1970s also began to more generally reflect the mood of the time. Shows were darker or grittier than before, which contributed to the success of many. The shadowy, deceitful environment inhabited by tortured soul David Callan, played brilliantly by Edward Woodward, brought a darker more contradicted world to our screens. *The Sweeney* showed a tougher edge to the police procedural, with hard men in run-down and seedy parts of London battling violent criminals against a backdrop of heavy smoking, fast cars and old-fashioned public houses. The shows of the 1970s felt different in reflecting the era, but were similar to their lighter and brighter 1960s predecessors in that most of the leads were male. Television in the 1970s presented a man's world, with the female 'lot' summed up by Ria Parkinson's character, in Carla Lane's series *Butterflies*, trapped in domesticity and motherhood. This male dominated approach to television drama was not something that Nation would follow in *Survivors* and *Blake's 7*. He would use the growing real-life dystopia to positive effect.

A dystopian backdrop suited Nation's style of writing. It immediately places a challenger against a system, or circumstance in the case of *Survivors*, thus offering interesting story lines. It also provides the opportunity for an intelligent subtext to the story by weaving in big social questions in areas such as morality, inequality and political systems. An oppressive and authoritarian regime, like that overseen by the Federation in *Blake's 7*, or the environment that *Survivors* was situated in, with most of the world wiped out by a pandemic, prompts storylines and dialogue on the prevailing or previous systems of power. This teases out ideological debate and stimulating discourse, bringing them into the homes of viewers as part of their 'primetime' entertainment and the chance to sub/consciously think on issues that may not occur to people in their everyday lives. As lead character Abby Grant says in *Survivors*: 'I just hadn't seen a political system as being one of our priorities' [7]. This is the second episode of the first series, *Genesis*, where Abby is discussing with former national union president Arthur Wormley how things might now change in society. Abby's thoughts, which up to then have focused on finding her son, and hopes of people coming together in unity [8], are met with Wormley's opportunistic and power hungry ideas. This moment is cleverly written and Nation has it doing so much more than a first viewing might suggest. It weaves into the story the political subtext of societal systems, indicating that this is going to be a source of trouble. It also signals to viewers, through Abby, that this is an opportunity to challenge the old systems of similar types of middle-aged men seeking power for themselves. Abby discovering that the house that Wormley and his men are in is not his but one that he has commandeered, only confirms her instincts. This is followed by Wormley summarily executing someone from another group, despite her pleas that he has no right to do this. "You murdered him!" she shouts before leaving [9]. Abby will forge her own way and this is an early sign that Nation is, through the storyline, showing the worst elements of current societal leadership. This is also a significant hint from Nation about the strong female lead role that Abby will take in the series. Nation's pen writes feminism in such a way so that nobody watching (or reading) this scene could possibly feel that this was an attempt at political correctness. It is a hugely political scene but fits seamlessly into the storyline and is carried along with pace, tension and drama. Powerful points made through skilful writing. This is something that he would repeat when writing *Blake's 7* a few years later.

Survivors and the first two series of *Blake's 7* were different in some clear ways. *Survivors* was set in the current day after an apocalyptic event and *Blake's 7* in the future, where space travel is common and life on other planets established. However, they also share many similarities. Both are clearly products of the 1970s' darker period, following each other in close succession, and covering primetime television slots from 1975 to 1979. They are also both distinctly dystopian, with a backdrop of constant and uncertain bids for survival. Authoritarian control or threats and challenges to liberties and normal freedoms are ever-present. There are, of course, the Terry Nation trademark pacey story lines, which can be seen in both series, bringing together action and suspense along with deadly countdowns and cliffhanging endings. They also both provide an interesting intellectual subtext with questions being asked about societal governance systems, justice and leadership. It is in the area of leadership that we see one of the most notable areas of similarity: gender. We see one of the strongest female leads on 1970s television in *Survivors*' Abby Grant, and then a similar picture of strong female leads in *Blake's 7* with Jenna Stannis, Cally and Servalan. The cult of Abby Grant, however, stands out in retrospect but has perhaps never properly been acknowledged.

Carolyn Seymour's portrayal of Abby Grant in *Survivors* was so powerful that it contributed hugely to the success of the series. Seymour herself was a strong-willed female, which in 1975 was not something that all were used to, or could take. 'It did feel exceptional, it felt exceptional that women were the sort of leaders of the drama' [10]. These are the words of Lucy Fleming, who played Jenny Richards, looking back on the series some thirty years later [11]. Lucy's comment suggests that Terry Nation's writing was ground-breaking at the time and therefore of significance when looking at British television in the 1970s. Ian McCulloch, who played Greg Preston, is clear that Nation's portrayal of women was no accident: 'We were told at the beginning that it was going to be more a sort of female oriented series than a male one' [12]. This was new, a female led series which also consistently delivered action, pace, suspense and drama. Carolyn Seymour was perfectly cast as Abby, playing herself in some key respects. She loved the character because Abby was so dynamic and strong, in a television world at the time where this was rarely seen – 'She was beautifully written' and 'I loved Terry's writing' she said [13].

The *Survivors* title sequence is worth watching alone for the story it tells and questions it raises. Stephen Brotherstone and Dave Lawrence in their first volume of 'Scarred for Life' provide a superb description of it [14], so I would simply say here that a laboratory accident, possibly in China, sees a virus infect a scientist who then decides to travel the globe causing worldwide outbreaks. The last border stamp of many we see is 'Immigration Office London'. We never, as viewers, find out what that was all about or whether the world tour was planned or impromptu. *Survivors* director Pennant Roberts said that 'the whole thinking behind the first episode was that it set out very clearly for the viewer the scale of the catastrophe' [15] which it certainly does. We then follow the actions of two lead females, Abby and Jenny. Jenny's character is more straightforward to follow; she has not been infected but her flat mate was and has died as a result. Jenny goes off to the countryside in search of others after her doctor friend explains the gravity of the situation. Abby, on the other hand, offers us a wonderfully complex introduction to her character, with contradictions and depth that mark the product of the coming together of Terry Nation and Carolyn Seymour's artistic talents.

The first episode of *Survivors* is in many ways the forging of Abby Grant. We are initially introduced to a wealthy suburban housewife in the Home Counties with tennis court, swimming pool, housekeeper and son in boarding school. Her husband commutes from the City, someone that we might imagine looks something like Guthrie Featherstone QC MP of *Rumpole of the Bailey* fame. We quickly find that in fact he is, in as much as he is played by the wonderful Peter Bowles. Sadly, for Peter Bowles fans, he is not long for the *Survivors* world, as Abby awakes from a virus-induced sleep to find him dead on the sofa downstairs and the village eerily quiet. In the space of the episode Abby, by necessity, moves herself through two years' grief. The history of apocalyptic fiction tells us that people act very differently when faced with such adversity. John Wyndham's 1951 book *The Day of the Triffids*, later a 1981 television serial, has a powerful scene where a doctor, finding out that he is blinded, launches himself through a fifth-floor window to his death [16]. The gravity and bleakness of the situation is just too much, he is overcome and clarity manifests itself in providing him with one option. The clarity in Abby's mind is different but equally powerful. We see a new Abby Grant emerge from the tragic circumstances with an objective that stays with her throughout the series: she must find out if her son Peter is still alive. A natural instinct of any parent, supported by a logic that if she has survived, then why might her son also not be a survivor. The steps that she takes are clear-headed and certain. Her discovery of children dead in their dormitory beds is harrowing enough but when you see her moving towards her son's bed the question emerges of what if he is also dead. Does this change everything? Will the Abby that we are starting to see emerge then move into the space of the doctor jumping from the window in *The Day of the Triffids*? This is a question which intriguingly remains unanswered, as Abby finds Peter's bed empty and she ascertains from the only surviving staff member there that one of the teachers took Peter and a group away from the school when things started to look bad.

The way that these scenes play out demonstrates Nation's dramatic skills. He had presented a dystopian world and, in Abby, delivered us a lead character with a purpose and reason to fight. Dystopian fiction does not work unless there are characters with objectives that are powerful enough to combat any setbacks. Surviving is strong as a motivation, but the search for your son is stronger. This now sets the stage for the 'new' Abby Grant to emerge. Upon her return home she cuts off her long hair to a shorter, more practical, style. She loads the car, which we may have already guessed is a Volvo estate, but in a lovely 1970s television historical touch, is the exact one 'DJH 180K' in 'of its time' yellow that is used by Jerry and Margo Leadbetter in *The Good Life* [17]. Its screen ownership, moving from the Leadbetters to the Grants is a short jump, Surbiton to a similar suburban setting. However, Abby is making a huge leap; she pours petrol around the house and sets fire to it with David's body inside, before leaving. These are powerful scenes, and we are in no doubt about the mettle of Abby Grant. We have seen a transformation and the emergence of one of the strongest female leads on 1970s television. Carolyn Seymour describes this wonderfully: 'I then go from being totally happy and content with my tiny little life to suddenly being a very aggressive warrior' [18].

Abby Grant is a natural leader in the series. Her role in leading a group of survivors was not sought and is never contested by the group that, with Jenny and others, collect around her. In *Gone Away* (S1 E3) Abby is the one who is not deterred by a hanging corpse in a supermarket labelled 'looter', whereas Greg wants to leave it and find somewhere else [19]. She wins out and they take what they need before having to violently defend their right to do so against what turns out to be Arthur Wormley's men. Later in the series, Greg demonstrates the group's reliance on Abby after finding out that Jenny has told Abby about a possible sighting of Peter. He is fearful of Abby leaving and berates Jenny with, "If she knows it or not, she holds this place together" [20]. This statement is backed up by more than her general ability to bring the group together; it is their reliance on her when things are difficult. One of the most challenging episodes to watch is *Law and Order* (S1 E9). A girl in the group is found murdered, with it implied heavily that she has also been raped. Everything points to it being someone in the group and the guilty party, Tom Price played by Talfryn Thomas, knows this. In an attempt to save himself, he tricks and wrongly implicates Barney, who has pronounced learning difficulties. A make-shift trial is held with a tied vote from the group on a decision to determine Barney's banishment or execution. Abby's character has clearly moved from where it was in the early encounter with Arthur Wormley as she decides that Barney should be executed. Harrowing scenes follow as it becomes known only to Abby and Greg that they convicted the wrong person. A decision is made not to let the group know, but this does not sit well with Abby whose character is genuine, but with extraordinary depth. A later storyline sees her make a decision to end the cancerous pain of friend Elaine Gorman by snuffing her life out with a pillow [21], something that would ordinarily be repugnant to us all, but in these circumstances feels like an act of humanity and one which will cost Abby greatly emotionally. Abby's subsequent disappearance to seek a friend with whom she has struck up a relationship previously is almost something of a relief when we see her able to unwind as the pressure of being the lone leader is lifted for a while.

This is ground-breaking television. Abby represents a new breed of television character, a strong capable female leader who gains the respect and trust of all those around her. The series shows the influence that Abby has through the confidence that this gives Jenny in standing her ground and coping with challenging situations. Abby's character works partly because of Nation's creative vision but also because she is played by someone who is able to project this so convincingly. The year is 1975 and Terry Nation and Carolyn Seymour have used one of the most influential mediums to begin wheels turning that move forward light years in gender equality. None of this ever feels 'forced'. Terry Nation has brought his vision to life and done so believably with action based, pacey and suspenseful storylines. You would hope that those overseeing the series would recognise this, not just because of the ground-breaking nature of the show, but also its popularity. However, this was 1975 so, sadly and perhaps inevitably, it was not seen by all as the progressive writing and performance that it surely was. It was viewed in some quarters as an example of women becoming too assertive; that certainly seems to have been the opinion of the series' producer, Terence Dudley.

The fact that writer Terry Nation, director Pennant Roberts, and actors such as Ian McCulloch were of the opposing view did not stop Carolyn Seymour ultimately being, in her own words, "fired from the show" [22]. There is, as so often, more than one reason for such a big change. Reflecting, Ian McCulloch felt that it was a 'pity because the dynamics for the three of us was good and she was a very successful character' [23]. He described Carolyn Seymour's removal from the series as Terence Dudley's decision, made because he found Carolyn's strong character 'a little difficult to take' [24]. Pennant Roberts stated that Dudley 'could not cope' [25] with the situation and that ultimately 'it was just a mistake of Terry Dudley' [26]. Seymour stated: 'He just didn't like me, he plain didn't like me' [27]. All of this suggests that Dudley did have a problem with the lead and it feels hard to rule out that one of the main reasons was that she was a strong woman. Nation's relationship with Dudley was no better: 'I fell out with him instantly, he didn't see it at all' [28] and this got no better when aspiring writer Dudley sought to take the series away from action and pacey storylines into a more sedentary show that focused on the self-sufficiency side of things. McCulloch felt that the project had moved away from Terry Nation's original idea: 'It now lacked pace, drama and confrontation and became rather boring' [29]. McCulloch himself wrote a couple of good episodes for the following two series, including his own exit. The loss of Nation's creative influence certainly changed the show. It took it away not only from the action-oriented stories, but also the opportunity to show feminism in a powerful and influential way. There were some notable exceptions to this, where strong storylines appeared, such as Roger Marshall's episode *Parasites* (S2 E10). This offers the viewer all of the best elements of a Nation script – pace, suspense and action – coupled with a well written unease that provides a leading role for the character Mina, who sees what the others have missed and acts on this. The loss of Nation, however, saw an overall reduction in the attraction of the series and episodes that followed, albeit with exceptions. The influence of Dudley had moved *Survivors* from something ground-breaking and special to just another good show. Terry Nation, however, was not done, as far as writing for 1970s television was concerned...

Nation's next big project was *Blake's 7* which drew in more than eight million viewers within the first few weeks of launch and ten million for the final ever episode [30]. It was a post-apocalyptic vision carrying classic dystopian traits, but with a twist: it was set in space. The backdrop is one of the controlling and authoritarian Federation. The state apparatus tells us immediately that we are in a dystopia, helmeted security guards patrolling the corridors, uniformity, loudspeaker instructions and surveillance cameras everywhere [31]. If we are in any initial doubt as to the deadly seriousness of the governing forces then this is quickly removed in the first episode, when we see mind altering drugs administered and the title character accused of child abuse, with 'evidence' falsified to secure a conviction. His crime, in reality, is resistance to the Federation. It is a bleak, grim backdrop but one that paved the way for Nation to deploy his favoured action and suspense, countdowns and cliff hangers. It also provided him with the opportunity to follow the missed opportunity of Abby Grant's longevity in *Survivors*, and place female characters in strong leadership roles to do battle across space. He does just this, undermining any notion that the creation of Abby was not a conscious thought process; the female co-leads in *Blake's 7* support the case that Nation was someone with an instinct for equality and an ambition to challenge viewers' preconceptions. However, this was still 1978 with inequality of the sexes. We would see *political* change a year later with Margaret Thatcher as the new Prime Minister, but television series were still largely a man's world. Nation understood this, which can be seen in his measuring of the scope at his disposal to influence viewers. A female lead character with a show of the same name might have been too much for many at this time. It would have perhaps been seen as making a point rather than anything else, which would have been a distraction to the series. It is also true that, as we saw with Dudley, the male dominated world of television production might not have supported a strong female character as the leader. In any case, Nation created a male leader of the pack, Rog Blake, played by Welsh actor Gareth Thomas.

There is, in *Blake's 7*, as we have seen before with Nation's writing, far more depth or layers than might be apparent on an initial viewing. *Blake's 7* gives us a mixed ensemble of characters to battle the evil forces of the Federation, brought together initially as a group of convicted criminals on their way to penal isolation on the planet of Cygnus Alpha. Whilst Blake is the leader and provides the impetus for revenging the Federation, in a ship handily left abandoned in space called the Liberator, the self-appointed captain is far from being a sexist male. Jenna Stannis, played superbly by Sally Knyvette, is cast – under Nation's pen – in a role that shows feminism at its strongest. Jenna is an equal in all things and respected by the group for her skills as a pilot, her intellect, wit and bravery. She is often the person that Blake turns to first 'in a fix' and she often outshines fan favourite Kerr Avon, again portrayed brilliantly by Paul Darrow, by leading without the need to add a sarcastic or pointed, barbed comment. Avon frequently and unhelpfully puts the pressure on Blake when he has made a tough decision, leaving the latter in no doubt that if it goes wrong then Avon will seek to capitalise. Whereas Jenna is the personality that you want alongside you in a tight spot: brave and intelligent without seeking to challenge the leadership position or be 'too clever'. Jenna is described in the *Blake's 7* 1979 annual as someone with 'remarkable qualities, not least of which is her exceptional ability to face the many dangers of space without turning a hair, she is one of the first space pilots in the business' [32]. For everyone of 'annual reading age' in 1979 this was culturally significant, showing an emerging equality on television with genuine female heroes. Nation confirms that whilst his intention was to entertain, because this is what attracts an audience, that 'within that, I like to say some things that I believe are valid and good and honourable. I hope it's subversive in that sense' [33]. Subversive in the best sense; he was changing the norms in primetime television by showing Jenna and co-star Cally, played by Jan Chappell, in *Mission to Destiny* (S1 E7), controlling the Liberator, but also then in other episodes, such as *Project Avalon* (S1 E9), out on dangerous missions, represented as equals. Jenna is a leader in her own right: "I've taught you too well" she says as Cally takes the ship's controls. The roles of Jenna and Cally are showcased well by Nation within Blake's group. A brief glance at the unconventional male co-leads helps to put the females in context. Vila Restal (Michael Keating) almost makes a comic point of being cowardly when it comes to doing anything that places him in danger [34]. Olag Gan, perfectly cast with David Jackson as the gentle giant of the group, is restricted by the fact he is fitted with a 'limiter' which controls his actions. Kerr Avon, the computer expert, gets involved physically when he needs to be, but there is never any sign of him wanting to play the all-action hero.

Surrounded by these males, it is the females onboard the Liberator who lead. They are tough and exciting, throwing themselves into gritty situations of Nation's making. Nation also places the ruling of the evil Federation in the hands of the wonderful Jacqueline Pearce as 'Supreme Commander' of the Federation, Servalan. Pearce leaves nobody in any doubt, including her chief assassin, Travis (Stephen Greif; later Brian Croucher) about who is in charge. Travis is often made to feel dispensable and a disappointment to Servalan as he fails to capture Blake. The role of lead females is set up well in the first and second series by Nation. In *Project Avalon* Travis has an efficient and ruthless all female army; Avalon is herself a female. In *Bounty* (S1 E11) President Sarkov's daughter Tyce also acts convincingly as his bodyguard and chauffeur. Tyce is a strong female in a more commonly male role for 1970s television. Cally plays a strong part throughout *Bounty*, leading the charge to rescue Sarkov. *Pressure Point* (S2 E5) is a great episode to show just how different *Blake's 7* was in terms of its approach to gender in comparison to many other television dramas at that time. Rebel leader Kasabi, played by Jane Sherwin, is taken hostage by Servalan with Kasabi's daughter, fellow rebel Veron. In an attempt to free her mother from Servalan, Veron deceives Blake, not knowing that her mother is already dead. Jenna comes to the rescue after Blake's capture, frees Veron and takes Servalan prisoner. It is a story full of strong female characters and one where we learn more about Servalan's ruthlessness in Federation training school where she reported Kasabi as a suspected rebel traitor. The usual reference point for this episode is the death of Gan who is killed as they try to flee, but there is more besides this in the way that Nation writes the female characters, even showing early signs of a change in Blake as he bursts into what he believes to be the Federation's

Control Centre shouting, "I've done it!" His reward for this bold, egotistical claim is deserved in this instance.

A great deal is made of Avon's character when *Blake's 7* is revisited and you can see why; he is enigmatic, intellectual, dry witted and for all of these reasons strangely attractive as a character [35]. Blake is simpler, clearer to understand. He does not hide his feelings or objectives and this transparency provides the others with a degree of certainty in him, and how he will behave in certain situations, arguably making him a good leader. The dystopian backdrop of the series surfaces questions of ideology in leadership and power; it shines a light on structures and balances of freedom and control. It can be difficult to surface these in a pacy storyline unless you have a mechanism to use. Nation appears to use Avon for this, as a challenge to Blake and someone who takes a different, often colder, detached and more material view of the predicaments that they find themselves in. Gareth Thomas and Paul Darrow deliver this contrast wonderfully but, set that aside, and it is the females that lead the show. Jenna, Cally and Servalan are central to all that is taking place. One is always in a lead role of the episode storyline, and they all are key to the soap operatic nature [36] of the background story being followed by regular viewers.

The first series established *Blake's 7*, proving a hit with viewers and, on the face of it, taking the opportunity that was lost with *Survivors* in bringing more equality to our screens, but not in an overtly didactic way. It works, and the Liberator lives up to its name in the way that the community within it live and work together. Terry Nation's brilliance, which could be put down simply to his great story telling, pace and drama, is about much more. He delivers the thrills, suspense and escapism for the viewer, but he was also ahead of his time in the way he did this. However, the 1970s, even late on, was perhaps not ready and set up for the kind of equality that Terry Nation brought to our screens. The series started to move away from Nation's original intent, with his influence significantly reduced, albeit not in the dramatic way that *Survivors* changed. Nevertheless, *Blake's 7* changes after the initial series, dramatically reducing the power and prominence of the females on the Liberator. This 'coincides' with Nation not writing many of the scripts or being so involved in the direction that the storylines were taking. [37] Sally Knyvette, who had up to now been at the forefront of most of the action, saw her role being dramatically reduced [38]. Knyvette felt that her role had 'disintegrated from a tough space smuggler to Blake's ship-bound work wife' [39]. Nation's writing had allowed her to play Jenna as an exciting and dramatic character, but she sensed that this changed to a 'humourless and uninventive' character always acting as the 'foil': 'It's very hard to *do* something when you haven't got the words written for you' [40]. Jenna's scripts started to lack the feminism that had contributed to them being so powerful, Knyvette left after the second series and was followed a series later by Jan Chappell who similarly felt that Cally's role had lost something [41]. 'I felt that the character as written initially changed and lost a bit of backbone' she said of Cally and felt that the aggressiveness of the character, that flowed from Nation's pen, had given way to passiveness [42]. The actors seemed to recognise that the progressive writing of Nation was the vital ingredient to the success of the show. Interestingly, actors on both *Survivors* and *Blake's 7* describe the changes as moving away from Terry Nation's original vision and express their unease at this [43]. The first series of *Blake's 7*, where all episodes were penned by Nation, had a political social conscience – it tackled issues such as tyranny, organised religion, interspecies prejudice, and the meaning of mercy and loyalty. Gareth Thomas felt that without Nation's writing that the show 'lost its grittiness' and was a 'betrayal of Nation's original intent' [44]. It would seem to be more than that; the opportunity to boost feminism in a positive and influential way was lost. Nation described Dudley as 'thick as a board' in relation to his decisions to change *Survivors* [45]. It does seem that those that could not see what Nation was doing did miss a trick.

Terry Nation knew how to create a story line and narrative that enabled him to deliver consistency and surprise across a series. His 'go-to' mechanisms of cliff-hanging endings and countdown plots provided the perfect escapism from a 1970s that was showing signs, in some parts at least, of catching-up and even overtaking fiction. However, Nation's writing did much more beneath the surface. He was able to capture political direction ahead of time in a way that did not detract from the entertainment and escapism. He saw that inequality of the sexes was not only wrong but was also providing indicators, for those that could see them, that this was ready for change. He placed females in leading positions without virtue signalling. He was operating the greatest of all social change mechanisms – *culture* change. Abby Grant was a credible character as an independent female in a believable role delivered perfectly by Carolyn Seymour. We see her strength in a narrative set by Nation where all of us as viewers are behind her. We acknowledge Abby as the leader of the tribe because she is the most natural character to hold that role. When we see the societal competition to Abby's group, in the shape of the entrenched union leader Arthur Wormley, we know something is wrong in society at that time. In short, we are subconsciously recognising feminism at its strongest and equality at its most powerful. Whether it was *Survivors* or with Jenna, Cally and Servalan in *Blake's 7*, he showed the value of change, all done with great skill so that we do not even recognise the move. As viewers we are not hit forcefully in the eyes with tokenism because of the blunt nature of the mechanism. Nation was instinctive and creative in his inclusiveness which was one of the reasons that his work endures and should be held up as progressive today.

© Stu Sterling

1. Alwyn W. Turner (2011), *The Man who Invented the Daleks, The Strange Worlds of Terry Nation*, Aurum Press Limited p. 19.
2. Cymru Online, (2013) *Celebrating the life of Terry Nation – creator of the Daleks.*
3. Alwyn W. Turner (2011), p. 19.

4. A Bingham (2004) *"An era of domesticity?" Histories of women and gender in interwar Britain*, pp. 225-33 in Cultural and Social History, Vol. 1.
5. Dominic Sandbrook (2013), Seasons in the Sun, The Battle for Britain 1974-1979, Penguin Books, p. 143.
6. Dominic Sandbrook (2013), p. 143.
7. Terry Nation (1976), *Survivors*, Futura Publications Limited, p. 75.
8. BBC (1975) *Survivors* Episode 3 'Gone Away'.
9. Terry Nation (1976), *Survivors*, Futura Publications Limited, p. 79 & BBC (1975) *Survivors* Episode 2 'Genesis'.
10. BBC (2006) *The Cult of Survivors*, DVD Extra in '*Survivors* All 3 Series box set', Disc 8 (2008) BBC Worldwide Limited.
11. BBC (2006) *The Cult of Survivors*.
12. BBC (2006) *The Cult of Survivors*.
13. BBC (2006) *The Cult of Survivors*.
14. Stephen Brotherstone and Dave Lawrence (2017), *Scarred for Life Volume One: The 1970s*, Lonely Water Books, p. 165
15. BBC (2006) *The Cult of Survivors*.
16. John Wyndham (1975 Ed), *The Day of The Triffids*, Penguin Books, p. 18.
17. BBC (2006) *The Cult of Survivors*.
18. BBC (2006) *The Cult of Survivors*.
19. Terry Nation (1976), *Survivors*, Futura Publications Limited & BBC (1975) *Survivors* Episode 3 'Gone Away'.
20. Terry Nation (1976), *Survivors*, Futura Publications Limited, p. 110.
21. Terry Nation (1976), *Survivors*, Futura Publications Limited, p. 161.
22. BBC (2006) *The Cult of Survivors*.
23. BBC (2006) *The Cult of Survivors*.
24. BBC (2006) *The Cult of Survivors*.
25. BBC (2006) *The Cult of Survivors*.
26. BBC (2006) *The Cult of Survivors*.
27. BBC (2006) *The Cult of Survivors*.
28. Alwyn W. Turner (2011), p. 221.

29. BBC (2006) *The Cult of Survivors.*
30. John Kenneth Muir (2006), *A History and Critical Analysis of Blake's 7, the 1978-1981 British Television Space Adventure*, McFarland & Company, Inc. p. 15 & 21.
31. Rodney Marshall (2015), *Blake's 7, A critical guide to Series 1-4*, Out There Publications p. 16.
32. British Broadcasting Corporation (1978), *Terry Nation's Blake's 7 Annual* 1979, World Distributors (Manchester) Limited, p. 5.
33. Alwyn W. Turner (2011), p. 288.
34. Rodney Marshall (2015), p. 68.
35. John Kenneth Muir (2006), p. 14.
36. Rodney Marshall (2015), p. 11.
37. Editor: As a breakdown of Terry Nation's script writing across the four series or seasons, he wrote 13/13; 3/13; 3/13; 0/13.
38. John Kenneth Muir (2006), p. 17.
39. John Kenneth Muir (2006), p. 17.
40. John Kenneth Muir (2006), p. 17.
41. John Kenneth Muir (2006), p. 19.
42. John Kenneth Muir (2006), p. 19.
43. BBC (2006) *The Cult of Survivors.*
44. John Kenneth Muir (2006), p. 16.
45. Alwyn W. Turner (2011), p. 220.

'WHAT YOU DON'T KNOW, YOU DON'T KNOW': MALCOLM HULKE'S 1970s WORK ON *DOCTOR WHO*

'In writing you're always looking for conflict...' Malcolm Hulke.

'To my mind the basic problem is that writers are by nature back-room-minded introverts and yet, in the publicity jungle, they find themselves pitted against an army of highly extroverted actors and actresses. I don't blame promotion people at all for taking the easy path of boosting the performers, if the writers fail to sell themselves as potentially equally good copy.' Malcolm Hulke.

Malcolm Hulke – generally known to friends and colleagues as Mac – was a successful writer for television, radio, cinema and theatre from 1958 to 1974. He wrote episodes for many of the most popular television series of those decades, including *Pathfinders in Space*, *Armchair Theatre*, *Danger Man*, *The Avengers*, *No Hiding Place*, *Gideon's Way*, *United!* and *Doctor Who* for which he is best remembered. My interest in him was first sparked by coming across the pamphlet *Here is Drama* (1963) which Mac wrote for Unity Theatre and which is preserved in the collection of the Working Class Movement Library. This led me, during the Lockdowns, to embark on writing a full biography of Mac which is still in progress.

Malcolm Ainsworth Hulke was born on 21st November 1924 in Hampstead, London. His mother was Elsie Marian Hulke while, until he was 21, Mac believed that his father was his mother's second husband, Walter Backhouse Hulke (who had died before his birth), this being what his mother had always told him. He wrote about how he discovered that this was not in fact the case, and that he was 'illegitimate' (as it used to be called) in an article, 'The stigma you can never escape,' which appeared in *The Observer* in the autumn of 1973:

'One day when I was 21, I decided to track down my father's relatives to find out why my recently dead mother always told me never to go near them. This well-to-do couple I found in a vast St John's Wood flat offered me afternoon tea. As she poured, the lady I thought was my aunt said, "Well, where do you think you fit into our family?" I explained I was the son of her long-dead brother and mentioned when I was born. "That's quite impossible," she said, "because my brother died two years before then. Do you take sugar?" I never called again. It isn't nice to go round shocking innocent householders. When you're illegitimate, you feel completely alone…You condition us to hide it. We are the totally silent minority.' [1]

Mac's mother led an itinerant and rackety life, often moving to escape debt and creditors, so often in fact that Mac never went to school. Mac recalled his childhood in a radio programme, 'I Never Went to School', broadcast on the Home Service on 01/08/1963. The script gives a valuable insight into his early life (with some characteristic asides from Mac):

'…although my mother didn't send me to school regularly, from time to time the thought would occur to her that I needed education. You see, she lived in a permanent state of reduction. Or that is to say, reduced circumstances, or more precisely, things weren't what they used to be. Actually, I sometimes doubt that things had ever been quite as she imagined they used to be. She was a woman with a vivid imagination. She would imagine that this or that business enterprise that she and her partner had embarked upon was going to flourish, or that this or that item of furniture which she had acquired on hire purchase was going to be paid for.

'She also imagined that I would, somehow, miraculously, go to Eton, and follow that up with Oxford or Cambridge. It never came within her sphere of thought that I might do better by going to a council school than by going to no school at all. Council schools were something to do with the working-class, like the Labour Exchange, free hospitals, council houses, and the Labour Party. In this attitude she was almost completely in accord with her partner, a lady in conjunction with whom she ran a succession of service-flats from one end of the Royal Borough of Kensington to another, thereby supplying food and five-shilling-a-week domestic servants to the younger sons of peers, the widows of admirals, and lesser members of the deposed Russian royal family. Indeed, reduced circumstances abounded, both above and below stairs, and in all degrees that you may like to name....

'My fourteenth birthday meant that we could all breathe a sigh of relief, for no more could there be the fear in our hearts of the knock on the door in the middle of the day, and the schoolman standing in the doorway. I shall never know how exactly we managed to get through the then nine compulsory without his ever calling. We changed our addresses fairly frequently, which may have made things more difficult for the inspectors – since it certainly did for our creditors. Or it may be that the schoolmen presume that all children will start school at the age of five and occupy themselves solely with chasing up those who didn't continue to attend regularly. [2]

In January 1945 Mac was called up, and spent his war service in the Royal Navy as an onboard canteen manager. He recalled:

'I so convinced the interviewing officer of my high standard of brightness that I was put in charge of a sea-going grocery on a corvette without even the delay one might expect by some training – that is to say, they were short of men at the time because corvettes sank so quickly. But no-one ever knew the agonies I went through, locked in my pint-sized canteen, as the corvette ploughed through darkened mine-fields, as I tried to keep the accounts straight. Unable to divide, multiply, or subtract, no surfacing U-boat struck more terror into my heart than the prospect of the NAAFI Inspector's check on my book-keeping on our infrequent return to harbour. But necessity being the mother of invention, I devised my own system of mathematics which worked so well that, six months later, in Dakar, Senegal, I was able to run a highly successful black-market in three different currencies for ten inglorious days that shook life into my bank balance.' [3]

Mac was discharged from the Royal Navy as medically unfit on 31st January 1946, his conduct recorded as 'very good'. (Presumably his nefarious and profitable activities as the canteen manager had not come to light.) Post-war, Mac worked in various menial clerical jobs, including a short period working for the Communist Party of Great Britain in its offices in King Street, Covent Garden. Mac had joined the party in June 1945, as many young people did at this time, inspired by the Red Army's role in defeating the Nazis. He appears to have remained a member until the early 1960s, although his relationship with the party leadership was fractious after he resigned from the party in 1951 whilst living in Cumberland (where his mother ran a guesthouse) and then clamoured to re-join a few months later when he returned to London. Reluctantly the party's stern Head of Organisation, Betty Reid, agreed in the end, although she remained very distrustful of Mac thereafter. Mac was only ever a peripheral figure in the party, but this did not stop Special Branch and MI5 monitoring his correspondence and preparing reports on him from time to time between 1948 and 1963.

In the mid-1950s, Mac made efforts to become a writer, firstly of trashy novels. With money as his holy grail, Mac brought his book-keeping skills to bear on his embryonic career as a pulp fiction writer:

'I calculated how fast I would have to write in order to earn by writing for this market at the same hourly rate I was earning by going out to work. It must, I discovered, be writing at one thousand words an hour, including plotting, correcting, and the physical job of typing. So I sat at my typewriter for two hours every evening for nineteen evenings, and produced the required thirty-eight thousand words. In due course, and without any nonsense and re-writing a word of this epic, I received my first cheque for professional writing – £18. Thus encouraged, the next step was to try television...' [4]

Mac began working with Eric Paice, who like he had also been involved with left-wing Unity Theatre, although in newspaper interviews they stated that they had met at an advertising agency. Both agreed that they wanted to break into the still relatively new medium of television where there was an increasing demand for drama on the BBC and also, after September 1955, on its new commercial rival, ITV. Their first success was *This Day in Fear*, broadcast in the BBC's *Television Playwright* series on 1st July 1958 which starred Patrick McGoohan as an IRA man in hiding from his former comrades. The police who come to call on him turn out to be IRA men intent on his death.

Television drama in the 1950s was still being made 'live' as though in a theatre, with actors hurrying between sets, getting there just in time for the camera shots (usually). The introduction of videotape from the US in 1958 allowed plays to be pre-recorded and – from the early 1960s – splice-edited for broadcast (with much less stress for all concerned), although it was an expensive medium, which is why the videotapes were often wiped and re-used for other recordings. No-one imagined that future generations of viewers might want to watch the lost programmes. Eric Paice looked back to this era in his book *The Way To Write For Television*, published in 1981:

'Until the invention and mass availability of the video recorder, a television play or series would appear before a mass audience for a brief hour, then vanish like the morning dew. And the television companies were extraordinarily profligate with material that seemed to them to be in unending supply. Most of the plays produced in the late fifties and early sixties were wiped so that the tapes on which they were recorded could be used again. To find any trace of them today you must rummage in the attics of writers with storage space to keep their old scripts. It was instant drama, with no shelf life.' [5]

Mac and Eric wrote four plays between 1958 and 1960 for *Armchair Theatre*, a series created in July 1956 by Dennis Vance and Howard

Thomas at the ABC television company, which had the franchise for weekend television in the Midlands and in the North until 1968. Canadian Sydney Newman was approached by ABC to become the producer of *Armchair Theatre*, Newman had made hundreds of documentaries in his home country, had worked in the USA for NBC, and also been head of drama at the Canadian Broadcasting Company where he pioneered a new approach, commissioning drama which reflected social issues. A number of these were shown on the BBC, attracting interest from Thomas and resulting in his approach to Newman.

Mac and Eric's plays for *Armchair Theatre* were: *The Criminals* (1958), *The Big Client* (1959), *The Great Bullion Robbery* (1963) and *The Girl in the Market Square* (1960). Sydney Newman also commissioned the pair to write a series of science fiction adventure serials for children, starting with *Target Luna*, broadcast in April and May 1960. *Target Luna* centres on a Rocket Research Station which is preparing to launch a space mission from Buchan Island, a remote Scottish isle. The head of the mission is Professor Norman Wedgewood, whose children, Geoffrey, Valerie and Jimmy, have come to spend the holidays with him. When he discovers that the astronaut Williams has become ill, Jimmy, aged 11, secretly takes his place and is launched into space in his stead, and he orbits the moon. As Jimmy re-enters the Earth's atmosphere he is tracked by Jodrell Bank and other stations. There is more danger as Jimmy falls asleep at the controls, but he wakes up just in time: the capsule comes in over Alaska and falls into the sea off the North Shetlands. Jimmy is rescued by two fishermen and taken to Buchan Island where his identity is revealed to the world.

Mac and Eric told the *TV Times* that they were keen to show a situation in which the different nations of the world unite. 'We soon see how the plight of one human being in an Earth-bound rocket catches the imagination of the whole world. Radar stations – Russian, American, British and others – are linked in a global effort to bring the rocket home. Space travel, it turns out, is a great unifying influence among the nations. The old law of the sea becomes the law of space, too.'

The six episodes were a success, leading Newman to commission three sequels from Mac and Eric: *Pathfinders in Space*, broadcast in September and October 1960, in which the adults and three children journey to the Moon; *Pathfinders to Mars*, broadcast between December 1960 and January 1961, in which they land on the red planet but find no Martians (or Ice Warriors) but only unfriendly plants; and *Pathfinders to Venus*, broadcast in March and April 1961, in which the space travellers find Venusians on the planet, living in their equivalent of the Stone Age.

Taken as a whole the four serials are a skilful mixture of adventure – the Pathfinders are almost permanently in peril of one kind or another, whether from meteors, cosmic radiation, sandstorms, giant lichen or lava – and science, with the viewers regularly provided with packets of information on numerous topics, whether it is the origin of the Moon, the mechanics of space exploration and travel, the possibility of life on other planets, and much else besides. Mac and Eric had clearly carried out a good deal of research in gathering both hard facts and speculative science to adorn their work. They also suggest that space exploration would be better served by co-operation, rather than competition, when they show the world working together to save Jimmy in *Target Luna* and the Russians sending a rescue ship in *Pathfinders to Venus*.

In the late 1950s his late mother's friend Winifred Boot sold the guesthouse which they had run jointly and moved down to London, where she and Mac bought a house, 33 South Hill Park, Hampstead which they set up as a lodging house, with Mac acting as the landlord and general handyman. The house sometimes held up to four lodgers. Eric Paice lived there for several years, as did Terrance Dicks, firstly on his own and then with his wife Elsa in 1964.

In addition to their work on television, Mac and Eric wrote two film scripts at this time. The first was *Life in Danger*, a film directed by

Terry Bishop, and produced by Butcher's Film Service, who released many low budget films in this period. The cast included Derren Nesbitt, Julie Hopkins and Christopher Witty and was released in January 1959. The other was *The Man in the Back Seat* which was produced by Lesley Parkyn and Julian Wintle (Independent Artists) and directed by Vernon Sewell. The cast included Nesbitt, Keith Faulkner and Carol White.

Malcolm's connection with Sydney Newman continued when he wrote nine episodes for the series *The Avengers*, which was created in 1961. Originally the series was a vehicle for Ian Hendry, following from his role as Dr Geoffrey Brent in the series *Police Surgeon*, which lasted for just one series in the autumn of 1960. In the new series he also plays a GP, this time called David Keel. It evolved over the decade from a black-and-white gritty crime and mystery thriller made on video, to a stylish and quirky fantasy series, filmed in colour, which combined English eccentricity with elements of 'Swinging London', carefully crafted to appeal to the American market.

Of these nine episodes, Mac co-wrote four episodes with Terrance Dicks who Mac asked to work with him on the scripts when he learnt that Dicks was very keen to write for television. In interviews Terrance has freely acknowledged the influence of Malcolm on his career, describing him as his mentor and recalled:

'The great thing about Mac, you see, from a technical point of view, was that he was a touch typist. He was always terribly efficient and well organised, a kind of human machine, and when he decided to be a writer the first thing he did was go to a typists' school and learn shorthand and typing. So the way we would work was that Mac would sit at the typewriter and we'd discuss a line or whatever, agree on it, and "zap", it would appear on the paper.' [6]

The episodes included *The Mauritius Penny*, in which a back street stamp-dealers is a cover for a neo-fascist plot to overthrow the government and institute 'the New Rule'; *The White Dwarf* in which financiers plot to make money on the global stock exchange by engineering a fake threat to the world by a rogue star; and *The Gravediggers* in which a threat to the country's early warning system is taking place under the guise of a funeral directors.

In January 1963 Sydney Newman was enticed over to the BBC to run their drama department. In the spring of that year Newman and his colleagues worked on devising a new children's programme for the late afternoon slot on Saturdays. What they came up with was a programme which they called *Doctor Who* in which a mysterious character called the Doctor travels through time and space, accompanied by his granddaughter Susan. To begin with, Newman had similar aims as he had in *Pathfinders*, i.e., to create a popular drama series for young people which would educate them about science and history.

The first episode was broadcast on 23rd November 1963, and it became a huge hit when its second serial introduced the Daleks, which sent the series off in a different direction with the Doctor and his companions regularly battling threats such as the ant-like Zarbi on the planet Vortis or the mechanical War Machines on the streets of London. The Doctor was played by William Hartnell from 1963 to 1966, Patrick Troughton from 1966 to 1969 and Jon Pertwee from 1970 to 1974. Mac was among the writers approached to write for the new series. In December 1963 he was commissioned to write a serial called *The Hidden Planet* and produced a number of scripts, but in the end it was not proceeded with, nor was another story about the last days of the Roman occupation of Britain. His first broadcast serial for *Doctor Who* was *The Faceless Ones*, written with David Ellis, shown in April 1967, which features aliens, known as the Chameleons, who have infiltrated an airport and are stealing the identities of travellers in order to take over the world.

Malcolm's next contribution to *Doctor Who* was *The War Games*, written with Terrance Dicks, now chief scriptwriter on the programme, and broadcast April to June 1969, stretching over ten episodes. It was written in haste, because, as Dicks admits in interviews about the serial, the production office had run out of scripts. The Doctor and his companions Jamie and Zoe land in what appears to be the First World War, but then discover other wars from history such as the American Civil War and Mexican Revolution are taking place in different zones. In fact, they are not on Earth at all, but on another planet where the war games are being run by an alien race so that they can create an invincible army to conquer the galaxy, assisted in this by a renegade Time Lord, the War Chief. The Doctor and his companions succeed in forming a resistance army of soldiers from different eras to storm the alien headquarters, but at the end the Doctor has to summon the Time Lords to finally resolve the situation and return everybody to their right time. In this story, Malcolm shows war as violent and pointless, controlled by ruthless leaders who place no value on human life. He adds to this by not giving the aliens names, only titles such as The Security Chief and The War Lord, and we never learn the name of their planet.

In early 1969 Patrick Troughton told the BBC that he wanted to leave the show, exhausted by the relentless production schedule of 44 episodes per year. There were other problems such as disputes amongst the producers and a drastic decline in ratings, with Troughton's last story *The War Games* garnering just 3.5 million. The series teetered on the edge of cancellation. In the end, the BBC decided to give it one more season, which many suspected might well prove to be the last.

Against the odds, *Doctor Who* was re-born in 1970 and re-established itself as a Saturday teatime must-see for another generation of young people. This was brought about by four factors. Firstly, the producers of the series opted for a new story line, anchoring the doctor on Earth as a scientific advisor to UNIT (United Nations Intelligence Taskforce), a quasi-military outfit first encountered by the Second Doctor in *The Invasion*. UNIT is led by Brigadier Lethbridge-Stewart, who had first appeared as a regular army officer in *The Web of Fear*. At the end of *The War Games*, the Doctor had been summoned to Gallifrey (the first time his home planet and the Time Lords had been seen in the series), where, after a trial for interfering in time and history, he is sentenced to exile on Earth and given a new appearance.

Secondly, the inspired choice of Jon Pertwee as Troughton's replacement, a surprise to many as he was principally thought of as a light comedian. Pertwee was born in 1919. After attending private schools, he went to RADA, but was expelled. During the Second World War he served in the Royal Navy intelligence service (if you look closely in some episodes, you can see his naval tattoo, allegedly acquired after a drunken night out). This wartime experience perhaps accounts for the air of authority he adopts as the Doctor; he is particularly short-tempered when faced with pin-striped bureaucrats and blustering military officers. After the war Pertwee forged a career as a comic actor on the radio, and also did some stage and film work. At the time he was chosen as the Third Doctor he was appearing in *The Navy Lark*, a long-running Radio Four naval comedy (still repeated on Radio Four Extra, by the way). Interviewed in 1994, he said, 'I wanted to play him straight, to be a figure that the children believed in, who have enough faith in the Doctor to say the doctor will do it, he will look after us and we'll be all right under his wings.' Pertwee was given a wardrobe which exactly suited his character and patrician personality, cutting an Edwardian dash in frills, velvet, hat and cape. They also gave him a retro car, Bessie. In the look of the Third Doctor there is an echo with a previous BBC series *Adam Adamant Lives*, also created by Sydney Newman and Verity Lambert, which starred Gerald Harper as an Edwardian gentleman adventurer frozen in 1902 and thawed out in Swinging London in 1966, where he resumes his fight against evil, accompanied by a companion (not a girlfriend) Georgina, played by Juliet Harmer. It ran for two series only and never achieved the popularity of *The Avengers* which frankly was much better.

Thirdly, the series was driven forward by script editor Terrance Dicks, and the new producer Barry Letts, who took over from Derrick Sherwin after the first episode *Spearhead from Space* had been filmed when Sherwin went off to rescue another BBC series, *Paul Temple*. Dicks and Letts formed a very close professional working relationship which was instrumental in popularising *Doctor Who* to a fresh audience.

Finally, *Doctor Who* was now filmed in colour which allowed a whole new look (although it was not without problems when the screen showed less than convincing monsters and fibre-glass sets). Of course, many people would still have seen it in black and white as colour television sets were very expensive to purchase to begin with and it was not until 1976 that the sales of colour televisions overtook their black-and-white predecessors.

The Doctor companions were Dr Liz Shaw (Caroline John), a scientist from Cambridge, an expert in meteorites, degrees in medicine, physics and a dozen other subjects; Jo Grant (Katy Manning), a fully qualified agent...safe-breaking, explosives and Sarah Jane Smith (Lis Sladen), a working journalist.

Mac contributed six serials to *Doctor Who* between 1970 and 1974 and helped on a seventh, serials which often had a political dimension. Terrance Dicks said: 'What we never did was commission a *Doctor Who* with a political message but nonetheless if you look at it there is a streak of anti-authoritarianism in all Mac's work: he doesn't trust the establishment.' [7]

Barry Letts concurred: 'You could be pretty certain that anything that he wrote would have an underlying political message which we didn't mind because we liked stories to have a reason.' [8]

Mac himself told an interviewer: 'Remember what politics refers to. It refers to relationships between groups of people. It doesn't necessarily mean left or right, Conservative or Labour, it refers to relationships between groups of people. So really, all *Doctor Who*'s are political, even though the other people look like reptiles, they're still a group of people if they're thinking creatures.' [9] In this era of *Doctor Who* the serials often dealt with issues of social concern such as pollution of the environment in *The Green Death*, the danger of unrestrained scientific advance in Inferno, mind-control in *The Mind of Evil*, racial segregation in *The Mutants* and class conflict in *The Monster of Peladon*.

Doctor Who and The Silurians: January-March 1970

Terrance Dicks' recollection of the origins of this serial is that 'we were looking for a story about a civilisation that rose and fell before Man. So I had an idea – no more than that – and asked Mac what he thought might have happened. And he said, 'Well, suppose they went into hibernation?' 'Why?' 'Well,' said Mac...and we kicked it around between us, discussing the reptile men, their hibernation, what wakes them up, and the whole thing unfolds. Then Mac was commissioned to go away and write a storyline, then the scripts and so on.' [10]

Mac recalled: 'I was asked to do something in caves. In science fiction there are only two stories: they came to us or we go to them. I thought, what about, they come to us, but they've always been here. I said, reptilian men...'Homo Reptilia' they were called by the Doctor. In the days of the Brigadier and the Master, you were told, we want the Brigadier in this or the Master.' [11]

In the opening scene, two men in caves are attacked by some kind of large reptile. Shortly afterwards UNIT is called in to investigate why an underground atomic research centre – seeking to provide cheap, unlimited power – is suffering problems with its energy supply and experiencing mysterious attacks on staff. One man who has survived an attack now spends his time drawing on walls like a caveman. The Doctor and his companion Dr Liz Shaw discover that in the caves below the centre an ancient race has been awakened, the Silurians, a species of highly intelligent reptiles who ruled the Earth millions of years before the evolution of the human race. They had gone into underground hibernation when they believed an approaching asteroid would destroy all life on the surface – and never awoke.

Mac explores a number of themes in this serial, including the threat posed by unfettered scientific research, relationships between races, and the military mind-set which believes that violence can solve all problems. The Doctor berates the Brigadier: "That's typical of the military mind, isn't it? Present them with a new problem, and they start shooting at it." The Doctor makes several attempts to persuade UNIT that they should not attack the Silurians, arguing that "they may not be hostile". When Doctor first encounters a Silurian, he tries to communicate with it, asking: "What do you people want? How can we help you? Unless you tell me what you want the humans will destroy you." Mac also shows divisions within the Silurians: while the elders are prepared to consider sharing the planet, the younger ones want to wipe out the humans with a plague.

The Doctor goes into the caves in an attempt to broker peace:

DOCTOR: But I still don't understand why you stayed down here.
SILURIAN: The hibernation mechanism was faulty. It did not function until a new energy source appeared.
DOCTOR: The power station at the research centre?
SILURIAN: Yes. We are now able to drain off its energy. But soon we shall revive our civilisation, and reclaim the Earth for ourselves.
DOCTOR: No, you mustn't, otherwise there'll be the most terrible war...But if you trust me, I think I can persuade the humans that you are prepared to live with them on this planet in peace.
SILURIAN: There is not room for both civilisations.
DOCTOR: Oh yes, I think there is. You see, your people are used to living in extreme heat, whereas these areas on Earth are of little interest to man. I believe with your advanced technology that you could build cities in parts of the world that man has hitherto completely ignored.
SILURIAN: Would your people agree to this?
DOCTOR: Well, they're not my people, but I think I could convince them, on the condition that you release those trapped men first.
SILURIAN: Those apes have only shown hostility to us.

DOCTOR: And you to them. Someone has to make a move, otherwise this whole thing will end up in complete catastrophe.

Despite the best efforts of the Doctor to broker a peace, suspicions on both sides prove insurmountable. The Silurians want their planet back, the humans are fearful of this alien invasion from below and at the end of the episode the Brigadier orders the destruction of the Silurians' base. The Doctor is outraged: "...that's murder. They were intelligent alien beings. A whole race of them. And he's just wiped them out". Mac gives Liz Shaw some sharp lines. When she is stopped from going into the caves with UNIT she enquires sarcastically: "Have you never heard of female emancipation?" When the Brigadier asks her to look after the phones, she snaps back, "I am a scientist, not an office boy." In 1970 the Women's Liberation movement was just beginning to make its voice heard.

Writing in *Doctor Who* magazine in 1984 Richard Marson wrote that *The Silurians* was:

'Very much the testing ground for the new *Doctor Who*. Whereas *Spearhead from Space* had been an adventure of exceptional pace, with new Doctor, companion, setting, format, and monster all introduced in one four-part story, *The Silurians* allowed time for a closer examination of the new face of *Doctor Who* and its length allowed an exceptional depth of characterisation and more scope for UNIT to work as a concept. *Doctor Who and the Silurians* was a successful, popular seven-parter, which combined all its elements into a well-made and well received show...' [12]

Marjorie Bilbow praised the serial in *The Stage* under the heading, 'A Fine Display of Craftmanship':

'This could have been a bore. It wasn't. Personality clashes were hinted at in tightly written dialogue leavened with humour arising out of *Dr Who*'s penchant for pricking the bubble of official pomposity with the direct question that served the double purpose of clarifying detail for the lay viewer. With an elaborate multiple set, adequately dressed with extras busying themselves with highly complicated machinery to provide a background of convincing activity, *Dr Who and the Silurians* promises to put many a million-dollar filmed fantasy to shame. It was not an enviable task for Jon Pertwee to take over the title role. Already he has created a brand new Superbrain with all the eccentric charm of his predecessors but with a humour and forcefulness all his own. The decision to turn the series into lightweight entertainment for adults instead of children has freed Caroline John from the need to act the well-meaning but irresponsible teenager and she makes Liz Shaw a worthy as well as an attractive assistant to the Doctor. Nicholas Courtney suggests hidden depths to the otherwise routine military figure of Brigadier Stewart by investing his dialogue with the sardonic humour of a man of action manifestly unawed by the wrangling boffins…And you know what? I bet that now *Dr Who* is being written especially for adults the kids will be flocking back in their thousands. A joke that will no doubt be savoured to the full by writer Malcolm Hulke, director Timothy Combe, script editor Terrance Dicks, and producer Barry Letts.' [13]

In *Running Through Corridors*, Rob and Toby's Marathon Watch of *Doctor Who*, Toby Hadoke writes:

'Malcolm Hulke's script continues to impress in that the research-centre characters are very believable, and have subtly drawn foibles …In Hulke's perception, Dr Lawrence's flaw of being a single-minded careerist is even greater than those of either Baker or Quinn. It is sometimes argued that the best *Doctor Who* stories entail a world already in progress when the Doctor shows up, and it makes for such great drama when Hulke plonks the Doctor onto the scene, and his presence shakes up the established relationships …Really, this story is about trust, and what happens when people do or don't allow themselves to exhibit it.' [14]

The Ambassadors of Death: March–May 1970

This was originally written for Patrick Troughton by David Whitaker and then had to be rewritten for Jon Pertwee. Terrance Dicks recalled that he had 'inherited this nightmare called *The Ambassadors of Death,* which was a good idea from David Whitaker, who was an excellent writer, but he'd been mucked about so much he sort of lost heart and direction. I decided I couldn't put him through any more rewrites because it just wasn't going to work and so I went to Barry and said they must pay David off, in full, for his six episodes – although he'd probably written about thirty-six by then – and then we took the basic idea and turned it over to Mac. He came to it fresh and went on from there and stretched it out by an episode for economy reasons.' [15]

The serial harks back to the first *Quatermass* of 1953 with its storyline of astronauts from a British space expedition to Mars who vanish before their capsule lands back on Earth. Instead, three alien ambassadors land in their stead who are kidnapped by a cabal of politicians and military men and who then force them to carry out a series of robberies using their extreme radioactivity to break into safes and military bases. Carrington, the leader of the conspiracy, is convinced that the aliens are a threat to the world.

The Doctor is blasted off into space to make contact with the alien race holding the astronauts:

DOCTOR: Why have you taken them prisoner?
ALIEN: Why have you not returned our ambassadors?
DOCTOR: Ambassadors?
ALIEN: An agreement was made. You have betrayed us. Unless our ambassadors are returned, we shall destroy your world.
DOCTOR: Ambassadors!...What you tell me is appalling. The authorities on Earth had no knowledge of this.
ALIEN: That is difficult to believe.
DOCTOR: Nevertheless, you must believe me. Now let me go back to Earth, and I will give you my personal assurance that your ambassadors will be returned to you.
ALIEN: But you do not even know where they are.
DOCTOR: From the information that you've given me, I'll find them. Now, please, you must let me try.

ALIEN: Very well. But if our ambassadors are not returned, we shall use our weapons to destroy your world.
DOCTOR: These three men, can I take them back with me?
ALIEN: They will remain here until our ambassadors are returned. Now you can go back to your spaceship.

At the end of the final episode The Doctor, UNIT and Liz Shaw defeat Carrington just as he is about to broadcast to the world and rescue the aliens, thus averting a space war. Despite his unfounded paranoia, Mac allows the viewer some sympathy for Carrington at the end as he is led away:

CARRINGTON: Had to do what I did. It was my moral duty. You do understand, don't you?
DOCTOR: Yes, General. I understand.

This theme of an establishment conspiracy occurs in a number of Mac's serials. Another theme is xenophobia about aliens - fear of the 'Other' - a highly relevant storyline in a Britain which was still coming to terms with the growth of new migrant communities from Asia, the West Indies, Ireland etc. The anti-immigrant racist organisation, the National Front, steadily grew in size and support throughout the decade until confronted by the Anti-Nazi League and Rock Against Racism in the late 1970s.

Robert Shearman writes:

'With both *The Silurians* and *The Ambassadors of Death*, we see the entire series turn on its heels, and adopt a far more adult stance towards the way it engages with alien cultures. It's not hard to see who is responsible for that; we now know that the vast majority of *Ambassadors* was written by an uncredited Malcolm Hulke. And that's what's critical to the way we perceive the Doctor from this point on, as a man of peace, as a diplomat - that in 1970s, the audience had 14 weeks of back-to-back Hulke to adjust to it....That superb ending, with Pertwee calmly walking away from aliens and humans, leaving them to tie up the loose ends themselves, presents a very new *Doctor Who* altogether.' [16]

Colony in Space: April-May 1971:

Barry Letts and Terrance Dicks had inherited from Derrick Sherwin the premise that the Doctor had been exiled on Earth by the Time Lords at the end of *The War Games* and could not leave in the Tardis, despite his endless, futile tinkering around in various serials with the dematerialisation circuit and other bits of electronics. Increasingly they saw this as a restriction and wanted to get The Doctor off the planet and back to having adventures around the universe as he used to do. *Colony in Space* is one of the stepping stones to achieving this.

In this second Jon Pertwee season The Doctor is given a worthy opponent, a renegade Time Lord known as The Master (Roger Delgado), playing Moriarty to his Holmes. At the beginning of the story The Master steals information from the Time Lords about a Doomsday weapon which could destroy the universe. The Time Lords therefore pluck the Doctor out of exile on Earth and send him into space with his new companion, Jo Grant (Katy Manning). It's her first trip in the Tardis.

They land on the planet Uxarieus in 2472, where a group of colonists (who with their long hair and clothes resemble a Californian commune) are building a new society. There is also a native race, the Primitives, who are telepathic and never speak. A mining company named IMC (the Interplanetary Mining Company), lands an expedition and plots to expel the colonists and extract the mineral wealth, using a robot to make attacks on the colonists and blame them on giant reptiles. The Master also arrives in the guise of the Adjudicator. The Doctor learns from the Guardian of the Primitives that they once had a very advanced civilisation which was destroyed by the radiation from the Doomsday weapon. At the end the weapon is destroyed by the Guardian, the Master is defeated, and the mining company is sent packing. There is a strong storyline in this serial about the environment and the rapacity of exploitative mining companies. The colonists have left Earth because of a population and environmental crisis which is killing the planet. In a key scene The Doctor argues with Dent, the leader of the IMC expedition:

DENT: The colonists shouldn't be here. My corporation has been assigned the mineral rights on this planet. Our preliminary survey indicates a very rich concentration of duralumin. You know how the Earth needs that mineral.
DOCTOR: Earth, or your corporation's profits?
DENT: What's good for IMC is good for Earth. There are one hundred thousand million people back on Earth and they desperately need all the minerals we can find.
DOCTOR: What those people need, my dear sir, are new worlds to live in like this one. Worlds where they can live like human beings, not battery hens.
DENT: That's not my concern. Minerals are needed. It's my job to find them.
DOCTOR: Even if it means turning this planet into a slagheap?
DENT: I can see we're on opposite sides, Doctor.

The other theme is the threat of nuclear destruction which in the 1970s seemed very real as the USA and the Soviet Union squared up to each other, both armed with colossal nuclear arsenals which could be launched in seconds. In a favourite device of Mac's, a moral argument, the Doctor and the Master argue in the cave of the Guardian:

MASTER: You must see reason, Doctor.
DOCTOR: No, I will not join you in your absurd dreams of a galactic conquest.
MASTER: Why? Why? Look at this. Look at all those planetary systems, Doctor. We could rule them all!
DOCTOR: What for? What is the point?
MASTER: The point is that one must rule or serve. That's a basic law of life. Why do you hesitate, Doctor? Surely it's not loyalty to the Time Lords, who exiled you on one insignificant planet?
DOCTOR: You'll never understand, will you? I want to see the universe, not rule it.

MASTER: Then I'm very sorry, Doctor.
(The Master aims his laser gun at the Doctor, and the Guardian's panel rises.)
MASTER: What's happening?
DOCTOR: Wait and see.
(The Guardian's throne comes out of the wall.)
MASTER: What is it?
DOCTOR: The ultimate development of life on this planet.
GUARDIAN: Why have you returned? What do you want here?
MASTER: I want to restore this city and this planet to their former glory.
DOCTOR: Don't listen to him, sir.
MASTER: You have here a wonderful weapon. Why, with it you could bring good and peace to every world in the galaxy.
DOCTOR: On the contrary. He'll bring only death and destruction.
MASTER: This planet of yours could be the centre of a mighty empire! The greatest that the cosmos has ever known.
DOCTOR: Tell me, sir, has this weapon of yours ever brought good to your planet?
GUARDIAN: Once the weapon was built, our race began to decay. The radiation from the weapon's power source poisoned the soil of our planet.
DOCTOR: Exactly. The weapon has only brought death, and yet he wants to spread that death throughout the galaxy! Unless you destroy this weapon, sir, he will use it for evil.
MASTER: No! You must be mad! Why, with this, we could control every galaxy in the cosmos! We could be gods!
GUARDIAN: You are not fit to be a god. I sense that if you have control of this weapon, you will bring only unhappiness and destruction to the entire universe.
MASTER: Then die!
(The Master points his laser gun at the Guardian, and it disappears from his hand.)
GUARDIAN: There is a self-destructor mechanism. You will please operate it.

DOCTOR: Not only does justice prevail on your planet, sir, but also infinite compassion.
(The Doctor goes to the console and touches a device. The Guardian shakes its head. Then he touches a lever and the Guardian nods, so he pulls it. The room shakes violently.)
GUARDIAN: You must leave at once, or you will be destroyed with the city.
(The Master leaves.)
DOCTOR: Thank you, sir.

Toby Hadoke writes:

'What I really like about this story...is Malcolm Hulke's pessimism. The truth is I never really bought Star *Trek*'s (albeit very laudable) optimism about the future...In Hulke's bleaker - but more morally complex - version of mankind's future, Earth is overpopulated, mining companies gut planets, entertainment systems have footage of real-life violence and we hear of an Earth where people routinely commit suicide...Caldwell...and Ashe give us hope in human-kind's inherent decency and keep this story from being so dark that you want to despair for the future.' [17]

The Sea Devils: February-April 1972.

In this story the exploration for oil in the Channel has re-awakened another group of Silurians in a base under the sea who begin to attack shipping. The Master (who is in prison on the coast) makes contact with them, offering an alliance to destroy the human race. The Doctor goes to their undersea base in an attempt to broker a peace, but this fails when a bumptious politician, Walker (Parliamentary Private Secretary) orders an attack. In the end the Sea Devils' base is destroyed.

The storyline echoes the first Silurian story with a valiant attempt by the Doctor to reconcile the two races, but ultimately failing, and ending in violence. A key scene occurs in the Sea Devils' underwater base when the Doctor argues for peace against the Master:

DOCTOR: I beg you not to listen to this man. He's the personification of evil.
SEA DEVIL: The Master is our friend.
DOCTOR: He wants only to provoke a war.
MASTER: I do not! I came here to help you revive your people.
DOCTOR: Why should you need his help?
SEA DEVIL: Our hibernation unit is faulty.
MASTER: And I can now repair it for you.
DOCTOR: But why revive your people only to have them killed? Let me try and negotiate that peace for you.
MASTER: As you did before, Doctor? The last time this man encountered your race, he tricked them. The humans destroyed them all.
SEA DEVIL: Is that true?
DOCTOR: Yes. I tried to make peace but I failed.
MASTER: You see? He admits it. Man is weak. Your conquest will be easy.
DOCTOR: Believe me, man is not weak. He's only too proficient at devising weapons of annihilation and using them.
SEA DEVIL: *He* says man is weak. *He* says man is strong.
MASTER: He's lying! He's trying to frighten you!
SEA DEVIL: No. I do not think he lies. Perhaps it would be better to make peace. I shall have to consider what you have said.
MASTER: Don't trust him!
(The Doctor raises his right hand and the Sea Devil puts its own hand against it.)

In an interview Mac said he thought that *The Sea Devils* 'was very well produced. It had the submarine which was very good trick photography...the people who do the trick effects for *Doctor Who* do a marvellous job. They really take it very seriously.' [18]

Robert Shearman writes:

'The definitive writer of the Pertwee era, Malcolm Hulke, clearly never felt very comfortable with the concept of the UNIT family. The scripts rely upon suspicion and antagonism...It's therefore quite clever that he uses the Royal Navy in this story, and a fresh set of military characters who can be less immediately trusting of the Doctor. It makes Pertwee's Doctor more of an outsider once more, and his prickly character thrives best in those circumstances.' [19]

Frontier in Space: February-March 1973

In an interview Mac said of this serial:

'The BBC said to me, 'We've just had a whole load of models of spaceships from a Lew Grade show on ITV. We can paint 'em up different colours, can you write a story which will use them?' It was obvious that with that amount of hardware, there has to be conflict because without conflict you've got no drama and this leads your thinking, fairly naturally, to wondering what was 'Frontier in Space' all about? A kind of 'Star Wars' – you've got two sides and who are they? Why are they at war? And the idea came of two great empires with an imaginary frontier drawn across them, across which their spaceships weren't supposed to travel, but of course they did and that's what gave us a story. All these problems have to be solved by drawing on sheer creative imagination and you have to think, 'What makes this story different?' because with science fiction, as with crime, romance, or any other genre of writing, there are only so many ideas and all the writer can do is keep shuffling them like a pack of cards and keep dealing out in a different way. And in the case of Frontier what made it different was that there was a third party which was manoeuvring the Ogrons to make each side antagonistic towards each other. That, incidentally, is a very political idea really. The two sides as far I was concerned were the Soviet Union and America and somebody else trying to tickle 'em up and get them at war with each other when they were quite capable of living in peace.' [20]

In this story the Doctor and Jo arrive in the 26th century where the Earth and the Draconian Empire are on the verge of war after a series of attacks on their spaceships which each blame on the other side. It turns out that the Master, in alliance with the Daleks, is seeking to provoke a war, and then move on unimpeded to conquer the galaxy. The dirty work of attacking the spaceships is carried out by a thuggish race, the Ogrons, who work for the Daleks. Suspected by both sides the Doctor finally convinces the humans and Draconians of the real threat and a joint expedition defeats the Master. Sadly, this is the last time that Roger Delgado played the Master as he was killed in a car crash in Turkey later that year.

As Mac openly acknowledged in the interview quoted above, this story is shaped by the Cold War when the United States and its allies confronted the Soviet Union and its allies. Both sides possessed vast arsenals, including nuclear weapons, and, on several occasions, came very near to war which unquestionably would have ended life on this planet. It's a very ambitious serial with scenes set on Earth, the Moon, Draconia, as well as on a number of spaceships, while the Doctor goes on a spacewalk at one point.

As in *Colony in Space* and *The Sea Devils*, Mac writes a scene in which the Doctor and the Master verbally joust, this time before the Draconian Emperor:

DOCTOR: May I have permission to address the Emperor?
EMPEROR: Wait!
PRINCE: This is an insult!
(The Doctor bows over the Emperor's hand.)
DOCTOR: My life at your command, sire.
PRINCE: How dare you address the Emperor in a manner reserved for a noble of Draconia?
DOCTOR: Ah, but I am a noble of Draconia. The honour was conferred on me by the fifteenth Emperor.
PRINCE: The fifteenth Emperor reigned five hundred years ago.
MASTER: Your Majesty, do not be taken in by this ridiculous story.
EMPEROR: Be silent! There is a legend among our people of a man who assisted the fifteenth Emperor at a time of great trouble when we were almost overwhelmed by a great plague from outer space. But you could not be that man. No Earthman lives so long.

DOCTOR: Your Majesty, this man that you speak of, was he not known as the Doctor? And did he not come to this planet in a spaceship called the Tardis?
EMPEROR: He did.
DOCTOR: Well, I am that man, sire. And I come from a race of people that live far longer than any Earthman.
EMPEROR: Even if I accept your claim, you have broken our law. Why did you violate Draconian space?
MASTER: Your Majesty, this man was, and still is, my prisoner.
DOCTOR: It is true, your Majesty. I did come here as a prisoner, but I came willingly, in order to warn you that this man is plotting a war between Earth and Draconia.
PRINCE: All Earthmen are determined upon war.
DOCTOR: Ah, but the Master is not an Earthman. I'm sorry to have to admit it, but he's a renegade of my own race, and he's using creatures called Ogrons to attack your spaceships and those of the Earthmen.
EMPEROR: The Earthmen who attacked our spaceships, they have been seen many times.
DOCTOR: I'm sorry, but there you are in error, sir. Your people have seen Ogrons, but they appear to them as Earthmen because of a hypnotic device.
JO: It's true, your Majesty. When Ogrons attacked the Earth ships, the Earthmen saw them as Draconians.
PRINCE: Silence! Females are not permitted to speak in the presence of the Emperor.
MASTER: Your Majesty, do not be deceived by the pathetic ravings of two criminals trying to evade justice.
EMPEROR: If what you say is true, it would explain much. We lived at peace with the Earthmen for many years, then suddenly they began to raid our spaceships. When we protested, they said that we were attacking them.
PRINCE: In order to cover up their own attacks, this is simply a plot of the Earthmen to lull us into false security.
(A Messenger enters.)
EMPEROR: Speak!

MESSENGER: Your Majesty, a spaceship from Earth seeks permission to land in the palace spaceport. They say they're on a special mission from the President of Earth.

PRINCE: This is a trick! You must not allow them to land!

EMPEROR: We are not yet at war with Earth. I shall hear what their President has to say. I give my permission.

MESSENGER: Your Majesty.

(The Messenger leaves.)

DOCTOR: A wise decision, your Majesty. For only by Earth and Draconia working together can we hope to arrive at the truth.

MASTER: I too welcome your wisdom, your Majesty. Nobody could be more devoted to the cause of peace than I. As a commissioner of Earth's Interplanetary Police, I have devoted my life to the cause of law and order. And law and order can only exist in a time of peace.

DOCTOR: You feeling all right, old chap?

MASTER: Only during a period of social stability, can society adequately deal with criminals such as this man and this unfortunate girl.

JO: Doctor, listen! That sound!

PRINCE: Silence, female!

JO: Quiet! It's the same noise that I heard on the cargo ship. Doctor, it's the Ogrons!

DOCTOR: Your Majesty, I beg of you to be cautious. Something is seriously wrong here. This ship that has just landed. I beg you, place it under guard immediately.

MASTER: Your majesty, please!

(Ogrons burst into the throne room, firing as they come.)

DRACONIAN: Earthmen!

MASTER: Seize them, fool!

(The Doctor knocks out an Ogron and the Master joins the other Ogrons.)

MASTER: Bah! You idiots! Back to the ship, all of you!

(The Master and his Ogrons leave.)

PRINCE: Now will you believe in the treachery of the Earthmen?

DOCTOR: Your Majesty, look down here and tell me. What do you see?

(The noise is still audible.)
EMPEROR: I see one of your Earth soldiers who attacked my palace and killed my people.
DOCTOR: Jo? Jo, can you still hear that sound?
JO: Yes, it's fading. It's almost gone.
DOCTOR: Your Majesty, I beg of you. Please look again.
PRINCE: Why do we delay? Destroy him!
EMPEROR: Wait! He has spoken the truth.
(The Emperor can see the Ogron.)

Mac makes the President of the Earth a woman (although we never learn her name), a forward-thinking idea at this time when politics was largely male-dominated. But he also indicates that this is a repressive society as the Doctor encounters members of the Peace Party imprisoned in the Lunar Penal Colony to which he is sent for a short time. Finally, Mac gives a great line to one of the Draconians: "The ways of the Earthmen are devious. They're an inscrutable species."

Richard Marson argues that this was Mac's greatest script: 'not only on the strength of the story but also because of the detail – his determination to create a future structure that whilst strong was also so well defined that you felt you had lived there for years.' [21]

Robert Shearman writes of Mac's script:

'Way back at the beginning of Pertwee's tenure, he was finding a way to take the 'trapped on Earth' format and end it, so that the expected cliché of alien invader was turned on its head before it had even had the chance to take hold. And now that the format has changed again, and we're now watching a series about *Doctor Who* 'exploring the stars', he's done the same thing, we might be expecting a story in which the Doctor helps humans fight in the future eon shiny spaceships, but instead we've got a situation where the Doctor and Jo are the monsters the humans are fighting...' [22]

Invasion of the Dinosaurs: January-February 1974

Mac said of this story:

'Now that again was very political. Because there you've got these people with a lovely idea of 'A Golden Age' but sometimes people with very good altruistic ideals can overlook the main issue, that's really what the message behind that one was. What they said to me was that the special effects department had found, if we liked, they could show monsters wandering around contemporary London, so could I think of some reason why dinosaurs were in contemporary London? So that was my brief. And I came up with this idea.' [23]

In this story the Doctor and Sarah Jane Smith land in a deserted London which was been placed under martial law. They learn that dinosaurs have re-appeared in streets of the capital, forcing the evacuation of the population. Eventually they discover a conspiracy of politicians, scientists and army officers who, concerned for the destruction of the environment and the threat of nuclear war, are planning to return the Earth to what they believe will be a pre-industrial Golden Age, using a device called Timescoop. The planet will then be repopulated by an elite group who have been fooled into thinking that they are in a spaceship going to a new world, but are in fact sealed in an underground bunker awaiting the New Earth. The Doctor defeats the conspirators, sending the leading scientist, Professor Whitaker, and the Government minister, Grover, back into the distant past after the Doctor has, of course, reversed the polarity of the Timescoop.

In a shock revelation the Doctor discovers Captain Yates from UNIT has thrown in his lot with the conspiracy:

DOCTOR: Just what are they going to do, Mike?
YATES: They're going to roll back time. The world used to be a cleaner, simpler place. It's all become too complicated and corrupt.
DOCTOR: Roll back time, I see. Can Whitaker really do that?
YATES: I believe so. All the preliminary experiments have been successful.

DOCTOR: Do you realise what'll happen if they succeed?
YATES: We shall find ourselves in the golden age.
DOCTOR: There never was a golden age, Mike. It's all an illusion.
YATES: Not this time. We're going to make it come true.
BRIGADIER: Really. How?
DOCTOR: Whitaker's machine creates a protective field, and anyone within that field will be unaffected. Anybody outside it will just cease to exist.
YATES: Quite right, Doctor.
BRIGADIER: Are we inside this protective field?
YATES: Perhaps, perhaps not. We're on the very edge of the zone here, but it doesn't matter.
BENTON: You mean it doesn't matter to you not existing?
YATES: I'm not important. The others will get there.
DOCTOR: Now listen to me, Mike, I -
(Yates turns his weapon on the Doctor.)
DOCTOR: Look, I understand your ideals. In many ways I sympathise with them. But this is not the way to go about it, you know? You've got no right to take away the existence of generations of people.
YATES: There's no alternative.
DOCTOR: Yes, there is. Take the world that you've got and try and make something of it. It's not too late.

Mac also includes a socialist slant on the environment crisis, giving the Doctor a speech at the end in which he says that at least Grover "realised the dangers this planet of yours is in, Brigadier. The danger of it becoming one vast garbage dump inhabited only by rats...It's not the oil and the filth and the poisonous chemicals that are the real causes of the pollution...It's simply greed".

Jon Pertwee left *Doctor Who* in 1974 to be replaced by the then unknown actor Tom Baker who went on to play the Doctor for seven years. Philip Hinchcliffe took over from Barry Letts as producer, while Robert Holmes took over as script editor from Terrance Dicks. Together they built on the existing success of the show and took it to new heights of popularity, but in quite a different direction, basing many of the stories on classic horror or gothic themes. Mac was never asked to write for the show again. In 1974 Mac won an award for his work on *Doctor Who* at the annual Writer's Guild awards for the best Children's Drama script along with Robert Holmes, Terry Nation and Robert Sloman. In a special issue of the *Doctor Who* poster magazine (1995) devoted to *The Sea Devils* it quotes Mac as follows:

'I think that in my stories the baddies aren't really baddies because they are doing what they think is right. I find it hard to imagine anyone as totally bad or totally inimical. In fact, there's great deal of ...well, although I say it myself philosophy and politics in my science-fiction stories since science-fiction, and *Doctor Who* in particular, is a great opportunity to get across a point of view. And the point of view I have is that, let's say a maggot that's just about to eat someone alive is not necessarily a bad maggot. That just the way he is. Maggoty. I never really write my stories with heroes or villains. They're just a selection of grey people doing grey things for grey reasons. I don't like the concept of heroes. Is the Doctor one? Perhaps, but not always.' [24]

In many ways this sums up Mac's approach to writing both *Doctor Who* and television drama in general. After the broadcast of *The Invasion of the Dinosaurs*, Mac never had anything else broadcast on television. Instead, he made a living from writing books, both fiction and non-fiction. In 1972 he and Terrance Dicks wrote *The Making of Doctor Who*, described by Gary Russell as 'the most important piece of work in the entire history of *Doctor Who* publishing'. *Doctor Who* is almost certainly the most written about programme in the history of British television with countless books and magazines, as well as numerous websites devoted to documenting and analysing (sometimes excessively so) every minute detail of the programme. In 1972, however, this book was ground-breaking and was seized on by fans, eager to know more about their favourite television programme. In the first chapter, 'How It All began', the authors go back in time to the creation of *Doctor Who* by Sydney Newman and his staff at the BBC in 1963:

'An idea as good as *Doctor Who* doesn't just happen. Like the building of a bridge, or the designing of a house, a great deal of thinking goes into a television series before you ever see it...People in television can only guess that their programmes will be successful. If their guess is wrong, then they can spend a lot of money producing a programme which nobody wants to watch.' [25]

The following chapters look at the role of the producer and script-editor, the impact of the Dalek on the series, the actors who have played Doctor Who, the various monsters – Cybermen, Ice Warriors, Yeti, Axons etc, UNIT, the companions, a glossary, 'How to Make a Monster', an explanation of how the programme is made in a television studio and a detailed production diary of a serial, *The Sea Devils*. A second edition was published in 1976, in which the script featured was *Robot* and in which the authors concluded:

'...in the dangerous and disturbing world of today there is a real need for a show like *Doctor Who*. It provides an escape into fantastic alien worlds, where the monsters and horrors encountered are safely distanced by their settings. Today the appetite for fantasy and wonder, with the much-needed release it offers, is greater than ever. Whatever happens to the Doctor on screen we can now be sure that many of his adventures will be preserved for posterity, though in rather different form.' [26]

The popularity of *Doctor Who* led to the publication of three novels based on the TV serials, beginning in 1964 with *Doctor Who and The Daleks*, written by David Whitaker and published by Frederick Mueller. This was followed in 1965 by *Doctor Who and The Zarbi* by Bill Struton and finally *Doctor Who and the Crusades* by David Whitaker. In 1973 Target books began publishing a new series of *Doctor Who* novels, many of them written by the original scriptwriters. Mac wrote seven novels for Target, six of which were based on his own work: *Doctor Who and The Cave Monsters* (January 1974), *Doctor Who and the Doomsday Weapon* (March 1974), *Doctor Who and the Sea Devils* (October 1974), *Doctor Who and the Space War* (September 1976), *Doctor Who and the*

Dinosaur Invasion (February 1976), and *Doctor Who and The War Games* (September 1979). The other novel he wrote was *Doctor Who and The Green Death* (August 1975), whose television script had been written by Robert Sloman. The remaining two stories that he had written for *Doctor Who - The Ambassadors of Death* and *The Faceless Ones* - were turned into novels by his good friend Terrance Dicks after Mac's death.

In an interview Mac explained how writing television scripts was different from writing novels:

'Remember that in a story you really have two stories going at once, the good guys and the bad guys. On television, especially in a show for younger viewers, you don't do very long scenes, people get bored. So therefore you cut from the good guys to the bad guys and from the bad guys to the good guys. In a book this would be very annoying if you got a half-page chapter, and then another half-page chapter. In a book you start the next chapter with 'Meanwhile' and you can go back in time to what the other people were doing ... Also, when you have a book to write you realise, 'I could make this a bit better...' You feel that you can, and therefore you should. You read through the old scripts and then you just start at the beginning...But you must expunge from your mind the possibility that they've seen it...you've got to describe things but also the role of people. You've got to try and get all this in early without boring.' [27]

Malcolm's *Doctor Who* novels are much more than just a straight retelling of the story using the original script. He alters the plots, often adds in extra scenes or references or new characters, and awards even minor characters a backstory.

Mac died on 6th July 1979 in Cambridge hospital. The notice in the press asked for donations to be made to the Royal Free Hospital Body Scanner Appeal while the funeral service took place in a crematorium. Terrance Dicks recalled that, as a convinced atheist, Mac had left orders that there was to be no priest, no hymns or any other ceremony at his funeral, and that therefore his friends sat by the coffin not knowing what to do. 'Finally Eric Paice stood up, slapped the coffin and said, 'Well cheerio, Mac' and wandered out. We all followed him.' *The Stage* carried an obituary which noted his work with Eric Paice in the late 1950s and then his branching out on his own in the 1960s. It also recorded that he was 'a passionate crusader for the rights of the writer and a man, as Eric Paice confirms, of restless creative energy….Last autumn he organised a highly successful week-end course for writers in Bognor, attended by a number of television and radio producers and had been hoping to repeat the event this year.' [28]

A common theme in a good deal of Mac's work was illusion and deception: the police in *This Day in Fear* are not police; the stamp collectors in *The Mauritius Penny* are not harmless philatelists; the aircrew in *The Faceless Ones* are human in looks only; the generals in *The War Games* are aliens, and so on…His message to the audience? Question what you think you see or what you are being told, especially by the powerful. Ask yourself what is really going on. As the Doctor says in *The Faceless Ones*: "Things are not always what they seem". As he wrote in the first chapter of his guide *Writing for Television* (1974), which he called 'What You Don't Know, You Don't Know': 'The more we learn about a complex subject, the more we realise there is to learn. And we can only start when we acknowledge there is something to learn.' The final word must surely go to Terrance Dicks. Mac was 'a very kind and generous man'.

© Michael Herbert

1. *The Observer*, 14th October 1973. The following issue contained a letter from Katya O'Brien who wrote: 'I hope that Malcolm Hulke's devastating article - one of the most powerful and necessary indictments of our laws I have read – will have some effect on, among others, those bottom-of-the -barrel-scraping script writers who still apparently believe 'barsket' jokes are a sure-fire way of raising a laugh,

to be rivalled only by 'unmarried mother' jokes for their brilliance. They might pause to remember that the one in 12 children born outside marriage and their mothers, being across-section, may make up one-sixth of the viewers, and of a nine million audience this means that possible 1½ million viewers are being insulted. One hopes in vain for a hiss from the sycophantic studio audience...though, of course, it wouldn't get past the studio anyway. I'm very glad you published this article.'
2. Malcolm Hulke, 'I Never Went To School', BBC radio broadcast, 1st August 1963.
3. Malcolm Hulke, 'I Never Went To School', BBC radio broadcast, 1st August 1963.
4. Malcolm Hulke, 'I Never Went To School', BBC radio broadcast, 1st August 1963.
5. Eric Paice, *The Way To Write For Television*, (1981), p. 1.
6. Richard Marson, 'The Incredible Malcolm Hulke', *Doctor Who magazine*, 91, August 1984.
7. Interview with Terrance Dicks, 'On Target', special feature on *The War Games* DVD (2008)
8. Interview with Barry Letts, 'On Target', special feature on *The War Games* DVD (2008)
9. Gary Hopkins recorded interview with Malcolm Hulke: *The Doctor Who Podcast,* 17th April 2013. So far as I know this is the only taped interview with Mac in existence.
10. Richard Marson, 'The Incredible Malcolm Hulke', *Doctor Who* magazine, 91, August 1984.
11. Gary Hopkins recorded interview with Malcolm Hulke: *The Doctor Who Podcast*, 17th April 2013.
12. Richard Marson, 'The Making of the Silurians', *Doctor Who magazine*, 91, August 1984.
13. *The Stage*, 5th February 1970.
14. Robert Shearman and Toby Hadoke, *Running Through Corridors, Rob and Toby's Marathon Watch of Doctor Who, Volume 2: The 1970s* (2016), pp. 15-17.

15. Richard Marson, 'The Incredible Malcolm Hulke', Doctor Who magazine, 91, August 1984.
16. Robert Shearman and Toby Hadoke, Running Through Corridors, Rob and Toby's Marathon Watch of Doctor Who, Volume 2: The 1970s (2016), p. 30.
17. Robert Shearman and Toby Hadoke, Running Through Corridors, Rob and Toby's Marathon Watch of Doctor Who, Volume 2: The 1970s (2016), p. 60.
18. Gary Hopkins recorded interview with Malcolm Hulke: The Doctor Who Podcast, 17th April 2013).
19. Robert Shearman and Toby Hadoke, Running Through Corridors, Rob and Toby's Marathon Watch of Doctor Who, Volume 2: The 1970s (2016), p. 86.
20. Richard Marson, 'The Incredible Malcolm Hulke', Doctor Who magazine, 91, August 1984.
21. Richard Marson, 'The Incredible Malcolm Hulke', Doctor Who Magazine, 91, August 1984.
22. Robert Shearman and Toby Hadoke, Running Through Corridors, Rob and Toby's Marathon Watch of Doctor Who, volume 2: The 1970s (2016), p. 123.
23. Gary Hopkins recorded interview with Malcolm Hulke: The Doctor Who Podcast, 17th April 2013.
24. Doctor Who poster magazine (1995).
25. Terrance Dicks and Malcolm Hulke, The Making of Doctor Who (1972), p. 2.
26. Terrance Dicks and Malcolm Hulke, The Making of Doctor Who (1976) p. 124
27. Gary Hopkins recorded interview with Malcolm Hulke: The Doctor Who Podcast, 17th April 2013.
28. The Stage, 12th July 1979

ADVENTURES ON EARTH, IN SPACE AND TIME

When Jon Pertwee stumbled out of the Tardis as the newly regenerated Third Doctor just after 5.15pm on Saturday 3rd January 1970 in episode one of *Spearhead from Space,* little did anyone know this heralded the beginning of a classic decade for television science fiction and fantasy. A rich variety of programmes from this genre reached British TV screens throughout the 1970s, covering a kaleidoscope of styles and themes, from exciting adventures set in distant galaxies to pessimistic tales of near future Earth; from superheroes to unlikely heroes; from comedy to the supernatural. In this chapter we will travel through the time vortex to reflect briefly on many of these programmes, pausing to explore three of the finest in more depth: *Doctor Who*, *UFO* and *Space: 1999*.

We first met The Doctor in the guise of William Hartnell, on 23rd November 1963 in a junk yard owned by the mysterious I M Foreman. Hartnell's portrayal as a kindly but irascible grandfather figure helped establish *Doctor Who* as a hugely successful family programme and throughout Hartnell's tenure in the Tardis it was broadcast every week for 11 months a year. This required a punishing all year-round production schedule equivalent to an episode per week. This schedule plus additional publicity requirements would strain any lead actor but, unknown to most people, Hartnell was also suffering from arteriosclerosis – a clogging of the arteries which restricts blood flow and oxygen supply to vital organs. The physical and mental effects contributed to Hartnell's bouts of ill-temperament and increasing difficulty in remembering lines. In 1966, the then producer Innes Lloyd took the revolutionary decision to change the lead actor in the title role.

So it was, after 134 episodes, on 5th November 1966 that William Hartnell's Doctor was 'renewed' into popular character actor Patrick Troughton (the term 'regeneration' was not used at this point). Unsurprisingly Hartnell was very upset his contract had been terminated but, nonetheless, Lloyd reports Hartnell as saying, "There's only one man in England that can take over, and that's Patrick Troughton." [1] The production team and Troughton correctly determined he should avoid imitating Hartnell's characterisation. Having rejected ideas such as playing the role wearing a Harpo Marx wig or like a tough windjammer captain, Troughton decided to play The Doctor as a 'Chaplinesque' and whimsical 'cosmic hobo' – though as he settled into the part this became an increasingly textured performance: comedic and dark, mischievous and mysterious. Due to the brilliance of Troughton's portrayal, this change was quickly accepted by audiences and this era is seen by fans as a particularly strong period, featuring stories with classic monsters like The Daleks, Cybermen, Ice Warriors and the Yeti.

Towards the end of the 60s, however, the programme's viewing figures were falling. Terrance Dicks who joined the programme in 1968 as associate script editor recalled rumours the BBC were considering cancelling the programme, although this is contradicted by Peter Bryant and Derrick Sherwin, then producer and script editor, who assert there was no prospect of cancellation. With Troughton deciding to bow out at the end of the decade, they felt there was a need for rejuvenation, however, and decided stories should be longer, set on Earth and with a series length reduced from 40 plus weeks to 25 or 26 weeks. These decisions were partly artistic but also logistic. From 1970 onwards *Doctor Who* would be made in colour and this sharply increased production costs. Longer stories set on Earth reduced the need for frequent changes of casts or expensive sets, whilst the absence of alien worlds allowed for more location filming and a less compact schedule facilitated rehearsal and production time.

Bryant and Sherwin's first choice for the Third Doctor was Ron Moody, but he declined. Their second was successful entertainer and actor Jon Pertwee, predominantly known for comedic roles on stage, screen and radio including several *Carry On* Films and – as Michael Herbert's previous chapter observes – the long running radio comedy *The Navy Lark* which Pertwee devised and which gave a platform for his prodigious talent for comedy characters and voices. He had also been the original choice for Captain Mainwaring in *Dad's Army*, but had turned down the role, partly due to Broadway theatre commitments. Tenniel Evans, a friend and fellow *Navy Lark* actor, suggested Pertwee put himself forward for the part of *Doctor Who*. Although Pertwee did not think he was right for the role, he asked his agent to contact the BBC only to discover that he was already in the frame. Bryant's thinking was that Pertwee would inject more humour into the role, but unsure how to approach the part Pertwee was advised by friend and Head of BBC Drama, Shaun Sutton to play the part as himself.

Therefore, other than occasional glimpses of comedy, Pertwee played the role straight, bringing much of his own personality to the role including his fondness for action, vehicles, and gadgets. He also, unintentionally, determined the Third Doctor's costume by appearing at an early photo-call dressed in his grandfather's smoking jacket. The BBC loved the look, and this became the template for the Doctor's style which also perfectly reflected his urbane, intelligent, heroic but slightly high-handed character. Pertwee's Doctor was a combination of tinkering scientist and flamboyant adventurer; modern day action hero and regency buck; a mixture of Adam Adamant, Quatermass with a dash of James Bond and a large dose of Pertwee himself. With his ingenuity, strong morality combined with an ability to look after himself in a fight, more than any other incarnation, Jon Pertwee's Doctor made the viewer feel safe.

The Earth-bound premise for the Third Doctor era was established in Troughton's final story, *The War Games* written by Terrance Dicks and regular co-writer Malcolm Hulke, which also introduced the Doctor's race, the Time Lords (they had never previously been referred to by name). At the end of the story, as punishment for his constant interference in cosmic affairs, the Time Lords exile The Doctor to Earth and remove his knowledge of time travel. They also force The Doctor to regenerate, however because Pertwee had yet to be cast at the time of production, it remains the only time in the programme's history to date that we do not see The Doctor regenerate into his/her next persona.

At the start of the Pertwee era, Terrance Dicks became script editor and Barry Letts took over as producer. Together they formed one of the great creative partnerships in *Doctor Who* history. Pertwee's first series is a little different from his others, however, because it was heavily shaped by outgoing producer and script editor Peter Bryant and Derrick Sherwin who had commissioned the scripts. It had a slightly more dystopian, adult tone and comprised just four stories starting with the four-part *Spearhead from Space* in which we first meet the Autons including the memorable scene where Auton mannequins break out of a shop window (although viewers do not see them break the glass). This was followed by three seven-part stories: *Doctor Who and the Silurians* (the only occasion the character's name featured in a story title), *The Ambassadors of Death* and *Inferno*. Each had strong storylines reflecting Quatermass-like themes of nightmarish consequence of human interference in science or nature and mysterious ancient or extra-terrestrial threats. Nevertheless, the seven-part stories arguably feel too long and somewhat padded.

The season did introduce key elements of the Third Doctor era and beyond, however. We first learn The Doctor has two hearts in *Spearhead from Space* whilst the Doctor acquires Bessie his famous yellow roadster in *Doctor Who and The Silurians*. Colour separation overlay (CSO) – also known as chromakey – was first used in this story. Whilst now looking very dated, CSO would be used as the predominant video special effects format in *Doctor Who* and other programmes for years. The Havoc stunt team first appeared and would go on to perform many large-scale action scenes in Pertwee stories. Although Troughton's Doctor was the first to use a sonic screwdriver, it becomes a regular fixture with Pertwee's Third Doctor. Most significantly, the Earth-bound Doctor now worked with UNIT (the United Nations Intelligence Taskforce) first introduced in the Second Doctor story, *The Invasion*. Pertwee's Doctor works closely with Unit scientist Dr Liz Shaw and develops a strong if occasionally spikey friendship, based on grudging mutual respect, with Brigadier Alexander Gordon Lethbridge-Stuart, played superbly by Nicholas Courtney who, over fifty years later, remains one of the favourite characters in the programme's history.

Letts' and Dicks' template for *Doctor Who* was firmly set with Pertwee's second season. They had never liked the longer story format, so this series returned to a mix of four and six-part stories. More controversially, they also felt the Liz Shaw character – played by Caroline John - was too strong and independent (almost an equal to the Doctor) and so dropped the character without even the benefit of a farewell scene. Caroline John was understandably upset but, unknown to the BBC team had become pregnant, so her time on the programme would have been limited anyway. Liz Smith was replaced by young, trendy, and feisty Jo Grant, played gloriously by Katy Manning. Although Jo was written to be less intellectual than Liz Shaw, she was brave and determined and perfectly fitted the programme style and Pertwee's Doctor. An ensemble Unit family cast was completed with the addition of Captain Mike Yates (Richard Franklin) and regular appearances of Sgt Benton (John Levene).

The second season also introduced an arch enemy Moriarty to the Doctor's Holmes in the form of The Master, played magnificently by Roger Delgado. Unusually, and perhaps mistakenly, The Master would feature in all five of the season's stories: *Terror of the Autons, The Mind of Evil, The Claws of Axos* and *The Daemons.* [2] The latter story, written by Guy Leopold (a pseudonym for Letts and co-writer Robert Sloman), is regarded as one of the decade's classic stories and an archetypal Unit family story. Set in the village of Devil's End, The Master is posing as the newly arrived vicar Mr

Magister and is using ancient black magic spells to summon Azal, a Devil-like creature whose spaceship is buried in a nearby barrow. Azal is the last of The Daemons, a race of aliens who visited ancient Earth and became the origin of satanic beliefs. Azal will appear three times before deciding whether to destroy the Earth or transfer his powers to another, which is The Master's plan. The Doctor, Jo, Benson and Yates join forces with local white witch Miss Hawthorne to stop him and his village followers. The story, which combines science and witchcraft, draws on many references of that period including Nigel Kneale's Quatermass and the Pit, Eric Von Daniken's book, *Chariots of the Gods*, the works of Dennis Wheatley and a general popular interest in the occult.

The on and off-screen teams were now firmly established. Pertwee's third season welcomed the return of the Daleks, after a five-year absence, in a time paradox story *Day of the Daleks*. Dalek creator Terry Nation was too busy working on ITC's *The Persuaders!* at the time and so the story was written by Louis Marks. *The Curse of Peladon* brought back another 'classic monster', the Ice Warriors whilst The Master was restricted to just two stories: *The Sea Devils* (an amphibious relation of the Silurians) and the final story, *The Time Monster*. Pertwee's fourth season was the tenth anniversary of the programme and commenced with *The Three Doctors* which united all his incarnations against Omega, a revered figure in Time Lord history who became trapped in a black hole when harnessing the power source that gave the Time Lords time travel but was now draining them of that energy. Shortly before filming, it sadly became clear that William Hartnell was too ill to play more than a pre-filmed cameo role in the story (explained by the First Doctor becoming trapped in a time eddy) and so Terrance Dicks had to extensively rewrite the story and reallocate much of his original role to other characters. Nevertheless, the interplay between Hartnell and Troughton and Pertwee in particular is sparkling, and the story is full of warmth and humour, making it a fitting celebration.

The six-part *Frontier in Space* featured the Draconians, Pertwee's favourite aliens from his time on the programme, whose distinctive appearance was created through John Friedlander's beautifully sculptured masks. It also heralded the return of The Master for what would sadly be Roger Delgado's final appearance. A further final denouement story between The Master and The Doctor had been planned but, as noted in the previous chapter, Delgado was tragically killed a few months later in a car accident in Turkey whilst preparing for a film. The closing episodes of *Frontier in Space* featured a surprise appearance by The Daleks which directly led to the next six-part story, *Planet of the Daleks*. These two linked six-part stories were conceived as a nostalgic nod to the twelve-episode First Doctor story *The Dalek Master Plan*.

The season ended with *The Green Death* written by Robert Sloman and an uncredited Barry Letts. It features the threat of lethal green slime and giant maggots created by chemical waste produced by an organisation called Global Chemicals which, it transpires, is run by a giant computer called BOSS with a will of its own. The story reflects Letts' concerns about humanity's impact on ecology which closely chimed with society's increasing environmental awareness. Its poignant conclusion sees Jo Grant leave for a new life with young environmentalist and scientist Professor Clifford Jones, very much a younger version of The Doctor. In a moving final scene, The Doctor sadly slips away from their engagement party, silently driving off in Bessie.

Katy Manning's departure and Delgado's tragic death were catalysts for Pertwee's decision to leave at the end of the next series, although he subsequently claimed that his decision was due to a request for an increased fee being unfavourably received. The season commenced with *The Time Warrior*, by Robert Holmes, which introduced a popular new monster, the Sontarans, but more significantly a new character in the form of journalist Sarah Jane Smith, played by the incomparable Elisabeth Sladen who would become perhaps the most beloved of all the Doctor's companions. Sarah's relationship with Pertwee's Doctor was forged through subsequent strong and varied stories: *Invasion of the Dinosaurs, Death to the Daleks, The Monster of Peladon*. So there seems real tenderness between them in the emotional conclusion to the final story, *Planet of the Spiders*, when Pertwee's Doctor collapses and regenerates leaving the Brigadier to remark, "Here we go again."

Barry Letts and Terrance Dicks decided to leave their roles as producer and script editor and were replaced by Phillip Hinchliffe and Robert Holmes respectively, destined to become another of the great *Doctor Who* creative partnerships. One of Letts' last duties was to cast Pertwee's replacement. Several actors were considered, including Fulton Mackay, Jim Dale, Richard Hearne, Graham Crowden and Michael Bentine, but eventually, at the suggestion of Bill Slater, Head of BBC Serials, he offered the role to Tom Baker who would become the longest serving Doctor and the actor most synonymous with the role even today. Baker had enjoyed a successful career on stage, small and large screen, but was still relatively unknown at the time despite recent prominent villainous film roles as Rasputin in *Nicholas and Alexandra* and Prince Koura in *The Golden Voyage of Sinbad*. Three other films in which he had gained major roles had been cancelled, however, and so in 1974, without employment, he was working on a building site to earn money and it was whilst working there that he was offered the part of The Doctor, something which changed his life.

The Fourth Doctor's costume resembled a late 19th Century Parisian bohemian with long coat, large floppy hat, and that famous long striped scarf. The scarf was created by happy accident when costume designer James Acheson gave multiple balls of wool to a woman with the extraordinary name of Begonia Pope who had knitted a scarf for his colleague. It was far more wool than was needed but Begonia Pope did not ask questions and so used all the wool to produce the incredibly long scarf which Baker loved. Baker's costume perfectly suited the Fourth Doctor's character: a brilliant, curious eccentric and eclectic outsider who often appeared distracted and detached and was prone to rapidly changing moods. In many ways like Pertwee before him, Baker was playing a slightly exaggerated version of his own personality. Although the Fourth Doctor would usually use wit and guile to outwit his enemies, just like his predecessor he was more than capable of fighting when required. Tall with a mop of curly hair, a beaming toothy smile and rich and resonant voice, Baker looked and sounded precisely how one imagined The Doctor would be.

Baker hit the marks with his Doctor straight away, helped by a brilliant first series of stories, two of which are regarded as classics. In *The Ark in Space* the Tardis materialises on the space station Nerva, to discover survivors of the human race held in suspended animation for thousands of years following their evacuation into space as solar flares threatened the Earth. An alien insect life form, the Wirrn, has visited the station and laid its eggs and as the humans are revived the larvae infects the leader (Noah) and threatens to destroy the remaining humans. Although the use of green bubble wrap to portray the larvae infection looks (to say the least) dated, this is a fine and genuinely creepy story. The first episode is notable for only featuring the three regular cast members: The Doctor (Baker), Sarah Jane Smith (Elisabeth Sladen) and Unit medical officer Harry Sullivan (Ian Marter). This is a wonderful establishing device to cement their characters' relationship both to each other and to the audience.

Terry Nation's *Genesis of the Daleks* reinvents the origin of the Daleks in a dark and gritty story which is part 'mad scientist' tale and part allegory of the futility of war and the perverted evils of Nazi Germany or another totalitarian regime. It also has a Shakespearean style, thanks to some wonderful speeches and brilliant direction from David Maloney. The Doctor, Sarah and Harry are sent to Skaro (the Daleks' home planet) by the Time Lords to the time of the long war between the Kaled and Thal races, with orders to prevent or change the development of the Daleks. Whilst the Daleks are an emerging threat, the real villain of the story is Davros, the brilliant but warped scientist who created the Dalek travel machine, devised to house future genetic mutations of the Kaled race and as the ultimate battle weapon. Michael Wisher's performance as Davros is astonishing, even more so as it is realised almost entirely through his vocal inclinations (bordering on a Dalek voice when angry). We cannot see Wisher's face behind John Friedlander's magnificent, sculptured mask and the character is confined to a mobile chair resembling the lower part of a Dalek casing and has only limited use of a shrivelled right arm. He is supported by an equally memorable performance from Peter Miles as Nyder, Davros' ruthless and sadistic acolyte.

Terror of the Zygons, the first story of Baker's second season was originally planned to be the final story of the first season. It sees the departure of Harry Sullivan originally devised as a character who could take on the physical action scenes if the Doctor was played by an older actor. With Baker in the role, this was unnecessary and so Harry was considered superfluous. Although a logical decision, it is regrettable as the trio of The Doctor, Sarah and Harry worked very well. It was also the last proper UNIT story and the last appearance of The Brigadier in the 70s. Holmes' and Hinchliffe's template for the programme was now set and the next two seasons became increasingly dark, drawing on themes of gothic and classic horror stories already referenced in The Fourth Doctor's first story *Robot*, inspired by King Kong (with Sarah Jane as the Fay Wray figure).

Planet of Evil drew on Robert Louis Stephenson's *The Strange Case of Doctor Jekyll and Mr Hyde* and the 1956 film, *Forbidden Planet*. *Pyramids of Mars* referenced Universal and Hammer Mummy films whilst *The Brain of Morbius* was inspired by various film versions of Frankenstein with also a nod to H Rider Haggard's *SHE*. *The Seeds of Doom* shares similarities to the 1951 film, *The Thing from Another World* and John Wyndham's *The Day of the Triffids*. *The Hand of Fear* referenced numerous films where individuals are possessed by a severed hand such as *The Beast with Five Fingers* (1946) or *The Hands of Orlac* (1924) remade as *The Hands of a Stranger* (1962). *The Robots of Death* draws on similarities to Agatha Christie's *And Then There Were None* whilst *The Talons of Weng-Chiang* is inspired by Edgar Allan Poe's *Murders in the Rue Morgue*, Gaston Leroux's *The Phantom of the Opera* and Sax Rohmer's *Dr Fu Manchu* stories.

Baker's third season was notable in several other ways. It saw the Doctor rediscover a second gothic style Tardis control room in *The Masque of Mandragora*, the emotional departure of Sarah Jane Smith at the conclusion of *The Hand of Fear,* and the introduction of new companion Leela in *The Face of Evil*. *The Deadly Assassin* saw the Doctor go back to his home planet which we discover is called Gallifrey. The story sees a cadaverous version of The Master return but also establishes numerous elements that have become Time Lord lore such as the Matrix, the notion that Time Lords can only regenerate twelve times, the Time Lord hierarchy and their distinctive ceremonial robes, reference to Rassilon and his symbols of office as well as introducing Cardinal Borusa who once taught The Doctor at the Gallifreyan Academy. The cliff-hanger to part three of *The Deadly Assassin* drew criticism from Mary Whitehouse, for ending on an extended shot of The Doctor being drowned. Whitehouse had been a critic of the increasing horror elements of *Doctor Who* for some time (even though children seemed to love them).

Philip Hinchliffe was moved on at the end of this season to produce the new BBC detective series, *Target* and was replaced by *Target*'s creator, Graham Williams. Robert Holmes would step down as script editor part way through the following season, to be replaced by Anthony Read, bringing to an end what many consider to be the peak of Baker's period. The programme had moved to a later, post-6pm start to reflect the darker tone but nevertheless BBC executives did feel that the horror elements should be curbed. Although the first story, Terrance Dicks' *The Horror of Fang Rock*, still reflected the gothic horror emphasis, there was a distinct shift throughout the season to more traditional science fiction themes and a more humorous tone so that the final story, *The Invasion of Time* which concluded with Leela's rather abrupt departure (as Louise Jameson had decided against renewing her contract) which is almost comedic. The programme continued to be immensely successful, however, and the introduction of the robot dog K9 was a real hit with audiences, though allegedly less so with Tom Baker.

The final full season of the 70s was a series of six linked stories under an overarching theme of 'The Key to Time'. This introduced two opposing figures of higher cosmic powers, The White Guardian played by Cyril Luckham (representing good) and The Black Guardian played by Valentine Dyall (representing evil). The Doctor is tasked by The White Guardian to find the six scattered and disguised parts of the Key to Time which, when assembled, will restore cosmic balance. He is also given (somewhat against his will) a new companion. Romana, a female time lord, is in many ways intellectually superior to The Doctor but a less experienced explorer. Over the season their initial mutual mistrust dissipates, and they form a close partnership. This season is a little patchy which partly reflects the under-developed Key to Time premise. There is a mixture of very good stories (*The Ribos Operation and The Stones of Blood*) and average ones. One of the latter, *The Pirate Planet*, was written by a certain Douglas Adams who would become script editor for the following season which took us from the 70s into the 80s.

Doctor Who was a popular staple of British television schedules throughout the 70ss, but many science fiction and fantasy programmes came and went with varying degrees of quality and success. This included imports from the USA. There was a raft of programmes about fantastic heroes or anti-heroes. One of the most successful was *The Six-Million Dollar Man* which premiered in the UK in 1974 and ran for five years. Astronaut Colonel Steve Austin (Lee Majors) is 'a man barely alive' after a NASA test crash. Today six million dollars might barely buy you a bionic foot but in 1974 it enabled Dr Rudy Wells (Alan Oppenheimer and later Marin E Brooks) to fit Austin with two bionic legs, which enabled him to run at great speed, a bionic arm which gave him great strength, and a bionic eye which gave him telescopic vision. Austin is recruited by the Office of Strategic Investigations (OSI) led by Oscar Goldman (Richard Anderson) as an agent for high-risk missions where his special powers prove invaluable. It was a fun and exciting series which spawned a spin off-series in 1976, *The Bionic Woman* starring

Lindsay Wagner as Jaime Sommers, Austin's childhood sweetheart who is recruited as an agent for OSI following a sky-diving accident after which she is given a bionic arm, legs and bionic ear enabling her to hear at great distances. Similarly successful, *The Bionic Woman* ran (literally) for three series.

Less successful, although still escapist fun, *The Invisible Man* lasted just 13 episodes in 1975. It starred David McCallum as scientist Dr Daniel Weston who discovers a means of turning himself invisible and ends up working for a Government Agency led by Walter Carlson (Craig Stevens of *Peter Gunn* fame). A remarkable lookalike mask and hands and clothes allow Weston to be seen normally when he wants to, though ironically he has to be naked to go undercover. Similarly unsuccessful, *The Man from Atlantis* had a decent premise which failed to deliver. Patrick Duffy played a mysterious amphibian washed up on the beach. Rescued and given the name Mark Harris, he is recruited by the Foundation for Oceanic Research where he initially seeks to discover if more of his race survive but also is embroiled in adventures involving assorted villains, sea monsters and strange beings. The series is remembered as much for Duffy's contact lenses, brief yellow trunks and extraordinary feet-only swimming action as it is for any stories.

For people of a certain age, Lynda Carter will always be *Wonder Woman*. Based on the DC comic character, Carter's Diana Prince may have been less Amazonian princess ad more ex-Miss USA with her tight-fitting star-spangled banner outfit, but she played the part brilliantly with a healthy mix of campness, knowing self-deprecation and bold action-hero. The first series, set in the 1940s, was not shown in the UK at the time so it was the revamped version, *The New Adventures of Wonder Woman*, which ran from 1978 that British viewers saw. Set in the 70s, Wonder Woman is recruited by the International Agency Defence Command (IADC) to fight a wide range of supervillains, aliens, and dictators. With its catchy but camp theme tune, and a nod to the 1960s *Batman* series in style, it may not be to everyone's taste, but the series was fun and deserves credit for featuring a strong female lead which was still relatively uncommon for the time.

Another television series based on a comic character, Marvel's *The Incredible Hulk*, premiered in 1978 and ran very successfully for five series. Bill Bixby is believable and sympathetic as mild-mannered scientist David (Bruce) Banner driven to seeking some form of super strength having failed to save his late wife from a burning car. An accident with gamma rays turns him into a Jekyll and Hyde character so that when angered he transforms into a giant green Hulk (played by ex-bodybuilder Lou Ferringo). The series follows a familiar US TV premise seen in *The Fugitive* (1963 -67) or *Kung Fu* (1972-75) where Banner's different adventures arise due to needing to move on from place to place seeking a cure for his condition but also pursued by reporter Jack McGee (Jack Colvin) who believes The Hulk is a killer. In fact, The Hulk usually 'saves the day', rescuing the weekly good guys and defeating the weekly villains. Much of the series' enjoyment derives from waiting for Banner to be pushed into a situation where, either angry or in pain, he transforms into his alter ego heralded by Bixby's eyes changing colour (through contact lenses which apparently caused him great discomfort), familiar eerie music and images of a ripped shirt revealing our green muscled anti-hero.

The Fugitive premise was also used in two spin-off television series from major movies, although neither series achieved the same level of success. *Planet of the Apes (1974)* starred the always watchable Roddy McDowall as the chimpanzee Galen who befriends crashed astronauts Virdon (Ron Harper) and Burke (James Naughton) and all three are pursued by gorilla leader Urko (Mark Lenard). The series reflects the original *Planet of the Apes* film but with notable differences such as the human characters, whist still subordinate to the apes, being able to talk. McDowall starred in four of the original five *Apes* movies and brings the same brilliant characterisation to the TV role with his mannerisms and slightly stooped walk whilst hidden behind the incredible ape make up. The series was well received in the UK, attracting high viewing figures but was less popular in the US and was cancelled after fourteen episodes.

The same fate befell *Logan's Run* (which was shown in 1978 in the UK). As with the original 1976 film, the series is set in 23rd Century where inhabitants of the City of Domes undergo voluntary euthanasia on reaching their 30th birthday through the Carousel ceremony. Those who refuse are hunted by the Domed City police, known as Sandmen. One of these, Logan (Gregory Harrison), is persuaded by Jessica (Heather Menzies) to escape the city and search for the mythical Sanctuary. They are accompanied by android REM (Donald Moffat), by far the most enjoyable character, and pursued by Logan's ex-friend and fellow Sandman, Francis (Randy Powell). Whilst the concept of the series, like the film, is truly chilling, the series was insipid with stories that were not particularly exciting. Just like *Planet of the Apes*, early cancellation meant that we never knew whether the characters achieved their goal.

Another short-lived series following a similar premise was *The Fantastic Journey* which ran for just ten episodes in 1977. A small scientific expedition becomes lost in the Bermuda Triangle and its members find themselves on a strange island where they meet a collection of characters from different time zones including Varien, a man from 23rd century (Jared Martin) and Dr Willoway played once again by Roddy McDowall. Like Dr Zachary Smith in Irwin Allen's 60s series *Lost in Space*, Willoway evolves from a not entirely trustworthy character to a principal lead and one of the best things about the programme. Reflecting another of Allen's 60s series, *The Time Tunnel*, the group cross multiple time zones encountering assorted people and adventures, searching for a way home. Sadly, we never discover their fate.

Writer, producer, director, and musician Glen A Larson was a prominent figure in US TV, particularly in the 70s and 80s. He produced programmes such as *The Virginian, McCloud, Alias Smith and Jones* and *The Six Million Dollar Man*. Larson was something of a magpie, happily borrowing ideas from other series and movies. According to James Garner's autobiography, Garner's production company complained that Larson copied several *Rockford Files* scripts for his own series, *Switch*. Allegedly, Larson then plagiarised *The Rockford Files* theme tune for another series which led to Garner punching him. Apocryphal or otherwise Larson's *Battlestar Galactica*, made in 1978, was heavily inspired by *Star Wars*, resulting in lawsuits from 20th Century Fox.

For all the accusations, Larson knew how to make an entertaining television show. *Battlestar Galactica* was an epic series with movie quality special effects from John Dykstra. Following a devastating attack by the evil Cylons, a caravan of spaceships carrying survivors of the twelve outer colonies travels under the protection of the remaining Battlestar Galactica searching for the enigmatic thirteenth colony – Earth. Led by Commander Adama (Lorne Greene) they encounter various alien races but also continually battle the pursuing Cylons. Drawing on pseudo-religious themes as well as reflecting programmes such as *Wagon Train*, Battlestar Galactica was hugely ambitious and highly entertaining. It was also enormously expensive. This meant that the programme was cancelled after one series and caused Universal Studios to insist that the opening episodes were initially turned into a movie and given a cinema release in the UK to recoup some costs. This meant that UK viewers did not see the programme until 1980 and the lack of a network slot affected its impact.

Television programmes dealing with threats and themes of 'the unknown' – in various forms – were hugely popular in the 70s and amongst the best of the small screen fantasy genre. In 1972 Nigel Kneale's play *The Stone Tape* terrified Christmas Day viewers. Rod Serling's *Night Gallery* presented stories of the supernatural, horror, science fiction and the unexplained over 98 half-hour episodes. *The Omega Factor* was a ten-part British series in 1979 which starred James Hazeldine as Tom Crane who possesses psychic powers and joins the secret Department 7, where he works with physicist Dr Anne Reynolds (Louise Jameson) and Psychiatrist Dr

Roy Martindale (John Carlisle) investigating cases of various paranormal phenomena and a possible conspiracy of world domination by mind control from a shadowy organisation called Omega.

Children of the Stones enthralled and frightened family audiences in 1977 with a tale of mysterious psychic forces generated from a stone circle which enslave all occupants of the village of Milbury (in reality Avebury in Wiltshire) into a state of docile happiness. Another children's programme *Sky* was also filmed near the stone circle of Avebury along with Glastonbury and Stonehenge. *Sky*, a mysterious alien boy with the power to compel people to his will, becomes trapped on Earth. He is befriended by a trio of children who try to help him return to his own dimension. *The Tomorrow People* ran from 1973 throughout the decade and featured the adventures of a group of teenagers who are the next stage in human evolution – homo superiors – possessing the powers of telepathy and telekinesis plus the ability to 'jaunt' – transferring from one location and appearing in another.

Kolchak: The Night Stalker starred Darren McGavin as world-weary reporter Carl Kolchak embroiled in stories featuring various monsters, such as Jack the Ripper, vampires, a werewolf, and a zombie but is never believed. Starting out as two made-for-TV movies, McGavin developed the character into a series of 20 episodes in 1974, but the series only appeared on British screens in some ITV regions in the 1980s. *Sapphire and Steel* started in November 1979 but is predominantly an 80s series. Nevertheless, we should not omit it here as it remains one of the finest and original British fantasy series. Created by P J Hammond, it starred David McCallum and Joanna Lumley in the title roles as time detectives who investigate strange events and threats from paranormal forces and time itself.

As radio's *The Hitchhiker's Guide to the Galaxy* proves, comedy and science fiction can combine very well but sadly this was not the case for most 1970s television examples. ITV's *The Adventures of*

Don Quick (1970) starred Ian Hendry in the title role and Ronald Lacey as his partner Sgt Sam Czopanser. Obvious from the fairly clumsy character names, this was a satire loosely based on Cervantes' *The Adventures of Don Quixote*, which sees inter galactic maintenance man Don Quick seek to right imaginary wrongs on each planet he visits, usually resulting in chaos. It was a bizarre and not very funny series which disappeared into the ether. *Holmes and Yoyo* (1976-77) was a similarly ineffective US detective comedy series. Starring Richard B Shull as detective Alexander Holmes and John Shuck (fresh from playing Sgt Enright in *McMillan and Wife*) as his robot partner, it ran for just thirteen episodes. Arguable worst of all, *Come Back Mrs Noah* (1977) was a rare misfire for sitcom geniuses David Croft and Jeremy Lloyd. Mollie Sugden was the title character, a 21st century housewife who wins a trip around Britain's space station and becomes accidentally launched into orbit along with a collection of other characters, with the UK Mission Control trying to return them to Earth. Despite the inclusion of other sitcom luminaries such as Ian Lavender, Donald Hewlett, Gorden Kaye and Michael Knowles, the one-trick concept soon wore thin, as did the humour.

The exception in this list is *Mork and Mindy* which premiered in the UK in 1979 and ran for 93 episodes. The massively popular programme was a spin-off from a *Happy Days* episode (*My Favorite Orkan*) and starred Robin Williams as alien Mork from Ork who visits Earth to observe human life and befriends Mindy played by Pam Dawber. The series gave full reign to William's brilliantly inventive improvisation and comic genius as well as his dramatic abilities. Mork is the innocent stranger in a strange world and the stories mix anarchic humour with genuine pathos and morality tales, neatly summarised at the end of each episode as Mork reports back on lessons he's learned to cosmic leader Orson, signing off with his regular greeting, "Nanu Nanu", which was adopted in playgrounds and offices across the globe.

In sharp contrast, many British 70s sci-fi/fantasy series were much darker, reflecting a distinctly dystopian view of the future. Many are covered in depth elsewhere in this book, but we will briefly highlight them in this overview.

Doomwatch (1970-72) was a 'sci-fact' series about a government department (Doomwatch) led by Dr Spencer Quist (Jon Paul) established to tackle the threat of dangerous scientific advances on the environment and humanity. Many of the stories were chillingly prophetic and dealt with themes such as manmade viruses, embryonic research, pollution, toxic waste, pesticides and manipulation of electronic personal data. The series also starred Robert Powell as Toby Wren and Simon Oates as Dr John Ridge and reflected increasing public awareness of ecological concerns and the potential harmful effects of scientific progress. The series was written by Dr Kit Pedler and former *Doctor Who* script editor Gerry Davis who had created the Cybermen. Some of the themes reflected stories from The Third Doctor's era - in fact Jon Paul facially resembled Jon Pertwee (minus the frock coats) with his character Quist sharing a similar disdain for authority figures. *Doomwatch* proved hugely popular, and viewers were shocked when the Toby Wren character was killed off at the end of series one. Davis and Pedler left before series 3 as they felt the series was being pushed to being more of a conventional drama.

Terry Nation's *Survivors* (1975-77) was a grim post-apocalyptic drama concerning a group of characters and their struggle to survive after 95% of the world's population is killed following the accidental release of a virus. Unsurprisingly this is not a series which people may have flocked to rewatch during the recent COVID pandemic, but it was hugely successful at the time and Nation's stories were full of believable characters, gripping drama, and emotion. Some contemporary critics criticised the lead characters for being too middle class but, in a way, this was the point of the series: people who were used to a relatively comfortable lifestyle suddenly having to cope with everything they knew being taken away and develop new skills and new ways of living in order to survive. Had the characters been experienced survival specialists, land workers, farmers, carpenters, and soldiers, it may not have had the same impact.

Based on a trilogy of books by Peter Dickinson, *The Changes* (1975) deals with a similar post-apocalyptic concept but this time combined with mystical elements. A strange noise emanating from machinery and technology causes people to reject and destroy them and revert to living in a pre-technical society. Teenager Nicky Gore (Vicky Williams) is one of a small group of people to be unaffected and discovers that the cause is a mysterious phenomenon created by the Necromancer, a living stone from the time of Merlin, which has been accidentally awoken. A similar 'end of days' theme is covered in *Quatermass* (1979) starring John Mills in the last outing for Nigel Kneale's classic character. Reclusive and world weary Quatermass seeks his missing granddaughter and finds a society in meltdown. Meanwhile, gangs of new age travellers are hypnotically drawn to ancient ritual sites including Ringtone Round (remember the earworm song 'Huffity Puffity Ringstone Round'?) where they are destroyed in beams of energy by a malevolent alien force.

A more traditional near-future dystopian world was covered in *1990* (1977-78). More thriller series than science fiction, this envisaged a UK which was a bureaucratic and tyrannical island police state run by the Home Office's oppressive Public Control Department (PCD) where the North Sea and Channel is equivalent to the Berlin Wall. Edward Woodward starred as journalist Jim Kyle working with a resistance movement to combat the PCD and help people flee the country.

One of the most popular and fondly remembered British science fiction series of this or any era was *Blake's 7* (1978-81). Roj Blake (Gareth Thomas) leads an unlikely group of anti-heroes against the totalitarian and oppressive Federation, with Kerr Avon (outstandingly played by Paul Darrow) stepping up to take over as leader following Blake's departure. The series had strong, dramatic storylines and was packed with memorable and superbly realised characters such as Avon, Vila (Michael Keaton), the villainous Servalan (a glorious Jacqueline Pearce) and the obsessive Travis (Stephen Greif and then Brian Croucher). Two years previously, Gareth Thomas appeared in a more bizarre Anglo-German comedy adventure production, *Star Maidens* (1976). Thomas is one of two escaping male servants fleeing the planet Medusa ruled by women and where men are regarded as servile. Once again Thomas' character is pursued by a powerful female villain, this time Supreme Councillor Fulvia (Judy Geeson). The programme was part role reversal satire on a male-dominated world and was a lavish production with an impressive European cast which included Dawn Addams, Pierre Brice, Lisa Harrow and Ronald Hines. Despite attracting worldwide sales, it was poorly received in the UK, however, and was only shown in some ITV regions.

Made a on a more modest budget *Moonbase 3* was a six-part BBC series from 1973 from the *Doctor Who* creative team of Barry Letts (producer) and Terrance Dicks (script editor) with none other than James Burke acting as script consultant. The series is set in 2003, reflecting the expectation that the 1969 moon landing and the recent Skylab launch would lead to a near future colonisation of the Moon. Earth's power blocs occupy different lunar communities at this point, with the Europeans living in Moonbase 3. Each story was an individual drama often focusing on the realistic fears and challenges people faced living in a lunar community. The programme starred Donald Houston as recently arrived Moonbase director David Caulder [3] along with Ralph Bates as his deputy Michael Lebrun, Barry Lowe as technical director Tom Hill and Fiona Gaunt as psychiatrist Dr Helen Smith. Although very well received, the programme lasted only one series.

Gerry and Sylvia Anderson's names are synonymous with 1960s action-adventure puppet series. However, as the decade segued into the 70s, ITC's Lew Grade invited them to draw on their 1969 science fiction film *Doppelgänger* and switch to live-action television productions. The result was *UFO*. Set in a near future 1980, it was reputedly the most expensive British television programme ever made at the time. The series drew inspiration from various sources, including the continuing public fascination with the possibility of extra-terrestrial visitors, conspiracy theories of government cover-ups of alien encounters, Christian Barnard's first human heart transplant operation in 1967 and Anderson's previous programme *Captain Scarlet and the Mysterons*. As in that series, where Spectrum protected the Earth from threats from the Martian Mysterons, *UFO* was about a secret organisation, SHADO (Supreme Headquarters Alien Defence Organisation), defending the Earth from alien attackers from an unknown world.

The programme re-used or redressed costumes and sets from *Doppelgänger* plus two futuristic gull-wing cars (similar to the DMC DeLorean car manufactured over 10 years later) designed by special effects supremo Derek Meddings and a Len Bailey, a Ford Motor company stylist. It also featured several cast members from the film, including the two main leads: Ed Bishop as SHADO Commander Ed Straker and George Sewell as his Deputy, Colonel Alec Freeman. Bishop was mesmerising as Straker, a brilliant but coldly logical and ruthless leader determined to get the job done at all costs. Sewell was also excellent as Freeman, an intelligent, loyal but more thoughtful and compassionate individual. They formed an effective partnership, with contrasting personalities which like Holmes and Watson together made a complete character.

The first episode *Identified* starts with a spectacular opening prologue set in 1970 when a police motorbike convoy and Rolls Royce carrying a younger Straker, and government minister (Basil Dignam,) is attacked by a UFO causing the car to crash. Fortunate to escape with his life, the prologue ends with rare photographic evidence of the UFOs being burned. Ten years later the episode concludes with the capturing of an injured alien who dies following a failed attempt to treat him. The post-mortem reveals the alien to have identifiable human organs indicating that the purpose of the alien visits is to harvest human beings for their organs to preserve the alien existence.

Like other Anderson programmes, *UFO* featured outstanding special effects and memorable vehicle designs. These included the craft which served as SHADO's three levels of defence. The Interceptors were three single-occupant space vehicles launched from SHADO's Moonbase when the long-range satellite Space Intruder Detector (SID), voiced by velvet-toned BBC newscaster Mel Oxley, alerted a UFO entering the Solar System. Each interceptor had a single nuclear ballistic missile to attack the alien craft. Purists may quibble why SHADO would rely on vehicles carrying only one missile, but this was for dramatic effect, allowing UFOs to slip past the moon defences into Earth's orbit (as was frequently the case). The Skydiver submarine was the next line of defence. The front of the submarine was superfast single occupant jet, Sky 1, which launched out of the water when Skydiver closed in on the UFO's trajectory. Sky 1 was usually successful in hunting down the UFO but if it landed or crashed to Earth the ground defence tank-like Mobiles would be deployed. The UFO itself was, perhaps, the most brilliant design of all. Following the familiar flying saucer shape, its spinning effect was achieved through a spinning lower hull revolving beneath a static Perspex dome.

SHADO HQ was based beneath the fictitious Harlington-Straker film studios, in reality ATV studios in Elstree. Artistically this served to preserve SHADO's secret identity but logistically it meant that the MGM film studios at Borehamwood and later Pinewood where the series was filmed could be extensively used as a backdrop, saving set construction costs. Barry Gray once again provided the music including its pulsating and memorable main theme which accompanied the exciting fast paced opening credits. Like many programmes of that era set in the near future, the show is dated by the costumes. Bright coloured collarless suits for the men but, most bizarrely, beige string tops for the Skydiver crew and purple wigs and silver miniskirts for the SHADO Moonbase female operatives, who monitored UFO and Interceptor positions akin to World War 2 war room personnel.

UFO stories were exciting but often dealt with dramatic adult themes and emotional conflict. *Confetti Check A OK* was a flash back episode about the formation of SHADO and how Straker's marriage broke down because of his secret work commitments and inability to divulge his real job even to his wife. *A Question of Priorities* was an emotionally charged episode where Straker is forced to choose between deploying an aircraft to transport a drug to save the life of his seriously injured son or reach an alien seemingly willing to defect. *Computer Affair* focuses on an emotional attachment between Moonbase Controller Lt Gay Ellis (Gabrielle Drake) and pilot Mark Bradley — who is also black — and whether this influenced a crucial command decision by Ellis. In *Survival* Colonel Paul Foster (Michael Billington) and an alien form a desperate alliance when lost on the Moon whilst in *The Responsibility Seat* Freeman faces a crisis when left in charge of SHADO whilst Straker pursues a journalist who has stolen a secret recording and to whom he becomes attracted.

As the series progresses, plots become more surreal as the aliens deploy increasingly extraordinary powers in their threats. In *Kill Straker* and *The Man Who Came Back* they control people's minds to become assassins. In *The Psychobombs* they transform three ordinary individuals into superpowered human bombs. In *ESP* they turn a man with latent ESP powers into an alien agent whilst in *The Cat with Ten Lives* they do the same with a SHADO pilot using a telepathic link with a possessed Siamese cat. In *Mindbender* they cause Straker to suffer dangerous hallucinations. In *The Long Sleep,* the aliens are able to resurrect and manipulate one dead victim and artificially extend another's lifespan whilst in *Timelash* they are able to freeze SHADO HQ in a time bubble. The closure of MGM studios created a forced production break after episode 17 and a delay in transferring to Pinewood studios meant that a number of the cast (including George Sewell and Gabrielle Drake) were no longer available and had to be replaced. Along with more bizarre plots this gave many of the final episodes a slightly different feel.

On every level *UFO* was a superior science fiction TV programme. Unfortunately, despite its quality and cost, like many other programmes at the time it did not secure a scheduled slot across the ITV network. Whilst ATV premiered *UFO* in 1970 in a peak timeslot, other regions showed it at different times, in some cases delaying broadcasting until 1971 or 1972. This might be because, historically, British channels have been uncertain about science fiction programmes, frequently not treating them as serious drama. Also, broadcasters were familiar with Anderson shows being aimed squarely at children or family audiences whereas *UFO* was much more difficult to pin down. Whatever the reason the lack of network scheduling impacted upon its UK success. In contrast, UFO proved immensely popular on public broadcasting services (PBS) in the USA, so much that CBS expressed interest in buying a second series. Plans were well advanced for a second series, which it was intended would move the base of the operations to an expanded Moonbase, when CBS changed its mind due to falling US ratings.

Thus, *UFO 2* was dead, but given the extensive pre-planning work undertaken, Gerry Anderson persuaded Lew Grade that a new series could be developed. Abe Mandell, Head of ITC New York, was an increasingly influential figure and he had already dictated that any new series should be spectacular and set on the Moon with no Earth-based stories. Anderson's initial concept was a cataclysmic event which saw the Earth destroyed but Mandell was concerned about public reaction, so Anderson rewrote the concept so that a gigantic nuclear accident blasts the Moon into deep space leading to a series of adventures for the crew of Moonbase Alpha. Although the concept relied on a heavy suspension of scientific credibility, Grade and Mandell liked the idea and so *Space: 1999* was born and would become (once again) the most expensive UK programme ever made at that point.

Husband and wife stars Martin Landau and Barbara Bain were contracted for the lead roles of Commander John Koenig and Dr Helena Russell, along with Barry Morse as Professor Victor Bergman. Actors in key supporting roles were Prentis Hancock as

Paul Morrow, Clifton Jones as David Kano, Nick Tate as Alan Carter, Zienia Merton as Sandra Benes, and Anton Phillips as Dr Bob Mathias. With additional funding from RAI Italy, the production values were of the highest standard. This included lavish sets like the vast Moonbase Alpha Main Mission; innovative design concepts such as the 'comlock' device, part electronic key, part communicator; superb makeup and costumes including the Alphan uniforms designed by internationally renowned avant-garde fashion designer Rudi Gernreich; cutting-edge special effects and models (a team led by Brian Johnson, as Derek Meddings was now working on *Bond* films) including the memorable Eagle Transporter craft. Episodes also attracted top directors including Ray Austin and Charles Crichton and an impressive list of guest stars such as Peter Cushing, Christopher Lee, Margaret Leighton, Ian McShane, Joan Collins, Richard Johnson, Leo McKern, Jeremy Kemp and Roy Dotrice who appeared in two episodes as Commissioner Simmonds.

Unlike similar sci-fi programmes such as *Star Trek*, the fascinating dramatic concept of *Space: 1999* was that human beings were plunged into deep space with no control over their journey, encountering strange beings and forces for the first time. They relied entirely on each other and their collective human ingenuity to deal with both the trauma of leaving behind their loved ones but also situations which were beyond their comprehension. Over 24 episodes this included: travelling through a black hole (*Black Sun*), parallel versions of themselves *(Another Time, Another Place)*, an alien made of energy (*Force of Life*), inexplicable pre-destiny *(Collision Course)*, a giant sentient spaceship (*The Infernal Machine*), the gift and loss of a temporary artificial moon atmosphere *(The Last Sunset)*, an anti-matter version of Helena Russell's missing husband (*Matter of Life and Death)*, psychic phenomena *(The Troubled Spirit)*, discovering origins of humanity *(The Testament of Arkadia)* plus various mystical cosmic beings and mysterious aliens.

In addition to great action and effects, the stories provided serious, intelligent drama up there with the best of any series of this genre. This was accompanied by a superb score by Barry Gray in what would turn out to be his swansong and some outstanding performances – particularly Martin Landau and Barry Morse who turned what could have been fairly stereotypical roles into textured and believable characters. Unfortunately, like *UFO, Space: 1999* suffered in the UK from bizarre and inconsistent ITV scheduling and failed to secure sales to a US network although, like *UFO*, it proved immensely popular on public broadcasting services (PBS). This encouraged ITC to order a second series, but this time geared more towards the US Market, the first of several disastrous decisions.

American producer Fred Freiberger was recruited to assist the series two US focus. Gerry and Sylvia Anderson's marriage had been strained for several years but had now completely broken down. Partly for this reason, Gerry handed considerable control for the second series to Freiberger who sought to Americanise the programme in the belief that this was what US audiences wanted (seemingly forgetting they had enjoyed the format of series one). He replaced the emphasis on intelligent drama with a focus on action and injected more lightness and humour along with obvious romantic relationships – particularly between Koenig and Dr Russell – feeling that this was missing in series one. Whilst somewhat true, this had reflected the more dramatic tone of series one which still contained plenty of emotion. Whilst series one episode endings were varied – sometimes hopeful, sometimes melancholic, sometimes reflective – series two episode endings would usually end with a jarring humorous scene tagged on.

Freiberger also changed the Alphan uniforms and replaced the large Main Mission set with a smaller Command Centre set believing that this would add intimacy and drama. In fact, the more restricted space reportedly created directorial challenges when shooting scenes. Most controversially, Freiberger jettisoned most of the series one cast and characters except for Landau, Bain, and Tate whilst Zienia Merton was brought back for a few episodes at Bain's insistence. No on-screen reason was given for the departure of so many popular key characters with Freiberger arguing no one would notice. However, combined with all the other changes, this caused confusion for viewers faced with a series which seemed neither new nor the same. There were two prominent new characters: Tony Verdeschi (Tony Anholt) who without introduction was suddenly Koenig's second in command and Maya (Catherine Schell), an alien with metamorphic abilities introduced in series two's first episode.

Not all the problems were caused by Freiberger. The budget for series two was drastically reduced which showed in some of the special effects, quality of design and sets and comparative absence of star guests. There also seemed to be a general air of confusion in the production. Gerry Anderson later acknowledged he should have exercised more control and prevented some series two changes – including the dropping of Barry Morse. On one visit to the studios, the influential Abe Mandell had insisted on the introduction of more monsters into stories – arguing this was what US audiences wanted – resulting in an increase in stories with hastily added clunky rubber monsters. On a subsequent visit Mandell queried why there were suddenly so monsters appearing, claiming that this was no longer what US audiences wanted! Whilst the precise level of Sylvia Anderson's creative input into the Anderson programmes is subject to considerable debate, many highlight her skill in dealing with people. Sylvia was apparently instrumental in making series one a happy working environment whilst, without her presence, it seems series two suffered from many off-screen tensions. In various subsequent interviews Martin Landau stated he frequently fought with Freiberger over many of decisions and tried to steer the programme back towards its series one approach.

Not everything about series two was wrong. Maya was a great character, brilliantly played by Catherine Schell even if the series fell into the trap of over-using Maya's metamorphic abilities to save the day. Martin Landau continued to be excellent as Koenig whilst Bain, Tate and Anholt were also highly watchable. Some of the stories were genuinely exciting and whilst not up to the same standard the quality of production and guest casts remained high. Nevertheless, whilst *Space: 1999* series one had been interesting, different, and full of intelligent and dramatic stories, series two was more comic book style, and resembled too many average sci fi programmes. It did not prove especially popular in the US, whist in the UK it had little advanced promotion and was once again scheduled in different timeslots including Saturday morning! Unsurprisingly, there was no third series, and this ended Anderson's association with ITC.

In between the two series, Anderson had been commissioned by NBC to produce a one-off special focusing on Einstein's theory of relativity, as contribution to an educational series using drama and entertainment to encourage teenagers to learn about scientific topics. The result was *The Day After Tomorrow* (also known as *Into Infinity*), a 50-minute story filmed in just 10 days at Pinewood and Bray studios using some of the *Space: 1999* cast and crew (including Nick Tate and Brian Blessed who had twice guest starred). Two human families are launched in a spaceship able to reach faster than light speeds dealing with cosmic hazards and experiencing the effect of the theory of relativity. At the end, the ship is forced through a black hole to voyage into the unknown. Uniquely for an Anderson programme, it was shown on BBC who (like Anderson) had hoped it might become a series. Despite the potential for an interesting *Lost in Space* like series, this never happened, leaving viewers to wonder what might have been.

© Trevor Knight

1. David J Howe, Mark Stammers, Stephen James Walker, *Doctor Who: The Sixties*, p. 68 (Virgin Publishing Ltd, 1993)
2. Editor: Trevor's comment reminds me of my personal feelings about the 'over-use' of the wonderful Servalan in *Blake's 7*. Less can be more.
3. Actor David Calder would go on to star as space detective Nathan Spring in a similar BBC series, *Star Cops*, in 1987.

CHILDREN'S DYSTOPIA

As we look back, as we remember, and as we attempt to rationalise our memories, we are apt to simplify and abstract the complex patterns woven by our accumulated experiences and the litany of contradictory events we recall, tidying and shaping what actually happened into a more acceptable and digestible form. Our recollections of childhood typify this assertion, as much as anything can.

The modern myth of childhood is strongly - even overwhelmingly - associated with the idea of innocence. However, this fixation on the uniform and absolute innocence of all children everywhere excludes any mitigation or qualification of the qualities of the individual child. Indeed, children taken as individuals are not always as moral nor as virtuous as the adult world would have one believe. Children can be, and often are, as cruel as any adult. The iniquities and inequalities of childhood are perpetuated into adulthood. Adult life is in many ways just a more sophisticated and more complex version of the playground. The privileged bully then, is the privileged bully now.

The 1970s are often viewed as a 'golden age' for children's television, especially by those who were children at the time. We all tend to idolise aspects of our own childhoods, even those who found their childhood to be traumatic. By extension, the 1970s can be viewed as much as a golden age of childhood itself as it is a golden age of television for children.

Television intended, at-least-in-part, for children naturally falls into a variety of closely related and complimentary yet distinct categories. First-and-foremost, 'Children's Television', a combination of education and entertainment. To this, we can add the more pedagogical and didactic television aimed at Schools and Colleges, as well as so-called 'family viewing' and the coverage of sports and events, be that Test Match cricket or Royal Weddings.

We can add to this News and Documentaries. This should not imply that children do not watch programmes other than those produced solely for them. Children and young people certainly watched many things other than children's programmes in the 1970s.

I for one certainly strongly recall watching afternoon repeats of the final series of *The Avengers* and ITC's *Randall and Hopkirk (Deceased)* long before I reached school age. Likewise, for *The Persuaders!*, though I seem to recall watching that in the evening. I may even have watched *Counterstrike* with Jon Finch, as I have strong memories of the other aliens sharing his appearance, though this is probably a false memory, as are so many. In a similar vein, Gerry Anderson's *U.F.O.*, originally intended as adult entertainment, was rapidly downgraded to children's television, becoming a staple of my Saturday mornings. Viewing these shows left their mark, and I love them still. An indelible impression was left on a mind that was then an open and receptive sponge rather than the hard and impermeable ball of bitterness and confusion it later became. I also recall, among many other childhood memories, being bored witless by interminable Sunday lunchtime discussions by prematurely aged farmers with defiant aggressive comb-overs debating the relative merits of different herbicides, pesticides, and fertilisers.

At the same time, at least when viewed retrospectively, the 1970s were also typified by something as distant from mythologised childhood innocence as anything one can easily imagine. This was something truly dark and malevolent, the concept of dystopia. Television – even television purposefully directed at children - showed us dystopia, real and imagined, and showed it to us in colour. The Television News was full of wildcat strikes and widespread industrial unrest, oil spills and power cuts. As we will see, dystopian drama was likewise spread through the popular television of the 1970s.

The start of any decade often shares much with the previous decade. The swinging 60s did not begin until mid-decade. The early 1950s was still living through the austerity of the 1940s. This phenomenon is less clearly marked for the 1970s, but it has been said that the 1973 fuel crisis was the defining moment of the decade. Certainly, the early 1980s were darker and even more desperate than the decade that preceded it, and shared much of its look-and-feel. For me at least, it was the darkest and most dystopic time I can recall, at least until the 2020s. Probably the brash 1980s did not emerge fully from the long dystopian shadow cast by the 1970s until, ironically, 1984.

In our discussion of dystopia and its dramatic realisation, let us begin, as I often do, by trying to define the word itself. What meanings are assigned to dystopia? As always, there are many definitions of the word. One runs: 'An imagined state or society in which there is great suffering or injustice, typically one that is totalitarian or post-apocalyptic.' Another has, 'An imagined world or society in which people lead wretched, dehumanized, fearful lives.' The word itself derives from a Greek root, meaning 'bad place'.

Dystopian fiction can trace a lineage at least as far back as the French Revolution, which induced a widespread fear that mob rule would yield dictatorship. In this, it can be seen as both a progressive and a regressive enterprise, at once warning against oppression and simultaneously supporting the *status quo*. Until the late 20th century, it was typically if not exclusively anti-collectivist. Dystopian literature can be seen as a response and a rejoinder to utopian visions of society. Such works are often satires of the world as it is and as satires of the world as it is presented in utopian novels. For example, Samuel Butler's *Erewhon* can be viewed as a dystopia, since the sick are punished as criminals while thieves are 'cured' in hospitals, something the citizens of Erewhon view as entirely natural.

Novels describing dystopias are legion. Perhaps the greatest and certainly the best-known novel of dystopia is *1984* by George Orwell (1903-1950). It has almost come to define the words dystopia, dystopian, and dystopic. *1984* also provides a *de facto* model for categorising and cataloguing fascism and totalitarian government. Of course, Orwell's novel did not exist in a vacuum, nor did it appear from nowhere. There were many antecedents to *1984* and many influences upon it.

Orwell has acknowledged his debt to the 1907 novel *What Might Have Been* by Ernest Bramah (1868-1942), later republished as *The Secret of the League* (1909). Bramah is now perhaps best known for creating Max Carados, the blind Edwardian detective. The character was brought vividly to life by Sir Robert Stevens (1931-1995) in the 1971 Thames series *The Rivals of Sherlock Holmes* based on the compilations of Hugh Greene (1910-1987), former Director General of the BBC, brother of Graham Greene (1904-1991), who was perhaps the greatest English writer never awarded the Nobel prize for literature. *What Might Have Been* is a strongly anti-socialist dystopia reflecting Bramah's political opinions, which were regressive and avowedly right-wing. In his essay *Predictions of Fascism*, originally published in 1940, Orwell says of *What Might Have Been* that it accurately prefigures the rise of fascism during the 1930s.

Many other works are believed or stated by Orwell to have influenced *1984*. These include works by famous authors and thinkers, with Arthur Koestler and Jack London among them. Amidst many other now quite obscure novels, there are several high-profile dystopias, of which *Brave New World* (1932) by Aldous Huxley and *We* (1921) by Yevgeny Zamyatin (1884-1937), are probably the most notable. Another important figure in dystopian literature who exerted a significant influence on Orwell was H G Wells, whose work *The Time Machine* (1895) is also widely seen as a prototype of dystopian literature. Wells' 1905 *A Modern Utopia* is said to be a direct influence on Orwell's *1984*, in style if not in substance. Another direct and specific influence, the novel *The Managerial Revolution* (1940) by James Burnham, promulgated perpetual conflict among three future super-states, a scenario that informs the internal logic of *1984*.

Perhaps influenced in part by the cold war and the implicit and explicit threat of nuclear annihilation, novels exploring different aspects of dystopia have - over time - proliferated. Notable amongst these are Anthony Burgess' 1962 novel *A Clockwork Orange*, *Fahrenheit 451* by Ray Bradbury, *The Handmaid's Tale*, and P D James' *The Children of Men*. All have been filmed or televised. All are by authors who are not condemned by the literati to virtual oblivion as mere 'science fiction writers'. Dystopias are popular and make good drama, whereas utopias are by comparison sterile and boring, lacking dramatic tension and engaging narratives. As the saying goes: the devil has all the best tunes. As a background motif, dystopian settings are also popular elements in young-adult fiction, providing stimulating settings for many novels and novel series. Examples include *inter alia* The Hunger Games series by Suzanne Collins, the *Divergent* series by Veronica Roth, and *The Maze Runner* series by James Dashner, to name but a few of the highest profile. All are popular, and all have been filmed, to greater or lesser acclaim.

In this regard, *The Handmaid's Tale* by Margaret Attwood is particularly interesting. Wikipedia summarises the dystopia described in the novel quite succinctly as 'a strongly patriarchal, white supremacist, totalitarian theonomic state'. This is precisely the kind of society that many people favour. Indeed, to the Donald Trumps and the Mary Whitehouses of this world, Gilead is not far short of a utopia. While some see the novel as taking a general situation that is already bad enough and making it worse, *The Handmaid's Tale* is arguably best seen in the context of the American evangelical right and their distorted Old Testament take on Christianity. Their recent ascendency has seen severe and widespread attacks on abortion rights and the right to equal marriage. Perhaps most sinister of all, is the demonization of Trans people, with its strong echoes of the historical demonization of other marginalised groups. Together, these are attempts to divide and undermine the LGBTQ+ community and, more generally, to push the Overton window of accepted morality back decades, if not centuries.

After this brief, superficial catalogue, we are left with the question: what exactly is a dystopia? How can we define the dystopian state? Like many things, a logically comprehensive and watertight definition is not readily forthcoming, but we certainly know a dystopia when we see it. We can broadly differentiate dramatic dystopias into stories that deal with Authoritarian and Totalitarian states versus those depicting the collapsed or collapsing of society. Thus, we have chaos versus repression versus the *status quo*. Dystopia is really about poverty, both spiritual and material. Dystopias can be characterised by poverty, be that material poverty, poverty of experience, or poverty of compassion. Ultimately, and emotionally, dystopia is about more than this. It is about lack of autonomy. The powerlessness of the individual against forces seen and unseen. These can be those oppressive forces operating at the level of the state or they can be other sorts of force acting at a much more local level. In Evelyn Waugh's 1934 *A Handful of Dust*, for example, the final chapters describe as dystopic a scenario as one could encounter, and certainly makes for a more compelling read than *Love Among the Ruins: A Romance of the Near Future*, Waugh's 1953 foray into dystopian fiction. Likewise, and somewhat nearer to home, ITC's *The Prisoner* can be read as an allegory of the loss of autonomy and individuality.

Whether or not the 1970s can be legitimately seen as a golden age of children's television, what is certainly true is that as children's television moved into the 1980s, it was taken over by a collective manic-ness. Children's television changed, perhaps out of all recognition. Some found 1970s children's television patronising and elitist, and so they replaced well-meaning attempts to educate and inform by pandering to the lowest common denominator. Instead of trying to raise the intellectual aspirations of working-class children, they dropped gunge on them. As society became more economically middle class and bourgeois during the 1980s, so children's television simultaneously became ever more commercialised and intellectually moribund.

This was, as anyone who has read *Scarred For Life* can tell you, a bleak time for everyone, not least children. Apart from Public Information Films – a place of dark and lonely water - there was existential bleakness that rivals anything produced for adults. It is not our theme here, but is worth exemplifying in passing. Take for example the *Shadows* episode with Clive Swift and Jacqueline Pearce. Likewise, the *Ace of Wands* episode *Peacock Pie* with Brian Wilde. Or *Escape into Night* or HTV's *King of the Castle*. At the other extreme, children's television had a preoccupation with children's homes, children in care, etc. Partly to bring home to middle-class children how comfortable their lives were compared to those endured by others.

Similarly, material poverty was everywhere in contemporary drama during the 1970s. The squalor and bleak poverty of the East End and impoverished London in the early-70s London was laid bare in the programmes of the time. For me at least, perhaps the most memorable such scenes are those of London Markets, as seen in the *Callan* episode *Where Else Could I Go?* by James Mitchell, PJ Hammond's *The Meddlers* (*Ace of Wands*), and the *Slaves of Jedikah* (*The Tomorrow People*). Almost as memorable are the remaining bombsites and ruined buildings that are a staple of London-based dramas from the 1970s.

In what follows, we will examine several different types of dystopia, touching more lightly on several more, contrasting dystopian dramas for children with dystopian dramas aimed at adults. Thus, in our consideration of dystopias and 'Children's Television', we must extend beyond the narrow definition of dystopias discussed above, and assay closely related areas. As well as dystopia, elements of bleakness and apocalyptic paranoia are almost endemic within children's television, as they were in adult drama during the 1970s. There is sheer existential despair evident throughout much of children's television during the decade, particularly when compared to what came after, and this, also, we shall touch on, however briefly. Moreover, there were of course many adult dystopias, and part of what we shall attempt here is a nimble if brief comparison between adult and children's dystopian and apocalyptical drama.

We shall examine a range of dystopias and dystopian scenarios. The dominant forms of dystopia are twofold. The dystopia of the strong organised functioning state. This is primarily the political dystopia of the totalitarian state as well as those arising from the ill-thought-through application of advances in medicine and technology. The other is the dystopia inherent within a collapsing society or failing state. The ecological dystopia is a special form of this second type, yet arises from the first. We shall also look at inter alia post-apocalyptic scenarios and the wider influence of dystopia on different aspects of life, as represented by television.

Political Dystopia

To begin at the beginning. Let us start with what is variously described as political, authoritarian, or totalitarian dystopia. By authoritarian, we mean enforcing strict obedience to authority at the expense of personal freedom. By totalitarian, we refer to a highly centralized system of government requiring total subservience to the state. Both of these structures suppress freedom of thought and freedom of action at the level of the individual citizen. However, totalitarian governments do this by exerting total control over the lives of individual citizens, while authoritarian governments expect the unquestioning submission of the citizen body to its authority. In many ways, political dystopia as we use the term here is the least equivocal of the several forms of dystopia that will be examined in this essay. Such societies are extremely oppressive, coercive, or intrusive with a strong centralised power that crushes and dehumanises the citizenry. For the most part, here government is strong, organised, well-orchestrated, and in control. Totalitarian regimes, be they nominally fascist or right wing, or communist or left wing in nature, figured widely in fiction during the 1970s, both in adult dramas and in television aimed directly or coincidentally at children. Yet the television of the 1970s was not the first to describe dystopic states; other, earlier decades also included much dystopian content.

ITC's *The Prisoner*, for example, was highly dystopian, showing us a total surveillance culture, something modern society is fast approaching if not already exceeded. Within a highly stylised and surrealistic location, the central conceit of *The Prisoner* is a futuristic world where the electronic scrutiny of the individual by the state is total. Screens are everywhere in *The Prisoner*. If no one can be trusted, then everyone must be watched. Strong echoes here of the total observation seen in Orwell's *1984*. Of course, with near-universal CCTV and our digital footprints, we are now living in a world characterised by the total surveillance promulgated in *The Prisoner*. Surveillance has now become the norm, albeit unnoticed by the public at large. One need only watch or listen to the seeming thousands of True Crime infotainment documentaries or podcasts to see how utterly reliant the modern police are on CCTV as well as forensic science for obtaining convictions. Better, I suppose, than their previous strategy of forcing confessions from the weak, vulnerable, and marginalised. Nevertheless, it certainly highlights how much urban life is now constantly filmed. What is available to the police is, for certain, available also to the wider state and the secret state. The watchers at home have, in their turn, become the watched. *The Prisoner* predicted a future which has become our present, and that is after all what speculative fiction is intended to do.

Beyond the trope of personal surveillance, *The Prisoner* has much that is dystopian about it. Number 2 and the organisation he or she controls represent palpable yet unseen forces working to control and regulate society. In *The Prisoner*, it is never entirely clear who can be trusted or why people do what they do. This concept of betrayal becomes a powerful if not wholly dominant trope, as it does widely throughout spy literature. Betrayal becomes a key plot element in the episodes *Free for All*, *The Chimes of Big Ben*, and *Checkmate*, amongst others. Despite its 'high technology' setting, the themes explored in *The Prisoner* derive in no small part from the paranoia saturating post-war espionage fiction. This is Cold War paranoia writ large: a world where no one can be trusted, where loyalties are fleeting or illusory, and where we might be betrayed by anyone, at any time. In *The Prisoner*, such paranoia was reinforced strongly by the technology, a topic we will revisit in due course.

Many of Nigel Kneale's works were also overtly dystopian in nature, including both adaptions such as his landmark version of *1984* broadcast in 1954, and certain of his original teleplays, such as *The Year of the Sex Olympics*. Despite being largely 'apocalypse postponed' stories where disaster is averted, Kneale's 1950s *Quatermass* stories have more than a touch of the dystopian about them, particularly *Quatermass II*. The *Quatermass Conclusion* (1978), which we shall mention more fully below, is by contrast a full-on dystopia, and in several ways, and for some the bolted-on final narration is among Kneale's bleakest works, lacking any consoling *deus ex machina* salvation.

Turning now to the 1970s, we shall commence our brief discussion by examining Terry Nation's *Blake's 7*, a programme that, despite its content and tone, somehow fell into the category of Family Entertainment, broadcast early in the evening, opposite *Coronation Street*. Nonetheless, the programme developed a strong and, for the BBC, ultimately an inconveniently loyal following among adults and children alike. Apart from anything else, what is special about *Blake's 7* is the texture of the personal interactions within the programme. *Blake's 7* concerns a group of people who do not get on. This is unlike almost anything I can think of, other than soap operas, where this aspect is accentuated to an unrealistic degree. They do not get on but nonetheless they function and succeed in spite of the tension, despite the bullying, the coercion, and personal blackmail.

Over its four series, we encountered, for example, references to paedophilia and child abuse that simply would not be countenanced in modern television, at least not in something aimed partly at children, as well as an instantiation of a fascist state, the use of state-administered mind-controlling drugs, drug use, and much else besides. The first episode of *Blake's 7*, *The Way Back*, as well as the last couple of episodes, are perhaps the most overtly dystopian, describing a highly regimented, closely controlled society that administers drugs to suppress and control dissent. The pacification drug trope can be traced at least as far as Aldous Huxley's *A Brave New World* and to Karin Boye's 1940 novel *Kallocain*, a novel set in a totalitarian world state where drugs control the mental landscapes of the individual. This also forms a key plot point in Robert Holmes' *The Sun Makers*, where an assault on the sublimation plant is a vital step on the route to revolution and freedom. Other episodes are also similarly dystopian. [1]

Rather than dwell obsessively on dystopias, much of the rest of *Blake's 7* concerns itself with the conflict between a small group of freedom fighters and the fascistic military of the Federation, and how this groups interacts with groups of much freer people far from the centres of Federation control. However, the bleakness of *Blake's 7* can be contrasted with the other programmes dealing with the near future. Here I am thinking specifically of *Moonbase 3* broadcast in 1973 and *Star Cops* in 1987, both BBC productions and decidedly non-dystopian, despite some of the content.

That other great stalwart, *Doctor Who*, also had many dystopian themes running through it, particularly ecological dystopias during the Jon Pertwee years, and many individual stories that reflect strongly various forms of dystopia. Of course, dystopia had been there from the start, or almost. The second full story introduced the Daleks, which were, or have become, a surrogate for fascists and fascism. Indeed, Dalek has become a synonym and euphemism both for fascists and fascism, as well as many other things. For example, Dennis Potter's famous quote about the demise of the BBC, which sadly continues to this day, describing BBC chairman Marmaduke Hussey and Director-General John Birt thus, "You cannot make a pair of croak-voiced Daleks appear benevolent even if you dress one of them in an Armani suit and call the other Marmaduke."

Turning to more specifically political dystopias, we can divide *Doctor Who* into stories that allow us to glimpse future dystopias and those that show us dystopias seen through the plot device of a parallel world. Future dystopias in *Doctor Who* include *Enemy of the World*, where the future is near, and now past, and *The Sun Makers*, where it is seemingly very distant. Parallel World stories include *Inferno* (1970) and *Day of the Daleks* (1972). We will leave discussion of *The Sun Makers*, which deals with an interesting variant on the political dystopia, until a little later.

Of course, there were many dystopian settings for *Doctor Who* before and after the 1970s. *The Macra Terror* and *The Happiness Patrol* both envisage repressive cultures with more than a little similarity to *The Prisoner*. *The Enemy of the World* is another 1960s *Doctor Who* story with strong dystopian overtones and undertones. Salamander is talked of as a dictator of the world. The guards and the wider security services are presented as harsh and asperous. In the shelter community, we see a grand realisation of the coercive deception, or major gaslighting, to use the modern vernacular.

Perhaps the most obviously dystopian story in *Doctor Who* appears in Jon Pertwee's first season. *Inferno* by Don Houghton depicts an explicitly fascist alternative Britain. It shows us two contemporary Earths: one the near future but difficult to date UNIT Earth and the other a parallel world where fascists took over during World War II. This fascist parallel world was a late addition to Don Houghton's script. There are overwhelming echoes here of the 1964 British black-and-white film *It Happened Here*, which shows the United Kingdom after being invaded and occupied by Nazi Germany, and the subsequent ascendancy of a regime run by British fascists. Both also have distinct similarities to the 1977 drama *An Englishman's Castle*, starring Kenneth More. It is set, like *Doctor Who*'s *Inferno*, in a world where the Axis powers won World War II.

The parallel world in *Inferno* is both dislocating and disorientating. People look different and act differently. The corrosive effect of living under a fascist dictatorship has turned our friends evil. Everyone is dressed in unfamiliar militaristic uniform with fascist overtones, even Liz Shaw's surrogate, who sports a different wig. The efficient and soldierly, kindly and avuncular Brigadier has become the sinister and petulant Brigade Leader. The 'Unity is Strength' posters, which showcase the BBC visual effects designer Jack Kine, are intentionally reminiscent of Orwell's 'Big Brother is Watching'. Visually, then, we are left in doubt whatsoever this is not our world, but the dialogue is more subtle, slowly revealing the situation without the overwhelming exposition we often encounter elsewhere.

There is talk of scientific labour camps, of party members, and slave labour. The parallel Greg Sutton says, "On a project like this you don't just need a good party member, you need a good engineer." The Brigade Leader says, "You are talking of the Republican Security Forces. And the reason we are here is that this is a scientific labour camp." To which the Doctor asks, "Staffed by slave labour, I take it?" Late in the piece, Sutton says, "You're still loyal to your glorious republic. I'd like to know what your precious dictator can do for you now." In perhaps the most in-your-face scene in *Inferno*, The Brigade Leader says, "I have full authority. Defence of the Republic Act, 1943." To which the Doctor responds: "Republic?" "Yes." To which the Doctor asks, "Then what's happened to the Royal..." The Brigade Leader's chilling response: "Executed. All of them."

One of the most dystopian *Doctor Who* stories is surely *Genesis of the Daleks*. To begin with, it has the Whovian surrogate for fascism, The Daleks. But it also contains the Kaleds and Thals, as well as Mutant scavengers and a 1000-year war. The Kaleds, at least as we first encounter them, are highly fascistic, evoking clear images of the Nazi state. Visually, in their jackboots and uniforms. We have Boy General Ravon, portrayed with youthful exuberance by Guy Siner. Nyder is a figure that draws equally upon officers of the Gestapo and SS, and upon concentration camp commanders. But the Thals are little better. They will use slave labour to build their rockets. Of course, when the drama requires it, both show a more amenable side. Ivor Roberts as Kaled Mogran and Harriet Philpin as Thal Bettan are, to different degrees, intelligent, reasonable, or heroic. The Thal-Kaled conflict has resulted in a 1000-year war. This has exhausted the economy and brought Skaro to the brink of environmental catastrophe, as well as creating mutant scavenging wanderers, such as Sevrin played by Stephen Yardley, who, in typical fashion, are as wise and honourable as anyone in the show. Again, the presence of the Daleks is almost a distraction, despite being used as well here as they ever have been in the programme, before or since.

Repressive regimes of one sort or another feature frequently in *Doctor Who*. While few of these are thought of as explicit dystopias, many are, should you choose to scratch the surface. There are feudal societies a plenty, and a feudal society surely fulfils most if not all the tick list of dystopic characteristics. Apart from stories such as *The Time Warrior* and *The King's Demons* which depicts medieval times, however inaccurately and tendentiously, Peladon is feudal, stereotypically so. Moreover, *The Monster of Peladon* (1974), in particular, contains a none-too-subtle nod towards domestic labour relations of the time, in that much of the plots concerns in one way or another the strained relations between badger-haired tri-silicate miners and the planet's ruling class. This mirrors *Doctor Who and The Silurians* (1970), where one can read a similar subtext into the story, or perhaps this subtext is only one that has been imposed retrospectively, since screenwriting should not let any message, however subliminal, obstruct the story, after all it is meant to be part of 'an exciting adventure in time and space'.

A number of other stories include dystopias where human populations have been enslaved by aliens with or without help from human facilitators. Among these, we find such stories as *The Day of the Daleks* (1972), *Planet of the Spiders* (1974), *The Sun Makers*, *Underworld* (1977), and *Horns of Nimon* (1979). In all these, there is typically a class of overseers or mentors, that stand between the aliens and enslaved masses. This is best realised in *The Day of the Daleks* and *The Sun Makers* where exploration of the collaborators, enablers, and quislings is put centre stage. In the best of these, then, one is put in mind of the quote by French Philosopher Simone de Beauvoir, "the oppressor would not be so strong if he did not have accomplices among the oppressed".

There are also several examples of alien worlds and alien populations enslaved or colonised by humanity. Examples include *Colony in Space*, *The Mutants*, and *The Power of Kroll* (1978). In *Colony in Space*, most of the natives we encounter have regressed to a state of near barbarism, with only a few of their race retaining technical knowledge. Fortunately, for them, the effect of the recently arrived colonialists has not affected them severely. In contrast, in *The Power of Kroll* the natives or 'swampies' of Delta Magna had been forcibly resettled "centuries ago" on its third moon after the planet's colonisation by humanity. Possibly the worst fate awaited natives in *The Mutants*, where the colonisers planned to alter the atmosphere of the planet Solos, making it breathable to humans but not native Solonians.

Thames Television's *The Tomorrow People* was in many ways the nearest that ITV came to a direct and long-lasting analogue to *Doctor Who*. While the premise of the show was amongst the most optimistic and utopian I can recall, it too had several dystopia components in its mix. These make for a dramatic counterpoint to the core concept of *The Tomorrow People*: that humanity is about to be liberated from its past, that my generation, and those who descend from it, are a new form of humanity freed from the desire to kill and possessed of special powers that place it beyond the limitations of all hitherto existing life. Utterly absurd, of course, but nonetheless compelling; or compelling enough, for *The Tomorrow People* to have been rebooted twice, which is not something that many series can boast.

We see several examples of dystopias during the eight series of *The Tomorrow People*. Amongst other instances, in the first season story *The Medusa Strain*, Count Rabinski describes the world of 2526, where telepaths have gained ascendency and relicts like himself, possessed as they are of rapacious yet pusillanimous personalities, have likewise become marginalised and oppressed. At least in his eyes. Even in the paradise of the future, someone loses out.

In the second season story *A Rift in Time*, we see the dystopia of slavery. Finding themselves in a parallel 1974, The Tomorrow People encounter members of a race of simian appearance known to Peter the Time Guardian as Trystans, one among countless alien races enslaved by the space-faring Roman Empire of the parallel present. Likewise, in the season five story *A much needed holiday*, we again encounter slavery, this time young natives from the planet Gallia enslaved by the villainous Kleptons, a cruel and despotic race that roam space exploiting indigenous cultures.

The Tomorrow People was not the only programme to address the concept of slavery and colonialism. While I will leave a proper discussion of this contentious issue to others, it is worth mentioning *The Georgian House* (1976), which used time travel as a dramatic device to address issues of slavery. It was written by Jill Laurimore and Harry Moore, produced by HTV, and starred an eclectic group of actors, including *Timeslip*'s Spencer Banks, Jack Watson, Janine Duvitski, and Brinsley Forde, later a member of 1980s reggae-pop band, Aswad. While its message was plain, couching it within an adventure story involving time travel necessarily made it more palatable. For me, however, the much more explicitly delivered message of *Roots* (1977) and particularly *Roots: The Next Generations* (1979) by Alex Haley, was a revelation that opened my eyes to racism and other injustice. *Roots* and *The Georgian House*, from the very different perspectives of Britain and America, both explored the tacit dystopia of slavery, discrimination, and racism.

Overt racism was of course endemic in 1970s Britain. It was everywhere on television from the *Black and White Minstrels* to the so-called comedians of the day such as Bernard Manning and Jim Davidson. The Overton Window has certainly moved since those days, but perhaps not as far as it might. *Till Death Us Do Part* may have started as satire on working class Tories, but the viewing public came to approve of Alf Garnett. Even the author Johnny Speight in time came to sympathise or at least empathise with his deeply bigoted, highly reactionary monarchist, most notably in the follow-up series, *In Sickness and In Health*. It is tempting to think that Alf Garnett would have been first in line to vote for Brexit.

Another similar aspect of the 1970s that is often quoted is that of sexism and misogyny. No one would doubt that it was a highly sexist age, and this is reflected in the way women were portrayed and their level of inclusion. There are, for example, no female characters in *The Deadly Assassin*. Yet it is too easy to overemphasize this point and by doing so distort the reality to support a particular political viewpoint. For dramatic reasons, there were strong women in abundance, but their ownership of narrative was greatly constrained. Fortunately, things are very different now. Likewise, for the representation of the LGBTQ+ community, though the sensitive and insightful portrayal of trans characters still lags far behind that of other minorities.

To qualify the above, what has not changed to anything like the same degrees is the representation of differently able characters in drama. They are not absent - Diana played by Sarah Sutton in *The Moon Stallion* is blind, Jean Taggart is a wheelchair user - they are still relatively thin on the ground, despite recent efforts, with the exception of a few high-profile performers, such as Liz Carr, who stars as Clarissa Mullery in the BBC's *Silent Witness*. One might ask, have we come that far from the early 1970s? In the 1972 series *Mandog*, one of its three juvenile leads, Carol Hazell who played the character Kate, as an obligate wheelchair user. Throughout most of the preceding and succeeding decades, such an eventuality was rare; having disabled actors was unthinkable. Then again, it is possible to argue that one can go too far the other way. In current television, it has become the norm for women and ethnic minorities - if not necessarily other marginalised groups - to predominate at senior levels within the police, the government, and other crucial organisations. It may thus appear to some that the battle for representation and equality has already been won, while in reality it is still being fought. One can argue that it is actually preferable to represent the world as it is, with all its inequalities, than as people wish it to be. Positive discrimination can thus prove counterproductive if it leads to stultifying complacency.

Returning to our discussion of *The Tomorrow People* and dystopia, perhaps the clearest and least equivocal example is provided by the second season story *The Doomsday Men*. This concerns a group of neo-fascist members of the Military, the Doomsday Men of the title, who wish to create a dystopia that preserves and glorifies war as a way of life. Very much the antithesis of the series. *The Tomorrow People* is, in the final analysis, deeply progressive, implying strongly that the future will be better than the past, rather than looking to the security and safety of the past, ossified rituals and unchallenged traditions, as our source of comforting reassurance.

We can contrast such programmes with more overtly adult yet thematically similar dramas of the 1970s, most if not all of which were broadcast after the 9pm watershed. Probably the best known of these are the BBC's *1990* with Edward Woodward (1978-1979) and *The Guardians* (1971). In LWT's *The Guardians*, a backlash against an economic and social freefall in Britain has led to a right-wing dictatorship supported by a ruthless paramilitary force. Visually, at least, there is more than a little nod to *The Guardians* in the 1987 series *The Knights of God*, another series aimed at children. The thirteen-part series showed the Britain of 2020, ruled by the eponymous Knights of God, a fascist, anti-Christian religious order that seized power in a civil war twenty years before. *1990*, as intimated by its title, was intended as more explicitly Orwellian. It describes a bureaucratic dictatorship with restricted freedom of information and a state-run press, directed by the repressive Public Control Department. The series was created by Wilfred Greatorex, and in many ways reflects his reactionary right-wing politics, which permeate much of his later writing.

There are also several other notable if now half-forgotten examples of adult dystopias. These include *An Englishman's Castle*, which has already been mentioned, two intimately linked dramas *The Donati Conspiracy* (1973) and *A State of Emergency* (1975), and, a little later, *The Aerodrome* (1983). *The Aerodrome* was based on the novel of the same name by Rex Burgess, and was much admired by Anthony Burgess, author of *A Clockwork Orange*. It concerns a dystopian vision of a future or parallel England, where a fascist and authoritarian government begins to build a heavily guarded, mysterious military airfield. This was a BBC adaptation of Rex Warner's 1941 novel of the same name. An archetypal village in an alternative England is taken over wholesale by 'The Air Force'. Living in the village is Roy (Peter Firth), who, undermined by revelations of his antecedents, joins the dashing and dynamic Air Force, in order to forge a new sense of identity. *The Aerodrome* is a complex and often humorous novel that both explores totalitarian dystopia and uses the concept to counterpoint personal relationships within the unfolding narrative.

Despite changes of cast, *The Donati Conspiracy* (1973) and *A State of Emergency* (1975) form a single, continuous narrative, with perhaps at most a few days separating the two three-part dramas. They feature an authoritarian regime under direct military control, echoing, perhaps, the way that Greek junta or Regime of the Colonel, a right-wing military dictatorship, had gained power in Greece from 1967 to 1974. *The Donati Conspiracy* stars Anthony Valentine as Paul Frederick and Michael Aldridge as Professor Michael Donati. In *A State of Emergency* (1975), Fredericks is recast as Patrick Mower, and Professor Donati by Michael Gwynn. Other notables include William Gaunt as Colonel Singleton, Richard Beckinsale as Robert Sadler and Janet Key as Frederick's wheelchair bound wife Jane. Valentine's performance in particular is noteworthy, being among his best. The series is given extra poignancy by the death of its author. In a similar manner to Ian Mackintosh - a former naval officer turned screenwriter, who had written *The Sandbaggers* for ITV and *Warship* for the BBC - whose untimely death in a helicopter accident in Alaska left the final series of *The Sandbaggers* unfinished, John Gould, writer of *State of Emergency*, died of cancer aged 36, leaving the final draft of *State of Emergency* uncompleted.

Together these two three-part dramas deserve a higher profile, and are easily comparable to, say, *1990* or *The Guardians*. All the trappings of fascism or totalitarianism are here - the rigged trials, arbitrary executions, torture, the works in fact - but they are handled with a light touch and considerable skill. Moreover, it underplays the exposition, which is sometimes overdone in *1990*; and the programme takes an interesting angle by presenting this parallel fascist Britain in a more favourable light perhaps than it deserves. Even opponents of the regime list its virtues. Jane Fredericks, for example, says, after being confronted by her husband, "... Ambitious for your system. For your cruel world that forces people to be happy; that doesn't allow them to be poor or dirty; or any of the things that keep people human." Indeed, this makes the series more compelling, not less, allowing us to almost side with the oppressive government, and by so doing realise how easy it is to be seduced by our potential oppressors.

As well as notable but now half-forgotten dramas centring on adult dystopias, there are several less well-known examples of dystopias aimed at children. Let us look at a few. First, *Mandog*. It is another BBC children's drama with a dystopian backstory. It is a six-part series of half hour episodes filmed in Southampton during summer 1971. I remember it well. Which is to say that I remember brief snatches of it, attenuated by time and reshaped by memory, but those snatches have remained with me strongly for 50 years, sufficient that on re-watching the sole surviving episode I could verify my recollection of both dialogue and individual scenes.

The programme dramatized the struggle between two factions, who have travelled back from the year 2600. One is a group of seven renegades, who call themselves The Group. The other comprise agents sent by a future totalitarian state. *Mandog* was written as original - rather than adapted – scripts, commissioned from acclaimed children's author Peter Dickinson, by producer-director Anna Home and Monica Sim, then head of BBC Television's children's programmes. Dickinson was the author of *The Changes* trilogy, soon to be adapted by Home as a 13-part series, of which more in due course. *Mandog* was later novelised by Lois Lamplugh.

Mandog adumbrates a future dystopia in its first episode. Levin, leader of The Group, has developed a time machine, and used it to flee - seemingly at random - to the early 1970s. Levin is played by Christopher Owen, an actor characterised by his ordinariness, a trait exploited by both *Callan* and *Doctor Who*. The secret police he and his compatriots are escaping from are known, somewhat incongruously, as The Galas. Levin says of them, "The galas, they are the secret police of our time. They rule by fear. They are supposed to be the servants of the government, but if the government defies them, it falls, and most of its members are thrown into Gala prisons. My father died, tortured in such a prison. We all know men and women who have suffered." Adding later, "Galas, they are our masters."

The choice of the name Gala is an interesting one. Again, if we look to the dictionary for a definition, we find the commonplace definitions: a competition; a showy and festive party; or pomp, show, or festivity. The word derives from romance languages, specifically the French, Spanish, or Italian gala, meaning 'festive occasion', and ultimately derived from the Old French gale, meaning 'rejoicing'. However, Gala has other meanings that may be more pertinent. Here, the dictionary defines the word as 'androgynous priests of the Sumerian goddess Inanna'. Inanna was an ancient Mesopotamian goddess linked to sex and fertility, love and beauty, as well as war, divine justice, and political power. Originally worshipped as Inanna in Sumer, and later by the Akkadians, Babylonians, and Assyrians as Ishtar. Likewise, a Gallus was in Roman times a eunuch priest of the Phrygian goddess Cybele and her consort Attis.

The linkage of political power with Inanna, and her caste of priests, may have prompted the choice of the name Gala for *Mandog*'s secret police from the future. However, to what extent this is coincidental or intended remains open to question; had we access to all six episodes we might be able to find out, otherwise any such speculation is merely conjecture. It is not at all clear whether Peter Dickinson, when writing his scripts, had radically different casting in mind for both the Galas and the renegades. Perhaps one influenced by Glam Rock, with more discernibly epicene and androgynous characters – I think here of Richard Speight's portrayal of Peter in *The Tomorrow People* stories *The Medusa Strain* and *A Rift in Time* - rather than the more obvious choices made in production, such as Derek Martin as the leader of the group of Galas.

While *Mandog* adumbrates parenthetically a future dystopia, with the action occurring on the then contemporary Earth, other programmes aimed at children looked instead to the past – as projected into the present or future - to power their own particular dystopic vision. In *The Tripods* (1984-1985), for example, we are presented with a world that is transformed into a pastoral idyll, evoking our collective recollection of some late Victorian or Edwardian rural utopia. Of course, as we shall discuss below, appearances are deceptive and it soon becomes clear that this is a post-apocalypse, post-alien invasion dystopia characterised by 'capping'. This is a process of mind control, whereby when children reach adolescence electronic caps are fitted, robbing the capped individual of free will.

Another excellent example of children's dystopia is provided by the 1976 antipodean serial: *The Lost Islands*. Despite its jaunty - not to say camp - theme tune and the endless sunshine, the series concerns itself with a personal dictatorship. A co-production between the Australian Ten Network and US studio Paramount, it comprised 26 episodes of 30 minutes filmed just north of Sydney in New South Wales. The premise of the show is neatly captured in the theme song, written and sung by Michael Caulfield: "...They didn't realise the ship had been blown across the reef, into the lost islands. Hiding in the bushes was a watchful pair of eyes. And living in the valley were people lost in time. Ruled over by a tyrant whose face was in a mask. The children must defeat him, so they can escape at last from the lost islands."

The Lost Islands, with more than a nod to the latter parts of Evelyn Waugh's *A Handful of Dust*, describes an authoritarian dystopia that perpetuates the past into the present. The dystopia here denies the progress and evolution or even just change that we expect intuitively in non-dystopias. By evolution, we can mean natural, neutral change rather than necessarily progress. Often things change but stay the same, as opposed to progress towards societal betterment or some chosen arbitrary goal. But, in *The Lost Islands,* its group of young protagonists confront an ossified society locked into the deep past. Here, the population is both directly oppressed and oppressed by unchanging tradition. It is a chastening thought that this unending sameness, with change - if change there was - coming with glacial slowness, is the condition under which the overwhelming majority of the 100 billion humans to have ever lived spent their entire lives.

Economic Dystopias

In this section, we shall discuss a different or at least a distinct form - or rather forms - of dystopia, which we will choose to categorise as an economic dystopia, for want of a better term. It is distinct from the kinds of political dystopia discussed above, in that the mechanism of causation operating here is a failing economy and the concomitant societal collapse that ensues. This type of dysfunctional dystopia is be characterised by chaos and anarchy, rather than the firm control and doctrinaire strictures we envisage in a fully functional political dystopia, such as those of an authoritarian, fascist, or totalitarian state. The collapse of a civilisation or society is typically characterized by the loss of socioeconomic complexity, cultural identity, extant governmental structures, the rule of law, and a concomitant escalation in violence.

Historically, potential causes of such a collapse have included *inter alia* war or natural catastrophe, pestilence or famine, a rapid decline in population, economic collapse, and mass migration. A collapsed society may then revert to a less complex and developed state or vanish completely. Would there be chaos and anarchy though, in a collapsing society? One would assume yes, but it is also likely to be mitigated at least initially by the sentiment and by convention, feelings that would atrophy quickly but not disappear all at once. The principal difference here from the apocalypse described below is the rate of onset. Here, the rate is relatively slow and meandering, at least when compared to the catastrophic transition from complete order to complete chaos, as we see in apocalyptic dramas, such as *The Survivors* or *Threads*.

Again, it may be useful to contrast dramas such as these from children's television with similar adult dramas, such as the BBC's *1990* and ITV's *Quatermass Conclusion* (1978). In other series, such as *The Guardians* (1971) or *The Donati Conspiracy* (1973) and *State of Emergency* (1975), economic collapse or the threat of it and ensuing anarchy, is given as the pretext for a move to autocracy, but the resulting societies seem relatively stable dystopias typified by strong and centralised government. In *1990*, one of the main driving forces of the plot arc is the economic collapse and the increasingly repressive measures used to maintain state control in the face of these pressures. However, in the *Quatermass Conclusion*, we see a society in free fall. Partly driven by external threats, not of this Earth, we see society unravelling before our eyes. A smorgasbord of terrorist groups, chronic underfunding of societal infrastructure, physical and psychological urban decade, all are here. But above all, we see a world that needs to burn books for heat.

Yet, you do not need to burn books: only ban them. The burning is symbolism. Hence, *Fahrenheit 451*. Indeed, as Bradbury makes clear, books are also just a symbol. Rather, knowledge and the desire for truth - transmitted in whatever form and via whatever medium - are what civilisation requires. Book burning is thus a metaphor for the ruthless and irreversible suppression of freedom of enquiry, and the opportunity for educated and intelligent people to think for themselves in a world of free and open discourse.

Preeminent among dramas that seek to explore the collapsing society, is *Noah's Castle* (1980). Produced by Southern Television in its dying days, the seven-part series was written by Nick McCarty from the 1975 novel by John Rowe Townsend. Townsend was also responsible for the novel upon which eight-part Granada series *The Intruder* (1972), featuring Milton Johns, was based. To quote the Simply Media DVD release, the series is "set in a time of social and economic collapse where hyper-inflation has led to food shortages, mass riots, and martial law. A desperate husband and father, Norman Mortimer (David Neal), takes his family to a large house in the country where he reinforces the cellar in order to store food and keep his family safe. But, as the situation worsens, the Mortimers arouse the suspicions of the starving locals and their sanctuary comes under threat as the news of their food store spreads." The higher profile series *The Changes* and *Survivors* evoke a similar scenario, but for different reasons; only more so. These dramas and many of those we describe in the section of post-apocalyptic worlds, all detail worlds where materials are scarce and fought over, and life precarious.

History also supplies us with similar scenarios of civilisation and society collapsing, perhaps the most iconic example is provided by the fall of the Roman Empire. HTV's *Arthur and the Britons* shows us an imagined picture of the so-called Dark Ages that followed the withdrawal of Roman occupation in 410 CE. In many ways, there is little to differentiate this world from other post-apocalyptic scenarios. Perhaps, the Romano-British had less far to fall, but for some it was still a very long way. Other programmes describe this period of a partial return to barbarism, including Thames Television's *The Boy Merlin* (1979), *The Legend of King Arthur* (1979), and *Merlin of the Crystal Cave* (1991), amongst many others.

At the other extreme, science fiction is also replete with examples. *Doctor Who* is full of them. *The Face of Evil* by Chris Boucher is a particularly fine example of a previously technical advanced society that in part collapses to barbarism and in part becomes bound by enervating and deceptive ritual despite retaining a technological veneer. Robert Holmes' *Mysterious Planet*, the first segment of *The Trial of a Timelord* presents a similar society. In Season 3 of *Blake's 7*, after the intergalactic war with Andromeda, The Federation is in retreat and the threat of chaos is ever present or at least constantly spoken of; though by Season 4, order and stability have reasserted themselves, reaching perhaps greater levels of control.

Having talked of *Doctor Who*, let us finally turn to *The Sun Makers*, a functioning dystopia with a violent end. *The Sun Makers* was a 1977 contribution to Doctor Who written by Robert Holmes. Holmes was, of course, a legend. In the words of Russell T Davies, "Take *The Talons of Weng Chiang*, for example. Watch episode one. It's the best dialogue ever written. It's up there with Dennis Potter. By a man called Robert Holmes. When the history of television drama comes to be written, Robert Holmes won't be remembered at all because he only wrote genre stuff. And that, I reckon, is a real tragedy." Had he written more, or been less able as a script editor, what might have been? Fortunately, for those who know and appreciate his work, *Doctor Who* provided Holmes with a forum that allowed him to escape the chorale imposed by popular television, offering him the scope to flex his imagination to the full, while simultaneously giving full reign to his metier for dialogue and plotting.

Of course, Holmes was part of a golden age of scriptwriters, fortunate - or unfortunate – enough to work in the milieu of embryonic television. Fortunate, because they were able - albeit within daunting technical and commercial constraints of the times, not to mention the stifling intellectual straitjacket of moral complacency and double standards - to write from the heart unfettered by the self-policing of latter days. Unfortunate, that they had no access to the fame and financial remuneration open to modern screenwriters and showrunners. Like Holmes, many of these wrote for *Doctor Who*, but others did not. Notable amongst these are Phillip Mackie; Jack Pullman, who adapted *I, Claudius* and wrote *Private Schultz* for the BBC; *Catweazle*'s Richard Carpenter;

Francis Durbridge; James Mitchell (*Callan*); Roger Marshall; or even more recent screenwriters such as Glenn Chandler, creator of *Taggart*. What might they, or any of the ITC stalwarts, have done with the unique format of *Doctor Who*?

Of course, *The Sun Makers* is not the only foray *Doctor Who* has made into economics. As mentioned above, both *Doctor Who and The Silurians* (1970) and *The Monster of Peladon* (1974) are said to contain less-than-subtle nods towards contemporary domestic labour relations. The truth of such assertions is open to question, though it seems rather clearer in *The Monster of Peladon*. In *Carnival of Monsters* (1973), the society of Inter Minor is divided into economic castes. There is talk of functionaries and official species. At one point, the character Orum makes the somewhat laboured jest, "They've no sense of responsibility. Give them a hygiene chamber and they store fossil fuel in it."

As a counterweight to this collapsing society trope, *The Sun Makers* promulgates a strong and stable dystopia, but one built on an extreme instantiation of capitalism rather than one based on a purely political oppression. Written, in part, as a parody of taxation, with death and other punitive taxes of all kinds on all aspects of life, with the vast majority oppressed and exploited, and even the elite no more than the deluded dupes of aliens. The world adumbrated by *The Sun Makers* is in many ways just a totalitarian society but one driven solely to meet the greed of the eponymous Company, and thus this framing gives this a wonderful and illuminating satirical edge. And should one choose to take it this way, it is as neat and dexterous critique of capitalism as has ever been written. With its escalating prices and punitive taxation, there is also a lesson for Brexit Britain in the age of austerity.

Technological Dystopias

Another type of dystopia is that arising from technology. Here again, we are reacquainted with the way dystopia and particularly its adjectives dystopian and dystopic have taken on connotations that the strict definitions of these words find elusive. Technological dystopias do not necessarily necessitate totalitarian states or economic collapse leading to violent anarchy. Instead, advances in technology can bring about similar levels of lost personal autonomy and ineluctable powerlessness that citizens might feel in Oceania. Science, technology, and scientific advance is generally treated well by 1970s children's drama. Science and scientists are typically heroes. When they are villains, they remain figures of authority. Science and technology in and of itself is a threat to no one. The ruthless industrialisation of technology for profit and its reckless instantiation on a global scale is the issue, and always has been. It is in scenarios such as this that the dystopian takes hold.

The beginnings of technological dystopian fiction can be traced back at least as far as *The Machine Stops*, a short story by E M Forster (1879-1970). *The Machine Stops* was itself televised in 1966 as episode one of season two of the BBC science fiction anthology series *Out of the Unknown*, starring Yvonne Mitchell as Vashti and Michael Gothard as Kuno. The story and thus the dramatization are both prophetic and deeply dystopian. EM Forster published *The Machine Stops* between *A Room with a View* (1908) and *Howard's End* (1910), both novels that explore the struggle between our external and internal worlds, and the contest between pretence and truth. Forster's story appeared in the same year as Italian poet Filippo Tommaso Marinetti's furious *Futurist Manifesto* in the French newspaper *Le Figaro*. It argued the opposite to *The Machine Stops*. In contrast to Forster, Marinetti embraced the machine. He contended that a modern speeding car was more beautiful than ancient static sculpture. The past was to him a decaying obstruction that must be extirpated to open our route to the future. There has always been a tension, even a conflict, between the pull of the future and the pull of the past. One is comforting and reassuring, the other exciting and progressive.

The anthology series was particularly good at exploring the potential societal impact of technology and future technology. It could, in each separate play, explore a different aspect of the many real and imaginary perils that science and the future threatened. Similarly, the BBC's *Doomwatch*. In a more formulaic dramatic context, *Doomwatch* (1970-1972) offered us, week in week out, cautionary tales of the impact of technology. While many rival its darkness of tone, few have ever rivalled its perspective, and few have been as uncompromising or prescient. The world of *Doomwatch* is the world of the unintended consequence. A world where the blinkered and self-serving perspectives of government and big business lead to the misuse of industrial science and technology. We have lived through many Doomwatch scenarios. The BSE crisis of the late 1980s to the early 2000s was as Doomwatch a scenario as one could imagine. That it did not lead to millions of deaths is both a blessing and a timely warning. As we will explore below, in climate change, and the environmental harm done by industrial technology, which in turn damages the biosphere that supports long-term survival, we are living through another, more inescapable, Doomwatch scenario.

The anthology series and *Doomwatch* were both perhaps at their most chilling and dystopian when dealing with the core of the human condition: its inevitable fragility; death, and the prospect of death. Indeed, we need look no further than *Doctor Who and the Cybermen*. Created by Kit Pedler and Gerry Davis, in 1966, The Cybermen, and their CyberPunk descendants *Star Trek*'s The Borg, are races of cyborgs - part human, part machine - conceived as having arisen as a quest for extended lives and virtual immortality. There are also clear similarities in name and appearance to the Cybernauts in *The Avengers*. While there were just three Cybernaut episodes, two in *The Avengers* proper (*The Cybernauts, Return of the Cybernauts*) and one in *The New Avengers* (*The Last of the Cybernauts...?*), the dystopian appeal of the Cybermen and Borg persists to the present day.

The 1970s and 80s also provided us with a plethora of programmes built around drama that discussed euthanasia and others built on scientific realisation of immortality, however spurious that might be. *Wine of India*, a play by Nigel Kneale, which aired as a

Wednesday Play in 1970, deals with government-regulated euthanasia in an ageless society where life span is licensed by the state. It was never repeated, the tapes wiped, and the play, like so many, lost forever. A similar single drama, *Dog Ends*, part of the *Play for Today* strand, aired in 1984, and starred Leonard Rossiter. It too dealt with state euthanasia, but in a society much closer to ours, one where longevity has increased to natural limits but with decades of frailty and illness, that typically accompanies it.

Agelessness is like cryogenic suspension, something yet to be realised. Immortality is impractical however compelling an idea. The scientific consensus contends that cryogenic suspension is both fundamentally implausible and unsound ethically. The strongest counter argument is that death is death. Any procedure that restores life to a corpse seems inconceivable. Someone ill but alive placed into suspended animation might be revived and cured, but not a cadaver. Similar is the idea of 'uploading' a human mind, with all its personality and memories, into a computer or robot. A very similar premise is dealt with memorably in *The Last Lonely Man* directed by Douglas Camfield and adapted from a story by John Brunner by Jeremy Paul, a 1969 episode of *Out of the Unknown*, starring George Cole and Peter Halliday. Like the prospect of immortality offered by cryogenics, it appeals to many, but repulses many others. Uploading a personality is essentially impossible from a scientific standpoint, particularly from a quantum physics perspective. While it might be possible to train an artificial intelligence system to mimic and thus reproduce the behaviour and thinking of an individual, it would ultimately be just a copy, necessarily lacking some elusive yet intrinsic quality unique to an individual. [2]

Very similar ideas even found their way into children's television. *Timeslip* (1970), dealt with a number of such concepts, including drug induced longevity and cloning. The second story of *Timeslip*, *The Time of the Ice Box*, gives us a vision of an alternate 1990. The Ice Box - or The International Institute for Biological Research to give it its full title - is undertaking controlled experiments on human volunteers. These include testing a longevity drug called HA57. The structure of this compound or identity of the mixture is known only to the head of the Ice Box, Morgan C Devereaux, played with typical gusto by John Barron. At the end of the story, Devereaux is revealed to be a clone.

HA57 is not the only longevity drug to be named in contemporaneous telefantasy. *The Spencer Bodily is Sixty Years Old* episode of ITC's *Department S*, written by Harry W Junkin, which also deals with longevity, is notable for naming BHT, an acronym for Butyl Hydroxy Toluene, described as mediating extended longevity. Known as an antioxidant, Butyl Hydroxy Toluene is used as a food additive, but is not licensed as a medicine, nor is it generally understood to lengthen life. BHT is also mentioned in the 1969 episode of *The Saint*, *The Man Who Gambled with Life*, also written by Junkin, BHT is once more a mediator of longevity, albeit only in Mimi the mouse.

In the third story of *Timeslip* we see a functioning technocracy dealing with a global environmental disaster. Technocracy is government by those with expertise, particularly technical or scientific knowledge. This contrasts with representative democracy, largely the province of lawyers and demagogues, where unskilled elected representatives are the prime arbiters of governmental decision-making. Selection is knowledge and performance not political affiliation, oratory, or popularity. Technocracy originally signified use of the scientific method to solving social problems. In its most extreme and hypothetical form, technocracy becomes a government run as a scientific, technical, or engineering problem. This is what *Timeslip* shows us, warning that the presumed lack of democratic oversight is the seed of its own destruction.

One of the landmark children's dramas of the 1970s addressed society's fear of technology head on. The BBC's *The Changes* (1975) was an ambitious attempt by Anna Home to mount an adaptation of *The Changes* trilogy, which comprised *The Devil's Children*, *Heartsease*, and *The Weathermonger*. The trilogy had been penned by the aforementioned Peter Dickinson, writer of 1972's *Mandog*.

After optioning the novels in 1971, Home then struggled for several years with scheduling and financial issues, though shooting the series entirely on film did reduce costs. Indeed, the project was almost cancelled in 1973. The series depicts an England regressing to a preindustrial state. The Changes of the title is not an external event such as a nuclear holocaust or even an economic collapse, but rather an internal or wholly psychological one, which causes the whole population to reject technology and wreck machines. The overall narrative of the series diverges significantly from the original trilogy, greatly condensing the complexity of the plot and reducing the number of characters, focusing on the main character of the final novel *The Devil's Children*, Nicola Gore, for the whole of the ten episodes. In *The Changes*, and in so many other children's dramas of 1970s, the depiction of what might then have been called ethnic minorities is by-and-large patronising and condescending, evoking the notion of the noble savage, so familiar to Voltaire and his contemporaries.

The rejection of technology seen in *The Changes* can be contrasted with *The Prisoner*, a series that has an equally strong if distinct technophobic core to its narrative. Both view conventional modern-day industrialised technology as a threat. In *The Prisoner*, Number 6 is menaced by current and work-a-day instantiations of technology, as much as he is by camera-eyed statues or delinquent weather balloons. Radios listen to him, or only play what others want him to hear. Telephones seem perfectly normal yet only work in the Village, and like everything there, technology while out of your control remains firmly in the control of others. Yet, it is not really technology itself that is being fought. Rather an authoritarian regime that uses technology to mislead and control us. As Isiah Berlin tells us, technology, and any system that nominally protects, will of need simultaneously remove our freedom. Poverty enslaves us all. If we take poverty away, as science and technology have done, it must be replaced with something.

Much has been said about *The Prisoner*, and perhaps at greater length and over a longer period than for any other programme.

Eclipsed today by the breadth - if not the depth - of discussion generated by the carefully orchestrated fandoms of many programmes, the detailed analysis of *The Prisoner*'s meaning remains an interesting topic in its own right and the programme likewise remains worth studying for this reason if no other. Even Patrick McGoohan struggled to rationalise the programme's legacy, leading him to attempt to reconcile the many inconsistencies of *The Prisoner* and seek its elusive and quixotic substance. He suggested that the programme was an allegory, reminding us that society had become too mechanised and consequently too regimented. That we had made significant technological advances, but at a rate too fast for society to manage effectively.

Ecological Dystopias

Doctor Who in the 1970s, at least when under the benign and spiritually enlightened stewardship of Barry Letts, had running through it a significant strand of environmental awareness that resonates strongly with current times. Most notably, the 1973 episode *The Green Death*, which dealt with chemical pollution and its environmental consequences. There were many other episodes displaying similar concerns, but *The Green Death*, above all others, presents the ecological dystopia at its closest to our own immediate experience.

The Green Death deals with one of the principal concerns of 1970s environmentalism, pollution, specifically pollution from the Big Oil and the wider problems arising from industrial waste being disgorged into the environment with no thought for the consequences. This and the issue of Nuclear Power, were the main issues of the day; it was only in the 1980s that the problem of carbon emissions leading to climate change came to dominate popular thinking about green issues.

However, beyond *The Green Death*, Barry Letts' ecological message is also clearly present in many stories, notably *The Colony in Space*, *The Mutants*, *Frontier in Space*, *Invasion of the Dinosaurs* - where it offers a pretext for some time travel shenanigans - and even *Robot*, although this is limited to a single mention by the Brigadier of the Doctor's interests in ecology during its first episode. Perhaps the only story after Letts' time to bring such concerns to the foreground is Robert Bank Stewart's *Seeds of Doom*.

In Colony in Space, we hear, "Scientists have turned to new means for providing accommodation for our ever-increasing population. These floating islands, rising to three hundred storeys, will make living space for five hundred million people." And, in response to a statement about how bad the planet is compared to Earth, we hear, "No room to move, polluted air, not a blade of grass left on the planet and a government that locks you up if you think for yourself." Dystopia indeed. In *The Mutants*, the Doctor says, "Well, the Earth these people know now, Jo, in the thirtieth century empire, is even more grey and misty. Land and sea alike, all grey. Grey cities linked by grey highways across grey deserts. Slag, ash, clinker. The fruits of technology, Jo."

In *Frontier in Space*, we see the dystopian nature of the Earth and its government. The Doctor asks, "Have you got many political prisoners here?" To which the reply is, "Thousands. Well, I mean, criticise the government and you're for it, aren't you?" Elsewhere, an announcer states: "...and the Bureau of Population Control announced today that the recently reclaimed Arctic areas are now ready for habitation. As a special inducement for those willing to live in New Glasgow and New Montreal, the first two totally enclosed cities to be opened, the family allowance will be increased to two children per couple." In what is largely a somewhat awkward and unsatisfactory combination of romp and mystery, *Frontier in Space* does occasionally drop in a few disquieting moments. In addition to the ones above, we also have the American Congressman Brook, who says "...and I warn the President that the people of Earth will no longer tolerate these insulting and murderous attacks! I hear the cries all about me. Attack Draconia! Attack now! Earth will not produce peace at the price of humiliation! There is only one solution now! War! War! War!"

Yet Barry Letts' environmental concerns were only a reflection of a more general zeitgeist present in the early 70s. Such concerns were widespread, even penetrating as far as popular television, more typically characterised as the principal medium supporting the concerns and priorities of the establishment and tasked with maintaining - at all costs - the status quo. They were there in everything, or at least many things. From Elizabeth Beresford's *The Wombles*, narrated by Bernard Cribbins, to *Doomwatch*, and the 1974 documentary series *A House for the Future*, as well as the Letts era of *Doctor Who*. Nor did they disappear completely. Environmental terrorists and activists were key protagonists in Troy Kennedy Martin's *Edge of Darkness* and *Natural Lies*.

Present concerns over climate change and the general warming of the planet are prefigured in various ways by many British television series of the 1970s and earlier. Before all of them, however, we had *The Day the Earth Caught Fire*. This is a 1961 film starring Edward Judd and Leo McKern, where nuclear tests rather than emissions of greenhouse gasses cause global temperatures to rise catastrophically, potentially rendering the world uninhabitable as it quickly turns to desert. Another example is *The Andromeda Breakthrough*, the 1964 sequel to the more famous *A for Andromeda* (1961), where Susan Hampshire replaces Julie Christie, except in some reused expensive exterior footage, where Andromeda is still clearly Julie Christie. The series describes freak weather, including severe storms and snowfalls, which result from deliberate interference with the world's climate. *The Year of the Burn Up*, the third of the four stories comprising *Timeslip*, also centres on a global ecological disaster. In another alternate 1990, interference with the Earth's climate has caused the temperature to rise dramatically, leading to a devastating environmental collapse. Survivors of the disaster are forced to seek refuge in caves where there is water and the chance of continued survival.

In the *Doctor Who* story *Inferno*, an alternative England, and possibly the whole of the parallel Earth, is destroyed by a super-volcano, brought about by the deliberate penetration of the Earth's crust by the Stahlman project. This is narrowly averted in our world but not in theirs. Whether or not this is the world consumed in flames that the Doctor describes in *The Mind of Evil* is never made clear; though one presupposes it is, since both stories were written by Don Houghton. *Alternative 3* was a hoax documentary, broadcast once in 1977, purporting to investigate the so-called 'brain drain'. It revealed a plan to terraform the Moon and Mars in the event of catastrophic climate change and a final environmental collapse on Earth. *Alternative 3* shares themes with *Doctor Who*'s *Invasion of the Dinosaurs*. Ben Elton's novel and 1997 television adaptation *STARK* is either a deliberate or unintentional reworking of many of the themes in *Alternative 3*.

Raven is a six-part serial made by HTV in 1977, starring a young Phil Daniels and Michael Aldridge, and written by Trevor Ray and Jeremy Burnham, better known for *Children of the Stones*. It concerns the fight to prevent construction of a nuclear waste disposal site in a system of man-made caves beneath a Neolithic stone circle, which also contain 5th-century rock carvings connected to King Arthur. Nuclear energy was, quite rightly, a key concern of the day; now eclipsed by climate change, yet an issue still, and one whose time shall come again. Ecological issues were also raised parenthetically in *The Moon Stallion*, with a vision of the future including technological collapse and by inference environmental disaster. Gerry Anderson's 1975 abortive pilot *Into Infinity*, with Brian Blessed and Joanna Dunham, mentions in its opening narration the squandering of natural resources. Environmental concerns were even set to music. The 1977 rock opera *Orion*, directed by Jeremy Swan for the BBC with a book by Melvyn Bragg of all people, is a science fiction musical, which tells of a group of people leaving Earth to find a new home.

American serials also had their own ecological catastrophes. In *Ark II*, broadcast in 1976, the opening narration sums things up nicely, "For millions of years, Earth was fertile and rich. Then pollution and waste began to take their toll. Civilization fell into ruin. This is the world of the 25th century. Only a handful of scientists remain, men who have vowed to rebuild what has been destroyed. This is their achievement: Ark II, a mobile storehouse of scientific knowledge, manned by a highly trained crew of young people. Their mission: to bring the hope of a new future to mankind."

All such environmental concerns were widely known and widely discussed in the 1960s and 1970s, yet this faded with Thatcher and the Big Bang, replaced and somehow side lined by the activism of the Green Party and Greenpeace. Yet here, above all, we see the dystopian drama at its most prophetic. History gives us many examples of authoritarian regimes, perhaps that is all it can show us. Likewise, with racist genocides. But in showing us the aftermath of ecological disaster, 1970s drama and particularly children's drama is showing us our as-yet-unseen yet likely future. Current projections of environmental disaster, of which climate change is but part, dictate immediate and radical world-wide action, yet current provision in even the most optimistic scenario is simply delaying the inevitable. The only truly sustainable solution is one where we want less. Fewer things. Less travel. Fewer children. Less of everything. Instead of constant growth, we need to adopt the Epicurean philosophy of desiring just what we absolutely need, not greedily consuming all that we want. We have to restructure society to put limits on the size of the population as we seek to reduce our personal consumption. This, of course, will never happen.

Post-apocalypse dystopias in 70s & 80s drama & children's drama

Beyond the ecological catastrophe, post-apocalyptic settings of various kinds were almost as common as dystopias. From one perspective, this is surprising, given we are discussing television, where we are told that the sun always shines. Then again, perhaps it is not at all surprising, given the era, that many television series had settings in one or other post-apocalyptic worlds. The word apocalypse has a Greek root and several common meanings. Apart from its more specific meaning within the context of Judeo-

Christian writings, apocalypse can mean a prophetic revelation, especially one relating to a cataclysm, where the forces of good triumph permanently over those of evil, or, by extension, any revelation or prophecy, particularly one relating to universal or widespread destruction or disaster.

On television, sometimes we were presented with the apocalypse itself; in other programmes, we saw a world left in the wake of some cataclysm or disaster. This was true of both adult and children's television. Some of these settings were also decidedly ghastly and dystopian, while others seem almost idyllic. Of all the apocalypses ever shown on television, *Threads* (1984) is perhaps the most compelling and frightening, because it is the most real, and immediate, at least to those of us who grew up in the shadow of the Cold War. Nucleomituphobia is a powerful thing. Putting *Threads* to one side, among 1970s series, arguably the most memorable series to address such a scenario was Terry Nation's *Survivors*. It was certainly a post-apocalyptic drama, but one in which we – through the experiences of its protagonists - live through the viral apocalypse itself, as well as the world the apocalypse leaves behind. Like *Threads*, the apocalypse itself, however lightly sketched, was a highly credible one. In light of recent events, a viral apocalypse seems more credible now than it did then.

Programmes other than *Threads* and *Survivors* also showed us what a post-apocalyptic world might be like. In *Z for Zachara*, a 1984 adaptation of Robert C O'Brien's posthumously published 1974 novel, starring Anthony Andrews as John Loomis and Pippa Hinchley as Ann Burden, we see the apocalyptic aftermath of nuclear war through the rather unlikely prism of a small valley with a self-contained weather system. Robert C O'Brien was the pen name of Robert Leslie Conly, who was a well-established children's author, and creator of *Mrs. Frisby and the Rats of NIMH* (1971). Much more memorably, we also saw the world plunged into anarchy and societal collapse by blindness in *The Day of the Triffids* (1981). A very faithful if somewhat updated version of John Wyndham's classic 1951 novel, the six-part series starred John Duttine as Bill Masen and Emma Relph as Jo Playton. One should also mention at this point the 1981 television adaptation of Douglas Adams' *The Hitch Hiker's Guide to the Galaxy*, which began with the destruction of the Earth, the point which most other shows never quite reach.

Turning now to children's television, there are many examples of shows that at least showed us post-apocalyptic worlds, if not necessarily the apocalypse itself. That is not to say that many children's programmes did not deal with the threat of nuclear weapons, as well as other similar if distinct threats to the world. Various adventure series concerned themselves with the threat from nuclear weapons and the potential for an ensuing nuclear holocaust. From programmes like Southern Television's *Freewheelers* (1968-1973) to HTV's *The Doombolt Chase* (1978) to the BBC's *Codename Icarus* (1981), nuclear weapons and other weapons of mass destruction, real or imaginary, provided copious peril for the watching audience. Even the *Doctor Who* stories *Robot* and *The Mind of Evil* both threaten nuclear annihilation. Earlier, in the 1960s, *The City Beneath the Sea* likewise dealt with the threat to the world.

Few - if any - actually showed us the aftermath of nuclear devastation. However, the idea was later used as the basis for parody. Though why it was thought necessary to parody the dystopian children's TV of the 1970s and 1980s is not a question I can readily answer. It formed the basis of comedy, if comedy it was, when this subgenre was satirised by 2002's *Cruise of the Gods*. Perhaps satirising is too strong; gently and affectionately poked at fun at would be nearer the mark. There is more than a whiff of *The Tomorrow People* in it, and its tone and texture reeks of *Scarred for Life*.

However, many other programmes did show us the aftermath of cataclysmic events of various sorts. As mentioned above, *Doctor Who*'s *The Day of the Daleks* (1972) showed as a dystopian world after a Dalek conquest of the Earth. *The Tripods* was set in 2089, in a world seemingly transformed into a pastoral utopia, styled after some late Victorian or Edwardian rural idyll. However, it soon becomes clear this world comes long after an alien conquest, with humanity now ruled through a combination of mind control, the abrogation of technology, and the direct intervention by the tripods. HTV's *Sky* written by *Doctor Who* stalwarts Dave Martin and Bob Baker also shows us a post-apocalyptic Earth after 'The Chaos', a largely unspecified global cataclysmic event. In a bolted on seventh episode, Arby Vennor, played by Stuart Lock, a teenager who has helped the eponymous Sky (Marc Harrison), is transported to a distant future where the remaining human natives live in a world of dank forests and freezing weather, and have become telepathic yet lost all technology, parodying it with meaningless rituals.

Utopias do not make for great drama, as I suggested earlier, while dystopias can provide gripping entertainment. Nevertheless, despite its frequently dystopian subject matter, children's television drama of the 1970s also offered some reassurance; hopeful glimpses of a 'better future', or of how the world *should* be, however unlikely or unattainable these may now seem to us as adults. *The Tomorrow People* and *The Lost Islands* both have groups of teenagers of different genders and ethnic origins coming together to fight evil. The suggestion in *The Tomorrow People* is that these teenagers will be better adults than the ones they replace. They are the next step in human evolution, but what is more important than their special powers of telepathy, telekinesis, and jaunting is their *moral* evolution. They cannot kill and they do not want to, which seems to me a most beguiling notion. The implicit promise of *The Tomorrow People* is that the world of the future will be a better, kinder, nicer one where everyone can live out a better, kinder, nicer life of deep fulfilment and contentment. No wonder the show has been remade twice. Ultimately, we might argue that at its best children's television – like Jonathan Swift's majestic Gulliver's Travels – combines elements of both utopian and dystopian fiction. A tantalising vision of a better future, but also a warning of the perils that lie ahead and outside in the real world, beyond both childhood and children's TV.

© DR Flower

1. Editor: Apart from the Federation itself, other memorable examples of dystopian worlds in *Blake's 7* would include: Vargas' quasi-religious control as the 'Supreme Power' in *Cygnus Alpha*; the Lost scientists' treatment of the Decimas in *The Web*; The Chenga hunting 'primitives' as organ 'donors' in *Power Play*; the Ultras' use of slaves in *Ultraworld*.
2. Editor: This is very much the theme – and message – of the outstanding *Black Mirror* story *Be Right Back*.

"SHUT IT!": A BRIEF OVERVIEW OF *THE SWEENEY*

The 1970s wasn't just avocado bathroom suites, garish wallpaper and dodgy haircuts. In fact, underneath all those stereotype images was a decade of civil turmoil. Mass inflation, political unrest, and a considerable increase in crime rates. At a time when only three UK channels existed, it was only fitting that a television series should be made that conveyed all these social issues, but from a specific perspective: the police.

The Sweeney ('Sweeney Todd', cockney rhyming slang for the Flying Squad) first appeared in the shape of an *Armchair Cinema* play called *Regan*, broadcast in June 1974. It centred around the title character Jack Regan, an individualistic and unruly Detective Inspector of the Flying Squad and his unorthodox methods in finding out the truth behind the murder of a younger officer. This role was reserved for and portrayed superbly by John Thaw, an already established actor and close friend of Ian Kennedy-Martin, the official creator of *The Sweeney*. Thaw's Regan, although quite the lone ranger, was given a sidekick, Dennis Waterman's Detective Sergeant George Carter. The pairing of Thaw and Waterman would go on to create one of the most iconic cop duos in British television history. Regan's unorthodox unruliness often leads to a clash with his superior officers, mainly the 'by-the-book' Detective Chief Inspector Frank Haskins, portrayed brilliantly by Garfield Morgan. An initial bane on Regan's existence, Haskins acted as a foil to the hot-headed Inspector, but as the series progressed the characters would develop a unique respect for each other. In effect, *The Sweeney* didn't simply create an iconic duo; a memorable trio emerged.

At a time when 'Clean Up TV' campaigner Mary Whitehouse reigned supreme, this violent and 'coarse' drama could have completely flopped. In fact, the pilot did the opposite, and attracted an audience of over 7 million, its grittiness awakening a craving for a 'new realism' amongst television audiences.

And so, *The Sweeney* was created. Made by Thames Television's relatively new Euston Films unit and shot on location using 16mm film, *The Sweeney* breathed new life into the evening's television listings with its fast-paced action scenes and roaring car chases. At its peak it drew in 19 million viewers. Its success also spawned two equally engaging and gritty spinoff films: *Sweeney!* and *Sweeney 2*. During its run, it covered a range of hot topics, from typical bank blags to drug smuggling and even police corruption. The relatively cosy world of *Z Cars*, once held up as an exemplar of TV realism, and the musings of Sergeant Dixon - "Evenin' all"- of the BBC's *Dixon of Dock Green* suddenly belonged to a different era. The fictional Dock Green and Newtown beats and their relatively harmless petty criminals were replaced by the real, mean streets of West London and 'villains' - hard men with shooters pitched against even harder coppers.

The Sweeney's gritty realism was conveyed in numerous ways, from brutal murders to unhappy endings. Regan and Carter weren't always victorious in their fight against crime, and more often than not the police themselves were seen as only being one step away from becoming villains themselves. This angle sometimes focused on Waterman's George Carter; in *Regan,* Carter mentions how he grew up with Tusser, one of the main villains of the plot, and in Trevor Preston's episode *Chalk and Cheese* we get an insight into Carter's past friendship with the villain Tommy Garret. Of course, the real villainous undertones are mainly present in the main character himself. From arranging a kidnapping in *Queen's Pawn* to passively partaking in the murder of a corrupt politician in the film spinoff *Sweeney!,* Regan's actions can be seen as far more villainous and treacherous than that of a petty 'tea leaf'. The creation of such a character conveyed the police force as something to be afraid of, something that was arguably needed to try and cure the rising crime rates of the 1970s.

In reality, some coppers actually were villains, most famously the disgraced head of the Flying Squad, Commander Kenneth Drury, who was involved in a sleazy corruption scandal in the 1970s. Drury's trial was ongoing during the run of *The Sweeney*, and he was eventually convicted on five counts of corruption and imprisoned for eight years in July 1977. It was expected that *The Sweeney* would cover this important topic of police corruption, but it had to tackle this carefully. Roger Marshall's *Bad Apple* covers the topic perfectly through the creation of two 'bent coppers', Detective Inspector Perraut and Detective Sergeant Huke, who are in charge of a protection racket and are even seen to steal money from the scene of an arrest. Perraut and Huke almost seem like an alternate and corrupt version of Regan and Carter; indeed, we see Regan himself tempted to pocket bribe money at the end of *Golden Fleece*.

However, had the writers made Regan's character simply a ruthless and corrupt cop it would have been a mistake, one which was arguably made by the BBC's later series (and its own take on *The Sweeney*) *Target*. The character of Regan is given considerable, subtle depth by both the impressive script writers and equally talented John Thaw. Underneath a hard-boiled surface consisting of shouting and scotch aplenty is a man of deep emotion and empathy. Haskins even describes him as "too emotional" in *Ringer*. Unlike the 'wooden tops' and 'pencil necks' of the police force, Regan often abandons the rule book in favour of his own ingrained sense of justice. He bends the rules, but never for his own personal gain, and indeed comes across as both human and humane. He is emotively sympathetic and supportive of Carter after the death of the latter's wife in *Hit and Run* and ignores the rule book to find his daughter's kidnappers in *Abduction*. Upon scratching away the surface, we discover a character not simply deserving our pity, but more importantly earning our admiration and respect.

Arguably, we identify most closely with Regan when, in the final episode *Jack or Knave*, he is wrongfully accused of corruption, ultimately leading to a final scene where the 'over-emotional'

Regan declares his resignation from the Flying Squad. After four ground-breaking series and 54 episodes, *The Sweeney* ended – a decision made by Thaw but supported by Waterman – whilst it was still going strong. Nearly fifty years on, the show retains its quality, power and shocking realism. The lead characters of Regan and Carter continue to be fondly remembered, and the line, "Get your trousers on, you're nicked!" is still guaranteed to raise a few smiles.

© Cailin Thomas

ROGER AND OUT: A PERSONAL VIEW OF *THE SWEENEY*

I have a distinct memory as a nine-year-old of secretly listening in at my father's study door and hearing him animatedly reading out some dialogue from a *Sweeney* script which he was working on. This was always his approach, as he wanted to be sure that the dialogue sounded crisp, 'real' and, where possible, witty. I would be lying if I said that I could recall any of the iconic lines which Roger was reciting, but I do remember how he would chuckle away both during the writing process and when we watched the filmed episodes. It was clear that writing for the show gave him enormous pleasure.

Later on, Roger retained fond memories of his time working for Euston Films, the film and television company which was founded in 1971. The Colet Court-based company had a vision: to make fast action, location-heavy television series on 16mm film – Arriflex 16mm cameras being much easier to use handheld, which would be the preferred style – rather than the studio videotape shooting technique which writers like Roger were used to working with at Thames. He had the privilege of writing the very first episode produced by Euston, *A Copper Called Craven*, for the revamped *Special Branch*.

In a 1987 interview, *The Marshall Chronicles*, Roger – who was not involved in the initial series of *The Sweeney* – suggested to Matthew Morgenstern that it was fellow writer Trevor Preston who provided the new show with 'a great edge', while also praising the 'marvellous chemistry' between the co-leads Thaw and Waterman: 'There was no sort of, 'He's hogging the limelight this week, I'll have to have a good one next week.' It was a very good relationship.' [1] Roger also recalled the changing culture in terms of the crew:

'Everybody, at the beginning of *The Sweeney*, were film technicians as opposed to television, so they all knew hardship, and what it was like to be out of work, so anything was possible. There was no, 'Oh dear, it's quarter past six, it's time for a break.' All the rules were put to one side and there was a marvellous feeling of, 'Let's get it done. OK, it's raining, we'll get wet. Lovely!' I'm not sure that lasted all the way through, but that's how it started. So there was great energy.' [2]

Roger felt that the quick turnaround of episodes in around ten days 'helped give it its injection of pace'. [3] His episodes cover several key thematic areas which, when viewed collectively, help to explain how *The Sweeney* represented something excitingly new within the genre of the British police series. *Hit and Run* and *Victims* poignantly centred on the personal lives of police officers; *Golden Fleece* and *Trojan Bus* placed two amoral thieves at the heart of the tales, semi-comic anti-heroes; *Taste of Fear* and *On the Run* – another two-parter – demonstrated the disturbing violence which the series often offered up; *Bad Apple*, in the words of *Sweeney! The Official Companion*, was 'one of the first stories on television to handle police corruption with a degree of intelligence.' [4] It helped to question the simplistic good/bad, copper/villain boundaries.

Hit and Run was Roger's first *Sweeney* story, broadcast in September 1975. He was given the task of killing off the character of Alison Carter, George's young wife. In a case of mistaken identity, Alison's 'accidental' death leads to unexpectedly emotive scenes between George Carter and Jack Regan. Part of the power revolves around George's lament, almost a soliloquy:

"A sudden death, a body on a slab. That's all. You can't relate to them all, can you? Only this time it isn't just a body, it's my wife's body. My wife's sudden death…A report on the death of Alison Mary Carter…29. Just 29…If this world runs for another million years, she'll still be 29."

Jack Regan finds listening to Carter's heart-felt speech deeply uncomfortable. His method of coping with the situation is male booze-bonding, supporting his mate by offering to share a bottle of whisky as they "drink down to the label". As *The Official Companion* notes, the construction of the script is key to the episode's poignant power. In the first act, we are given examples of the loving but pressurised relationship between George and Alison, with long working hours eating into their private lives. We invest time in them as a couple, which helps to make her death shocking. Some of those domestic details are then revisited following her death, such as a half-finished letter, or the cup of tea Alison left for George beside the bed, now as cold as her body in the morgue. It is the type of nuanced, emotive drama one does not naturally associate with 'action television'. There is an interconnected narrative involving a drug ring and one of Alison's fellow teachers who makes regular school trips to France, but it is the impact which her murder has on George which resonates. There is even a sense of guilt, as she had stepped outside the school to post George's football pools when the bungled assassination takes place. The episode ends with Carter alone in his bedroom, in a house which now feels empty. The professional distance which a police officer normally feels from a corpse in a morgue has been effectively and emotively closed. This is a body *and* a person we can all relate to.

Golden Fleece, broadcast in October 1975, combines the semi-comic capers of two Australian robbers – Colin McGruder and Ray Stagpole – with the serious theme of police corruption and internal complaints. Sometimes, the light and dark are daringly mixed, as in the teaser which *The Official Companion* describes as 'blackly funny – and nasty'. [5] The villains use a shotgun to destroy a piece of bedroom furniture in their latest victims' house: "Stand and deliver, your money or your wife! On second thoughts, we'll just take the money!" There is a decidedly mid-70s feel to Colin and Ray's casually sexist and homophobic language and behaviour. Nevertheless, the viewing public's positive reaction to Patrick Mower and George Layton's characters suggested that the duo somehow captured the general mood. Did their popularity also reflect an ambivalence towards the police force? McGruder and Stagpole are almost like an inverted Regan/Carter double-act, with viewers clearly enjoying their 'cheeky' villainy. With the Flying Squad's Haskins having a bank account for his snouts' services, there is, despite his stitch-up, a suggestion of blurred boundaries between the law enforcers and law breakers. This is also one of those *Sweeney* episodes – like its sequel *Trojan Bus* – which calls into question any labelling of the series as 'straight' police drama. Both episodes arguably send the show over the edge into comic strip caper territory, particularly the runaway London bus with a bewildered Austrian tourist in traditional stereotype costume on board. The Colin/Ray episodes, in addition, continually and playfully reference other television series, films and actors, including *Kojak*, Paul Newman and a musical score which echoes *The Sting*. The *Official Companion* suggests that 'this was the most outrageous the series got. A parody of *Butch Cassidy and the Sundance Kid* that also satirises the way that cinema can glamorise such characters.' [6] It is hard to argue with the writers' remarks. Roger Marshall would later suggest that *Trojan Bus*' direction 'went over the top' [7]; in reality, the scripts themselves were pushing the boundaries of the realistic police procedural. Throughout its four series run, *The Sweeney* was happy to experiment, moving between tough character-driven stories like *Hit and Run*, the 'comedic anarchy' – as *The Official Companion* terms it – which is threatened here, and the more authentic or sober depictions of violence and the criminal underworld we have in *Taste of Fear* and *On the Run*. What *Trojan Bus* also offers us is a glorious visual tour Thames-side of a London docklands caught somewhere between post-Blitz bomb sites and Wapping gentrification.

Golden Fleece and *Trojan Bus* essentially draw on the same formula: McGruder and Stagpole using a glamorous female insider to profit from the weak security points inside the gold/art trade. The characters' popularity – Marshall was even tentatively approached about creating a spin-off series – reflects the mid-1970s where a pair of 'flash monkeys' might seem more attractive to viewers than the Establishment coppers seeking to arrest them. As if aware of this, Regan is keen to observe: "I don't like the way they give the impression they're lovable jokers, colonial clowns. They're not, they're vicious. They carry a shotgun...If you carry a gun, you're gonna end up using it." Regan's comment is spot-on and (almost) addressed to the audience. Part of the problem is that the viewer has possibly sided with the criminals here, and the subversive comic tone of *Trojan Bus* means that the potentially deadly shoot-out at the end is unable to return us to a more serious mood. This is *The Sweeney* in danger of losing its identity, with its lead characters marginalised, and it is little wonder that a potential third episode with Mower and Layton was vetoed by Thaw and Waterman. As Marshall noted, 'They said, quite rightly, 'Come on, it's our show!'' [8]

Taste of Fear, broadcast in October 1976, provides us with the type of shocking teaser which had Mary Whitehouse hurrying to her complaint hotline. The sight of George Sweeney's unhinged Tim Cook in action plunges us directly into a robbery which could easily turn in to a murder scene. The kneecapping which he delivers to the Irish homeowner introduces us to a topical British Army/IRA theme which is never fully developed, despite the suggestion that Cook's violent behaviour may be partly explained as a case of PTSD. Norman Eshley's Robert Hargreaves provides the episode with a subplot involving class conflict and the stark contrast between academic qualifications and real-life experience of the 'war' being fought on the streets. Rather than being depicted as a one-dimensional stereotype character, Hargreaves is seen as a man capable of intelligently investigating leads – it is easy to forget that it is he who, effectively, solves the case – but who is out of his comfort zone when the going gets rough. The conflict which arises between Regan and Hargreaves is a result not only of the latter's inadequacies but also the former's prejudices: "He doesn't swear, he doesn't smoke...when he *does* drink, it's cider, in halves...and ten to one he's a God botherer." Regan is as narrow-minded and bigoted as Hargreaves and his ambitious young wife are. The direction of the violence in the story, with so-many close-ups of faces, boots, and some scenes shot in a single take, left its mark with the viewer, as Roger observed in the *Official Companion*: 'I thought David [Wickes] did it extremely well. The violence and the anti-Irish angle were very frightening.' [9] In this respect, George Sweeney's Method approach to the verbal and physical violence also played a key part, the actor happily putting his fist through a mirror.

As in *Hit and Run*, Marshall provides another downbeat ending, this time with Hargreaves cowering in a public telephone box, having run away from the shoot-out at a travel agency. In reply to Carter's observation that it is a hard world, a world-weary Regan replies, "Yeah, but keep it to yourself, George. No one else wants to know." There is dry humour here, but also a hint that the public do not necessarily care about the day-to-day risks which police officers face on the mean streets. *Taste of Fear* offers us a grim world of seedy bedsits, rundown caravan sites, and a volcanic violence which can erupt at any moment – including unnecessary beatings by police officers as well as by Tim Cook.

Given George Sweeney's electric performance in *Taste of Fear*, it is unsurprising that Roger was encouraged to spring Tim Cook from prison for *On the Run*, first broadcast in December 1976, the final episode in the third series. Unlike the McGruder/Stagpole sequel, where the two-dimensional Aussies are simply brought back for a second, somewhat similar outing, Tim Cook – given more screen time second time around – is allowed to grow and develop, becoming a psychologically complex character. On the one hand, we have Cook's psychotic explosions of violence, dramatically aided by Ron Geesin's thumping 'Frenzy' score. Conversely, we are forced – almost against our will – to feel for him. Haunted by traumatic events from his time in the Army, terrified by confinement, be it attics, cellars, or the caged cricket pavilion he hides out in, he is, in some respects, as much a victim as he is a criminal on the run. His complex relationship with gay prisoner Pinder hints at a desire or need to repress his own homosexuality in the macho, heterosexist worlds of prisons and society in general. Nevertheless, his affection for 'Pinhead' is also demonstrated in a strangely touching scene and, later on, we see him unwilling to leave him for dead in the forest, just as he saved him from a homophobic attack in prison. Within the affluent, refined, homoerotic world of 'Uncle' Woodhouse he is equally an outcast, dyslexic and lacking the veneer of manners or educational polish to fit in. As Pinder tells Uncle: "He's not a Greek. More a Roman." There is an effective contrast between the tormented, cabin-fever Cook we see contained in buildings and the almost boyish, carefree Cook we see liberated out in the woods. His Army experiences become, paradoxically, both his strength and his weakness. The finale manhunt in the woods almost has a Wild West feel to it, as Cook takes out one policeman after another, leaving us with the inevitable showdown with Regan and the almost clichéd conclusion as a semi-concussed Carter comes to the rescue. Yet this is a story which finds room for almost Wildean dialogue, as Uncle warns Pinder: "There's nothing banal about money. Not having it, that is banal." The downbeat ending, with a freeze-frame close-up of Jack Regan's battered face, offers us the ultimate in downbeat 'tags'. As *The Official Companion* notes: 'With the benefit of hindsight, *The Sweeney* production team believe that it would have been better to have finished the programme after three series. *On the Run*, with drama, action, a memorable villain and an ominous low-key ending, would have been a dramatic and satisfying conclusion.' [10] I would agree wholeheartedly with that. Once again, it is an episode which bounces us between genres and also reflects a police force in cultural transition: far-sightedly willing to use a psychiatrist as part of their investigative work, yet still deeply closeted in prejudice, specifically homophobia. As a final observation about this truly memorable episode, for the eagle-eyed viewer with a long memory, the whitened grass of the cricket field in this episode is a reminder of the long summer drought of 1976, the one during which my dad's script was filmed.

Bad Apple, broadcast in October 1976, saw Roger tackle the sensitive subject of police corruption which, as Cailin Thomas observed in her essay, was a highly topical subject in the media at that time. The scriptwriter stated that this episode was set out of London because Regan was too well-known in the city to go undercover there; *The Official Companion* suggests that this relocation had more to do with avoiding the public connecting the fictional story to the ongoing investigation into corruption in the real Flying Squad. I guess that setting *Bad Apple* elsewhere made sense on both counts. The two 'bent' police officers in the story – DI Perrant (Norman Jones) and DS Huke (John Lyons) – are like a warped version of the Regan/Carter duo, rotten to the core, involved in a wide range of illegal activities: protection rackets, blackmail, bribery, framing, taking stolen money. It is almost as if they are rogue sheriffs in a Wild West town, as sleazy as the Blue Parrot pub/nightclub they use as their own private pleasure dome. If Regan's moral code initially finds the idea of investigating fellow officers repellent, it is nothing to the ultimate disgust which the uncorrupted DI feels when Perrant and Huke's veneer of swagger is removed: "Every copper on every beat has to pay for what you are, has to live you down." *Bad Apple* offers a bleak vision of a morally grey world in which legitimate whistle-blowers are ostracized by the police force and officers like Huke genuinely or cynically feel that their deceptions are acceptable so long as they keep an eye or lid on the bigger picture of major crime in their 'manor'.

Roger Marshall's final *Sweeney* script, *Victims*, was first broadcast in December 1978. It takes us back to his first story in the sense of a narrative centring on the personal life and tragedies of a police officer. While Waterman had arguably given his finest performance in *Hit and Run*, here it is Garfield Morgan who shines. The actor who played DCI Frank Haskins was always grateful to be given the chance to escape from the limitations of his usual deskbound role: 'It is always interesting to develop other sides of a character. Roger Marshall wrote really good scripts that were a joy to play.' [11] The 'boss' in cop shows is often side-lined from the action, and Roger was keen to correct that, particularly bearing in mind what a fine actor Morgan was: 'Garfield was a good actor and I wanted to give him something meaty. Haskins was so often the part no one wanted to explore.' [12] *Victims* also continues the theme of corrupt coppers examined in *Bad Apple*. The two narrative strands of Doreen Haskins (Sheila Reid) suffering from a mental breakdown and informant Jimmy Park hiding from the police connect in several ways. First, their desperate situations are both linked to the police force: Doreen is ravaged with guilt and misses her two sons, sent away to boarding school seemingly to protect them from their father's professional world; Jimmy has shot a 'bent' policeman who squeezes money out of him like a leech and refuses to let him take a job and go 'straight'. We find both Doreen and Jimmy hiding out in abandoned buildings, both victims in their own ways. Just as George Carter was too busy with his work to attend a family party in *Hit and Run*, here Haskins has missed his mother-in-law's funeral and not accompanied his wife on a recent visit to see their boys at school. The Flying Squad is seen here as both all-consuming and far from 'clean'.

Once again, much of the power of the piece comes from the emotive details Roger adds: Doreen pushing a doll in a pram which she talks to; voices and faces from the past haunting her; lost in that past as she gardens in the back yard of their boarded-up former home; a postcard sent to one of the boys with a short quote from Stevie Smith's poem: 'Not waving, [but] drowning'. The ending of this episode is about as bleak as it gets: a zombified Haskins on the point of resignation and left to help his terrified wife pick up the proverbial pieces; a furious, distraught Eve Fischer (Lynda Marchal) blaming Regan for her lover's death in a shoot-out, describing the police as "fascist pigs" and "filth". Nothing positive has been achieved by the Flying Squad in a memorable, penultimate episode.

Roger Marshall wrote eight *Sweeney* episodes in total, seven of which I have examined here. They offer a taste of the wide range of stories, themes and moods found in the series as a whole, one which certainly broke new ground in terms of both subject matter and filming style and method. It was a journey – enjoyed by up to 19 million viewers – which my father was proud to share with the Euston Films crew.

© Rodney Marshall

1. Roger Marshall interview with Matthew Morganstern, *The Marshall Chronicles*, *Primetime* magazine, 1987.
2. *The Marshall Chronicles*.
3. *The Marshall Chronicles*.
4. *Sweeney! The Official Companion*, p. 151.
5. *Sweeney! The Official Companion*, p. 121.
6. *Sweeney! The Official Companion*, p. 128.
7. Roger Marshall, cited in *Sweeney! The Official Companion*, p. 128.
8. Roger Marshall, cited in *Sweeney! The Official Companion*, p. 128.
9. Roger Marshall, cited in *Sweeney! The Official Companion*, p. 149.
10. *Sweeney! The Official Companion*, p. 186.
11. Garfield Morgan, cited in *Sweeney! The Official Companion*, p. 121.
12. Roger Marshall, cited in *Sweeney! The Official Companion*, p. 121.

AVENGERLAND IN THE 1970s: A BRAVE NEW WORLD

The debate has raged ever since *The Avengers*, the iconic series that captured and shaped the 1960s zeitgeist in equal measure, was revived seven years after its demise. While the original *Avengers* series owed its success to its ability to evolve – moving from two male leads to a male/female pairing, black and white to colour, videotape to film – the shift from the 60s to the 70s was, and remains, a point of contention for some fans. The arguments against *The New Avengers*' legitimacy as a continuation of the original series are myriad, but many of them boil down to the idea that there is something ineffably, quintessentially Sixties about *The Avengers* and its surreal, whimsical fantasy landscape, 'Avengerland', in which eccentrics and strange happenings were permanent fixtures. Detractors across the decades have argued that it is nigh-on impossible for this world, created within the confines of the brightly hued and optimistic 1960s, to be recreated in the harsh reality of the 70s. This put the series in a difficult position from the start. Had *The New Avengers* presented a faithful recreation of the 1960s *Avengers* series, it would have been (and in some cases was) accused of offering an unoriginal anachronism rendered absurd rather than charming by the harsher 70s landscape. At the same time, any attempts made to modify the series and its universe to be more in keeping with the ethos of the new decade were criticised as rendering the series 'un-*Avengers*-ish'. And so, over 45 years later, the question remains: did *The New Avengers* successfully recapture the original series' ethos while modifying it to be in keeping with the braver, harsher world of the 70s?

Before we can answer that question, it is necessary to determine what, exactly, made the original series '*The Avengers*'. When many fans describe a character, episode, or plot as '*Avengers*-ish', they typically mean that it is in keeping with the look and feel of the colour Emma Peel and Tara King episodes. However, while those stories are by far the most famous of the series' run, they represent only about half of its 161 episodes. Often overlooked are the first three seasons starring Ian Hendry as Dr. David Keel and Honor Blackman as Dr. Catherine Gale. These early stories are grounded in the grittier crime and espionage genres and possess a very different feel compared to the colour stories due to plots involving the likes of drug dealers and crime syndicates, the studio-bound 'live' method of recording, and the often conflict-habituated dynamics between Steed and his partners.

This diversity amongst the series' various seasons is one of the ingredients that drove the show's success. Unlike in other series, *The Avengers*' creatives were unafraid to make radical changes to the show's feel, format, look, writing, and characterisation to keep things fresh and move with the times. The varied seasons also allow it to appeal to a much wider audience – those who prefer a more grounded, gritty take on the series' universe will enjoy the earlier seasons, while those with a predilection for out-there tele-fantasy stories can immerse themselves in the surreal and sci-fi stylings that marked the series' later incarnations. Similarly, the rotating roster of lead characters provides viewers with plenty of options from which to choose a favourite. However, while this ever-changing nature played a large part in the series' success, it is also undeniable that, because of it, there is actually very little that ties the series' myriad incarnations together. This poses a problem when defining what, exactly, *The Avengers* is. A quick survey of the whole of the series' run from 1961 to 1969 reveals that the only elements present in each season are:

- The character of John Steed, as played by Patrick Macnee (although even he was omitted from two stories in the series' first season)
- Steed works with at least one partner, who was not necessarily female (the first season found him collaborating

with both Keel and Keel's nurse Carol Wilson in some stories, while Season 2 gave him a rotating roster of assistants that included Cathy Gale, nightclub singer Venus Smith, and Dr. Martin King)
- Steed and co. investigate some sort of mystery that is not necessarily bizarre, unusual, or typical of Cold War espionage. Some of Steed's earliest cases concerned protection rackets (*The Frighteners*), drugs (*Hot Snow*), insurance fraud (*A Change of Bait*), and arson (*Ashes to Roses*)
- The word "Avengers" in the title

If this sparse collection of elements is all that ties *The Avengers* together, then it is undeniable that *The New Avengers* is a continuation of what came before, as it meets all of the criteria. Even its overseas filming in France and Canada cannot be held against it. Though filmed entirely in the United Kingdom, episodes of the original series were set in far-flung locales such as Peru, Colombia, and Jamaica, while *Mission to Montreal* largely takes place on the Atlantic between Britain and Canada. Most notably, *They Keep Killing Steed* was originally going to be filmed in Spain before it was ruled untenable, suggesting that the series would have ventured beyond British borders if logistics and its budget had allowed. And while it is true that the whole of the original *Avengers* series was produced in the 1960s, had the show received funding for an additional season, production would have inevitably spilled over into 1970. Would that season, made under the same conditions as the Tara King episodes by the same cast and behind-the-scenes personnel, not have been considered part of the *Avengers* canon simply because it was made in a new decade? What if another season had been produced after that, and another after that? If the show had never gone out of production and *The New Avengers'* two seasons had come at the end of an unbroken run stretching from 1961 to 1977, would anyone question that its 26 episodes were as much a part of the series as any story featuring Cathy Gale or Emma Peel? Of course, there is more to what makes a show than the technicalities of its production. Like *The Avengers*, many series transform so dramatically over the years that they become, in essence, a different show, despite being part of the same unbroken run. However, if we are willing to accept that the whole of the original series' run, from Keel to King, is *The Avengers*, albeit different flavours of the same, then there is no reason to not accord *The New Avengers* the same privilege merely because of the decade in which it was made.

Even laying these technicalities aside, however, the answer to the question "Is *The New Avengers Avengers*-ish?" is an unequivocal 'yes'. Not only was it *The Avengers* in the sense that it met the same loose criteria that bound its predecessor together, but it also drew on the original series' ethos, sampling elements from virtually every season, while at the same time mixing in new innovations and touches that were uniquely its own, thereby evolving the series' formula just as every era of the show did before it. Combining the new and familiar was a difficult task, complicated by the requirement to relocate Avengerland to a harsher 70s context, but it was one that *The New Avengers* pulled off with more success than it is often given credit for.

Everything New is Old Again

As Rodney Marshall notes in the Preface, there is a tendency to look at the 60s through rose-coloured glasses. Mention the decade, and what instantly springs to mind is a period marked by optimism and revolutionary change, be it sexual liberation or women's rights, as well as brightly-coloured fashion, Op-art, iconic music, and a carefree, swinging zeitgeist. However, this image of the 60s ignores the fact that it was not always an innovative, progressive, hopeful time, either in reality or onscreen. Indeed, the television shows produced in the early years of the decade were, in many ways, more in keeping with the conservative stylings of the 50s, from the demure, knee-length sheath dresses and traditional suits worn by the stars, to the casting of women in either secondary roles to the male lead or as decorative guest stars, to the filming of episodes in black and white. The music was similarly 50s-tinged, leaning heavily toward regimented, quick-stepping tracks or jazzy compositions. The theme for the first season of *Danger Man*, which is sonically similar to a vintage news broadcast, is one example of this 50s influence, as is the jaunty military-esque theme for *Gideon's Way*. Composed at the beginning and in the middle of the decade, respectively, they are markedly different to the theme for the decade-closing series *Department S*, possibly the most quintessentially groovy, Swinging 60s piece of music in existence. All three pieces were penned by Edwin Astley, but the stark difference in style between the first two and the third demonstrates how much the televisual culture shifted from staid to swinging over the course of the last half of the decade.

It is the later, technicolor incarnation of the decade that people typically envision when they think about the 60s, and, by the same token, it is the version of *The Avengers* that existed during this period, the colour Emma Peel and Tara King stories, that most often comes to mind when people recall the series. These episodes were made when the 60s were at their most swinging, and therefore captured the mood and feel of the period while also helping to shape it, with Diana Rigg as Emma Peel being the first woman on television to don the miniskirt. These episodes also benefited from the show's largest international audience, the culmination of years of gradual expansion of the series' reach beyond British borders. As the existing Keel episodes only became available internationally decades after their original broadcast, the show did not venture outside the United Kingdom until the Gale episodes, when countries such as Canada and Australia picked up the series. After the black and white Emma Peel episodes were sold to the United States, however, overseas sales picked up steam, with the result that countless international audiences were treated to at least the colour Emma and Tara stories. In some countries, these were the only episodes to be broadcast regularly – or at all – and thus formed the basis upon which many worldwide viewers formed their impression of *The Avengers* as a show that embodied the Swinging 60s, one that could not possibly exist at any other time.

Of course, *The Avengers* had begun years before the 60s began to swing. Early episodes took place in a more grounded, gritty world, placed a heavier accent on realism, and featured noir stylings that were far removed from the later seasons' lighter-hearted technicolor adventures. As a result, these early seasons were much closer in feel to 1970s series, and, therefore, *The New Avengers*. This similarity between 1970s and early 60s series may not have been coincidental. One could argue that, culturally, after the highs of the 1960s at its most swinging, the 70s were the morning after the night before, the tonic used to sober up after the party. *The New Avengers*' feel and ethos were in keeping with this return to reality, with the show sobering up from late-60s flights of fancy to return Avengerland to its grounded Keel and Gale era roots. Brian Clemens alluded to this stylistic change when describing the difference between *The New Avengers* and the original series: "The old series was a humorous spoof, with dramatic overtones. *The New Avengers* is dramatic, with humorous overtones." [1] It is a neat shorthand way of contrasting the two series, but again compares *The New Avengers* only to the Peel and King stories. If one compared *The New Avengers* to the Keel and Gale eras, the descriptor "dramatic, with humorous overtones" would be equally applicable to all of them.

There are other elements in common. Many episodes in the series' first three seasons and *The New Avengers* touch on similar subject matter, such as drug dealing (*Hot Snow*, *Trap*), suspended animation (*Dead of Winter*, *K is for Kill*, *The Eagle's Nest*), doppelgangers (*Man with Two Shadows*, *Faces*), the weaponization of deadly viruses (*The Golden Eggs*, *The Midas Touch*), corrupt British army units (*Esprit de Corps*, *Dirtier by the Dozen*), and mysticism (*Warlock*, *Medium Rare*). The Keel era was the first to experiment with the three-person team format that would become *The New Avengers*' template, with Carol Wilson occasionally working alongside Keel and Steed to form an early avenging triumvirate. While Carol did not feature in every story, her role in the series was considered to be significant enough for actress Ingrid Hafner to be given the same status as Macnee and Hendry on the cover of the March 10, 1961, issue of *TV Times*, and for *TV Times* and the *Manchester Evening News* to run small features on Hafner akin to pieces written about her two male co-stars. Carol also played leading roles in the likes of *Ashes of Roses*, in which she goes undercover at a hair salon, and *Girl on the Trapeze*, in which she becomes the earliest incarnation of the *Avengers* action heroine, using an injection to knock out an opponent.

There is also early season influence at work in *The New Avengers'* characterisation of its leads. Purdey shares Cathy's cool, sharp-tongued personality and penchant for motorcycles, and is the first *Avengers* woman since Cathy to be shot (Cathy's wound comes in *The Wringer*, Purdey's in *Complex*). There is also something of Steed and Cathy's fractious, conflict-habituated relationship in Purdey and Gambit's verbal sparring (though theirs is infinitely more affectionate than that of their forebears), while Keel and Cathy's clear-eyed assessments of Steed also have a successor in Gambit's wry observations about him a decade and a half later. In *Three Handed Game* and *Hostage*, Gambit indirectly describes Steed as "ruthless" and "a master of the double-play". This calls to mind Cathy's chastisement of Steed about his methods, ruthlessness, and callous nature on a number of occasions, most notably when she conveys her disgust at his willingness to allow a woman to marry a double of the man she loves in *Man with Two Shadows*, and when she argues forcefully with him in *Conspiracy of Silence*, to the point that Steed's frustration and anger with her become so acute that he seems close to physically striking her:

Steed: I'm going to threaten him. Either he gives us that information or I'll have him deported. By Monday he'll be canning tomatoes in Naples.
Cathy: You're fighting fire with fire.

Steed: He's scared. It's the only language he knows.
Cathy: You're wrong.
...
Steed: You're an idealist.
Cathy: And you're a cynic.

Similarly, in *Toy Trap*, Keel is so enraged at Steed for using a young woman for whom Keel was responsible to help capture the villains that he pushes Steed off of a swing. The ensuing exchange nearly results in them coming to blows:

Keel: If you ever do anything like that again, I'll beat the living daylights out of you.
Steed: What the devil do you think you're doing? Nobody –
Keel: I'm doing something I should have done a long time ago.
Steed: What the hell are you talking about?
Keel: Knocking sone sense into that bigoted head of yours.
Steed: (LOSING TEMPER GRABS KEEL) Steady on boy, people don't talk to me like that.
Keel: (GRABBING STEED) Well here's one that does. Now you listen to me. If you ever go behind my back again, I'll take you apart.

While tempers did not flare quite as dramatically in *The New Avengers*, it was the first incarnation of the show since the Keel and Cathy eras to depict a physical confrontation between the leads [2], with Steed knocking out Gambit in *Hostage* when the latter arrives to arrest him. *Target!*, meanwhile, has Steed physically remove a desperate Gambit when the younger man grabs Dr. Kendrick by the lapels and demands to know why the doctor has not found a curare poisoning antidote for Purdey. Overall, Gambit's relationship with Steed is more amicable than the one he shares with Keel and Cathy, though the fact that Gambit is willing to speak plainly about the kind of man Steed is and refuses to let him skate by on charm alone – "I can't let you get away with everything," he tells Steed in *Faces* – means that he is similarly able to hold him accountable.

Of course, *The New Avengers* did not solely draw upon the first half of its legacy, but incorporated plenty of elements from the Emma and Tara eras, as well. Indeed, in many ways, *The New Avengers* picked up where the Tara era left off, retaining and building upon many of the same themes and characteristics. One recurring Tara era theme is the trustworthiness of the leads, with Tara forced to go on the run after her loyalty is called into question in *Who Was That Man I Saw You With?*, while Steed undergoes conditioning to assassinate Mother in *Stay Tuned*, has his reputation undermined by a plethora of murderous doubles in *They Keep Killing Steed*, and is prevented from working cases until his name is cleared in *All Done with Mirrors*. Even Mother himself is suspected of being a criminal mastermind in *Take Me to You Leader*. This theme was also prominent in *The New Avengers*, with Steed's loyalty being called into question in *Medium Rare* and *Hostage*, while *Faces* finds Purdey and Steed regarding each other as potential doubles.

The Tara era also includes some early examples of Steed losing old friends. In *Get-A-Way!*, his friends and colleagues are systematically murdered by escaped prisoners, while *Take-over* places his old chums the Bassetts in mortal peril and sees their loyal butler, Sergeant Groom, killed. Such losses would become regular occurrences in *The New Avengers*, with Steed losing several friends to either death or betrayal in the likes of *House of Cards*, *Dead Men are Dangerous*, *Medium Rare*, *Angels of Death*, and *Faces*.

Notably, there are hints that the Tara era might have eventually instituted a two-men-and-a-woman format had it continued production into the 70s, with Tara occasionally partnering with younger male characters, such as Baron von Kurt in *They Keep Killing Steed* and Captain Cordell in *Bizarre*. While these characters were largely included to free up Patrick Macnee to shoot other episodes, his waning interest in, but continued loyalty to, the series may have eventually resulted in him appearing in further seasons in a reduced capacity, and a new permanent male character being introduced to share the load. The resulting format would have been very similar to *The New Avengers*, but regardless of whether it would have been implemented, there is a sense that von Kurt and Cordell were Gambit prototypes used by the writers to experiment with the idea of adding a younger male character to the mix.

Elsewhere in the show's final season, we see the first glimmerings of *The New Avengers*' 'thicker cardboard' characterisation, with Brian Clemens offering an early version of his vision for *The New Avengers*' leads while discussing Tara's evolution throughout her run: "Part of the humanising process is that Tara has a chronological development, which Cathy Gale and Emma Peel never had. She has achieved our purpose. *The Avengers* was two-dimensional – now it is two and a half. The cardboard is a little thicker." [3] Along with Tara's evolution, the show offered a peek into the leads' love lives, with Tara pursued by Teddy Chilcott in *My Wildest Dream* and flirting with Baron von Kurt in *They Keep Killing Steed*, much as Purdey would engage in flirtations in the likes of *Target!*, *To Catch a Rat*, *Three Handed Game*, *Trap*, and *Hostage*. Like Tara's Teddy, some of Purdey's suitors also go bad, such as Cromwell (*To Catch a Rat*), Spelman (*Hostage*), and Larry Doomer (*Obsession*). Steed also gets in on the romance, reuniting with ex-girlfriend Janice in *The Curious Case of the Countless Clues*, whom he greets with a kiss, an intimacy his onscreen flirtations typically lacked. That moment anticipates Steed's active love life in *The New Avengers*, which sees him romancing a series of eligible ladies in episodes such as *The Midas Touch*, *House of Cards*, *The Last of the Cybernauts...?*, *Trap*, and *Hostage*. Meanwhile, Tara's Uncle Charles in *Wish You Were Here* marks the first onscreen depiction of a member of an *Avengers* lead's family, a predictor of things to come, with Purdey's step-father and uncle appearing onscreen in *House of Cards* and *Dirtier by the Dozen*, respectively, while her mother makes a vocal cameo in *Hostage*.

Perhaps most notably, the Tara era establishes a more institutional slant for the series, with stories focusing on the inner workings of 'The Ministry' (Steed's department) for the first time since the series' early years, when Steed was briefed by a handful of different superiors – such as One-Ten, Five, and Charles – and was sometimes called on to investigate his own people (such as his department's resident interrogator in *The Wringer*). In the Tara era, this institutional focus was most obviously revived in the form of Steed's superior, Mother, and his one-time replacement, Father. Some fans disliked the addition of Mother, preferring the identity of Steed's employers to remain a mystery, as in the Emma Peel episodes. However, as the first three seasons of the show demonstrate, it was the Peel stories that were the anomaly, being the only era of the show in which Steed lacked some kind of superior. In *The New Avengers*, Steed became the authority figure for his team, but frequently interacted with higher-ups such as McKay in *Hostage* and a host of senior bureaucrats, ministers, and military types in the likes of *Faces*, *Angels of Death*, *The Tale of the Big Why*, *The Lion and the Unicorn*, *K is for Kill*, *Complex*, *The Gladiators*, *Emily*, *To Catch a Rat*, and *The Tale of the Big Why*. The fact that Tara and her one-time substitute Lady Diana Forbes-Blakeney are professional agents is another sign of the series' institutional focus. All of Steed's previous partners were 'talented amateurs', i.e., civilians possessing useful skillsets but who were not trained agents. In contrast, Tara is introduced as a trainee agent in *The Forget-Me-Knot* and the development of her skills is a recurring theme throughout the season, with Steed initially acting as a mentor and offering helpful tips (e.g., about her judo technique in *Invasion of the Earthmen*), before Tara eventually becomes proficient enough in the art of espionage to run missions solo (as she does in *All Done with Mirrors*) and take on important assignments, such as testing security (*Who Was That Man I Saw You With?*).

The New Avengers continued this trend by making both Purdey and Gambit professional agents, with Steed once again serving as mentor to his younger colleagues and passing on words of wisdom about the job (Gambit mentions that Steed always tells him to cultivate his instincts in *Sleeper*, while Steed instructs Purdey on the tricks of the trade in *The Midas Touch*).

Part and parcel of this increased focus on the Ministry itself were insights into its inner workings. Examples of this in the Tara era include the issuing of a 'pink and purple' pass to agents when they are granted leave (*Killer*); the psychiatric evaluation of agents and the reductions in security rating and removal from active service of those deemed unfit (*Stay Tuned*); a rest home for agents recovering from injuries sustained in the line of duty (*Noon Doomsday*); and the Ministry's not-so-friendly rivalries with other intelligence departments (Mother is annoyed that MI12 has been assigned to investigate in *Super Secret Cypher Snatch*, and experiences schadenfreude when his department is called in after MI12's agent goes AWOL). Though it is not a legitimate operation, the interrogation training program featured in *The Interrogators* is so easily accepted by the agents who are called on to drop everything at short notice and submit to being put through the wringer that it is clearly akin to legitimate Ministry programs.

The New Avengers reveals similar insights into the department's operations. Rather than receive a pink and purple pass, we learn that all agents must run a target range and pass a medical before being allowed to take leave (*Target!*), and that records of deceased individuals are destroyed (*Faces*). We see the ID cards issued to Gambit and Stannard, which the former uses to demonstrate his authority to ask Penny Redfern questions as part of his investigation in *Dead Men are Dangerous*. We also see how internal investigations are conducted, with McBain compiling evidence about Steed which ultimately results in him being put under house arrest in *Medium Rare*. A similar process unfolds in *Hostage*, with Steed followed, his mail intercepted, and Gambit assigned to investigate him when his loyalty is called into question. Routine surveillance at known opposition drop-off points is also established (*Hostage*), as is the need for agents to submit to regular medicals, which are conducted by resident physician Dr. Kendrick when he is not doing autopsies (*Target!*). The Minister's role in the department is also flagged, with *Hostage* bringing news of a ministerial visit, while *To Catch a Rat* has Steed and Gambit investigating the connection between the Minister and ex-operative Irwin Gunner. Interdepartmental collaborations are highlighted in the same story, with Cromwell from D16 involved in the investigation. The department's internal hierarchy is also subtly depicted through Steed's role, which has him overseeing a stable of agents, including Stannard and Terry (*The Eagle's Nest*, *The Last of the Cybernauts...?*), while other agents, like *Three Handed Game*'s Larry, run parallel investigations to Steed's own, but still check in with him (if only to gloat). Steed also confirms that the department's officiousness is alive and well, referencing the layers of bureaucracy required to grant him permission to learn about Professor Mason's research in *The Last of the Cybernauts...?* The same episode provides an insight into the department's procedures when an individual imprisoned by an agent is released, with Fitzroy informing Steed that old foe Goff is out. We also learn about the department's informant system, as administered by paymaster Freddy Mason (*Medium Rare*). Peeks into security procedures are also provided, from McKay's safe, which records the last time it was opened (*Hostage*), to the bulletproof, soundproof room used by the members of Steed's brainchild, the 'three handed game', to record their recitations of the contents of a top secret document. There are also insights into how operations have advanced, or not, over the years, with Morse Code still employed (*To Catch a Rat*; *The Midas Touch*), but codenames no longer fashionable (*To Catch a Rat*). The darker sides of the organisation also emerge, most poignantly in the case of Steed's old friend and fellow agent Freddy (*The Midas Touch*), who buckled under the pressure of the job and turned to drink to prop up his nerve. No longer fit for duty, the Ministry terminated his services, leaving him to fall into alcoholism and homelessness, rather than providing him with the support he so desperately needed – and deserved – after working in such a high-stress profession. Another dark side is the seeming lack of loyalty the department engenders, with many of Steed and co.'s own colleagues unmasked as traitorous, including Spelman, Coldstream, Felix Kane, Wallace, Bradshaw, and Harmer.

An increased focus on the department came with a corresponding focus on Steed and Tara's fellow agents and other colleagues, some of whom appear in the likes of *False Witness*, *Noon Doomsday*, *All Done with Mirrors*, *Wish You Were Here*, *The Interrogators*, and *The Curious Case of the Countless Clues*.

The New Avengers builds on this, featuring a host of Steed, Gambit, and Purdey's fellow agents, contacts, and other associated Ministry staff, including Stannard in *The Eagle's Nest*; Roland in *House of Cards*; the duplicitous Felix Kane in *The Last of the Cybernauts...?*; the ill-fated Merton and Turner in *Cat Amongst the Pigeons*; disgraced ex-agent Freddy in *The Midas Touch*; the ill-fated McKay, Talmadge, Palmer, and Myers, plus Ministry physician Dr. Kendrick and target range administrators Bradshaw and Jones, in *Target!*; the amnesiac Irwin Gunner, records man Finder, and women manning the Morse Code stations in *To Catch a Rat*; bureaucrats Torrance and Bilston in *Faces*; Larry in *Three Handed Game*; George Ratcliffe in *Gnaws*; records clerk Sandy in *Dead Men are Dangerous*; administrators Manderson and Coldstream (plus his secretary, Jane) and fellow Ministry man Carter in *Angels of Death*; overseers Wallace and McBain, paymaster Freddy Mason, and scientist Roberts in *Medium Rare*; superior Tommy McKay and agents Walters and Spelman in *Hostage*; the late Williams and double agent Murford in *Trap*...the list goes on. Indeed, it is difficult to find an episode that does not feature one or more of the triumvirate's colleagues, be they agents, top brass, or those assisting with science, administration, or medicals. Even when the trio ventures overseas, they pick up new colleagues in the shape of Commander Leparge (*The Lion and the Unicorn*) and Colonel Martin and Dr. Jeanine Leparge (*K is for Kill*) in France, while in Canada they collaborate with intelligence head Baker and agent Greenwood in *Complex*; head of security Peters in *The Gladiators*; agent Bailey, intelligence man Milroy, and tech expert Murford in *Forward Base*; and double agent Collings and intelligence man Reddings in *Emily*.

In keeping with these appearances by various Ministry personnel are numerous peeks into the departmental headquarters itself. The Tara era offered a few glimpses of Ministry facilities and infrastructure in episodes such as *Noon Doomsday* and *The Forget-Me-Knot*, opening the door for *The New Avengers* to venture inside Ministry headquarters on a regular basis. Over the course of the series, we see The Ministry's dojo (*House of Cards*, *Hostage*, *Dead Men are Dangerous*); target range, medical exam room, and morgue (*Target!*); Morse Code operations and file room (*To Catch a Rat*); corridors, offices, and second morgue (*Faces*); infirmary (*Three Handed Game*); records room and second infirmary (*Dead Men are Dangerous*); meeting room, office, and computer lab (*Angels of Death*); other offices and lab (*Medium Rare*); and corridor and McKay's office (*Hostage*). Gambit also makes reference to an (unseen) shooting range used to test out new weapons (*Hostage*). These regular appearances by the leads and their colleagues in their workplace, rather than only out in the field or in their flats, may, as some suggested with the inclusion of Mother in the Tara era, reduce the sense of mystery inherent in the way Steed and his colleagues operate. However, what is lost in mystique is more than made up for by the living, breathing universe that these glimpses into the Ministry help to establish. While visits to any kind of institutionalised setting in the Peel episodes were always purposeful and plot-based, such as the trip to the Ministry archive in *The See-Through Man*, scenes depicting Steed, Purdey, and Gambit wandering the Ministry's corridors, socialising with colleagues, attending meetings, conducting research, and keeping their skills sharp (in the dojo or at the target range alike) give the audience an insight into their lives between assignments, enriching their characterisation as a result. They also establish a sense of normality that, in many ways, is not far removed from the daily routine of the average office dweller, and which throws the leads' high-octane espionage antics, such as car chases, shoot outs, and fights, into sharp relief. These scenes also allow us to imagine them engaging in other mundanities, including writing reports, drinking (probably terrible) coffee in the break room, eating lunch at the canteen, and exchanging idle gossip (which is hinted at by Purdey's references to the departmental rumours she has heard about Gambit's love life in *To Catch a Rat*). The use of corridors, stairwells, or offices in Pinewood Studios' Heatherden Hall for many of the Ministry scenes results in a unified aesthetic that further cements the impression that everything takes place in the same multistory building, adding to the series' realism and world-building.

As with the Keel and Gale eras of the show, there are plenty of plots that echo adventures in the Emma and Tara stories in *The New Avengers*' repertoire. Of course, *The Last of the Cybernauts...?* is the most obvious throwback, continuing the Cybernauts saga begun in *The Cybernauts* and *Return of the Cybernauts* by reviving Professor Armstrong's creations in the hands of another wheelchair-bound villain, but plenty of other non-sequel stories are cut from the same Emma/Tara cloth. Recurring story elements include seemingly-innocuous animals being instructed to kill (*The Hidden Tiger*, *Cat Amongst the Pigeons*), deadly automated buildings (*The House that Jack Built*, *Killer*, *Complex*), B-movie sci-fi antagonists (the man-eating plant from space in *Man-eater of Surrey Green* and the giant rat in *Gnaws*), mind-transfer (*Who's Who???*, *Three Handed Game*), doppelgangers (*Two's a Crowd* and *They Keep Killing Steed*, the latter sharing *Faces*' manufacturing of doubles through plastic surgery), a race for something of value (*Dead Man's Treasure*, *The Tale of the Big Why*), murder by stress induction (*The Fear Merchants*, *Angels of Death*), psychics (*Too Many Christmas Trees*, *Medium Rare*), surreal, depopulated landscapes (*The Hour That Never Was*, *The Morning After*, *Sleeper*), and the leads' loyalty being called into question (*Who Was That Man I Saw You With?*, *Medium Rare*, *Hostage*). These parallel plotlines demonstrate that *The New Avengers* incorporated sci-fi and fantasy stylings as often as it did the espionage and crime stories that characterised the original show's early years.

Eccentrics, another signature element of the later seasons of the series, were also included in the *New Avengers*' canon through the likes of the forgetful Hara (*The Eagle's Nest*); bird-mad Bridlington (who has a series of 'no cats' signs that calls to mind a similar set of anti-dog signs in *The Hidden Tiger*); rose enthusiast Roland (*House of Cards*); snakehead-infused alcohol lover Professor Lopez (*Target!*); Grant, who enjoys playing with toys in his bubble bath (*To Catch a Rat*); Purdey's ice-hating uncle Colonel Elroyd Foster (*Dirtier by the Dozen*); despotic bureaucrat Titherbridge (*Target!*); and fake medium Victoria Stanton (*Medium Rare*). While such eccentrics are not as numerous as in the Emma and Tara years, by sprinkling them throughout its episodes, *The New Avengers* infuses itself with some of the original's offbeat British charm.

The sense of humour that characterised the original series' later seasons is also alive and well in *The New Avengers*, with much of it coming from Purdey and Gambit's exchanges, during which Purdey typically goes off on bizarre tangents, be it raising an old debate from last Tuesday (*Forward Base*) or questioning the directorial credentials of *Treasure of the Sierra Madre* (*The Midas Touch*). Many of these exchanges position Purdey as 'New Avengerland's' preeminent eccentric, rivalling even Steed himself, who maintains his offbeat charm in the new series by apologising to chickens for stealing their eggs (and leaving them money, in *Emily*) and mixing up fragrant rat bait in his best silver (*Gnaws*). Mike Gambit, in contrast, is the sane man of Avengerland, but when not engaging in bizarrely-humorous exchanges with Purdey, he also doles out his share of quips that run the gamut from pitch black humour ("Need to warm up a little first?", a line delivered as he pushes a baddie toward a crematorium in *House of Cards*) to endearingly bad jokes (his "undercover" quip in response to Purdey's inquiries about his liaison with the so-called 'Russian countess' in *To Catch a Rat*). Also inherent in the humorous exchanges between Purdey and Gambit is the ongoing flirtation that characterised so many of the original series' partnerships, particularly the Steed/Peel relationship.

The appearance of familiar elements from the Keel, Gale, Peel, and King seasons in *The New Avengers* establishes that it drew on all eras and aspects of its lineage. However, the series is also unquestionably distinct from its predecessor, and, like every season before it, created its own version of Avengerland, one that was shaped by its 70s context as much as what had come before.

Everything Old is New Again

While much of 1960s pop culture packs more weight and meaning than meets the eye, as the decade gave way to the 70s, there were hints that people had had their fill of its style over substance tendencies, and were hungry for something a bit more substantial. Music moved beyond short and sweet (and slightly tinny) pop ditties, to longer, richer songs in a variety of genres with multi-layered arrangements and meaningful, clever lyrics that took their time – or, in the case of progressive rock, the whole album – to tell their stories, rather than hurrying to return to a catchy chorus. Television leaned toward grittier, realistic stories that reflected the happenings of the time. Even fashion pushed for more substance, quite literally calling for extra fabric with which to craft midi dresses rather than miniskirts, while men swapped their too-small 60s jackets and stovepipe trousers for flares, wide ties, and jackets with full skirts. This love of substance went hand and hand with an increased consciousness of, and cynicism regarding, the issues of the day, from the state of the economy to the possibility of nuclear war, all of which made the naïve, 'make love not war' idealism of the 60s feel dated at best.

Into this substance-hungry, less-optimistic landscape came *The New Avengers*. Reviving a light-hearted 60s series in an era typified by a preference for realism and substance was a tall order. Brian Clemens recognised this, and knew that, to have any chance of success, the series would have to make changes, not only to keep up with the times, but because evolution had always been an essential component of the *Avengers* formula. In crafting the new series, Clemens met the new decade's demand for realism and substance by placing an accent on drama over humour, crafting 'thicker cardboard' characters who were more fleshed out than the previous series' protagonists, incorporating weightier plots and themes, and establishing a more grounded Avengerland.

New Avengerland

Over the years, the original series' setting, dubbed 'Avengerland', has become synonymous with the show itself, defining its tone and atmosphere, and therefore the types of stories and characters it featured. Serving as the backdrop for *The New Avengers'* characters and their adventures, 'New Avengerland' similarly established the show's overall feel, and is best described as an expansive place of consequence, with strong connections to the real world and a sense of history.

From a sheer physical standpoint, *The New Avengers'* universe feels bigger than what had come before, and not only because over a quarter of its stories were filmed in France and Canada. The original series' world, particularly in the Peel and King eras, is carefully curated to create a charming, offbeat image of Britain, which, as Brian Clemens observed, drew more on people's ideas about the country than reality. The curated artificiality of the Peel/King Avengerland lends it the feel of a pocket universe – small, perfectly formed, and insular. The extensive use of the studio, even after the transition from videotape to film, allowed for more location shooting, compounding this sense of Steed and co. existing in a surreal fantasyland limited in geographical scope. This is by no means a criticism, as the studio-based 'outdoor' sets cultivated a feel and atmosphere all their own, and allowed the series' creatives to control the show's aesthetic to a greater degree than they could on location. However, the use of such sets, along with locations in close proximity to the studio, reinforced the sense that Avengerland was a small, self-contained place, not one that stretched out into infinity. In contrast, *The New Avengers* made more use of location work than its predecessor, employing the grounds of Heatherden Hall at Pinewood Studios to great effect, as well as a bevy of urban and rural locales. While the use of Pinewood and its environs, as well as some of the surrounding areas, lends the show some of the unified aesthetic and self-contained feel of the original series, many episodes give expansive, sprawling locations starring roles, which serve to push back the world's horizons. Locations exemplifying New Avengerland's increased scale and scope include the moody environs of Eilean Donan castle in Scotland in *The Eagle's Nest*; the labyrinthine gas works through which Purdey and Gambit pursue their quarry in *The Midas Touch*; the converted windmill at which Steed and Perov have their stand-off in *House of Cards*; the Pinewood Sanatorium, used to great effect as the target range in *Target!* and the eerily empty and overgrown Base 47 in *Faces*; the silent London streets of *Sleeper*; *Dirtier by the Dozen*'s army base, surrounded by crisp, green, rolling hills through which Purdey and Gambit flee; the ominous disused picture palace in *To Catch a Rat*; the Wimbledon theatre, the grandly theatrical setting of the final fight in *Three Handed Game*; the Victorian Folly, where Mark Crayford makes his last stand in *Dead Men are Dangerous*; and the stark, bleak landscape of the missile site in *Obsession*. These locations, coupled with roving outdoor journeys in episodes such as *Trap*, *To Catch a Rat*, *The Tale of the Big Why*, *Emily*, and *The Gladiators*, allow *The New Avengers* to cultivate an expansive background to its universe, an Avengerland without borders – literally so in the case of the series' overseas forays to France and Canada – the openness of which lingers on in the mind even when the action is studio-based.

At the same time, the series' extensive location filming shows us another side of this 70s Avengerland. While the series' leads live in attractive flats and country houses, and pay visits to manors and government offices as part of their work, there is another, less polished side to the series' universe. While the Peel and King eras of the original series favoured a sophisticated, idyllic aesthetic, consisting of green, rolling hills in the English countryside, grand houses, charming villages, and smart London flats and neighbourhoods, *The New Avengers* went back to its grittier roots, reviving the earlier seasons' willingness to show the less savoury and polished side of the country. Many have commented on the show's extensive use of derelict locations, such as the disused gasworks in *The Midas Touch*, the abandoned Pinewood Sanatorium in *Target!* and *Faces*, the ramshackle picture palace in *To Catch a Rat*, the abandoned multilevel building in *Faces*, the rather shabby-looking shopping complex and riverside café in *Sleeper*, and the derelict funfair in *Hostage*. These less-than-glamorous locales ground the series' events in the real world, acknowledging the harsh economic realities that existed at the time and had taken a toll on the country's infrastructure. By embracing pockets of dereliction and decay, *The New Avengers* therefore allowed its aesthetic to align with its characterisation and plots, both of which acknowledged real-world issues beyond the middle- and upper-class concerns of the Peel and King years. At the same time, the series did not dispense with the slickness and sophistication that had characterised the series at its height, but instead forced it to sit beside some uncomfortable realities about how the world had moved on (or not), rather than gloss them over for the sake of fantasy and illusion. To hammer home the point, the series carried this grittier aesthetic into the studio, creating the likes of the murky sewer in *Gnaws*, the shabby assassin's flat in *Medium Rare*, the derelict funfair interior in *Hostage*, and the mission house in *Faces*. The decision to include such settings, even when the creatives were able to exercise complete control over how the sets looked, demonstrates that the rundown, derelict locations were used intentionally, rather than reluctantly chosen from whatever was available. This aesthetic was a harsh shot of realism to inject into what had become an idealised English fantasyland, but was also an indicator of the series' willingness to face reality, rather than elide it.

Along with the aforementioned physical confinement, the original series' Avengerland was also limited temporally. While it possessed hints of continuity in its earliest episodes, with some of pilot story *Hot Snow*'s story threads picked up in second episode *Brought to Book*, Leonard White soon issued a memo dictating that continuity should be avoided in future stories in favour of self-contained plots, enabling viewers to tune into any episode without knowledge of what had come before and not be at a disadvantage. With a few exceptions (the Cybernauts and Dr. Armstrong's assistant Benson in *The Cybernauts* and *Return of the Cybernauts*; Brodny in *Two's a Crowd* and *The See-Through Man*), this stricture was largely adhered to throughout the original series' run, and references to Steed's previous partners were sparing (Cathy is name-checked in *Too Many Christmas Trees*; Cathy and Emma's names are glimpsed on files in *Pandora*). What this lack of continuity allowed for in terms of accessibility had the side-effect of narrowing the scope of the series' universe. Characters that departed virtually ceased to exist, while events that occurred and information imparted in the course of one story were essentially erased to make way for the next, the world of the show effectively rebooting not only between seasons, but with each new episode.

The New Avengers changed things by introducing a thread of continuity. In doing so, it opened 'New Avengerland' up temporally, pushing the borders of its world back through time to absorb the whole of the original series' continuity and bring it back to vivid life. The references *The New Avengers* made to the series' decade-long history were not so prevalent as to spoil the enjoyment of viewers unfamiliar with some or all of the original series, but acknowledging what had come before instilled a subtle, but very real, sense that there was a whole *Avengers* universe beyond what *The New Avengers* showed on the screen, humming along in the background. Now more than ever, one felt that, say, Emma Peel had not simply winked out of existence the moment she drove offscreen with her newly-revived husband. Instead, references to Emma scattered throughout the show demonstrated that she was not only alive in Steed's memory, but that other characters who had never met her were aware of her and her work with Steed. As a result, it was easier to imagine Emma living out her life in some other, off-screen corner of Avengerland. Indeed, *The New Avengers* went so far as to offer us a taste of that off-screen Avengerland in *K is for Kill: The Tiger Awakes*. While Emma's appearance is underwhelming in its presentation – consisting of recycled original series footage which quite literally freezes Emma in time, portraying her as wearing the same clothes, sporting the same hairstyle, and living in the same flat as she did in the 60s – it does give us a small peek into her life a decade later, one in which she still fondly thinks of Steed and their time together, spots connections between current events and her old cases, and is "not Mrs. Peel anymore", implying that she and Peter Peel divorced sometime after their reunion. Steed replies that he knows, but that she is "still Mrs. Peel" to him, a sign that his affection for her remains undimmed. When that 'appearance' is coupled with references to Emma throughout the series, which include a photo of her on display in Steed's home in *House of Cards* and *The Last of the Cybernauts...?*; a glimpse of her name on a file and an appearance by the green Bentley driven by Steed during her adventures in *Dead Men are Dangerous*; a recounting of her and Steed's two previous encounters with the Cybernauts by Purdey and Gambit in *The Last of the Cybernauts...?*; and her 1967 'flashback' appearance in *K is for Kill: The Tiger Awakes*, Emma emerges as a living, breathing character who exists in the broader *Avengers* universe in a way she did not in the Tara King era. Other references to Cathy Gale and Tara King (on the aforementioned *Dead Men are Dangerous* files and bracketing Emma's photo at Steed's) similarly create the sense that these characters, too, are living their lives in the wider world of Avengerland and are never far from Steed's mind. Some criticise *The New Avengers* of setting too much store in nostalgia, reviving memories of the original series' past glories instead of developing its own feel and ideas. What this perspective fails to recognise is that *The New Avengers*' sense of history *was* part of its originality – it used the considerable legacy of its forebear to infuse its take on Avengerland with rich detail and background. At the same time, that nostalgia for the series' past was frequently tinged with melancholy, just as likely to bring pain as evoke warm memories of the good old days – Steed's Peel-era Bentley is blown up in *Dead Men are Dangerous*, while Emma's call in *K is for Kill: The Tiger Awakes* has her wistfully reminiscing about "long, happy memories" of her time working with Steed, something both seem to believe will never happen again. As a result, *The New Avengers*' tone could be more sombre, or at least bittersweet, than its predecessor, but what some moments may have lacked in levity, they made up for in substance and gravitas.

Also adding gravitas, as well as realism, to 'New Avengerland' was its treatment of violence. The harder edged, crime-noir stylings of the original series' earliest seasons resulted in less stylised, grittier depictions of violence, whether unleashed by the villains of the piece; a ruthless, sometimes gun-wielding, Steed; or a brawling Dr. David Keel. However, the recording of these early stories in black and white made the depiction of blood much more difficult, with wounds losing some of their impact when tinted an inky grey-black rather than vivid red and rendered less distinct due to the poorer picture quality and limited number of close-ups that came with recording 'live' on videotape. By the time the series made the switch to film, gritty violence was on its way out, replaced with an increasingly stylised fantasy landscape in which blood made only sporadic appearances, and was generally declared verboten. Indeed, the series' deaths scenes were once described as being so innocuous that viewers could imagine the actor playing the deceased getting up afterwards, collecting his paycheque, and going home. This attitude toward violence cemented the transformation of the series' setting into a quasi-child's fantasyland in which the leads 'played' at being spies, then went home at day's end, diabolical plots evaporating into insubstantial wisps of imagination.

The New Avengers' consequentialist ethos resulted in a less-stylised treatment of violence that packed more punch. Deaths were not so easily brushed aside, and blood made a not overwhelming, but noticeable, return to the screen. This acknowledgement of the consequences of violence allowed the series to retain some credibility with its audience in the less fanciful decade that was the 70s, even if it steered clear of the extremes of other series of the period, e.g., the at times shockingly brutal *The Hanged Man* (1975). Gambit's earliest fight scenes, in particular, demonstrate the series' grittier attitude toward violence, with him executing brutally efficient takedowns of enemies via a series of hard-hitting, expertly-placed blows doled out in a blur of speed, bracketed by moments of composed, controlled stillness. Gambit's combination of stillness and brutal yet controlled attacks could be viewed as a metaphor for the series' attitude toward violence – willing to depict it, but keeping a tight handle on it to ensure that it never strayed into gratuitousness, something that even the hardest-edged take on Avengerland could not censure without losing the spirit of the series. Even so, the show sometimes danced close to the edge, and, in the case of *The Gladiators*, crossed the line. The episode featured several fight scenes that, while tame by today's standards, included bareknuckle brawls and depicted characters being hit or thrown with such force that they broke walls, doors, and other fixtures on impact. Graphic violence was also implied in a slightly queasy scene in which Purdey and Gambit follow circling carrion birds to a police car, the trunk of which contains the mangled, decomposing remains of two policemen. Gambit opens the trunk, takes one look at the ugly sight within, quickly closes it, and looks sick. Purdey, curiosity piqued, asks to have a look, waving off Gambit's attempts to deter her by assuring him that she is not the "fainting kind". She quickly regrets her decision, remaining riveted by the carnage until Gambit breaks the spell and closes the trunk to hide the grisly mess from view. A queasy Purdey weakly suggests that "a girl can always change her mind." It was all too much for broadcasters, with ITV pre-empting the episode for its violent content and relegating it to a later timeslot, while in other cases it was not shown in the initial run, or was transmitted in edited form, most notably with a scene removed in which a fighter has his ears boxed, a move it was feared young viewers would emulate. While the series did not suffer any other notable instances of censorship, this episode is often cited as the best evidence of the series' more brutal, violent edge, though there were many other examples that gave it a run for its money, including Gambit's decimation and interrogation of Ralph in *The Eagle's Nest*, during which he attempts to force Ralph's mouth open to retrieve a suicide capsule, and his delivery of lightning cavalcades of blows to take down Turner in *The Tale of the Big Why* and Madame Sing's bodyguard in *The Midas Touch*. Another near-the-knuckle scene in *House of Cards* finds Gambit putting the villainous Cartney's hand near the flames of a crematorium to force him to drop his gun, then pushing Cartney toward the same when he refuses to talk, implying that he will use the fire to loosen his tongue, if necessary. *Hostage* has Gambit at both the giving and receiving ends of violence, with Steed landing a low blow to knock him out and goon Marvin throwing him bodily around, before an exhausted, dishevelled Gambit finally gains the upper hand. *The Last of the Cybernauts...?*, meanwhile, features a high-impact shot of him being struck by a car.

Of course, Gambit is not the only player to up the series' violence quotient. *Dirtier by the Dozen* showcases Colonel 'Mad Jack' Miller's brutally outdated methods of disciplining his men, from lashing them to a gun carriage and pulling them over uneven terrain to executing them by firing squad. *Three Handed Game* freeze frames on an image of 'Tap' Ranson taking a right hook to the jaw, while agent Larry's watcher is murdered and left in a grotesque tableau, his cigar smashed into his mouth. Some violence gains added impact with the inclusion of blood. The malevolent and sinister fishhook attacks in *The Eagle's Nest* cut both Stannard's cheek and Purdey's hand, while in *House of Cards*, Gambit bleeds from a knife wound inflicted during a fight to the death with Spence. Both Steed and Purdey are shot, in *Dead Men are Dangerous* and *Complex* respectively, with blood shown on Steed's fingers after the fact. *Cat Amongst the Pigeons*' shot of raw meat would be graphic enough for Avengerland, but the ante is upped with blood on Purdey's palm after a nasty peck, and, while we are spared the sight of Turner being clawed at by birds, we do see the results in the form of his heavily scratched hands and arms, injuries that were omitted on similarly scratched and clawed victims in *The Hidden Tiger* and *The Winged Avenger*. *The New Avengers*' decision to show the cuts on the shaken, catatonic Turner (who later dies from shock) could be interpreted as a statement by the series on its attitude toward blood – it does not wallow in it, but uses it to depict the harsh reality of death with a clarity the later seasons of the original series did not. Unlike the actors in the original series, one cannot imagine Turner's portrayer simply getting up after the character has died and going home. These deaths are meant to stick, and the stakes are elevated in the series' universe as a result, to the point that even the leads are depicted as carefully putting on their safety belts before engaging in a high-speed car chase (*The Last of the Cybernauts...?*) or espousing the dangers of smoking (*K is for Kill: Tiger by the Tail*), moments that highlight their mortality rather than portraying them as immune from the dangers of car crashes and cancer.

Plots and Themes

While many of *The New Avengers*' plots were similar to those in the original series, it regularly put its own unique twist on familiar material by imbuing it with the weightiness that its more grounded version of Avengerland demanded. The show achieved this by putting a greater emphasis on realism, spotlighting social and political issues, and, most importantly, introducing and emphasising a more relatable, human element. Characterisation is *The New Avengers*' greatest strength, and it uses its well-drawn leads and guest players, along with their actions and fates, to bring the myriad issues it explores or touches on to vivid life.

One example of the series' weightier take on familiar subject matter is *The Eagle's Nest*'s explicit description of the human cost of an enemy takeover. While its spiritual predecessor *The Town of No Return* generally leaves the details of the townspeople's fates to the imagination – with the notable exception of the dishevelled

Mark Brandon, who collapses and (presumably) dies from the injuries inflicted by his pursuers – *The Eagle's Nest* refuses to let us off the hook, with Father Trasker explaining, with stomach-churning blitheness, that anyone – women, children, the elderly – who did not submit to the will of their new overlords was either slaughtered or used for experimentation. The content of Trasker's words is horrifying enough, but his casual delivery as he describes people being killed and tortured hammers home his stunning lack of humanity and ratchets up the story's stakes by illustrating the great evil that will be unleashed on the world should the avenging trio fail to stop him.

Cat Amongst the Pigeons, in contrast, offers a less clear-cut villain in Zacardi, who uses his control over birds to murder a number of individuals. However, unlike the selfish motives of the wranglers of the killer cats in *The Hidden Tiger*, Zacardi's motivation is environmentalist in nature – he targets men who advocate the culling of the bird population to prevent them from competing with humans for resources. Though his motivation does not justify his murderous actions, Zarcardi's death at the episode's close leaves a bitter taste in the mouth, and there is a sense that our heroes, despite preventing him from killing more people, have failed to address the broader issue at play, which is still crying out for a more humane solution.

Faces and, to a lesser extent, *Gnaws*, address the issue of homelessness and the corresponding dehumanisation of those who suffer it. The occupants of the mission house in *Faces* are used as nothing more than raw material, their bodily integrity and identity cut away by the plastic surgeon's knife. When one of the men dies, he is buried under a name that is not his own, while Prator and Terrison/Craig, who know his true identity, lament his passing only as a waste of the time and effort put into transforming him. While the homeless men they recruit are not sympathetic in that they appear to be happy to go along with the plot's requisite murder and deception, there is no avoiding the fact that to do so they must give up who they are, as well as their independence, forced to remain under Dr. Prator and Terrison/Craig's thumb and pass on information in order to earn their keep. That lack of independence makes one question whether the men are able to freely choose whether to participate in the scheme. Do Mullins, Terrison/Craig, and Prator threaten to kill those who refuse – and follow through with those threats? Do some agree because the shelter and support of the mission will be withdrawn if they do not cooperate, or because they are in such dire straits that they see it as their only way out? The episode does not answer these questions, but they are worth considering, as is the abuse and exploitation that characterise Mullins and Prator's dehumanising treatment of 'Terry Walton'. Having identified 'Walton' as a potential replacement for Gambit, they manhandle and imprison him, revealing the inhumane treatment that they undoubtedly subject all of their potential charges to. Not caring a jot about that fact that the supposedly alcoholic 'Terry' could die from being forced to go 'cold turkey', Mullins only tells him that, in a few days, they will know whether he will be of use or can go "back on the scrap heap". Previous doppelgangers in the likes of *Man with Two Shadows*, *They Keep Killing Steed*, and *Two's a Crowd* were not portrayed as being so readily abused, but rather as professional agents or other self-interested individuals happy to give up their identities for the sake of their work. *Faces*, in contrast, leaves one with a lingering sense of sadness and horror at the thought of how many men likely met their ends as a result of such harsh treatment, doled out without their consent, their say in the matter reserved until they had 'dried out'. The fact that both Mullins and Terrison/Craig were once homeless themselves adds an interesting wrinkle, demonstrating that even those who would be expected to be the most empathetic to the plight of the homeless are as capable as anyone of treating them as disposable once their fortunes change. The homeless sewer dwellers in *Gnaws* do not receive the same share of the spotlight as their counterparts in *Faces*, but the series' willingness to once again depict a segment of society that is often overlooked and ignored is meaningful in and of itself, as is Steed and Gambit's respectful treatment of them. The homeless men's scenes highlight the grimness of their plight – which includes sourcing drinking water from a sewer outlet – and demonstrate that society only pays attention to them when they become enmired in a significant event, in this case being attacked by the giant rat. The series had featured homeless individuals before, including Hickey in *The Hour That Never Was* and Kermit the Hermit in *The Living Dead*, but their portrayals are less sympathetic. Hickey's lifestyle is one of choice and rife with hypocrisy (he is a conscientious objector who frequents only military dustbins and loves wartime for the plentiful salvage opportunities it provides), while Kermit allows himself to be paid off rather than tell the truth about the ghosts and allow for the rescue of those who have been abducted. *The New Avengers*, in contrast, casts such characters as human beings deserving of respect and vulnerable to being preyed upon.

K is for Kill raises another serious – but very different – issue in the form of the spectre of another world war, a familiar plotline in *The Avengers* and countless other Cold War era series, but muddies the waters with the character of Toy. A Russian friend of Steed's who has no interest in conflict with the West, he attempts to dissuade, then arrest, his warmongering countryman, Colonel Stanislav, who ultimately frames Toy and sends him on the run from his own people. Even so, Toy still attempts to warn Steed of the danger, only to lose his life in the process. Toy and Slanislav therefore offer two opposing philosophies on East-West relations, yet both are willing to sacrifice the preserved soldiers, their own people, for their respective aims – Toy decides that they must be exterminated to maintain world peace, while Stanislav is willing to use them as cannon fodder to incite the world war he so desperately wants. Their conflicting perspectives and goals paint a complicated picture that diverges from the typical Cold War stereotypes. This is evidence of *The New Avengers*' generally nuanced presentation of countries and nationals who are typically framed as the 'enemy'. Just as *K is for Kill* does with Russia, opening episode *The Eagle's Nest* offers two polar opposite visions of Germany: one looking to the past, the other to the future. Trasker and his followers raise the spectre of the evil and horrors perpetrated by Nazis during the Second World War. Trasker whips his troops – all kitted out in their old uniforms – up into a fervor as they scream old rallying cries and plot how to revive their leader and help him achieve world domination, plots that would undoubtedly trigger another world conflict. On the other end of the spectrum is the forward-looking Dr. von Claus, a man who never bought into the horrific ideology that took hold of his homeland, and insists that it should be consigned to the past. A kind, good man who seeks only to help people by developing techniques to freeze the sick and dying and revive them when they can be treated, he singularly refuses to test his methods on a real human being until the monks present him with a subject they insist will die without his assistance. When von Claus learns the true identity of the man who they want him to revive, he refuses to help them on pain of death, only relenting when the monks threaten his wife and daughters. However, he does not go quietly, pushing back forcefully against everything Trasker says, from making scathing comments about his treatment of the island's inhabitants – "Oh, yes, that battle cry has been the excuse for a great deal of bloodshed" – to blithely dismissing Trasker and his followers as nothing more than the "last bastion" of the wartime legions. Despite his principles, von Claus does not value the sanctity of human life at all costs, willing to let his evil patient die for the good of humanity when Steed and Purdey interrupt the revival process. Gerda, the German historical records expert Gambit visits for research assistance, also paints a flattering picture of Germany, not only helping Gambit, but flirting with him, neither holding the other's nationality against the other. Gambit also refers to "our German friends" being as "cooperative and efficient as usual" with his inquiries, pointing to generally cordial relations between the two countries. Taken together, the episode presents a more balanced, nuanced picture of Germany through its people, showing that, while they do not deny the horrors of their past, they are generally forward-looking, embracing former enemies as friends and allies.

More nuanced portraits come in *House of Cards*. While Perov fakes his own death and activates the 'House of Cards' sleeper scheme in a bid to locate and kill Professor Vasil, his replacement, Olga, works against him, standing guard outside Steed's home to prevent an attempt on his life. Unlike Perov, Olga values *détente*, and knows there is more to be gained by keeping Steed alive and maintaining good relations with him than attempting, as Perov does, to achieve victory at all costs. The sleepers that make up the 'House of Cards' are also a diverse bunch, with the likes of David Miller and Dr. Tulliver enjoying their lives in England and not wishing to harm their adopted countrymen. Tulliver only embarks on his mission with reluctance, while Miller attempts to warn his friend, Steed. Others, like Spence, who tries to kill his old friend Gambit; Frederick, who targets his employer's friend, Roland; and Joanna, who plans to kill her lover, Steed, put the motherland before their personal loyalties. Undertaker Cartney has no scruples or loyalties whatsoever, not only aiding Perov in his plot and keeping him hidden from his countrymen, but blithely revealing that he has been conning the customers of his funeral parlour for years, reusing the same coffin rather than sending it through the crematorium. Another Russian character, Chislenko in *Gnaws*, is similarly complex, expressing admiration for Purdey, who he declares "fight[s] good...for a woman", and embracing her after she joins him in a Russian-style toast. Purdey later returns the sentiment, expressing concern for Chislenko when she finds him nursing a bullet wound. Despite this mutual affinity, Chislenko holds fast to his loyalty to his country, confronting Gambit with accusations about Britain bugging the Russian embassy and later lying to both Purdey and Gambit about his intention to call off the search so that he can continue it solo. Chinese characters come in for similar treatment in *The Midas Touch*, with operative 'Hong Kong Harry' on friendly terms with Steed despite repeatedly lying to him, while cultural attaché Sing, in contrast, goes to extreme measures to stop Gambit from asking questions about Turner's location so that he can rescue the kidnapped Purdey. However, after Gambit defeats her bodyguard and delivers an intense monologue about Midas' horrifying ability to kill with a mere touch, Sing gives him the information he seeks. This demonstrates that, despite being fiercely loyal to her country, Gambit's speech affected Sing so much that she chose to follow her conscience and help prevent Purdey's death. That act, coupled with the growing fear and horror that spreads across her face as Gambit speaks, imbues her with a sense of humanity that overcomes her cool, composed, confident demeanour. These depictions are meaningful as they look beyond black/white, good/bad dualities, presenting 'enemy' countries as composed of people with complicated motivations and loyalties who are not wholly against their British counterparts. While the original series also depicted 'friendly enemies', it did not do so with the same frequency, and the likes of *The See-Through Man* and *Two's a Crowd*'s Brodny were played largely for laughs. *The New Avengers* also featured characters of this ilk, most notably the ridiculous Tarnokoff in *The Gladiators*, who fawns over Steed, and unfortunately also featured insulting racial stereotypes (such as Soo Choy in *Trap* and the aforementioned 'Hong Kong' Harry), but, on many occasions, it makes a deliberate attempt to present 'enemy' agents as more than automaton henchmen who indiscriminately hate and destroy.

The danger posed by innovations in science and technology is another recurring original series theme that was carried over to *The New Avengers* and given a harsher, character-driven twist. Research into freezing and reviving people was conducted by the villainous Dr. Kreuzer in the Keel era episode *Dead of Winter*, but *The Eagle's Nest* has a good man, Dr. von Claus, conducting such research in the hopes that it will save those with terminal illnesses. However, his good intentions are quickly twisted by Father Trasker and his fascist colleagues, who kidnap him in order to force him to use his techniques to revive their leader. The prospect of evil people, thought long dead, being revived to continue their reigns of terror has a chilling effect on the optimism and hope originally associated with von Claus' techniques. One wonders if this insight into how his research could be used for evil rather than good made von Claus reconsider whether to continue it. *The Midas Touch* sees Professor

Turner offer an alternative to cold storage, instead managing to keep a terminally ill man alive with drugs. However, this new lease on life comes with deadly consequences, with Turner infecting his subject, 'Midas', with a host of fatal diseases that render him literally untouchable, the slightest contact with his skin resulting in death. However, Midas is not a sympathetic guinea pig – he trusts Turner implicitly and lacks any compunctions about using his powers to kill. One is left lamenting what Turner's work could have achieved if it was used to aid good people suffering and dying from incurable diseases. Instead, it is employed for the selfish end of acquiring the not-so-good professor more gold, while Midas demonstrates that it is not only the morals of the scientist that can have deadly consequences for the world at large, but those of his subject, as well. Felix Kane's actions similarly taint his cybernetic augmentations in *The Last of the Cybernauts...?*. In the real world, such technology is (happily) being used to increase the mobility of people with disabilities. Kane, however, is not satisfied with his new lease on life, and uses the newfound strength of his artificial limbs to seek revenge on the leads, who he blames for his wheelchair-bound existence. Another piece of technology that could potentially benefit the world is Zarcardi's bird-controlling flute. Fellow bird lover Bridlington attempts to develop a similar device in an effort to control the bird population, rather than cull it, but with limited success. If Zarcardi had offered his flute and expertise to Bridlington, together they may have achieved Zarcardi's objective without bloodshed. Instead, like all of his aforementioned fellow villains, Zarcardi uses his skills to cause harm, killing those that would kill his beloved birds.

Other misuses of technological and scientific advances abound, often with a nastier twist than in the original series. *Faces* sees advanced plastic surgery techniques lift homeless people out of poverty, only to strip them of their identity and independence and turn them into intelligence-gathering ciphers, an exploitive twist lacking in *They Keep Killing Steed*. *Sleeper* takes the S-95 gas, invented to peacefully defuse hostage situations by knocking out the hostage-takers, and uses it to paralyse a whole city in order to strip it of its riches, a greater perversion of a development intended to save lives than the misuse of the dentist's drill in *The Hour that Never Was*. *Three Handed Game*'s mind-swapping technology is infinitely more invasive than that in *Who's Who??*, which at least left the victim's mind intact when relocating it to another body. *Three Handed Game*'s technology is quicker and dirtier, harvesting memories from a victim and leaving them at best with huge gaps in knowledge, at worse as empty vessels or hosts to a new consciousness. Unlike the computer-run prison tailormade for Emma Peel in *The House that Jack Built*, *Complex* offers an automated building constructed for good, intended to protect the Canadian intelligence services, but which is revealed to be programmed to work for the other side. *Gnaws* finds research scientists quitting their government jobs so they can reap the financial rewards of their miracle growth formula rather than use it to help countries suffering from famine, then resorting to murder to cover up the havoc their serum wreaks in the sewers. Their actions, unlike those of the scientists controlled by the alien plant in *Man-eater of Surrey Green* (who were not responsible for bringing said plant to Earth), are totally voluntary. While the original series featured many such cautionary tales in which science was used for nefarious purposes, in *The New Avengers* there is a more of a sense that the negative uses of these scientific wonders will lead to research into, and the use of, them being curtailed and shut down, lest they cause more trouble. Steed explicitly channels the show's pessimistic conclusion that science and technology, no matter how well-intentioned, inevitably causes suffering in *The Last of the Cybernauts...?* Musing that a government facility only devises new ways to kill people, the woman giving him a tour of the facility disagrees, proudly informing him that it has recently found a cure for a nasty bacterial infection. "That you devised," Steed infers wryly, to which the woman defeatedly responds, "Well, yes."

An issue incorporated into many of the series' scripts that reflects society's darkest side is that of sexual violence, the threat of which is frequently levelled against Purdey. Other female *Avengers* leads had also faced such threats, particularly Emma Peel, who endured Fitz menacingly unzipping her catsuit in *Dial a Deadly Number*, John Cleverly Cartney attacking her with a whip while she was dressed as the 'Queen of Sin' in *A Touch of Brimstone*, and Paul Beresford making stomach-churning comments about what he planned to do to her while she was under his control in *Return of the Cybernauts*. However, such instances were scattered infrequently across the series. Purdey, in contrast, is threatened with sexual violence on more occasions despite *The New Avengers*' much shorter run. While these scenes are unpalatable and uncomfortable to watch, the fact that *The New Avengers* acknowledges that female spies would, sadly, face additional threats in the field that their male counterparts would not is evidence of the series' willingness to enter the uncomfortable territory that comes with its more realistic world. The series made this willingness clear from the very first episode, *The Eagle's Nest*, in which Main employs a 'stun' fishhook to knock Purdey out, rather than one that would kill her, because he "fancied other things". *The Midas Touch* finds her doubly threatened: first by Midas, who asks Turner to "give" her to him; then by her guard, Froggart, who, forbidden from touching her, circles her with a lascivious gaze while she is bound to a chair, and, in one skin-crawling scene, runs his fingers along the ropes covering her breasts. The super-soldier trainees in *The Gladiators*, meanwhile, muse about using her for "pleasurable" purposes.

It should be noted, however, that when Purdey is threatened, she is never cast as a helpless victim. Instead, such scenes provide her with the opportunity to show her mettle as an agent, able to keep a level head and devise a variety of methods to defeat or foil her assailants, often singlehandedly. She baffles Main by saying she "fancies" a *steak au poivre*, turning his lascivious comment into something innocent, and later swiftly dispatches him in combat. She insults, then flirts with, Froggart to distract him and give Gambit an opening to knock him out. She defeats Midas with a few high kicks, and levels several of the 'gladiators' in a quick brawl. She is equally capable when propositioned by fellow agent George Myers, who places his hand on her bare thigh (*Target!*); head of D16 Cromwell, who runs his hand along her shoulders and neck, leans in for a kiss, and asks her out for dinner, then pronounces that they are in a "relationship" before they have even sat down at the table (*To Catch a Rat*); soldiers of the 19th Special Commando, one of whom rests his hand on her leg (*Dirtier by the Dozen*); and Packer, one of her kidnappers, who has a penchant for calling her "sweetheart" (*Hostage*). Purdey deals with these situations with the same equanimity and deftness of touch that she does the threats, lightly plucking Myers' hand from her leg; deflecting Cromwell's attentions by telling him to put on his newly-mended trousers, teasing him about claiming to be "just passing by" when he arrives at her flat to ask her for dinner, crisply questioning what "relationship" he presumes that they have, and subduing him before the kiss can take place; plucking the soldier's hand from her leg with a quip that parries his "You like a touch of danger" comment with the brilliant rejoinder, "The danger, not the touch"; and defying Packer by tartly replying "I'm not your sweetheart" and throwing a cup of water in his face.

Cutting even closer to the bone than any of the sexualised threats and advances Purdey endures are the infinitely more personal events of *Obsession*. While earlier seasons of the show had depicted abusive relationships, they involved the guest cast rather than the leads, and were used to emphasise just how nasty the villains were. In *Obsession*, however, this issue comes to the fore through an exploration of Purdey's relationship with ex-fiancé Larry Doomer. Scenes throughout the episode reveal Larry's inability to let Purdey go seven years after their breakup and his tendency to relate to her with possessive and controlling behaviour. In the course of the story, he rests domineering hands on her shoulders, attempts to force her to kiss him, asks Purdey if she "belong[s] to someone", claims to own her ("She's mine. She belongs to me."), and, at the episode's climax, uses emotional blackmail to stop her from killing him, before attempting to shoot her himself. However, none of these scenes possesses the shock value of a moment in the 1970 flashback sequence. Having stopped Larry from murdering the man he holds responsible for his father's death, Purdey attempts to comfort him, only for Larry to slap her face in response. It is a stunning moment. While Cathy, Emma, Tara, and Purdey herself are regularly attacked by male opponents, the blows those opponents land are intended to stop the women from interfering with their plans, differ little from the attacks they level at their male colleagues (barring any erroneous assumptions made about the 'weakness' of their sex), and are not struck in the context of a personal relationship. Larry's slap, in contrast, is very personal indeed, perpetrated against Purdey by an intimate partner. In a series that had done so much to depict its female characters as strong, capable, and easily able to physically best a man, the sight of an *Avengers* woman being attacked and victimised by someone she loves and trusts is shocking and unexpected to say the least. Adding to the shock value are Purdey's conflicted feelings about Larry. Though she chose to end their relationship, she still expresses concern for Larry's well-being during his missile run and when he drops his glass at the party, and is unable to bring herself to kill him in order to stop the destruction of the Houses of Parliament.

Depicting an *Avengers* woman as being emotionally vulnerable and having been victimised would seem to undermine all of the work the series had done to depict its female leads as strong and capable, but to view it in that way is to misconstruc the new, more realistic direction in which the series was pushing its characters. Purdey's struggles with Larry do not make her weak, but a complicated, multi-faceted human being. Throughout the series, she demonstrates time and again that she is strong, intelligent, and capable of repelling opponents both verbally and physically. Her decision to cut off all contact with Larry after the slap, rather than entertain any apology he might have offered for his abuse, is further evidence of her strength, demonstrating that she will not allow anyone, even someone she loves, to mistreat her. At the same time, her conflicted feelings about Larry are in keeping with the reality that even strong, capable people have flaws and vulnerabilities. To put it simply, even the strongest people are *human*. Rather than paint Purdey as a flawless superhero incapable of making mistakes and who remains coolly objective in the face of any situation, *Obsession* offers us an *Avengers* woman for a new Avengerland, one whose past has left its mark and who cannot forget her feelings for Larry despite knowing that she does not want to – and should not – be with him. Purdey's conflicted emotions are not only humanising, but realistic, conveying an inner turmoil experienced by countless abused women (and men), for whom the understanding that their partner's treatment of them is unacceptable is tangled up with feelings of love and affection. In acknowledging Purdey's flawed humanity, the story also shows that capable people at times need help from others, with Purdey's inability to deal with Larry requiring Gambit and Steed to step in to stop him. This should not be perceived as undermining Purdey's character. She saves both of her colleagues on several occasions throughout the series, and Gambit and Steed are not framed as 'weak' for requiring her assistance; there is no reason that Purdey's need for help in dealing with Larry should be framed any differently. The episode's depiction of a complex, multi-faceted female lead is significant in itself, but its decision to use her to shine a light on the uncomfortable issue of domestic violence is an exceptionally brave one for an adventure series, arguably *The New Avengers'* bravest from a realism and social commentary standpoint.

Obsession is one of many plots with a personal dimension in *The New Avengers*. Of course, *The Avengers* also featured personal stories, most notably its debut episode *Hot Snow*, which found Dr. David Keel entering the world of crime-fighting to avenge the murder of his fiancée, Peggy. This was followed by the likes of *Six Hands Across a Table*, which found Cathy Gale romantically entangled with Oliver Waldner, who is revealed to be at the heart of Steed's investigation; *Don't Look Behind You* and *The Joker*, revenge tales centred around men who believe they have been personally wronged by Cathy and Emma Peel, respectively; *The House that Jack Built*, in which Emma is trapped in a mechanised house programmed by a disgruntled former employee; *Murdersville*, in which Emma suffers, and then avenges, the death of her childhood friend, Paul Beresford; *Get-a-Way*, which finds Steed trying to protect his old friends from being killed by escaped prisoners; and *Who Was That Man I Saw You With?*, in which Tara King is forced to go on the run when her loyalty is called into question. However, such plots were generally exceptions to the rule. *The New Avengers*, in contrast, disproportionately weaves a personal dimension into its stories. Felix Kane in *The Last of the Cybernauts...?* is driven to kill the triumvirate because their pursuit of him led to a car accident that left him disfigured and wheelchair-bound. In *Trap*, Soo Choy's convoluted plot is conjured up in order to save face after the trio's interference in his drug deal damages his reputation amongst his fellow crime lords. *Dead Men are Dangerous* revolves around Steed's childhood friend Mark Crayford's quest for revenge after a lifetime of being 'second best' to Steed. *The Lion and the Unicorn* turns on the Unicorn's longstanding rivalry with Steed, as Steed's attempt to get the best of him leads to a plethora of unanticipated complications when the Unicorn is accidentally killed by his own people. Spelman's plan to undermine the Ministry in *Hostage* hinges on framing Steed as a traitor, exploiting his affection for Purdey, and turning Gambit against him. Even those stories that do not place the leads at the centre of the action often have some personal dimension. In *House of Cards*, Steed discovers that both girlfriend Joanna and old friend David are sleeper agents, while Gambit has a similar shock when his old friend and karate teacher Spence attempts to kill him in cold blood. The *Midas Touch*, *Faces*, and *Sleeper* all find Steed losing old friends. *Obsession* deals with the fallout of Purdey's broken engagement. Gambit is motivated to bring down Colonel 'Mad Jack' Miller to avenge the murder of his friend Travis in *Dirtier by the Dozen*, and faces an old enemy, O'Hara, in *The Gladiators*. Purdey, meanwhile, suffers the losses of many potential paramours, including Stannard (*The Eagle's Nest*), George Myers (*Target!*),

Marty Brine (*Trap*), and Larry (to brain-draining in *Three Handed Game*) and is betrayed by others, such as Cromwell (*To Catch a Rat*). Though the series may sweep the emotional fallout of these events under the rug in subsequent episodes, the fact that the leads are shown as being affected by said events lends the stories, characters, and wider universe gravitas, painting 'New Avengerland' as a place of lasting consequences.

Characterisation

In keeping with Brian Clemens' 'thicker cardboard' dictate, characterisation was prioritised in *The New Avengers* more than in any other era of the show, and, consequently, became its greatest asset, offering interactions that entertained and delighted, even when the plot did not. While this attention to character benefited all players, as evidenced from the more nuanced portrayals of guest stars that allowed for the conveyance of certain themes and examination of social issues, the leads received the most attention in the character stakes, a decision that bore fruit on multiple levels. Not only did the fleshing out of the leads up the stakes in the many plotlines that had personal relevance for one member of the trio, and further ground 'New Avengerland' by depicting it as a place populated by multi-faceted individuals, but it also allowed the audience to become more intimately acquainted with the avenging triumvirate and connect with them on a personal level.

One important tool used to establish the series' multi-faceted characters is continuity, which demonstrates that the leads' memories stretch back further than the beginning of each fifty-minute instalment, and therefore imbues the trio and their relationships with substance and intimacy in the form of old in-jokes and familiar dynamics. Examples of this character-based continuity abound. Gambit makes recurring wry observations about Steed's way of operating, calling him "ruthless" and "a master of the double play" (*Three Handed Game*, *Hostage*), and stating that he trusts him in "everything but cards" (*The Tale of the Big Why*).

The Midas Touch connects to *K is for Kill: The Tiger Awakes* via Purdey and Gambit's mirror exchanges – "We wanted him alive." "Difficult decision: Him or you?/Conflict of interest: I wanted you alive." – which occur after one has killed someone to save the other. Gambit's knowing delivery of his line in *K is for Kill: The Tiger Awakes*, and Purdey's equally knowing smile in response, suggests that both remember the previous exchange. The duo also tip each other out of bed (in *The Eagle's Nest* and *The Last of the Cybernauts...?*) and have a penchant for referencing old movies, discussing *The Treasure of the Sierra Madre* in *The Midas Touch*, while Purdey quotes, "Play it again, Sam" in *Cat Amongst the Pigeons* and cliched Western dialogue about "head[ing] 'em off at the pass" in *Trap*. Most notable is the "Mike Gambit, one of these days."/"I know. I'm looking forward to it." exchange, which the pair reiterate with such frequency that Gambit comments on it in *House of Cards* – "You keep saying that." – and, as 'Terry Walton', is instructed to learn it as part of his training to replace the 'real' Gambit. The fact that this exchange is not only recurring, but known to characters other than Purdey and Gambit, reinforces the sense that this version of Avengerland is vested with a living memory that survives from episode to episode.

Continuity also applied to the leads' biographies, parts of which were not simply introduced to meet the demands of the plot and then forgotten, but often referenced on more than one occasion. These repeated references contribute to the 'thicker cardboard' nature of the characters, transforming them from ciphers who shapeshift at the whims of the writers into three-dimensional characters with backstories that have implications for their daily lives and actions. The most frequently referenced biographical tidbit is Purdey's previous career as a ballerina with the Royal Ballet, to which she attributes her unique, high-kicking method of combat in *The Eagle's Nest*. While this reference to Purdey's previous career could have been a one-off, the series instead repeatedly reminds us of her time as a ballerina. Some of these references, such as the presence of a barre in her flat at which she is shown doing ballet-influenced workouts or performing a few casual plies (*The Last of the Cybernauts...?*, *Faces*), add nothing to the plot, but simply serve to reinforce Purdey's love of dance and the continuing role it plays in her daily life. *Obsession*, in contrast, takes us from the present to the past, providing a flashback to Purdey's time as a dancer in which she is shown readying herself for a performance in full ballerina regalia. This sense of history is reinforced by other characters' references to Purdey's dancer past. Larry Doomer, upon seeing Purdey for the first time in seven years, asks if she is doing a show in the area, to which Purdey replies, "I don't dance anymore, Larry." In *Medium Rare*, Purdey tells Victoria Stanton that, "Steed doesn't like the ballet", prompting Steed to quip, "Only ballerinas." Further augmenting her dancer credentials are revelations that her repertoire extends beyond ballet to tap (*Three Handed Game*) and disco (*Trap*). Emma Peel was a businesswoman and Cathy Gale an anthropologist, but neither of their professions garnered such frequent references in their episodes.

Character continuity is used to flesh out Gambit's biography and character, as well. He obliquely references his time in the Navy in *Dirtier by the Dozen*, quipping, "I know all the nice girls love a sailor", before telling Penny Redfern he joined when he was fourteen in *Dead Men are Dangerous*. His extensive karate training is also repeatedly mentioned, rather than simply implied by his fight scenes. Spence in *House of Cards* claims he taught Gambit everything he knows, but Gambit replies that he's learned a few things since. Some of that new knowledge presumably came from his current karate master, who he quotes in *K is for Kill: The Tiger Awakes* while pondering whether to use the art form to attempt to crack a tree trunk. After pulling off said trick, he grumbles that he must have a word with his karate master while rubbing his aching knee. Other episodes find him in the Ministry's dojo. He beats Spelman in a practice bout in *Hostage*, takes on Spence in a friendly fight that quickly turns deadly in *House of Cards*, and instructs Purdey in karate in *Dead Men are Dangerous*, a scene that reveals him to be an expert in his own right. Gambit's love life is also a recurring theme, with potential paramours appearing in *The Eagle's Nest*, *Three Handed Game*, *Dead Men are Dangerous*, *Angels of Death*, *Trap*, and *K is for Kill*, and more implied through references to his little black book of women's telephone numbers. First mentioned by 'Terry Walton' in *Faces*, Gambit brings the book up again in *Sleeper*, much to Purdey's surprise, a neat moment of continuity that suggests that she believed the original reference was a fictionalised detail invented by the equally fictitious 'Walton'. Elsewhere, Gambit's preference to sleep without wearing pyjamas is first mentioned in *The Last of the Cybernauts...?* and reaffirmed in *Sleeper*, while his revelation in *The Midas Touch* that he took up motor racing – "Le Mans. Spa. Monza. Daytona. I crashed at them all." – also pays dividends, not only explaining his fast, expert driving earlier in the same episode, as well as the likes of *The Eagle's Nest*, but also his propensity for crashing, as exemplified by *The Lion and the Unicorn* and *The Gladiators*.

While Purdey and Gambit's character continuity creates connections between *The New Avengers*' 26 episodes, Steed's character continuity further strengthens the ties between the new series and its predecessor. Call-backs to Steed's original series past include two appearances by the Bentley he drove while working with Emma Peel (in *Dead Men are Dangerous* and *K is for Kill: The Tiger Awakes*) and reaffirmations of his trademark dislike of guns – "I abhor violence, and loud gunshots make me blink." (*The Eagle's Nest*); "I don't even have a gun, except for an old Colt 45, and that's just for sentimental reasons." (*Medium Rare*). The series also re-establishes Steed's love of horses and expert horsemanship, showing him riding with Gambit (*Target!*), grooming the animals (*Medium Rare*, *To Catch a Rat*), gifting one to Laura (*The Last of the Cybernauts...?*), and looking on as Joanna tends to another (*House of Cards*). Other episodes reaffirm his love of clay pigeon shooting (in *Faces*, harkening back to a scene in *Quick Quick Slow Death*), his penchant for indoor golf (in *Angels of Death*, as first seen in *The Murder Market*), and his preference for historical and military inspired décor. All of his signature character traits are also present and correct, including his love of champagne; his preferred wardrobe of tailored suits, Chelsea boots, bowlers, and umbrellas; his genteel demeanour and underlying ruthless, devious streak; and his legendary status as a master spy who has won the respect of members of the opposition, with the likes of Ambassador Brodny (*Two's a Crowd*, *The See-Through Man*) now joined by attaché Tarnokoff (*The Gladiators*) and master spy the Unicorn (*The Lion and the Unicorn*) in his long list of admirers.

At the same time, *The New Avengers* was not slavish in its depiction of its leading man. Instead, it developed its own internal continuity for Steed, now in his fifties and with many years of experience – in both life and espionage – behind him, and used it to convey to the audience how the character they knew and loved had grown and changed with the passing of the years. The most notable example of this internal continuity is the increased focus on Steed's private life. While the original series featured an occasional friend or acquaintance, *The New Avengers* introduces a number of Steed's friends, some of whom he has known since his youth. These characters not only provide a window into Steed's pre-*Avengers* life, but reveal his emotional, at times melancholy, side as he grieves their untimely demises, which pepper the series with such frequency that some fans have mocked them as a tired, overused trope. It is true that the list of Steed's dearly departed chums makes for grim and/or ridiculous reading, depending on one's perspective. Over the course of the series, he loses the likes of Mark Crayford (*Dead Men are Dangerous*), Mark Clifford (*Faces*), Hardy (*Sleeper*), Freddy (*The Midas Touch*), Toy (*K is for Kill: Tiger by the Tail*), Manderson (*Angels of Death*), David Miller (*House of Cards*), and Derek Wigmore and Freddy Mason (*Medium Rare*), amongst others. While one could dismiss the frequency of these deaths as a product of the writers' creative well running dry, they can also be viewed as evidence of the grim reality of Steed's line of work. In a nice continuity moment, Purdey notices that a morbid pattern has emerged, acknowledging Steed's repeated losses in *Angels of Death* by asking why, rather than taking bereavement leave, he insists that "the show must go on". Steed simply replies that it must, a response that Purdey finds unfathomable, but which demonstrates the extent to which Steed has become inured to the tragic realities of the job, understanding that, while the chances of him surviving as long as he has in the business are extremely slim, the odds of him not losing any comrades over the course of his long career are even slimmer. From this perspective, the frequency with which Steed endures losses can be seen as realistic – the longer someone lives and works in an area, the more people they will come to know and form attachments to, and the more likely it will be that some of those people will pass away, particularly if their work is high-risk. Rather than a sign of creative deficiency, Steed's loss of those close to him is part of the series' acknowledgement of the harsh realities of his chosen profession, as well as life in general, which is in keeping with this harsher take on Avengerland.

Further evidence that Steed's repeated losses were a conscious creative choice, rather than the result of a dearth of creative inspiration, is the fact that Purdey and Gambit experience similar losses, albeit with less frequency. Having lost her father ten years earlier, Purdey also loses her ex-fiancé Larry Doomer, as well as colleagues and prospective love interests such as CIA agent Marty Brine (*Trap*), George Stannard (*The Eagle's Nest*), George Myers (*Target!*), and Larry (*Three Handed Game*), and is inconsolable when she believes Gambit (*Faces*) and Steed (*K is for Kill: The Tiger Awakes*) have been killed. Gambit, meanwhile, contends with the betrayal and loss of karate teacher Spence (*House of Cards*) and colleague Bradshaw (*Target!*), as well as the death of fellow agents and friends Travis (*Dirtier by the Dozen*) and Harlow (*Gnaws*), whose deaths he feels deeply and works hard to avenge. While the series does not spend the whole of its runtime dwelling on the themes of grief and loss, its willingness to convey the emotional toll the job takes on the leads further enriches their characterisation and contributes to New Avengerland's consequentialist bent.

The series also deepened the characterisation of its leads through the dressing of their homes. While the original series gifted the leads with a series of stylish flats, those abodes were often more decorative than functional, with key rooms never shown onscreen. Cathy Gale's abodes had some interesting features, such as sliding metal doors and a surveillance system to enable her to identify visitors, but her bedroom and kitchen were rarely shown, and one incarnation lacked the adornment and extensive library one would expect of the home of an intelligent, educated woman who had lived overseas and studied anthropology. Emma Peel's first flat benefits from Harry Pottle's inspired set design, with the modern circular fireplace in the centre of the room adding visual flair and creating a focal point for the space. However, there is again very little adornment, save for a few porcelain figures that fail to reflect Emma's fascinating array of interests, while her kitchen is rarely featured and her bedroom is only glimpsed through the open doorway. Her colour flat is much the same, with both its pre- and post-renovation incarnations sparsely adorned and consisting of a living area and little else. Items of interest, such as a chemistry set and a large work-in-progress ceramic sculpture, occasionally fill the space, but are transitory. Tara's home is a welcome break from the sparseness, chock full of knickknacks that include ceramic wig mannequins, a collection of telephones, and eclectic wall art, but again the whole space is a lounge/living area equipped with one small dining table, with the bedroom, bathroom, and, presumably, kitchen all located beyond a door that we never see behind. Steed fares the best, with his Peel and King era abodes particularly well thought out, featuring art, books, antique furniture, and quirky touches – such as a tuba containing flowers – that reflect its occupant's traditional aesthetic and eccentricities, as well as a kitchen that sees regular use, all of which allow them to feel like homes rather than sets.

The New Avengers built on this 'lived in' quality in constructing its leads' homes, creating spaces that reflected people with lives beyond their careers and the story of the week, and thereby bolstering the 'thicker cardboard' characterisation of the occupants. While original series characters' bedrooms were mostly left to the imagination, the series shows us Gambit's green-themed guest room, furnished with art, a phone, and a side table, as well as the retractable bed in the living area that he prefers to sleep on – and actually shows him sleeping on it. When the bed has reverted to a couch, the set dresser's attention to detail is such that the pillow Gambit sleeps on remains tucked in one corner of the couch's seat. That attention to detail extends to the kitchen, which comes complete with dishes in the drying rack and bottles and glasses crowded on one corner of the countertop, while the large 70s smoked glass dining table is seen with books and other items arranged on it, suggesting actual use. A full bookshelf, drafting board, stereo with a host of records (some of which Gambit takes out to play in *The Tale of the Big Why*), and a weapons collection add to the personalisation of the space, suggesting a three-dimensional person with an interest in music, reading, collecting, and drawing. The inclusion of Op-art prints, a large silver Buddha head, a plant, and a large white statue, meanwhile, establish his eclectic taste and aesthetic and allow the space to avoid the depersonalising lack of adornment that marked previous principals' abodes. Even after Gambit's flat is redecorated in the second season, the set dressing retains elements of the previous incarnation, such as a large piece of Op-art, a realistic touch that reflects the fact that people rarely shed all of their belongings when redecorating.

Purdey's flat is also generously dressed with an array of adornments, from beaded curtains used to divide the open space into a kitchen, living area, and bedroom, to plants, fringed hanging lamps, stuffed animals, an open cabinet containing a bust and various knickknacks, and a piano. Small touches make the space feel lived in, such as magazines scattered across the coffee table, books on the nightstand, and stacks of records by the record player. Adding to the lived-in quality of the space is Purdey's engagement with it: using her ballet barre for workouts, sleeping in her bed, looking in the mirror, playing a game of Scrabble on the coffee table, and sweeping aside the beaded curtains as she moves from room to room. The epitome of that engagement comes in *Medium Rare*, in which Purdey is shown redecorating her flat, with later episodes depicting the finished product in another of the series' wealth of continuity touches.

Steed's country seat also adds to the continuity stakes, with the military-themed paintings, *objets d'art*, and antiques scattered about the space calling to mind the décor of his previous flats. The large leather couch and chair that dominate the living area are reminiscent of similar furniture in his Stable Mews flat, and a drum repurposed as a side table calls to mind the flower-filled tuba in its quirkiness. The country house's sizeable library is also familiar, reminiscent of Stable Mews' full bookshelves. Being a more expansive residence than those inhabited by Purdey and Gambit, we only see a small section of it, namely the living and dining area, the entryway, and a small staircase that presumably leads to living quarters, but all of it is used rather than being merely for show, with characters coming and going through the front door, Steed popping upstairs, and the trio working out their next move at the dining table, in the living room, or on the staircase. Steed's grounds also see use, rather than serving as nothing more than a backdrop, with characters riding horses or playing cricket on the grass.

Having established its deeper characterisation through everything from the leads' flats to continuity strands, the series then used it as a lens through which to examine certain social issues. One of the most notable uses of this lens by the series was to break new ground on the issue of class. While working-class incidental characters featured in the original series, particularly in the first three seasons, the leads were primarily middle- or upper-class. As the concept of Avengerland was further refined, a rule was implemented to remove working-class characters from the mix. With the dawn of the less-fantastical 70s, the series' creatives clearly believed that the exclusion of working-class characters from

The New Avengers' ranks would not be realistic or acceptable. The decision to make one of the series' three leads, Gambit, working class was therefore a revolutionary one, and signposted the new direction in which the series' creatives were taking Avengerland. However, Gambit's admittance into what was still a relatively rarefied world of powerful or upper-class individuals did not come without comment or compromise. While Gambit is not shy about his working-class roots, mentioning the small yard in which he played as a child (*Dead Men are Dangerous*), that he never went to prep school (*The Eagle's Nest*), and his time in the Navy (*Dead Men are Dangerous*), he has adopted certain upper-class characteristics, particularly in speech and dress. The former is a product of actor Gareth Hunt's drama school training, which smoothed away his self-described original cockney accent. Gambit may not share his portrayer's training, but the fact that he does not speak with a working-class accent suggests that he made a conscious choice to adjust his way of speaking in order to blend into his new surroundings. The same logic applied when choosing his wardrobe, with Gambit opting for tailored suits rather than the more casual jeans and bomber jackets that Hunt himself would have preferred to wear. Brian Clemens explained that Gambit would have to frequent the corridors of power as part of his work, and his wardrobe was specifically chosen to allow him to blend in amongst government ministers and civil servants. Though one can follow Clemens' logic, it essentially requires Gambit to adapt to his new, elevated environment rather than the other way around, his admittance to the rarefied echelons of Avengerland society conditional on him sacrificing some of his identity. Furthermore, even after making such sacrifices, Gambit's presence is sometimes merely tolerated, with some individuals not even bothering to conceal their scorn at having to speak to someone they deem to be beneath them, such as the huffy Brown-Fitch in *The Eagle's Nest*. Such snobbery exists even within the trio itself, with Steed needling Gambit in *Faces* about his 'unsuitable' choice of shotgun, before 'forgiving' him by saying "you can't help your background." Gambit reacts to the slight by shooting Steed's clay pigeon out of the sky and telling his boss that he will not let him get away with everything, a retort Steed takes with good grace, but the very fact that he makes the remark at all indicates that there is a certain amount of snobbery at work even amongst those who hold Gambit in high esteem. Purdey, in contrast, seems to have a complete lack of consciousness of the difference in status between Gambit and herself, despite her upper-middle-class stylings. Off-handed comments, such as, "You were weaned from prep school too early", demonstrate that she has never turned her mind to the probability that Gambit never attended a private school, and yet his reply that he did not fails to raise any sort of reaction from her. Indeed, though Purdey and Gambit make a habit of debating just about every topic under the sun, they never discuss class, though there is no sense that either of them intentionally avoids the topic. It simply does not seem to enter Purdey's mind at all. Even when she attempts to out-do him in their latest debate, her superiority is always based on having the better (or more bizarre) argument, not her inherent status as a social 'better'. For her, class is a non-issue, one that she does not consider or factor into her interactions with others. It is her refreshing perspective that points the way forward for 'New Avengerland'.

Another issue the series tackled through its characters was sex. While the original series was rife with sexual overtones, from Cathy Gale and Emma Peel's leather catsuits to Steed's flirtatious banter with his female partners, it generally steered clear of romantic entanglements when it came to its leads. Though it was implied that Steed bedded some of the women he flirted with, Cathy began a serious romance with Oliver in *Six Hands Across a Table*, and Tara flirted with temporary partner Baron von Kurt in *They Keep Killing Steed*, the series generally thrived on ambiguity, innuendo, and meaningful glances, fading to black or cutting away without confirming or denying that anything had happened or would occur. This coyness persisted even as the 60s began to swing, bringing increased sexual liberation. While the creatives' vision of a fantasy Avengerland dictated that explicit sex, blood, and violence be left offscreen, there was also a measure of prurience at work. While Cathy Gale and Emma Peel were depicted as strong, capable, intelligent, independent women, the series' creatives still felt it necessary to make them both widows (or, in Emma's case, a presumed widow) in order to make their spending time with Steed while unchaperoned socially acceptable. The thinking behind this decision was that, as married women, Emma and Cathy would 'know what it was all about', i.e., they had acquired sexual knowledge through the respectable institution of marriage, and therefore could spend time alone with Steed without having to worry about keeping their virtue intact. Similar reasoning undoubtedly dictated the show's treatment of earlier *Avengers* women, Carol Wilson and Venus Smith, both of whom were unmarried. The relationship between Steed and Venus was characterised as fraternal by producer Leonard White, while Carol was kept at arm's length by David Keel, who was still grieving his fiancée, and the need for Steed to keep the true nature of his work from her limited the intimacy of their interactions to the odd dinner. It was only with *The Avengers*' final female lead, Tara King, that the show broke with tradition, allowing her to engage in an 'are they?/aren't they?' flirtation with Steed without the benefit of a deceased husband to lend a veneer of respectability. However, Tara was granted full sexual licence, not at the instigation of the series' creatives, but that of Tara portrayer Linda Thorson who, in crafting her character, rejected the creatives' proposal that she be another 'Mrs.' Thorson's reasoning was that it was much more respectable for Tara to be spending time with Steed if she were unattached than if she had a husband: "They suggested it might seem indecent for a single girl to be shown in his flat and perhaps having stayed overnight. I thought it was highly indecent for a married woman to be staying with him. So I persuaded them that it was much better for Tara to be single." [4] It seems unlikely that the creatives intended for Tara to have a living husband, and instead meant for her to be yet another widow, but whether 'Mr. King' was alive or dead, the implications were the same: Tara could only be sexually active after a 'legitimate' relationship with a man.

Amazingly, Thorson got her way and Tara became 'Miss' King, but the fact that this otherwise progressive series waited until its third main female lead to break this taboo demonstrates how deeply rooted conservative beliefs surrounding women and sex truly were. This was further attested to by the fact that, despite her singleton status, Tara was not depicted as seriously romancing men, while her relationship with Steed followed the template set by her predecessors, with plentiful suggestive scenes and innuendo, but no concrete indication that anything actually occurred between them.

By the time *The New Avengers* came on the scene, however, social mores had shifted, and the tide of opinion regarding the depiction of sex, particularly in relation to women, had well and truly turned. To this end, Purdey topped Tara King by being an unmarried woman who worked closely and unchaperoned with not one man, but two, while also enjoying the romantic attentions of many other men, typically fellow agents, some of whom she agreed to dinner dates with (Spence in *House of Cards*; George Myers in *Target!*), flirted with (Larry and Masgard in *Three Handed Game*), was shown having dinner with (Cromwell in *To Catch a Rat*), or it was implied she had gone out with in the past (Spelman in *Hostage*; Stannard in *The Eagle's Nest*). Most notably, *Obsession* establishes that Purdey was sharing a bed with Larry Doomer during their engagement, thus providing onscreen confirmation that she was engaging in pre-marital sex. The matter-of-fact framing of this scene, with Larry's absence rather than earlier presence in her bed serving as the source of the drama, demonstrates that the series' creatives no longer found the idea of Purdey being sexually active problematic, or even particularly notable, a massive shift from the conservative attitudes at work less than a decade earlier.

Like Purdey, Steed and Gambit's sex lives were also opened up to the audience. While the 1960 saw something of a double standard at work, with male leads allowed to romance women with abandon while their female counterparts could only do so if they were widows, *The Avengers* did employ a measure of subtlety in the depiction of its male leads' romances. *The New Avengers* shakes things up by presenting onscreen evidence of Steed's love life, showing him entertaining a series of girlfriends with whom he goes riding (Joanna in *House of Cards*; Laura in *The Last of the Cybernauts...?*), has dinner (Suzy in *Hostage*; an unnamed woman in *The Midas Touch*), kisses (Laura in *The Last of the Cybernauts...?*; Miranda in *Trap*), and invites to parties (Tricia and Laura in *The Last of the Cybernauts...?*). While Steed was always depicted as, in Macnee's words, "a wolf with the women", his romances were generally left to the imagination. *The New Avengers* removed that mystery by providing onscreen evidence of its perennial leading man's sex life, a creative choice in keeping with a 'New Avengerland' that was less interested in playing coy than in depicting a realistic state of affairs. Gambit's sex life is similarly out in the open. While the original series would have probably used flirtations and references to his little black book to get the point across, he is instead allowed to make dinner plans (with Gerda in *The Eagle's Nest*, Dr. Leparge in *K is for Kill*, and Penny in *Dead Men are Dangerous*), kiss love interests (Penny in *Dead Men are Dangerous*; Jane in *Angels of Death*; Purdey in *Sleeper*), and have women in his flat (Penny in *Dead Men are Dangerous*; an unnamed girlfriend in *Trap*). It is also implied that he spends the night with Dr. Leparge of *K is for Kill*, while both Purdey and he acknowledge his proclivity for getting "carried away" with attractive women in the course of his work (*House of Cards*), and he himself admits to taking his "undercover" work with the (so-called) Russian countess "literally" (*To Catch a Rat*).

There was more flesh on display to go with this increased focus on sex. The original series occasionally called on the female leads to show skin, with Emma Peel donning a series of skimpy costumes in the black and white episodes, including her Queen of Sin ensemble (*A Touch of Brimstone*), harem girl outfit (*Honey for the Prince*), and see-through bodystocking featuring strategically-placed feathers (*The Girl from Auntie*), before there was a noticeable move away from such provocative outfits in the colour stories. This wardrobe philosophy was maintained for Tara King, who appeared in a short robe in *The Forget-Me-Knot* and a series of minidresses, which, while revealing, were still much more modest than Emma's most risqué costumes. Elsewhere, Steed went shirtless in *Dragonsfield* and *Immortal Clay*, stripped down to his undergarments in *Mr. Teddy Bear*, and donned swimwear in *The Removal Men* and *Castle De'Ath*, while Cathy appeared in her underwear in *Death Dispatch* and *Man with Two Shadows*, and Emma's bra was shown while she was changing in *The Joker*. All in all, however, skin was shown by the leads relatively infrequently across the original 161 episodes, whereas *The New Avengers* packed in almost as many examples in a mere 26. Gambit poses nude for Helen McKay in *Three Handed Game*, and also appears shirtless in *Dead Men are Dangerous* and *The Last of the Cybernauts…?*, while Purdey is shown in her underthings in *House of Cards*, *Target!*, and (partially) *Faces*, not counting the flashing of her stocking tops in the likes of *To Catch a Rat*, *Target!*, *Cat Amongst the Pigeons*, and *Three Handed Game*. Both Lumley and Hunt disliked these sexualised scenes, with Lumley in particular rallying against the push to make her character 'sexy', but the fact that this proved to be an issue at all is evidence of the show's sexual boldness compared to its predecessor. Notably, while Steed showed skin considerably less often than his female co-stars, Gambit appears shirtless as often as Purdey is shown in her underwear. Though Purdey easily 'wins' in the sexualization stakes if her stocking shots are added to the tally, *The New Avengers* at least distributed its sexualising scenes more evenly between the sexes than its predecessor.

This fundamental equality in the sexualising stakes may come as something of a surprise, but is evidence that *The New Avengers* subverted sex and gender norms just as frequently as its predecessor, albeit more subtly. The original series had broken ground with its upending of male/female dynamics, with Steed dressed and acting as the debonair, genteel English gentleman, while his female partners were clad in leather or other action wear and took on the lion's share of the physical combat. Cathy Gale's leather gear quickly became iconic for its sexual overtones, but also, more importantly, for imbuing the character with a sense of toughness and formidability that was typically associated with men. That aggressive look, combined with Cathy's strong personality – an intelligent, forceful woman who knew her own mind and was unafraid to make her opinions known – was necessary to break new ground and prove to the audience that a woman could be every bit as physically and intellectually capable and uncompromising as a man. Cathy's show of strength and intelligence set a precedent that allowed Emma Peel to reclaim her femininity in both dress – phasing out Cathy's leather look in favour of miniskirts and colourful 'Emmapeelers' – and personality – incorporating more flirtatiousness and humour and dropping Cathy's forceful moral arguments with Steed – while still being taken seriously as a brainy action woman. Tara King was allowed to be even more traditionally feminine, played as young, inexperienced, and often dependent on Steed for assistance, and occasionally donning even more feminine fashions, such as silk and velvet minidresses.

However, even Tara was not as outwardly feminine as Purdey. While Tara had donned tomboyish outfits consisting of culottes, western-style shirts, and colourful vests paired with trousers, all paired with low-heeled boots, Purdey was marketed as an ultra-feminine, 'stockings and suspenders' girl. Brian Clemens himself described the character as bringing the concept of the *Avengers* woman full circle, her liberation now so well-established that Purdey "won't have to burn her bra – she can put it back on." [5] This vision for the character seemed to be borne out by her wardrobe, which largely consisted of an array of midi-length dresses and skirts featuring soft, flowing, gossamer fabrics, bright colours, feminine patterns, and high slits, typically paired with footwear featuring far higher heels than anything donned by her predecessors. She typically engaged in her balletic, panache-style of combat (itself a mark of her femininity) in such ensembles, rather than designated 'action' outfits, and even the likes of her green bodystocking in *The Eagle's Nest*, a pseudo-Emmapeeler in all but name, was feminised, paired with high heeled red lace-up boots and layered over with a metallic blouse and skirt. Purdey also wore more jewellery on a regular basis than her predecessors. While Cathy Gale wore her wedding ring, Emma Peel occasionally sported a ring or bangle, and Tara donned the odd pair of earrings, Purdey always wore at least one ring and earrings, and often a thin chain around her neck. Her flat was similarly ultra-feminine, painted in shades of lilac (later white), and featuring the likes of floral wallpaper, a blue and purple piano, and stuffed animals. Purdey was also vocal about her femininity and womanhood, proclaiming "I'm a girl!" (*K is for Kill: Tiger by the Tail*) and asserting that "women are allowed their idiosyncrasies" (*Gnaws*).

However, these outwardly feminine trappings do not tell the whole story, with Purdey, like her predecessors, regularly upending and subverting assumptions about femininity and womanhood. Her largely feminine wardrobe is peppered with masculine trouser suits, some of which even feature ties, while her short hair is both tomboyish and practical. She possesses a formidable physicality, which allows her to easily traverse a military obstacle course while interviewing an SAS lieutenant, in some cases managing to scale the various obstacles faster than him. When he expresses incredulity that she belongs on the course at all, she shoots down his sexist remarks by sarcastically asking him in which traditionally feminine domain she 'belongs': "Where would you prefer me? In the kitchen? Tending the nursery? In bed?" (*The Midas Touch*). This comes after she requests that the lieutenant address her by one name, like her male colleagues – "Just Purdey." – completely ignoring the question of whether she is a Miss or Mrs. Purdey is also depicted as having a high tolerance for alcohol, a characteristic typically associated with 'manliness'. She adds vodka, gin, and bitters to fizzy lemonade in *Dead Men are Dangerous*, guzzles Chislenko's vodka – and throws it with Russian gusto – in *Gnaws*, and takes a swig of moonshine without so much as blinking in *Emily*, while her favourite drink is a gin, with a dash of bitters and ginger ale (*Dirtier by the Dozen*). She also throws lethal right hooks in amongst her balletic fight moves, is an excellent shot (she earns a score of 99% on the target range), and, rather than nibbling at salads, has a prodigious appetite – she fantasises about *steak au poivre* in *The Eagle's Nest*; prides herself on her ability to make a good omelette (*The Midas Touch*, *The Lion and the Unicorn*); devours marshmallows in *To Catch a Rat* and bakes them into a pie in *Three Handed Game*; eats orange slices mid-car chase in *The Midas Touch*; complains of hunger pangs in *The Tale of the Big Why* while fantasising about Italian food, before munching on an outsized sandwich at a roadside stand when Gambit opts not to go to a restaurant; whips up (giant) tomato salad in *Gnaws*; and pilfers a chip from the unconscious policemen in *Sleeper*. She rides a motorcycle, barely makes a fuss about being shot (*Complex*), is proficient at cricket (*Dead Men are Dangerous*), is competitive about equalling Steed's target range record (*Target!*), and keeps her cool in moments of peril – she is unfazed when Steed confirms that they will probably be killed in *The Eagle's Nest*; replies to Colonel 'Mad Jack' Miller's statement that they will not make allowances for her as a female prisoner with, "You mean you haven't got a hair dryer?"; handles Main and Froggart's sexual threats in *The Eagle's Nest* and *The Midas Touch*, respectively, with equanimity; grins broadly mid-attack by gun-wielding opponents in *Sleeper*; stares down her captors in *Hostage*; tricks her kidnappers in *The Tale of the Big Why* into untying her feet to free them up for high-kicking; and chastises the Russian occupants of *Forward Base* for interrupting her train of thought. She also makes empowering statements about her sex – "You must stop being so gallant, Steed. We're liberated now." (*The Last of the Cybernauts…?*); "I'm striking a blow for womanhood and purity." (*Dead Men are Dangerous*) – while also, at times, being cynical about it – "It has all the vindictiveness of a woman…Inside every woman there's a degree of pure cat." (*Dead Men are Dangerous*). Along with such cynicism, rather than being a stereotypically empathetic, considerate woman, she possesses a sometimes-acerbic sense of humour that can occasionally slip into the callous, even cruel. She flippantly posits that the death of George Stannard (with whom she had gone out to dinner) by fish poisoning may have been caused by "one oyster too many, or a herring bit him". When interviewing the brain-drained Larry, Gambit, perhaps seeing the cards from Ivan's game of solitaire, wonders if the unfortunate agent is repeating the word 'game' because he wants to play cards. Purdey, who had been espousing Larry's attractiveness hours earlier, responds to his plight with a quip: "Maybe he's a bridge addict." She can be similarly insensitive where Gambit is concerned. Recognising that her colleague's attraction to her runs far deeper than that of a passing flirtation, she delights in toying with his emotions by hinting that she reciprocates his feelings (kissing him in *Sleeper*; mouthing 'love' when saying "I do love you" in *Target!*; pushing him onto his back and leaning seductively over him in *Dirtier by the Dozen*; drawing him away from Dr. Leparge in *K is for Kill: Tiger by the Tail*) or making him jealous (waxing lyrical about Larry's virtues in *Three Handed Game*; flirting with the Unicorn in *The Lion and the Unicorn*; describing Marty Brine as "handsome" in *Trap*). She is also not above humiliating him for her own amusement (she takes every opportunity to catch a glimpse of him unclad when his blanket slips in *Three Handed Game*, before making a rather cruel jab). Purdey therefore subverts expectations, presenting as the picture of femininity in dress, décor, and fighting style (as well as previous career as a 'dainty' ballerina), before quickly deconstructing that surface image as soon as her personality comes to the fore. This demonstrates that Brian Clemens' assertion that Purdey could put her bra back on was an accurate one. Her predecessors' groundbreaking depictions of strong, capable women allowed her to have the best of both worlds, being overtly, unapologetically feminine in some respects without losing her credibility as an agent and action woman. At the same time, Purdey's characterisation continued the pioneering work of her predecessors in redefining gender tropes by pairing the most extreme examples of femininity yet seen in an *Avengers* woman with traditionally masculine traits, demonstrating that, rather than being irreconcilable, such traits could coexist comfortably in the same person. As a result, *The New Avengers*, through Purdey, was able to challenge sex and gender stereotypes surrounding women in a more subtle way than the original series, presenting a surface image of traditional femininity that it then delighted in subverting.

The series pulled the same trick with Mike Gambit. The original series had used Steed to challenge conventional ideas about masculinity, particularly through the character's approach to fashion. Patrick Macnee's inspired crafting of his character's signature image transformed the city businessman's suit and bowler hat from a stiff uniform into a paean to elegance and impeccable tailoring. Ironically, Macnee achieved his timeless, unstuffy look not by looking forward to the latest trends, but by reaching back into the past, drawing sartorial inspiration from his jockey father, Naval commanding officer, and the Regency period, which Macnee termed "the most flamboyant, sartorially, for men". [6] Macnee used those myriad inspirations to subtly reshape the suit, reinjecting the flourish and visual interest that had been stripped away from men's clothes over the centuries through the inclusion of velvet collars, embroidered waistcoats, longer jackets, and braiding, while at the same time eschewing breast pockets and reducing the number of buttons on the jacket to ensure a better fit. The 70s built on these and other innovations in male fashion that had been pioneered by 60s men who were keen to get away from the stultifying confines of the traditional suit and its palette of muted colours. As a result, the 1970s embraced a host of feminine touches in its outfitting of the well-dressed man. Colour, once taboo, became almost mandatory, with a veritable rainbow of hues, from traditional browns and blacks to powder blues and pinks, tinting fashionable male ensembles. High heels, an originally male fashion innovation used to improve a horse rider's grip on his stirrups and later to bolster the wearer's status, were reclaimed by fashionable men. Hair lengthened to the point that it rivalled, or even became the inverse of, women's pixie cuts and (Purdey) bobs. An abundance of fabric in tailoring sent the too-small 60s suit packing, leading to longer jackets that nipped in at the waist before flaring out into a long skirt that reached well down the thigh. Flaring also extended to trousers, the free-flowing fabric of the legs akin to the movement of a skirt, while ostentatious jewellery, particularly chains and rings, also became fashionable.

The 1970s' deep delves into traditionally feminine style choices obviously go far beyond the subtle detailing introduced by Steed. However, while Gambit was positioned as the younger, modern counterpoint to Steed's traditional conservatism, the series' creatives opted for Steed-like moderation when styling Gambit, allowing him to adopt some of the feminine touches of the period without going to extremes: boots with a significant, but not ostentatious, heel; three-piece suits in traditional materials and muted palettes, but featuring flares, long-skirted jackets lined in coloured silk, shirts in green, blue, and yellow, and coloured silk-backed waistcoats; hair longer, but not extremely so; jewellery worn regularly, but in the form of a non-ostentatious watch, ring, and thin chain. This limited embrace of the decade's femininization of men's style allowed Gambit to remain fashionable while retaining a traditionally masculine silhouette and appearance.

Along with giving him the requisite 'camouflage' needed to blend in in the corridors of power, the restraint exercised in crafting Gambit's look was part of a bid to cast him as the 'hard man' of the trio, as was the series' publicity, which featured shots of Gambit looking grim and deadly, sometimes with gun drawn. Other hallmarks of the classic square-jawed action man appeared in the series itself, with Gambit depicted as being a good shot, proficient in combat, occasionally ruthless when extracting vital information from an enemy (*The Eagle's Nest*, *House of Cards*), and steely-eyed in a stand-off (*The Eagle's Nest*, *K is for Kill: The Tiger Awakes* and *Tiger by the Tail*, *The Tale of the Big Why*). The series also has him perform suitably action-oriented stunts, be it leaping onto a moving car (*Dead Men are Dangerous*) or airplane wing (*The Tale of the Big Why*), cracking a tree trunk with a flying two-foot kick (*K is for Kill: The Tiger Awakes*), or diving through a plate-glass window (*Target!*,

Angels of Death, Complex). He also accrues corresponding action man injuries, including knife wounds (*House of Cards*), bad bruising (*Dead Men are Dangerous*), broken bones (*The Last of the Cybernauts…?*), and bullet wounds (*Angels of Death, K is for Kill: The Tiger Awakes* and *Tiger by the Tail*), and endures brutal beatings (*Dirtier by the Dozen, The Lion and the Unicorn, Hostage*) and being knocked out (*The Last of the Cybernauts…?, Hostage*). Adding to his action man credentials is his expertise in weaponry. Steed refers to Gambit as the team's resident armoury expert (*Trap*), a title Gambit backs up by listing the relative merits of his and Trasker's guns during their stand-off in *The Eagle's Nest*, dating the last use of an X5 pin grenade to within a year in *K is for Kill: The Tiger Awakes*, and identifying a bullet as the type used by assassins in *K is for Kill: Tiger by the Tail*. His flat also reveals that he collects weapons, with torpedoes, rifles, and antique duelling pistols on display. Also bolstering Gambit's action man credentials is his previous career in motor racing, during which he drove at Le Mans, Spa, Daytona, Monza (*The Midas Touch*).

Taken together, these characteristics would seem to be conclusive proof that Gambit is a stereotypical, macho action man. Like Purdey, however, Gambit subverts his traditionally masculine image as soon as one looks beyond the deadly, professional agent to the man underneath. Indeed, the series often goes out of its way to shatter Gambit's hard man image by depicting him as unquestionably and unashamedly human, showing him on the losing end of fights (*The Lion and Unicorn, Emily*), looking heavenward and breathing a sigh of relief after standing in the path of an oncoming car (*Obsession*) and making ill-judged decisions (e.g., declaring victory too soon in *Trap* and getting himself captured as a result; letting Steed get close enough to land a blow in *Hostage*). Further undercutting the stoic action man image is Gambit's sometimes goofy sense of humour and penchant for corny jokes, examples of which include a favourite gag about a plastic fig leaf (*Angels of Death*); bad puns about doing "undercover" work with the Russian Countess (*To Catch a Rat*) and diving to the bed of the lake (*Forward Base*); his amused response to Steed's quip "come in boat number five" (*Emily*) and champagne bubbles going up his nose (*K is for Kill: Tiger by the Tail*); and his quip about Steed's party being an "anniversary" of the same party he had the year before in *Obsession* ("No idea what that was for, either.").

Perhaps most surprising, given his casting as the 'hard man', is Gambit's softer side, typified by demonstrations of emotion, vulnerability, and loyalty. He is kind, feeding a little sparrow he has named Charlie every morning and asking after Steed's wellbeing when he notices that he is worried about Hardy (*Sleeper*). He is visibly affected by the deaths of fellow agents and Ministry men Terry (*The Last of the Cybernauts...?*), Harlow (*Gnaws*), and Bradshaw (*Target!*), and is deeply upset when his long-time friend and karate teacher, Spence, tries to kill him (*House of Cards*). He is also extremely loyal, defending Steed against accusations that he has turned traitor in *Hostage* even as the evidence piles up, and working to prove his innocence in spite of the anguish investigating his friend causes him. Even after Steed knocks him out when Gambit confronts him about his actions, Gambit still gives his friend the benefit of the doubt, calling Purdey's mother to check Steed's story about Purdey being taken hostage before riding to his friends' rescue. He is similarly loyal when Steed is under suspicion in *Medium Rare*, pushing Victoria Stanton to conjure up predictions about Steed's future, willing to pursue every avenue, no matter how far-fetched, to prove Steed's innocence. With that loyalty comes a protective streak, with Gambit willing to quite literally risk life and limb for the sake of his colleagues and friends. He takes a bullet while rescuing Purdey and Steed from the maze in *Angels of Death*; endures a brutal beating to save them in *Hostage*; takes bullet wounds to both hands while assisting Purdey in *K is for Kill: Tiger by the Tail*; is hit by a car while guarding Purdey's flat in *The Last of the Cybernauts...?*; falls off of a car while attempting to catch Mark Crayford after he shoots at Steed in *Dead Men are Dangerous*; is beaten while attempting to rescue Purdey in *Dirtier by the Dozen*; and runs the deadly target range to retrieve the antidote for a poisoned Steed and Purdey in *Target!*. Even more painful than these physical trials is the toll the events of *Obsession* take on Gambit's friendship with Purdey. Initially worried when Purdey turns down the 'plum' job Steed has arranged for her, Gambit's concern for her only grows when Larry arrives at Steed's party and he intuitively senses that Larry poses a threat to Purdey. He appears on the scene shortly after Larry attempts to assault Purdey and instantly recognises that something serious has happened between them. He stops Larry from following Purdey back to the party, before warning Larry that he is "a close friend" who will protect her if need be. Later, he makes gentle inquiries about the nature of Purdey's relationship with Larry, and is not dissuaded from helping her when she tells him to mind his own business. These signs of friendship pale in comparison to the events of the episode's climax, when Gambit kills Larry to stop him from killing Purdey, a deed she is unable to do herself. He then saves Purdey from harm a second time, holding her tight to prevent her from running straight into the path of the missile and quietly enduring her screams of anger and anguish straight into his ear. Even when Purdey has calmed down and he attempts to explain his actions, he relents when Steed tells him to let her go, putting her own pain above his own. Gambit's attempts to help those he cares about reveal him to be, not a robotic killing machine, but a man with a huge heart who feels things deeply. Such moments fly in the face of stereotypical action man tropes that dictate that 'manliness' is incompatible with showing concern or emotion.

Another emotion that comes to the fore on Gambit's part is equally irreconcilable with the action hero label: love. Though Gambit does conform to the ladies' man secret agent stereotype to the extent that he flirts with women and keeps a little black book of telephone numbers, he also upends that trope with intimations that, where Purdey is concerned, there are deeper feelings at work. In *The Last of the Cyberanuts...?*, when Purdey asks if she has forgotten anything in her summary of the Cybernauts, he suggests, "Only that you love me very much." In *Target!*, Purdey teasingly revving her car when she says the word 'love' in "But I do love you" leads a hopeful Gambit to ask her to repeat the sentiment. Later in the same episode, he is desperate to save her life, vowing to hunt down and kill those responsible if she dies. In *Forward Base*, Purdey recounts a debate from the previous Tuesday about the capability of men to commit. Purdey's argument was that men are "more changeable and more restless", while Gambit disagreed, claiming that "no man would ever up and leave a woman, not if he really cared for her." In *Hostage*, he expresses a fervent wish to meet Purdey's mother, and ends a call to the woman herself with, "By the way, I hope to have dinner with you sometime." In *Dirtier by the Dozen*, he surrenders to Colonel 'Mad Jack' Miller and risks World War Three to save Purdey from a minefield. Rather than painting Gambit as a heartless lady-killer only interested in sex, Gambit's recurring comments to Purdey regarding love and commitment, which are backed up by his actions, reveal deep feelings for her, rather than a desire for a shallow or casual tryst.

Gambit also defies macho stereotypes by extending the same respectful treatment he accords Purdey to the other women he romances. While Purdey regularly endures advances by men that involve – often proprietorial – physical contact, Gambit's method of flirting is respectful, conveying his interest in a non-aggressive manner. Indeed, more often than not, it is the women, not Gambit, who make the first move. Gerda in *The Eagle's Nest* is the aggressor, enthusing about Gambit's attractiveness and practically demanding a dinner date. Gambit, in contrast, keeps her at arm's length until he has completed his professional duties, and, while he acknowledges Gerda's attractiveness and glances appreciatively at her figure, that glance is subtle rather than a leer, and his flirting is strictly verbal, not physical. Artist Helen McKay in *Three Handed Game* is similarly forward, boldly asking Gambit to take his clothes off. It transpires that Helen only wants Gambit to pose for her latest sculpture, but Gambit does not react to this development with anger or disappointment, nor does he use his state of undress as an excuse to take advantage of or harass Helen, the pair instead engaging in a light verbal flirtation while he poses. Dr. Jeanine Leparge in *K is for Kill* is also not bashful, asking Gambit to her apartment for dinner and seductively telling him he can choose what they will "do afterwards". Gambit does make the first move with Penny Redfern in *Dead Men are Dangerous*, but the pair quickly fall into a rapport that conveys their mutual interest, with Penny suggestively asking Gambit how well he mixes a martini. Jane in *Angels of Death*, whom Gambit catches off-guard with a kiss, would seem to be an exception to his hands-off approach. However, this situation is quite different, as Gambit knows that she may be able to assist him with his investigation into fellow Ministry man Coldstream, for whom Jane acts as secretary. Harbouring suspicions that Coldstream might be a traitor and that Jane may have knowledge of, or be complicit in, his traitorous dealings, Gambit puts his professional duties first and, instead of his usual respectful form of flirtation, uses the best method at his disposal to literally disarm Jane, who holds him at gunpoint. Sensing she is unsure of what to do with him despite her threats, he discombobulates her with a mixture of charm, humour, and unexpected behaviour, giving her instructions on how to frisk him, taking her gun, returning it, and kissing her. The result is that the confused Jane, rather than staying on the offensive, asks what he wants, allowing Gambit, having neutralised the immediate threat posed by the gun, to get down to brass tacks and question her about her boss. It should also be noted that, even if Gambit is unusually forward in this instance, Jane signals her attraction to him long before he kisses her, the gun she is holding on him wavering briefly as she looks him over approvingly, and she is nonplussed by the kiss, rather than offended by it. Furthermore, once Gambit has established that she is not a threat, the rest of their encounter unfolds in Gambit's typically respectful way. This encounter therefore serves to illustrate that Gambit does not distinguish between the sexes when dealing with (potential) villains and will use whatever means necessary to get the job done and ensure the security of Queen and country. Jane's brandishing of a gun and employment by Coldstream lead Gambit to peg her as a potential enemy whom he cannot afford to treat with his usual decorum, and he uses whatever methods he can employ to disarm and get information from her, just as he would if he were dealing with a male villain. However, when his professional duties do not require him to take extreme measures, his flirtations are always respectful.

This goes double for Purdey. Despite their closeness, Gambit's physical contact with her is usually employed as a necessary part of their work, be it putting his arms around her to pretend they are lovers to prevent a man they are tailing from becoming suspicious of their presence (*Forward Base*) or holding her tightly to prevent her from running into the path of a missile (*Obsession*). His most physical flirtatious overture toward her is extremely demure: covering Purdey's hand with his own in *The Last of the Cybernauts...?* When Purdey withdraws her hand, Gambit accepts the rejection rather than pursuing her. And while Gambit does give her figure the occasional appreciative once-over, he usually looks her in the eye. Purdey herself tacitly acknowledges that Gambit's method of flirtation is respectful in *Faces*. Playing her double 'Lolita', Purdey scolds 'Terry Walton' for pinching her bottom, exclaiming, "Gambit wouldn't do that!". While she claims that his behaviour runs counter to the reports about Gambit that she has been given, she is undoubtedly speaking from her own experiences with Gambit. Gambit, for his part, treats 'Lolita' disrespectfully partly as a way to maintain his cover as the unscrupulous 'Terry Walton', but also in an effort to drive 'Lolita' away before she is called on to kill and replace Purdey. Unable to break his cover or contact Steed or Purdey, harassing 'Lolita' is the best tool Gambit has at his disposal to keep his partner safe, and his interactions with her serve as another example of him not distinguishing between the sexes when it comes to dealing with the enemy. In the rare situation where Gambit improperly gains an advantage over Purdey, such as when he waits until she has undressed to reveal his presence in her flat in *House of Cards*, Purdey quickly turns the tables and makes her displeasure known, in that instance by stepping on him in retaliation, punishment Gambit accepts without protest. Furthermore, in *Three Handed Game*, she takes more advantage of him than he did her, openly attempting to catch glimpses of his naked body whenever the blanket he is using to preserve his modesty slips. Each also tips the other out of bed while they are naked, save for the sheets wrapped around them – Gambit does the honours in *The Eagle's Nest*, while Purdey returns the favour in *The Last of the Cybernauts...?* These encounters demonstrate the fundamental equality that characterises the pair's relationship, with Purdey not the only one being objectified. In fact, Purdey has the advantage when these encounters are tallied up – when Gambit catches Purdey in a state of undress, his gaze is more casual than lingering, while in a similar situation, Purdey openly gapes at his naked body and revels in his embarrassment. If these scenarios were to play out between other people in different circumstances, however, they would unquestionably cross the line. The fact that both Purdey and Gambit instead react to these situations with only annoyance or mild pique, rather than perceiving them as a threat or violation, is indicative of how comfortable and safe they feel with each other, how much they trust one another, and how well they understand one another's (innocuous) intentions. Furthermore, Gambit's admiration of Purdey's form is always secondary to his concern for her well-being. In *Target!*, Gambit finds her unconscious, dressed only in her slip, but is so worried about her welfare that he seemingly fails to register her state of undress. Just as notable is the way the series establishes that Gambit's relationship with Purdey is not solely based on the prospect of sex or romance, but a strong friendship. The pair regularly spend time together outside of work hours, playing Scrabble (*The Last of the Cybernauts...?*) and tennis (*Trap*), dancing at the disco (*Trap*), going out to dinner (*The Tale of the Big Why*) and parties (*The Last of the Cybernauts...?*, *Obsession*), and participating in karate bouts (*Dead Men are Dangerous*). Even when they are on duty, their conversations often stray to other topics, such as old movies (*The Midas Touch*), relationships (*Forward Base*), and their personal histories (*To Catch a Rat*). This demonstrates that, to Gambit, Purdey is always a person first, someone he cares about and enjoys spending time with rather than constantly sexualises.

Overall, Gambit's behaviour toward women is a subversion of his casting as the series' action man, a role that suggests that he should conform to the stereotypes typically associated with such characters and callously use and discard women with abandon. Instead, Gambit treats women as equals whose enjoyment of their time together matters as much as his. Compared to the more forward, often physical passes made at Purdey by other characters which typify the behaviour often modelled in the popular culture of the time, Gambit's approach offers an entirely different, respectful way of relating to and expressing interest in the opposite sex, one that is mainly verbal, involves focusing on a woman's face rather than her body, and allows her to be the instigator of the flirtation. By having a younger male lead who displays the traditionally 'masculine' qualities of aptitude in combat and desirability to women model such behaviour, the show tacitly endorses Gambit's way of doing things, implying that his approach is not 'unmasculine' and that the aggressiveness displayed by male incidental characters toward Purdey is no proof of manhood, a significant statement in the 70s landscape.

Gambit's treatment of Purdey also feeds into the series' continuation of its forebear's ground-breaking depiction of equality between the sexes. While Steed's relationships with both Purdey and Gambit are fundamentally unequal due to his professional seniority over them, Purdey and Gambit share a dynamic marked by equality, despite their surface styling as traditionally masculine/feminine characters. As in the original series, the pair take turns rescuing one another, with Purdey coming to Gambit's aid in *The Midas Touch*, *Emily*, and *The Lion and the Unicorn*, while Gambit returns the favour in *House of Cards*, *The Midas Touch*, and *Target!* The duo work in tandem to defeat enemies, including a Cybernaut and a group of soldiers (*Dirtier by the Dozen*). They also value each other's areas of expertise, with Gambit providing insights into mathematics, probability, martial arts, and weaponry, while Purdey is knowledgeable about languages and esoteric topics (such as churches), as well as having keen insights into how people behave. If both are equally knowledgeable about a topic, they engage in mutually respectful debates. When they are mid-assignment, Gambit only pulls rank on Purdey when her relative inexperience as an agent makes him, the more senior operative with experience in the Army and Navy, better equipped to make certain decisions that could have serious consequences for one or both of them. It should also be noted that both Gambit and Purdey benefit from Steed's received wisdom on everything from cultivating instinct to giving others space in difficult times, meaning Gambit is not depicted as always knowing 'better' because of his sex.

Conclusion

As the 60s turned into the 70s, new, weightier realities set in, displacing the carefree optimism that characterised the last few 'swinging' years of the earlier decade. In response to this shift in the zeitgeist, *The New Avengers* set about building a rich, grounded world populated with three-dimensional characters who felt things deeply, were flawed, and had lives, backstories, friends, lovers, families, and homes that extended their existence beyond the confines of the story of the week, predicting today's trends in television characterisation. The fleshed-out world and characters were accompanied by a willingness to allow a certain amount of consequence and emotional messiness to come into play, and a refusal to hide from real world issues, instead facing them with an, at times, unflinchingly clear-eyed perspective. At the same time, the show still held fast to the original series' sense of humour and fun, while also offering familiar plots and themes and reviving its history and beloved characters. This balance of old and new was a difficult one to strike, and the series was not always successful at striking it, but *The New Avengers*' ability to incorporate elements from every one of its predecessor's distinct seasons, while adding its own unique twist to the material, has been underappreciated.

For that reason, despite being made for a braver, harsher decade, *The New Avengers* deserves to be considered as the rightful continuation of the original series' long legacy.

© JZ Ferguson

1. Dave Rogers, *The Complete Avengers*, p. 223.
2. One cannot count Emma and Steed's fight in *Man-eater of Surrey Green*, as Emma is under the plant's hypnotic control at the time and is not responsible for her actions.
3. *TV Times*, March 1-7, 1969.
4. Dave Rogers, *The Ultimate Avengers*, p. 209.
5. *The Ultimate Avengers*, p. 249.
6. Piers D. Britton and Simon J. Barker, *Reading Between Designs: Visual Imagery and the Generation of Meanings in The Avengers, The Prisoner, and Doctor Who*, pp. 46-47.

OPENING PANDORA'S BOX:
SHADOWS OF FEAR & *THRILLER*

For many television historians and critics, the (elusive or mythical) Golden Age of television drama was that of the early anthology series of single plays: shows such as *Kraft Television Theatre* (1947-58) – including Rod Serling's Emmy award-winning *Patterns* (1955) – and *Playhouse 90* (1956-60) in the US, or *Armchair Theatre* (1956-74) in the UK. In the 1950s these tended to be live broadcasts, adding to the sense of a one-off theatrical performance for the small screen. In the early days of *Armchair Theatre*, the producers often drew on classic plays, but as the 1950s segued into the 60s, Canadian Sydney Newman was determined to present challenging, contemporary drama written by exciting new playwrights; he also wanted to move away from what he saw as stuffy, class-specific material:

'The only legitimate theatre was of the 'anyone for tennis?' variety, which, on the whole, presented a condescending view of working-class people. Television dramas were usually adaptations of stage plays, and invariably about upper classes. I said, 'Damn the upper classes – they don't even own televisions!'" [1]

This democratising vision – coupled with the often-controversial subjects tackled by dramatists such as Harold Pinter – proved hugely successful, with many of the one-off plays both critically acclaimed and popular with the viewing public. *Armchair Theatre* was undoubtedly an inspiration for many of the anthology series which followed, including *Studio 64* (1964), *Theatre 625* (1964-68), the BBC's *The Wednesday Play* (1964-70), *Play for Today* (1970-84), *Second City Firsts* (1973-78) and *BBC2 Playhouse* (1974-83).

If we consider the single play anthology to be a dramatic form of television, then *Journey to the Unknown* (1968-69), *Shadows of Fear*

(1970-73) and *Thriller* (1973-76) might be seen as belonging to a sub-genre, one in which elements of the supernatural, horror or psychological fear are added into the mix. These three series are quite different from each other yet, as their distinctive title sequences and unsettling scores warn us, in each case we will be entering a strange, disturbing, twisted, dramatic landscape. All three owe a creative debt to both Alfred Hitchcock's playful suspense and Rod Serling's ground-breaking *The Twilight Zone* (1959-64), *Journey to the Unknown* in particular.

In the well-known Greek myth, curiosity gets the better of Pandora who opens a jar – later mistranslated as a box – and unwittingly unleashes all manner of physical and emotional curses and evil on the world. One online dictionary – *Merriam-Webster* – defines Pandora's Box as 'a prolific source of troubles.' It goes on to suggest that 'anything that looks ordinary but may produce unpredictable harmful results can thus be described as a Pandora's Box.' Pandora had been warned not to open it, but – in modern parlance – she could not help herself. Part of the charm of Thames Television's *Shadows of Fear* and Brian Clemens' ATV *Thriller* is their 'unpredictable' nature. You are never sure what is going to leap out each week. Nevertheless, the iconic theme music and opening titles of these shows – as already mentioned – warn us to expect trouble. However, as Pandora discovered to her cost, curiosity is a powerful emotion. In addition, as the ancient Greeks acknowledged, we have always gained a perverse pleasure from unleashing something frightening, albeit from the relative safety of a book or screen.

Shadows of Fear has an unusual broadcast history. A pilot story (*Did You Lock Up?*) was transmitted in June 1970, topped the ITV ratings for that week, and this led to the green light being given to nine further tales which were shown in a run between January and March 1971. A final drama – with a period setting, only half the length of the others and broadcast at 11 pm – emerged almost two years later, possibly in a half-hearted attempt to relaunch the series in a glossier, shorter format, but arguably adding a false, final note.

One of the episodes (*Come Into My Parlour*) was a remake of a wiped 1967 *Armchair Theatre* and was recorded in black-and-white, due to a strike by ITV technicians. The connective tissue was an almost Hitchcockian, psychological fear or suspense, often with a cruel or chilling twist in the tale. As the series title suggests, the stories often revolve around the 'anticipation of the bang', rather than on-screen violence.

The quirky, animated opening titles offer us a mix of the mundane – terraced streets and a tower block – and the disturbingly surreal – indistinct or twisted faces silently screaming from windows – hinting that this combination of social realism undercut by the macabre will be at the heart of the narratives. Both the main writer, Roger Marshall, and the principal director, Kim Mills, had worked on *The Avengers* and *Public Eye* in the 1960s, while writer and producer John Kershaw arrived after two years as producer and editor of *Armchair Theatre*. For this chapter, I will be exploring some of the more effective plays in this anthology, before briefly reflecting on why others did not (arguably) work quite as well.

Did You Lock Up? was inspired by a real-life event. Months earlier, writer Roger Marshall had returned home from a weekend away with the family, only to discover that we had been burgled. My parents experienced the rollercoaster of emotions which millions of others have gone through: numbed shock and confusion, dismay, anger, a sense of violation. As they surveyed the damage and made a mental note of what was missing – such as a much-loved wedding clock – the phone rang. It was executive producer Lloyd Shirley. Roger said he was too angry to talk, but when Shirley heard about the break-in, he encouraged Marshall to channel his frustrations into script form. Writing the pilot became a cathartic process, one in which the homeowner gains the ultimate revenge. Thames received a flood of letters from viewers who said that they could identify with Peter Astle and that they fantasised about doing the same thing.

Peter and Moira Astle (Michael Craig and Gwen Watford) are swiftly established as a loving, middle-aged couple enjoying a wedding anniversary at a hotel. If they come across as comfortably middle class, *almost* smug, this impression is then rudely interrupted. The pop of a champagne cork segues into the smashing of a window as their empty house is broken into. The juxtaposition works well, dramatically, and continues as we move between the couple celebrating and the burglars ransacking their house, the vandalising of a sofa with a flick-knife marking the latter out as unnecessarily sadistic. The 'morning after' return sees Moira as the one who reacts emotionally – including her expressed desire to encounter the thieves – while Peter appears to respond in a calmer, practical manner: telling his wife not to touch anything, working out the burglars' methods. This sets us up for the gradual twist and transformation as we watch his descent into paranoia and vengeful planning.

"How do you forget it? You know what I'm really doing? Up here? [points to his mind] I'm operating a rack with our burglar on it. He's about nine feet long already, and the louder he screams, the more I turn. Every time a window rattles, my hair bristles. A paper drops through the letterbox, and I nearly fall through the bottom of the bed. We go out for twenty minutes and dash back expecting to see the house being driven off on the back of a truck. And you say, 'Forget it'."

The emotive speech establishes Astle as a character who is unable to 'move on'. He seems increasingly unaware of, or disinterested in, his wife's needs and emotions, and a second Peter Astle emerges, almost a Mr Hyde. His mission for revenge is a combination of Old Testament blood justice – "I want my eye for an eye" – and a paranoia which also reflects his inbuilt class snobbery, suspecting builders, the odd-job man, window cleaner, greengrocer, cleaning lady. In Peter's universe, "Everybody [who is working-class] is guilty until proved innocent."

Sergeant Newman – stylishly played by Ray Smith – provides Astle with several things: grim 1970s burglary statistics; crime prevention advice; and the dire warning that the robbers will almost certainly return to this "burglars' paradise" within a few months, once the couple have spent the insurance money on replacement items. His bleak picture of the future does little to dissuade Peter from hatching his plans. There is an intriguing undercurrent of class conflict between Newman and Astle, reinforcing our sense of the homeowner as being smugly pleased with himself.

Despite the increasingly dark nature of the story, Marshall injects some black humour. As Peter turns the family home into a prison with sliding steel gates, Moira drily observes, "We get burgled, we end up behind bars". Watford delivers her dry remarks with wonderful aplomb and Kim Mills' direction allows us to witness the couple conversing from either side of the newly installed barrier, an irony Mrs Astle is acutely aware of. This main set – the Astle's house – lacks any particularly interesting features and the lack of exterior filmed inserts means that we must rely on the dialogue to imagine its remote location. That the story works so well is down partly to the central characters being expertly drawn by the writer; the excellent performances of most of the cast; some inventive camera angles created by Mills in both the antique shop and the Astle house; also, the daring final twist which Marshall leaves us with: two (amoral) men left to rot in a trap partly of their own making. While some viewers clearly shared Astle's extreme sense of poetic justice, arguably far more subtle and interesting is the story's depiction of Astle himself. Events have stripped Peter Astle of his veneer of charm and respectability, revealing something far less edifying, a running leitmotif in *Shadows of Fear*.

As mentioned earlier, *Come Into My Parlour* started life as a (now lost) April 1967 *Armchair Theatre*, *Will You Come A Little Closer?* starring Freddie Jones and Caroline Mortimer. In the remake, they were replaced by Peter Barkworth and Beth Harris. Both versions were written by Roger Marshall and directed by Kim Mills. The fact that a technicians' strike forced the production team to record it in black-and-white is a reminder of the early 1970s context, with both television and the print press affected by industrial action. Ironically, this also allowed the story to offer a noir visual appeal which is, arguably, perfect for this stand-out story.

Come Into My Parlour immediately creates a downbeat feel as we encounter Deanna Ward (Beth Harris) in a drab-looking bedsit, with a full ashtray and rain dripping down the windowpane. Like an actress preparing for an audition, she is practising her lines or pitch as a salesperson for a cosmetics company, clearly down on her luck and out of her comfort zone. As the episode title appears, we are offered the unsettling image of a fly trapped by a spider, a visual piece of foreshadowing. The long corridor set of a block of flats, with its closed doors, nicely conveys both the humiliation involved in 'cold calling' and the potential danger which might lie behind any one of them, particularly for a lone female.

There is an effective contrast between the shifty gaze of John Dolby (Peter Barkworth) looking at Deanna through his front door peephole – director Mills offering us his fish-eye view of her – and his friendly, well-spoken voice as he invites her in. What Dolby offers her seems to be a performance of his own, full of melodramatic hand gestures: a bad luck story about a lost Tube ticket leading to a criminal record and his dismissal from a firm of solicitors. A true story, or a self-deluding fantasy? We never find out. His stream-of-consciousness tale hints at his racism, sexism, snobbery and an obsession with the legal system. Bizarrely, it also encourages Deanna to open up, with a backstory of her mental breakdown and a confession that she is without family or friends. Are they becoming secret sharers? Or is she simply the perfect female lone victim?

When Dolby reveals that his first name is John, the fact that it brings Gielgud and Lennon to mind for Ward, but serial killers Haigh and Christie to him, should set alarm bells ringing in her head. As should his request to photograph her. Is her relief at human contact, the hint of friendship, and the promise of a sale enough to blind her? Seemingly so. Mills offers us a return to that sinister fish-eye lens peephole as Dolby watches Deanna depart at the end of Part Two.

With Dolby having convinced his cleaning lady Mrs B (Peggy Bullock) that he and Deanna are engaged, our fears that Part Three will see his web finally and fatally trapping Deanna Ward escalate as he refers to 'Dr Crippen' and asks her views on the death penalty. Is the champagne drugged, or the cigarette which he takes out of a silver case? Peter Barkworth offers a disturbingly creepy performance as the role-playing fantasist John Dolby, full of sexist zeal. When Ward demands her money, he compares her to the "sordid" women who perform his manicures, calling her "frigid" and "cold". The comparison takes us back to his earlier, uncomfortably sexual speech:

"My one vice. A fortnightly manicure. Ten minutes of sensuous luxury. Warm, cosy, cocooned in this white sheet. Half-closed eyes. And this blue-smocked goddess, hair smelling of perfume, paddling my palms and pinching my fingers with soft hands. Pass her in the street with your hat on and she wouldn't recognise you. But just for that moment, you're the master."

John Dolby considers manicurists, masseuses and door-to-door saleswomen as teasing, money-focused prostitutes: "tart, hustler, whore, streetwalker". His role-playing law court game, in which Deanna is in the dock and he is the prosecuting lawyer, provides him with the power to be the "master". It appears that neither sex nor her murder was his aim. Indeed, when a humiliated, confused, dazed, and provoked Deanna Ward finally plunges a knife into his back in the late twist, one is left to wonder whether that was Dolby's sado-masochistic aim all along, instigated when he presented the blade to her earlier as, "Exhibit A: the murder weapon. Next time you see it, there will be a little tag and string attached to it." With Ward left to knock on a neighbouring door in a zombified state, *Come Into My Parlour* is almost as dark as *Shadows of Fear* gets. Only the gothic horror of *The Death Watcher* will match it in terms of disturbing drama.

The opening of Jeremy Paul's *Return of Favours* provides us with an immediate tease. In an apartment, Gordon Marsh (George Cole) is busy stuffing women's clothes, handbags, shoes and jewellery into a suitcase. When an amorous couple let themselves into the same flat, he hides himself until they are busy in the bedroom, at which point he plays detective, searching a handbag, and discovering a wallpaper order book in a coat pocket. He even settles himself in the kitchen with the book, which contains coded messages for sex *rendezvous* like the one which is taking place now. Almost ten minutes in, we have not established who any of these three characters is.

When the three finally collide, one mystery is lifted: Maureen – Gordon's wife – has been allowing her friend Judith (Jennie Linden) to use the apartment on Wednesday afternoons for sex with a married man, decorator Roger (Robin Ellis). What makes the opening intriguing is both Judith and Gordon's reactions to their meeting. She seems genuinely amused to be found in his bed. While he initially appears to be angry, he is soon smiling to himself while making tea. Jeremy Paul's script now sends us into Pinter-esque dialogue:

Roger: *Tea*?!
Gordon: Yes. You'll stay for tea.
Roger: Well, no. Look...It's very kind of you -
Gordon: I've made it now.
Roger: We really ought to be getting along.
Gordon: Why? You'd still be here if it hadn't been for me.
Roger: Yeh, I know -
Gordon: For *God*'s sake! It's the least you can do.

The following conversation, over a civilised cup of tea, about redecorating the (locked) spare room is equally, delightfully odd. Why is it locked? Why was Gordon packing up his wife's possessions? Why did he ruin her geraniums? How did he injure his heavily bandaged hand? At this point in the play, one might even wonder if she has been 'disposed' of, something Gordon playfully hints at as a long, entertaining Act One (25 minutes) ends.

With the arrival of Maureen (Caroline Blakiston) in Act Two, we flit between the two couples, Judith's fear for her friend's welfare and Roger's desire to do nothing about it leading to a similar disconnect between the lovers as the one we see between the Marsh husband and wife. The couples appear to be polar opposites: one pair only connected by sex, the other distanced by the complete absence of it. If Maureen's appearance comes as a surprise to Judith, it is part of a double twist as Gordon creates the ultimate double bluff by murdering her – off-camera – and then framing Roger for the crime. The wearing of the bandages can now be revealed: they fulfilled the role of an assassin's glove. There may be one or two plot holes, such as how Gordon Marsh already knew about the lovers, but Jeremy Paul provides us with a stylish, witty thriller. Caroline Blakiston plays such a minor role in *Return of Favours* that this is almost a three hander, and Cole, Linden and Ellis all excel in their parts.

Writer Jacques Gillies specialised in one-off television plays, having worked on a dozen different anthologies. *The Death Watcher* opens with two intriguing snippets of conversation: a husband and wife – Robert (Michael Hawkins) and Emmy Erikson (Judy Parfitt) – discussing a forthcoming experiment in psychic phenomena which she has agreed to take part in, and a Dr Pickering (John Neville) praising Emmy's brilliance but "lack of balance" with his helper, Dawson (Victor Maddern), in addition to a worrying reference to involuntary mental health patients. Pickering's dress and manner create the impression of a character from a Gothic horror, deepened when he observes that the isolated setting of his country house has been described by some as "suffocating in Suffolk".

Pickering and Emmy's initial chat about the possibility of communication with the dead – including the theory of dualism – seems to counteract her earlier avowal that she has an open mind. Having suggested that she is no longer willing to be involved, but unable to return to London that night, the warning that Caesar – a supposedly vicious but silent Rhodesian Ridgeback – is set loose in the house at night and the fact that guests are locked in their sleeping quarters add to the sense of a country house trap. The bars on her nursery attic bedroom window nicely reinforce this impression.

In the morning, any lingering doubt for us is swiftly overcome: "in the interests of science" Emmy Erikson is now a prisoner/patient. There is an effective contrast between her increasing panic and the 'rational', 'civilised' breakfast table responses from the serene, twisted Doctor Pickering. The regular use of flashbacks of Robert's warnings – "Sounds an out-and-out quack!" "I bet his theories are quite potty!" "I think you're mad to go!" – work superbly in reinforcing Emmy's growing sense of panic. Having earlier come across as a willing participant in the scientist's warped trap, Dawson reveals that there are papers to 'prove' that Emmy is a former inmate of a psychiatric prison, locked up for murdering her child. Is convincing him that these are fake Emmy Erikson's only hope of escape from Pickering's chamber of horrors?

As Emmy awakes, tied and trapped in a metal coffin, with a large monochrome photo of the scientist on the wall, we have entered genuinely disturbing territory: "I believe that just as we can imprint parenthood in the first weeks of life, in the same way we can imprint just before death. My image is the last thing you will see." Despite the happy resolution, the final news – that Pickering has killed himself, with a photo of her in his hand – continues the horrific idea of the death imprint. Horrific, but horrifically great entertainment, thanks largely to a superb script and Parfitt's performance. *The Death Watcher* is probably the closest that *Shadows of Fear* comes to *Thriller* territory in terms of its content and style.

Shadows of Fear scripts revolve around *psychological* drama, never venturing into the supernatural. Their success relies heavily, therefore, on the central characters being both believable and if not likeable at least being fully developed and three-dimensional, having intriguing layers and depth to them. In the cases of killers, we require a motive for a murder, be it revenge, love, lust, hate, jealousy, paranoia, or insanity. When the stories fail to deliver, it is usually down to unsatisfactory characterisation, rather than glaring plot holes or a fault with the actors themselves. John Kershaw's *Sugar and Spice* delivers a clever twist in the tale – a teenage girl getting away with murder by planting false evidence – but provides us with no reason why she killed her (unseen) little brother. Neglect? Jealousy? There is no explanation or backstory for the disturbing fratricide; the 'Why?' is never answered, which leaves us, as viewers, frustrated and feeling cheated. Roger Marshall's *Repent at Leisure* is a beautifully crafted narrative with lots of clever red herrings in the plot, yet the superficial, rich widow Isabel (Elizabeth Sellers) does not possess a single redeeming feature. Had her new, working-class husband (George Sewell) genuinely been plotting her demise we would have been unmoved. We are left wondering why the sweet-natured Harry fell in love with her in the first place. It may be a question of 'love is blind', but it still feels like a flaw. Richard Harris' *At Occupier's Risk* delivers in terms of atmosphere, helped by the castle setting, whistling wind and harpsichord score. However, not one of the characters is remotely believable, or empathetic, leaving a fine cast – Gemma Jones, Anthony Bate and Annette Crosbie – with an impossible job.

Despite the false notes, at its best *Shadows of Fear* offers us some impressive one-off plays. The studio-bound stricture is perfect for creating claustrophobic dramas and there are a number of scintillating acting performances, from Gwen Watford, Judy Parfitt, Peter Barkworth, George Cole and Margery Mason among others. They are fascinating time capsules which occasionally centre on working-class households but, more often, offer us insights into an affluent 'Middle England' – the "adultery belt" of suburbia as one character calls it – of glossy Sunday Colour Supplements, where murders are plotted by seemingly respectable people amidst the jars of marmalade and cups of tea.

Brian Clemens (1931-2015) was, without doubt, one of the most prolific and popular writers in the history of British television. Despite his prodigious output across seven decades, his name is inextricably linked to *The Avengers*, although it is an urban myth that he created the iconic series. Nevertheless, he did creatively drive the show during its filmed era and reincarnated it in the 1970s as *The New Avengers* (1976-77). Between these two, he wrote two intriguing films: *And Soon the Darkness* (1970) and *Blind Terror/See No Evil* (1971). Sometimes labelled as 'horror', they are probably better described as psychological thrillers. Despite their differences, they share connective tissue, including the disturbing spectacle for the viewer as we are forced to watch a young female being stalked by a male predator. There is a sadistic suspense at the core of both narratives. While Avengerland had been a far lighter, increasingly tongue-in-cheek meta world, Clemens had demonstrated his ability to add darker elements in episodes such as *The House That Jack Built*, *The Joker* and *Pandora* which all centre on a female being trapped inside a country house. In many respects, Clemens' two films take Avengerland and drain it of any lighter touches, leaving us in menacing spaces, be it the agoraphobia of a flat, deserted French countryside or the claustrophobia of a Home Counties mansion. There is no doubt that these paved the way – creatively – for the anthology series *Thriller* (1973-76), forty-three tales which were all story-lined by Clemens and the vast majority scripted by him as well. [2]

Unlike most of the series distributed and/or sold by ITC in the 1960s and 1970s, *Thriller* offers us a theatrical rather than cinematic experience, with its predominantly studio-bound stories. While the later *Hammer House of Horror* (1980) looks superb in its High-Definition transfer, as a collective body *Thriller* arguably suffers, visually, from being made on videotape, with 35mm film inserts. Ironically, some critics see this restriction as being an advantage in terms of creating a 'foreboding atmosphere':

'What would nowadays be considered glacial pacing (the long, deliberate tracking shot across an empty room accompanied by sinister oboe cadence was something of a motif, for instance) was integral to the atmosphere. Rather than cut rapidly from shot to shot, the direction took its time, almost taunting the viewer with its creeping progress. When all the other elements were working, a vivid sense of foreboding was the result...Being mainly studio-bound, with a couple of sets...and a minimal amount of location filming, they look visually primitive these days. However, this simplicity had the virtue of putting the emphasis firmly on script and action, in lieu of fancy camera angles. In fact, the technical limitations had an atmosphere all of their own: the videotaped interiors were claustrophobic and tense, while the grainy, overcast countryside film inserts looked like they could be hiding untold menaces.' [3]

I would, overall, agree with this general assessment. It is worth observing, however, that techniques such as using four-wall sets and floor lighting are effectively employed. *When* all the ingredients are in place, the theatrical style of shooting *Thriller* can enhance the stories in terms of mood. There is plenty of variety in terms of genre, from traditional whodunits to Hitchcock-style suspense, horror and the supernatural. There is, arguably, also a wide range in terms of quality, from some stories which work brilliantly, to others where the baffling hook is not backed up by a satisfying narrative. This is unsurprising, given the speed with which the episodes were being written, predominantly by one man. [4] This section of my chapter will offer a brief journey through all ten tales which were broadcast in the initial series (April-June 1973), offering a flavour of *Thriller* as a whole.

The first episode to be broadcast in the UK – on April 14th, 1973 – was the expertly crafted *Lady Killer*, renamed *The Death Policy* in the US. This represents a restrained Clemens at his very best, with characters cleverly held back, several twists in the tale and a satisfactory moral comeuppance for the main character. It is a nice touch that the 'Tony' character who conman/killer Paul Tanner furtively telephones on several occasions – but who remains unseen – turns out to be Toni, a woman. Equally, that the mysterious Jack Hardisty is an unwelcome 'secret sharer', almost as corrupt and shady as Tanner. The story benefits greatly from the brief filmed inserts, establishing the isolated location of the stone lodge and the clifftops, with rocks and pounding waves beneath. We instinctively know that at least one character will dramatically plunge to their death. The sets are equally effective. There is a tired, old-fashioned feel to the hotel which helps to create a sense of the boredom one might experience in such a seaside location out-of-season, providing the perfect opportunity for an attractive stranger to charm a young female guest. Paul Tanner is a superbly created character, but much of the credit must go to Robert Powell who offers up a flawless performance as a coldblooded opportunist. Tanner is, essentially, an actor who can change his face like masks and who will offer his new wife a full range of moods from romantic charm, through histrionics, to fury. Powell is utterly, horribly convincing in each of these masks or moods. [5] In terms of characterisation, one might argue that American Jenny Frifth is less believable. A vast amount of circumstantial 'evidence' has stacked up before she becomes properly suspicious: mysterious night-time phone calls, lies about the house and a previous marriage, the bizarre present of his first wife's second-hand dress, the unknown occupation of her 'businessman' husband, a doctor calling about a forthcoming cardiogram...Given her trusting naivety, the *sang froid* she demonstrates at the end requires a certain amount of suspension of disbelief from the viewer.

Lady Killer benefits from an excellent cast, with Barbara Feldon impressing in a difficult role as the naïve newlywed, Linda Thorson wonderfully sultry as Toni Tanner and TP McKenna magnificent as one conman attempting to blackmail another. It is Powell, though, who is magnetic as the embodiment of human evil and avarice, including the split-second, cliff-top change of mind about killing Jenny when she reveals that she is worth $1 million.

It is worth observing at this early point that the impressive cast list for almost every *Thriller* episode helps to explain the series' critical and commercial success. Viewed as a collective body, it is a veritable who's-who of 1970s stars, including young ones yet to reach their career heights, such as Helen Mirren, Dennis Waterman, Stephen Rea and Michael Kitchen. As was the case in *Journey to the Unknown*, there is often a US or Canadian actor in the story, in a bid to attract an American audience; some of these choices were fascinating ones, such as hiring two actors well-known for iconic 1960s US TV shows: Paul Burke (*Naked City*) and George Maharis (*Route 66*). Given the fact that *Thriller* was never going to revolve around lavish location shoots, or a central star, it was vital that a well-structured story was matched by interesting set design and the quality of the actors cast. [6]

The second episode broadcast, *Possession*, threatens to take us into the realms of supernatural horror, before providing a twist that drains away the paranormal element. The teaser offers us a time-shift back to 1953 and an eerily filmed murder – the silhouette of a stabbing – in a detached country house. We immediately sense, as the murderer drags a body into the cellar while casually whistling and then clicking his fingers, that these mannerisms will be reused in the main body of the story. Post-titles, we are in the same location twenty years later. We seem to have all the ingredients for a ghostly horror tale – a cellar doubling up as a graveyard, the creepy whistling of Greensleeves, rooms wrecked as if by a poltergeist, a psychic medium revealing the lingering presence of a killer. Despite memorable performances by John Carson and Joanna Dunham as a newly married couple, it is Hilary Hardiman as the spiritualist Cecily Rafting who stands out, convincing us of the possibility that past incidents can remain or linger in a place long afterwards:

"You must have had a favourite place as a child, a hideaway, or a picnic spot perhaps? When you return there, those long-past incidents still remain, so vivid you can almost hear the childish laughter."

It is a memorable, elegiac piece of poetic prose and Cecily Rafting is an intriguing, instantly likeable character. John Carson is an outstanding actor, and he plays the two Ray Burns with great skill: the loving husband and the finger-flicking, whistling 'possessed' man. Burns genuinely is a Jekyll and Hyde of the 1970s, with money and social standing his sole motives. Joanna Dunham portrays the increasingly terrified Penny with restrained subtlety, never resorting to hysteria. The supporting characters are equally well cast: Athol Coats as a vaguely creepy handyman and James Cossins as an uncaring estate agent solely interested in selling High Pines, which he is doing once again in the final, cyclical scene.

We are, ultimately, tricked, by both the story itself and its title. What we have witnessed is a murder mystery, albeit an atmospheric one. Unlike *Lady Killer*, there are serious plot holes here, such as how Penny Burns could hear whistling in the house when the perpetrator, her husband, is lying beside her asleep; the same applies to their dining room furniture being smashed while they are both in bed. These incidents work well on a first viewing, while we still think it is a ghostly tale. However, once that has been revealed as a red herring, we feel cheated. As in *Lady Killer*, there is a moral twist in the tale, as Ray Burns tumbles to his death in the cellar, but it is perhaps a little too neat: the killer dying on the exact spot where he buried two of his victims.

Nevertheless, John Cooper's direction creates a suitably creepy atmosphere here, with the camera panning through the house and down into the cellar when Greensleeves is being whistled and while the medium is calling out for the killer to "come to me". Equally effective is the way we continually cut between Penny chopping up carrots as she prepares dinner and the plumber hammering through the concrete cellar floor where – as the teaser has already established – there will be a grisly discovery. The séance is beautifully written and shot, with Madame Rafting reliving that fateful day in 1953, including the dialogue between Elizabeth Millington and her murderer. With the exception of a couple of establishing shots of High Pines and its driveway, the episode is studio bound which reinforces the sense of us being stuck in another of Brian Clemens' memorable country house traps. It is a theme and setting which suited both the writer and the series.

Despite attracting Donna Mills to play the co-lead role relatively soon after her appearance in the iconic film *Play Misty for Me* (1971), *Someone at the Top of the Stairs* – a fans' favourite – for me does not work as a story. The seedy boarding house – with its peepholes and odd tenants – is an intriguing set-of-sets, but there is something not simply deeply unpleasant but even tasteless about the tale, including a small child spying on a naked woman and a kitten thrown to its death, albeit off-camera. Here, the twist that none of these characters exist anymore and that there is a Dorian Gray type mastermind living in the attic, renewing his own life through their deaths, takes us into both the supernatural and horror, including the rising body count in the basement. Mills and Judy Carne offer convincing performances as young, trendy 70s students, but I find little else to commend it for. None of the other guests in the house come alive – no pun intended – and David de Keyser's Cartney is like a twisted Dickensian character out of a gothic melodrama. However, I am probably in a tiny minority with this one.

An Echo of Theresa (*Anatomy of Terror* in the US) provides us with a stylish mystery thriller set in London. It benefits greatly from the generous amount of location filming, these inserts providing a genuine feel of autumnal 70s London. Having established himself as a household name in the US over the course of 99 episodes of *Naked City* (1960-63) as Detective Adam Flint, Paul Burke is cast as businessman Brad Hunter, enjoying what he describes as a "second honeymoon" with his wife Suzy (Polly Bergen) on their first ever trip to England. A single glance at the London *Times* newspaper triggers a series of strange reactions, from anger and violence to genuinely schizophrenic behaviour, such as describing himself as an English gentleman – "Never corrupt good Scotch with ice" – and ordering cigars when he does not smoke. As Hunter begins to demonstrate knowledge about locations and names which should be impossible, part of the charm of the story is waiting to discover whether there is a supernatural element to the story or a realistic drama centring on mind games. Burke is excellent in the lead role as his character veers between confusion and anger. Just when you sense that the narrative has exhausted the exploration of a bewildered husband and wife – is he or is he not losing his sanity? – Clemens drops in a succession of mysterious villains and arguably the story's star character, private investigator Matthew Earp (Dinsdale Landen). Earp – "I exist on suspicions" – allows the mysterious strands to begin to weave together and injects humour, pace and energy into the episode. Landen plays the part with stylish aplomb, from his initial meeting with the Hunters to his confession to the villains at the very end that there were no bullets in his gun. Clemens and Landen combine to create a fun character slightly larger than life, but never ridiculously so. (It is no surprise that the actor/character was brought back for *The Next Scream You Hear*, 1974. One could easily imagine a spin-off series involving Landen's Earp). The reveal that 'Theresa' is many things, including a phone number – from the time when UK telephones combined letters and figures – a code, and a person, is a clever touch and the 'echo' in the title can ultimately be connected to the fact that Brad Hunter has started reliving forgotten past events: his brainwashing in the hands of the enemy. 1950s mind games have, inadvertently, created a confused 'sleeper' agent. The reveal that the Eastern Bloc spy cell leader intends having the Hunters terminated adds a darker edge to the puzzle's endgame. Coming on the back of three very different tales, this espionage (almost time travel) mystery reinforces our early sense of the bewilderingly exciting range of stories which we are going to be offered by Brian Clemens' anthology.

In some respects, *The Colour of Blood* (*The Carnation Killer* in the US) takes us back to the suspense territory of *The Lady Killer*, with the familiar male predator/female victim scenario. Except that here Clemens weaves a more complex and morally grey narrative, providing us with a tale where the 'lone female victim' is a red herring. Indeed, almost all the central characters will turn out to be disturbingly amoral or clinically cold.

The memorable, wordless teaser opens by panning across a bleak, deserted landscape with the surreal sight of an impeccably dressed man wheeling a pram towards a quarry. Director Robert Tronson offers us an artful reflection of his figure in the water, before the twist as the man sends the pram crashing into the dump below, with a young, dead woman falling out of it. The man, Anthony Page, places a carnation in his suit jacket, and we see that the corpse has one as well, in its lifeless hand. He even offers her a casual wave goodbye. We are, therefore, unsurprised to discover, post-titles, that after his arrest and trial he has been deemed 'guilty but insane' by the authorities. Norman Eshley's performance as a woman-hating, mentally disturbed serial killer will, arguably, be as compelling as Robert Powell's was in the opening story.

The crash and subsequent escape of Page from a prison van is effectively filmed and, after the story has brought him together with solicitor's clerk Julie Marsh at Waterloo Station, Eshley cleverly conveys Page's innate animal intelligence and ability to think on his feet. Particularly disturbing is the way he stares forensically at his next potential female victim and picks up on any double meanings, such as Marsh's observation that their train left "dead on time". He is uninterested in either sex or money, it is all about the pursuit for him: "anticipation can be better than the event itself". The 1970s train, with its private spaces (sliding door compartments), reminds us of the dangers and menace which train travel involved, particularly for lone women, in an era before open carriages and CCTV.

Much of the power of this dark tale initially stems from the way we feverishly switch between settings: the train taking Page and Marsh (Katharine Schofield) into the countryside, detectives impatiently awaiting updates about an escaped killer in a busy police station, the wait for news about Miss Marsh in a solicitor's office, and the journey which Marsh's co-worker, Peter (Garrick Hagon), has set out on for a mysterious romantic rendezvous. This allows the story to maintain pace and the sense of interlocking narratives.

Once again, Clemens draws upon his favoured location of an isolated country house trap, drawing on a full range of thriller clichés, including stuffed animals, furniture covered in dust sheets, and an unplugged telephone. Equally effective is the way we, as viewers, are tricked and teased: for example, an off-camera bedroom scream from Julie Marsh turns out to be because she has seen a rat.

In terms of the characters, with the sole exception of the police officers, we have a set of unscrupulous individuals. The real client Michael Graham (Geoffrey Chater) is clearly a furtive, dishonest businessman, while solicitor Baverstock – played with his usual conniving charm by Derek Smith – is more interested in his reputation than his young, female employee's safety. As soon as Clemens delivers the triple twist that Peter and Julie are lovers, that they are planning on killing the client and taking his money, and that the deserted house is not the real one, we are left to reassess the situation. We no longer have the clichéd sexploitation scenario of an innocent female locked in a house with a male killer. Instead, we now have the strange spectacle of waiting to see which of the villains will triumph. Clemens creates dark humour amidst the dramatic tension. Julie and Peter are planning to drug Page's glass of white wine, but the killer puts this on hold, commenting ominously that "everything should be allowed to breathe – for a little while". Since when did white wine need to breathe? Unlike in *The Lady Killer*, where a happy ending is created, there is an inevitability here that the lovers will die, their bodies left in the locked tomb of a house no one will find, with the scattered bank notes and their corpses left for the rats, the final creatures we see as they scamper across the tiled floors.

The Colour of Blood is a genuine thriller, with twists and turns in the plot, and cleverly directed to keep us on edge. It is well cast, with Eshley magnetic in the central role. Arguably, though, the lack of any empathetic characters leaves us feeling strangely detached from the bleak ending. The story is captivatingly thrilling, but it leaves us with no one to care about. This is not a weakness, as such, in what is a cleverly crafted narrative. It is simply my observation that some of us feel the need to emotionally invest in at least one character.

Murder in Mind takes us into the realms of meta fiction, as the story centres on a writer of crime thrillers, George Drew (Richard Johnson), planning on committing a murder of his own, and a policeman attempting to interpret clues from both Betty Drew's fragmented ramblings and from the novelist's own texts and method of writing: piecing together the various plot elements "like a jigsaw puzzle" in George's words. In theory, it is a clever, playful approach.

Pre-teaser, Betty (Zena Walker) has inadvertently heard her own murder being planned through the "hollow voices" (of her husband

and his lover) coming through the bedroom fire grate, but her confusion has led to her 'assuming guilt', leading to an intriguing teaser where she arrives at a police station and confesses to a murder which – it turns out – has not taken place. Yet.

Unfortunately, as soon as the alleged victim, 'missing' secretary Jill Pembury (Christina Greatrex), turns up safe and well, we have all the ingredients we need to solve the mystery: the real intended victim, the motive – Betty and George's wealth is "financially inseparable" – the method to be used – a fake break-in – and the time, echoing Drew's novel *Murder Her At Midnight*. The second half of the story therefore simply becomes a question of whether DC Patterson will understand how the fragmented pieces of Betty's confession fit together and whether he can arrive in time to thwart the murderer.

What started out as a nicely puzzling concept gives way for a predictable, straightforward tale. To make things worse, the central characters and the acting performances of Johnson, Walker and Greatrex are flat. It is left to the police trio of Gee, Ronald Radd as his tough-but-fair boss, and Anthony Boden as the calm, philosophical station sergeant to raise the bar. Donald Gee does a good job of portraying a young, keen, and dogged Detective Constable working on instinct rather than evidence. Sadly, despite his interesting character and performance, there is little else to praise here. Secretary/lover Jill Pembury refers to Drew as "churning" out his novels. Here we have a sense that *Murder in Mind* has also been churned out. In the absence of inventive sets or direction, there is nothing to mark the story out as extraordinary. Patterson's arrival in the nick of time leads to a lifeless, theatrical battle in the bedroom and, while there is a happy ending, this scene mirrors my overall sense of a story which fails to spark or excite.

A Place to Die takes us firmly into the realms of horror, with the teaser plunging us into the clichéd nightmare of a young, fair-haired woman in a bright frock, or nightdress, being pursued through woodland at night-time, ending with a deathly scream. The hand-held camera adds to the sense of frenzy, panic and confusion. What follows is a story which combines elements of the Hammer tradition, folk horror and the type of picture-postcard village setting favoured by Clemens in several *Avengers* episodes, most notably *Murdersville*. Indeed, Laurie Johnson's score here is, at times, very similar to the one he composed for that 1960s story. Thematically there are also similarities between the two: the arrival of outsiders looking to start a new life in the countryside; the use of medieval devices by the villagers of Little Storping, such as the ducking stool and chastity belt, and the strange behaviour and olde-world customs of the locals in *A Place to Die*.

Dr Bruce Nelson describes moving to a village and taking over a local practice as an exciting opportunity to be his own boss and to escape "the rat race". Yet his attitude – for a highly intelligent man of the world – is a dismissive, closed-minded one. Despite the mounting evidence of strange goings-on – villagers talking about the full moon, almost everyone limping on the same foot, odd gifts given to his young wife, a crucifix and clove of garlic left by his predecessor in the surgery, letters from that previous GP which were written, sealed, but never sent off, a voodoo-type doll with a broken neck – he dismisses it all as the result of "inbreeding" and "closed communities". Bryan Marshall plays the role with great skill, conveying the sense of a decent, warm-hearted man, even if he is one who feels superior to his patients. Less convincing is doe-eyed Alexandra Hay as his young American bride, Tessa. In all fairness, it is a thankless role as the intended village sacrifice. The part mostly consists of expressing panic, fear and confusion through her eyes.

The village store seems to double up as community hall. It is a strange set, more like a warehouse than shop and most of its visitors are simply one-dimensional, undeveloped figures: blacksmith, gamekeeper, gardener, dressmaker...Whenever Jill (Sally Stephens) or Tessa Nelson enter, there is an uncomfortable undercurrent of sexual tension, with all the men hungrily eyeing them up; yet this aspect (mercifully) is never properly developed. If Tessa is destined to become the bride of Satan – and Jill sacrificed as her bridesmaid – then this is intended as the way to provide "eternal Satanic power for the village", rather than sexual gratification for 'Crazy Nick'. Juan Moreno plays the part of the mute Nick with great skill, as we see his character twist from Shakespearean 'village joker/idiot' to the Prince of Darkness, as it were.

A Place to Die is another of those stories where someone – Dr Nelson here – arrives in the nick of time to provide a happy ending. Yet, as Bruce examines the dead Nick's deformed foot, he steadfastly dismisses the cloven hoof as "an inbred deformity". As a (narrow-minded) man of science, he demands a rational explanation. Are the writers – Brian Clemens and Terence Feely – leaving it up to us to decide whether the locals are genuinely possessed, or simply deluded? That certainly seems to be the opinion of critic Kevin Lyons, who goes on to offer the following summary:

'*Thriller* was always a bit hit-and-miss…*A Place to Die* is never boring but it also never quite engages as it should. The plot is littered with inconsistencies and things that are never quite worked out properly but as an early example of "folk horror" (it was broadcast several months before *The Wicker Man* was released) it's of some historical interest. It may not be one that you'll want to come back to all that often though.' [7]

Overall, I would agree with these general observations about the series in general and this particular episode. In terms of inconsistencies, there is a major plot hole in *A Place to Die*. The villagers greet the arrival of the beautiful, limping Tessa as "the expected one" and yet it has been made clear to the evil housekeeper Bess – and therefore to the village in general – that she is temporarily suffering from a ski accident injury. Therefore, their shock when they discover that her foot is not deformed after all makes no sense.

Nevertheless, this story once again illustrates the range which *Thriller* offers in its opening series. While Lyons suggests – in contrast to the *TV Cream* review – that the videotape nature of *Thriller* is detrimental to creating 'atmosphere', I feel that in *A Place to Die* a chilling atmosphere *is* created, by the creepy villagers themselves, the score – including pan pipes and flutes wafting from the woods – and the 'props' which Tessa discovers scattered around the house. She comments at one point, "What can happen in a sleepy old English village?" In the fertile imagination of Clemens and Feely, just about anything.

File It Under Fear provides us with a teaser which takes a clichéd scenario but gives it some intriguing twists. A woman walks along a pavement at night, watched by a man dressed in a military or security guard uniform. He hides in the shadows as she prepares to descend into a pedestrian subway, before peering down after her. We expect her to be attacked in the tunnel, but she emerges and, as she subsequently walks across a canal side wooden footbridge, she apprehensively looks behind her, as if instinctively sensing danger. Suddenly, an unseen figure strangles her, she drops the books she was carrying, and the camera focuses on those hardbacks and her lifeless hand. Is the uniformed man a red herring, or a killer? Why are the books significant? These two unanswerable questions lift the teaser above the ordinary.

Post-teaser we are swiftly taken to three different locations: a corner sweet shop where that same man (Gerry Masters, played by American Richard Pendrey) is flirting with shop girl Betty (Jenny Quayle); a police station when a Superintendent is annoyed to have had his game of golf interrupted by murder; and a town library where the killing is being discussed by two young librarians. The book theme is quickly reintroduced. Head Librarian Liz Morris has a theory that "you can judge a person's character...by the books he reads." Miss Morris reads romance, although she seems keen to keep that fact to herself. One quickly senses that we have been playfully offered lots of clues already, leaving it up to us to decide which ones are genuine.

Unlike in *A Place to Die* where most of the characters remain crudely sketched 'types', here Clemens' script – both in terms of dialogue and pace – and the excellent casting allow the characters to be quickly and effortlessly established as fully-rounded people. Superintendent Cramer (James Grout) is an instantly interesting character. His annoyance at having his golf match interrupted might come across as callous, yet he immediately strikes us as a thorough policeman, and one who instinctively senses that the killer will strike again. Equally intriguing is Miss Morris (Maureen Lipman), a friendly, highly efficient woman who is clearly lonely and looking for love. Her young assistants George Bailey (Richard O'Callaghan) and student Gillie Randall (Jan Francis) inject some youthful energy into the library, while John Le Mesurier's early arrival as library dweller Stubbs has us wondering whether he is simply a lonely man looking for company and reading material, or someone more sinister.

Clemens continues to build the suspense at a rapid lick: Betty telling Gillie that she is meeting a married man by the bridge that evening, the Super's theory that the strangler is a "trained" killer, Stubbs' frantic confession that he is desperately lonely, and the reveal that George is reading a book about karate and has been mocked by Betty for being physically immature and lacking 'masculinity', a verbal humiliation which he reacts to in a threatening manner. In a stylishly, darkly playful touch, Gillie's warning to her friend, "I think you are a fool. I mean, where's it going to get you?" cuts into Sergeant Truscott telling his boss about "the morgue". With Gerry Masters lurking around the library at closing time, and the introduction of the Morris' furtive lodger Steve (John Nightingale), we are surrounded by potential victims and killers.

There is, of course, an inevitability that the killer will strike again, something which adds to the dramatic tension rather than takes away from it. When it does occur, it is effectively captured in the shadows. Filmed inserts allow us to see police frogmen scouring the canal for evidence, reinforcing the laborious, painstaking nature of a murder inquiry. At the halfway stage of this whodunit, we genuinely have no firm idea who the serial killer is.

As the circumstantial evidence stacks up against both Gerry Masters — seen with the missing Gillie, standing on the footbridge by a dead body then running off, and lurking in the library, before taking out books such as *The Psycho Murders* — and Steve Kerroway — scratch marks on his face, uncharacteristically heading out each evening, first arrived in the town soon before the initial murder — it all seems too obvious or neat. Instead, our suspicions turn to both George and the lonely Stubbs. One has already expressed his desire to prove his 'manhood', the other has a Naval background and is unhealthily interested in the young female victims. George, though, is a coward and fantasist, in addition to being someone who lacks the 'trained' background profile. That leaves the elderly Stubbs, a man who has offered several damning comments about young women in the 1970s, referring to "girls of today" as being "easy". Clemens provides us with several cunning twists late in the tale: Gillie turns up safe and well, having been working with Gerry Masters to uncover the killer who the serviceman wrongly thinks is George; Liz hurls a bookcase down on to Masters in the belief that he is the killer. This leaves us with the ultimate irony, that she could not have been further from the truth when she said that you can judge a person's moral character from the books they read. If only she had listened to Stubbs' moral judgements about young women's supposedly 'loose' sexual attitudes, she might have caught a killer, rather than killed an innocent man. Having judged Gerry Masters (partly) by the books he reads, she has now killed him with a bookcase of them.

File It Under Fear is a cleverly plotted whodunit. When we look back, it is the library which is at the heart of the narrative, but it is the overheard snippets of conversation which are key, not the books which people have chosen to read. Clemens creates some superb characters in the story, in particular the dogged Superintendent Cramer and Liz Morris who, by her own admission, has become "a dried-up old spinster" at the age of 29. On a second viewing it becomes more obvious early on that Stubbs is the serial killer, but then hindsight is a wonderful thing. As so often in the series, the casting is spot on, in particular James Grout, Maureen Lipman and John Le Mesurier. Lipman's performance is a highlight of the series. Liz Morris is a genuinely tragic figure, someone who lives out her private life in a fantasy world of romance novels while real life passes her by. Rose Hill, as Liz's mother, offers us a welcome injection of humour with her morbid love of reading about violent deaths in the newspaper: "I do like a nice murder."

File It Under Fear offers us some delightful sets. The corner shop is a mid-70s snapshot, with its jars of sweets and adverts for ice lollies such as Cider Gold. The substantial library has upper-storey galleries and spiral staircases, allowing the camera some lovely, elevated shots and coming into its own in the unexpected finale. As was the case in *Journey Into the Unknown*'s *Matakitas is Coming*, it provides the perfect claustrophobic setting, with dark corners and recesses; the potential for faces to suddenly appear between books on a dusty shelf.

The screenplay for *The Eyes Have It* was written by Terence Feely, but it draws on not only Clemens' storyline but also material from several earlier stories of his. Clemens had already used the idea of a house being picked out by villains as the perfect spot for an assassination in both *The Baron* episode *The Maze* and *The Avengers* hybrid Nation/Clemens episode *Take-Over*. He had used the plot of a blind victim trapped in a building in his film *See No Evil*. Here, the two scenarios are successfully brought together.

Many of the *Thriller* episodes have quite complex plots with twists and red herrings often thrown into the equation. Here, the storyline is delightfully simple. In a variation on the ticking time bomb theme, it becomes a question of whether a group of blind students can draw upon their collective mental and physical resources to thwart the assassination of a "man of peace" who will be passing close by their Clinical Training Centre. The teaser tricks us into thinking that this is a perfectly normal group of medical students, until the almost surreal moment when cold-blooded Anderson (Peter Vaughan) shoots the tutor and we watch a sightless Sally (Sinead Cusack) grinning on the other side of the glass screen, oblivious to what has just happened.

The Eyes Have It relies on the crackling dramatic tension created in a slow-moving drama. Both Alun Armstrong and Dennis Waterman impress as blind students, but it is Sinead Cusack who drives the narrative. Sally uses all her instincts and senses: smelling the villains' gun oil, feeling Anderson's distinctive gold ring, questioning everything which takes place, from the mysterious arrival of 'plumbers' to the disconnected phone line. Cusack steals every scene she is in and her "bloodhound" character demonstrates that Anderson was foolish to believe that "nothing can go wrong in the kingdom of the blind."

An extra layer of drama is created by the tension between the Organisation's observer Moore (Leslie Schofield) and the hired assassin Jeffries (William Marlowe) who seem as intent on killing each other as they are on wrecking the Heads of State peace talks. All three villainous roles are stylishly played by the actors, with Vaughan always reliable as an imposing, menacing figure and genuine sparks flying between Marlowe and Schofield.

Several moments are particularly memorable, such as the scene where Sally thinks she is practising on a surgical dummy only to discover George Mallard's corpse, and her escape through the dumb waiter and cellar only to realise that the helping hand which greets her is Anderson's.

At times the script arguably overdoes the blind/sight gallows humour jokes, particularly at the end when the television commentary refers to the parade as an event that "really is something to see". Nevertheless, *The Eyes Have It* is a fascinating thriller which is very different from any of the previous tales.

Spell of Evil completes the initial series of *Thriller*. Although it takes us firmly into the supernatural, unlike the folk horror setting and feel of *A Place to Die*, here there is a decidedly 1970s vibe created by the clothes, the décor and the principal sets: both the Mansell split-level modern house and the glass-fronted offices with their river views. Tony Mansell's lower floor den – with its open-tread staircase, brown leather sofas and huge copper fire hood – gives the story a contemporary, modern feel, offering a clever contrast with the subject matter at hand: ancient witchcraft. Gothic horror meets 70s interior. It is made clear to us – but not to Tony (Edward de Souza) – early on that the mysterious Clara (Diane Cilento) has the ability to make strange things happen through her powers: a dating agency letter vanishes from his office desk, PA Liz (Jennifer Daniel) is physically injured by a coffee percolator and a glass frame, business rivals die in a car crash, all accidents manufactured by her, remotely. Her only sign of weakness is a shocked, fearful reaction to finding the first Mrs Mansell's crucifix necklace. As viewers, we are left to conclude early on that Tony's wife's death in the teaser was caused or created by Clara. (After all, we have witnessed how devastated both the husband and housekeeper were by her demise, in addition to the fish-eye hint that she saw a plunging dagger in her final moments.) This leaves us with several intriguing questions. What is Clara's motive? Will Tony realise what is happening? Is there anything which can be done to stop her?

At the halfway point of the story, Clara jokingly tells her husband, "Didn't I tell you, darling, I'm a witch?" It recalls the old adage:

'Many a true word is spoken in jest.' With Tony bedridden and the faithful Mrs Roberts (Iris Russell) knocked down by a car soon after, one senses that it will be up to the equally faithful – and suspicious – Liz to do something about Clara before it is too late. Liz, in effect, becomes a self-hired private detective. The pleasure, for the viewer, is in watching how the final third of the story pans out, with two equally determined women fighting it out, figuratively speaking.

Despite the dark content, there is plenty of humour injected by Terence Feely. When Tony and business partner George (Jeremy Longhurst) first hear the gravelly voice of Clara on the phone, George warns him: "Don't get too excited. I had an uncle with a voice like that." Later, when Clara first meets Liz, she offers the wonderfully condescending: "Oh! You're the *secretary!*" As the frantic finale takes place, the witch expert brought in by Liz takes time out to marvel at Clara's fetish 'killing image': "Oh, it's a beauty!"

Spell of Evil does not contain any star names in its cast, nor is there a single acting performance which stands out. However, as a piece of dramatic entertainment, it keeps the viewer hooked throughout and there is an exciting pace to the story, which is not always the case in the *Thriller* series.

Looking back on that first series, we have great variety in terms of genre, from whodunits to whydunits, from conventional thrillers to psychological horror and supernatural tales. Sometimes we are unsure, initially, which type of story we have been plunged into. *Lady Killer, The Colour of Blood, File It Under Fear* and *The Eyes Have It* are, for me, all first-class pieces of drama and even the less successful offerings all have intriguing elements. Most of them offer us fish-eyed insights into or reflections of Britain in the mid-1970s, from unfashionable seaside holiday towns, a growing student culture, the trend of people moving out of the city, aspirational middle class living...in other respects, some of the themes covered, such as male voyeurism, or murder committed out of a desire for monetary gain, are timeless ones.

The earlier Thames Television thriller series *Shadows of Fear* (1970-71) remained grounded, largely speaking, in realism, with psychological fear being the running leitmotif. Here, the canvas was far wider and, arguably, more ambitious. Brian Clemens was, at that time, arguably one of the only British script writers who could have 'sold' an anthology series single-handedly to a television company, and it is testimony to his prolific imagination and speed of writing that he could storyboard each one of the stories. Understandably, as the subsequent *Thriller* series progressed, we start to see recycling, variations on already established themes, including the lone woman trapped in a country house. There are, after all, weaknesses as well as strengths to a show dominated by one writer. In this initial run, Robert Powell, Norman Eshley, Maureen Lipman and Sinead Cusack each produces a spellbinding acting performance and the casting, in general, is first rate. There is enough connective tissue between the ten tales to give a sense of each belonging within a series; yet part of the excitement generated by *Thriller* is, as I suggested at the very start, that sense of the unknown, the unpredictability, as we switch on a new episode and re-open Pandora's Box.

Ultimately, there is a lovely contrast between *Shadows of Fear* and *Thriller*. The older anthology benefits from the intensity of small casts, its studio-bound claustrophobia, and greater social realism. *Thriller* brought greater variety in terms of both genre and the 'exotic', transatlantic nature of many of its cast lists. Both anthologies offered great 'theatrical' entertainment, although part of their appeal today is nostalgia: the fun of uncovering each episode's cast of stars, the slower pace of drama – not necessarily a weakness – even the 70s interiors. The stories are also a sad reminder that one-off TV drama is, largely, a vanished art form. Part of the fun of anthology series, from *The Twilight Zone* to *Black Mirror*, is that bewildering sense of journeying into the unknown, of exploring a new world each week, populated by different characters. In the case of both *Shadows of Fear* and *Thriller*, certainly the clothes, hairstyles and technical limitations date the tales, yet many of the stories themselves have lost little of their magic, as we happily plunge into a veritable Pandora's Box.

© Rodney Marshall

1. Sydney Newman cited in *Armchair Theatre*, an article in *The Wayback Machine, Television Heaven* online.
2. In some respects, *Thriller* looks back to the more fantasy-driven Hammer anthology series *Journey into the Unknown* (1968-69), which made great use of transatlantic casts and often created a similar sense of claustrophobic menace in episodes such as *Matakitas is Coming*, where Vera Miles' character finds herself trapped in a locked library at night-time with a serial killer.
3. *TV Cream* website, June 21st, 2010.
4. *TV Cream* refers to 'the old school approach: four days in the studio, one day on location, bash it out, onto the next one.'
5. Just a few months later, Robert Powell would be seen in a remarkably similar role as a 'charming' cold killer, Brian Godfrey, in the *Zodiac* episode *Sting Sting Scorpio*, broadcast on 25/03/1974. Norman Eshley also reappears as a villain in *Zodiac* story *The Strength of Gemini*, first shown on 11/03/1974. For all their differences, *Zodiac* and *Thriller* share connective tissue. The offbeat Anton Rodgers/Anouska Hempel mini-series is explored by JZ Ferguson in the following chapter.
6. In a tweet sent to me, Martin Marshall, author of *A Thriller in Every Corner*, argued that the "creative directorial input" was "pushing multicamera studio recording beyond its usual boundaries". (Twitter message, 11/05/2022).
7. Kevin Lyons, the EOFFTV Review, 22/05/2018.

ZODIAC: LESSONS FROM THE STARS

The title of the show is *Zodiac*, but do not let that fool you. It is true that Roger Marshall's 1974 series' premise is that one can solve crimes using astrology, the study of the movements and positions of stars and other celestial bodies and the supposed influence of them on people and their lives. As a result, each episode featured suitably astrologically themed titles and plots. (A second season of six stories, which would have allowed the show to spotlight all twelve signs of the zodiac, sadly failed to materialise.) However, while the show delivers plenty in the way of horoscopes and star signs and their influence on the 'star-crossed' victims and perpetrators of crime, it is much more interested in drilling down into the psychology, actions, and characterisation of its two principals, Detective Inspector David 'Grad' Gradley and astrologer Esther Jones, as well as those of the players in the mysteries that they investigate, and extracting some valuable life lessons that can help us to not only survive, but thrive. These 'existential survival skills' are as relevant today as they were in the politically and economically harsh 70s landscape in which they originated.

A World of Contradictions

In all crime series, characters employ a measure of deception or illusion to protect their secrets, regardless of whether those secrets have a direct bearing on the crime of the week, in order to preserve the image of themselves that they and others believe to be true. In the process, such characters will often act in ways that are antithetical to what they profess to believe or stand for. While such intentionally deceptive characters appear in *Zodiac*, the most notable and interesting contradictions are found in the depictions of the two leads, Grad and Esther. These contradictions provide insights into Grad and Esther's psychology that, in turn, form the basis of many of the series' life lessons, or 'existential survival skills', which can be used to change one's life for the better.

Lessons from Detective Inspector David 'Grad' Gradley

Be open to new ideas and reassessing your convictions (even if you do not completely abandon your old ones).

Of the two leads, Grad provides the more obvious example of contradictory beliefs and behaviour in the series with his opinion and use of astrology. Grad and Esther's relationship begins in *Death of a Crab* with him mocking what he believes to be a pseudoscience. While exploring Esther's flat, Grad discovers a pack of tarot cards, a ceramic hand laying out the fundamentals of palmistry, and books on astrology, and makes his disdain for Esther's beliefs known: "An astrologer?...Shouldn't you be... polishing your crystal ball?...I hear your union is pressing for a unilateral ban on tea bags. Any truth in it?" Esther counters with a knowing, "Bigot or sceptic?" to which Grad responds, "Neither. I just think it's a load of old Taurus." Other derisive comments about astrology and 'mystical' powers follow. In *The Cool Aquarian*, he mocks Esther's belief that he is focusing on the wrong suspect by sarcastically asking, "[Are] your bunions twitching?". Similarly, in *Saturn's Rewards*, he teases a glum Esther about being unable to guess a man's birth sign after she failed to guess the sign of Grad's brother, rubbing salt in the wound with the jab "Another clanger?". In the same episode, he dismisses her astrologically based theory of the case by claiming that he does not need "bed, book, and candle." In *Sting, Sting, Scorpio!*, he mocks her astrological beliefs and abilities when she takes over her fortune telling mentor's old shop: "Well, I never thought I would see the day...Everything from Taurus' tea leaves to day trippers' bunions." Grad pairs this derisive attitude toward mysticism with strong advocacy for traditional investigative techniques. He states his crime-solving philosophy in *The Cool Aquarian* – "I like evidence, right? Concrete evidence...black and white" – before adding that he generally does not take people's words for things, and believes that they often lie. In the same episode, he utilises conventional investigative methods, such as door-to-door inquiries, surveillance, and investigating known criminals, while working a case. In *Saturn's Rewards*, he describes good police work as being down to "perspiration and shoe leather", and uses logic to hypothesise that a murder was committed before the curtains were closed, and therefore was potentially witnessed by someone. In the same episode, he claims that he has no need for Esther's assistance in solving the case as long as he sticks to the facts. In *The Horns of the Moon*, he takes umbrage when Esther believes that creating horoscope charts for each of the suspects will help to solve a case, preferring to use 'tried and true' techniques to draw conclusions instead. When Esther asserts that one of the suspects could not be the killer because his chart shows that he is incapable of murder, Grad dismisses her theory as nonsense.

However, though Grad makes no secret of his disdain for astrology, Esther casts doubt on his conviction that it is nonsense in their first meeting. On sight alone, Esther correctly predicts that Grad was born between March 20 and April 21, and provides a remarkably accurate sketch of his character, telling him that he is resolute, forthright, egotistical, adventurous, and in need of patience. She also tells him that he is prone to headaches, sudden tempers, stomach upsets, and sinus problems. "Still sceptical?" she inquires, to which Grad replies, "Yes, but less than I was five minutes ago." Minutes after meeting Esther, she has already planted a seed of doubt in his mind, and, despite his continued emphasis on facts and evidence, Grad finds himself giving Esther's astrologically based theories and pronouncements more weight than he cares to admit, when he is not blatantly relying on them. In *The Cool Aquarian*, he seems to have become an out and out convert, despite continuing to insist that he prefers concrete evidence, asking Esther to use her powers to help him pin down the nature of a criminal act that he has heard is going to occur on a specific day. Later, he asks Esther to hold a missing woman's locket to see if she can get a reading that will tell him what has happened to her. When Esther admits that she feels nothing, Grad sighs about having to go back to the old standards of criminal records and fingerprints, even though such old standards are the kind of policework he always insists is the key to cracking cases. He also asks Esther to cast the missing woman's horoscope and, when Esther discovers that the woman is being held near water, he reads out water-related words until Esther feels an affinity for one, which helps them to determine the missing woman's location. Throughout the story, Grad never seems to doubt Esther's predictions or abilities for a moment, relying on them rather than questioning or mocking them, and using them alongside traditional policework. Other episodes also find him implicitly or explicitly acknowledging the veracity of Esther's powers and the usefulness of astrology. In *The Strength of the Gemini*, Esther's ability to pick a winning horse with long odds has Grad taking her hand and desperately running it down the racing listings in the hopes of getting her to repeat the trick for his own benefit. In *Saturn's Rewards*, Grad is proud to solve a case without Esther's assistance, but reluctantly admits that Esther's astrological reading of an MP as being incapable of murder was correct. In *Sting, Sting, Scorpio!*, Esther's sixth sense impression that a woman has been murdered by drowning – so vivid that she smells the sea – is taken extremely seriously by Grad. A highly effective pullback, showing Grad leaning in and speaking intently to Esther about what she has just experienced, emphasises both the gravity of what has occurred and Grad's total belief in the truth and accuracy of what Esther has told him. After Esther explains her astrologically based theory about the circumstances of the woman's death to a member of the Brighton police force, the man mocks her and Grad laughs along with him, albeit nervously, unwilling to let on that he believes Esther's theory is correct. He makes up for his hypocrisy later on, when he expresses admiration for Esther's accurate prediction about the common thread between all of the significant events of the case: water. These moments would seem to run counter to Grad's derisive comments about astrology and emphasis on using logic and evidence to solve crimes, but Grad's complicated and contradictory views on Esther's powers and astrology have a lesson to teach us, one that Grad himself hints at in an exchange in *The Horns of the Moon*:

Esther: Do you accept the fact that astrology has a scientific basis?
Grad: I'm not sure. I accept the fact that you think it has and sometimes you make me believe it.

Grad therefore entertains the existence of Esther's powers while maintaining a healthy scepticism. Grad's openness of mind and willingness to live with the tension between these two opposing belief systems – rather than force himself to choose one way of thinking over the other – lead to improvements in his life, as Esther's abilities offer him another tool with which to solve crimes. Grad's complex, contradictory take on astrology therefore offers a model of how to be cautiously open-minded, one that involves entertaining new ideas without being staunchly rigid in our beliefs or abandoning them in the face of the smallest challenge.

Our assessments of our talents and abilities are not always accurate. Re-examine the evidence to determine whether you are as bad at something as you or others believe.

Another of the contradictions inherent in Grad's character provides us with this lesson. In *Death of a Crab*, Grad tells Esther that he is under no illusions that he is, or ever will be, a good policeman. He backs up this conviction in *The Cool Aquarian*, in which he claims that others were similarly convinced that he was not cut out for the force: "I always was unobservant – they said so at police college." However, Grad's self-assessment of his proficiency at his job is not borne out by his professional performance in the series. In fact, *Death of a Crab*, the very episode in which he is critical of his professional proficiency, reveals him to be clever and quick-thinking when conducting his investigations. While attending a crime scene in a penthouse, Grad receives a telephone call from Esther, whom he has yet to meet. Rather than identifying himself as a police officer, he pretends to be the occupant of the penthouse in order to glean information from Esther while her guard is down. When Esther comments that his voice sounds odd, i.e., unlike that of the penthouse's owner, Grad thinks fast and stuffs a chip into his mouth, telling Esther that he is eating breakfast. While at the same crime scene, Grad also demonstrates that he is observant and detail oriented, noticing small things that others might miss or dismiss. He spots an almost-invisible stain on the carpet and not only identifies the substance as malt whisky, but notes that there is no bottle of that alcohol anywhere in the penthouse, raising questions about where the stain came from. He also notes that the victim, who everyone has assumed to be the wealthy occupant of the penthouse, is wearing worn, out-of-fashion shoes, calling the body's identity into question. Grad's suspicions turn out to be valid, as the victim is revealed not to be the wealthy penthouse occupant after all. When the real occupant turns up and gives his version of events, the observant Grad queries why, upon returning home, the man went straight to the bathroom and checked the bath – the location where the body was discovered – pointing out that it is an odd thing to do before even taking one's coat off. He is similarly detail oriented in *The Cool Aquarian*. After listening to a recording made by a kidnapped woman and sent to a rich businessman, he intuits from the content of the message that the kidnapper knows the businessman very well, a hypothesis that is confirmed when it emerges that the kidnapper is the businessman's colleague. Grad's observational skills also come to the fore in *The Horns of the Moon*, in which he notes that a gun, believed to be the murder weapon, has suddenly appeared in a room. He is also observant in *Saturn's Rewards*, in which he picks up on a Member of Parliament's suspicious slip-up while he is asking the MP questions about a murder that took place in the flat opposite the MP's. The MP mentions a murdered woman before Grad has told him that a murder has taken place or the victim's sex, causing the MP to scramble for an explanation and claim that he heard about the murder from his gossipy hall porter.

Grad also brings logic and deductive reasoning skills to his chosen vocation. In *Saturn's Rewards*, Grad works out the entire sequence of events that unfolded during a murder using logic and evidence. Rather than relying on her 'crystals', he instead uses Esther as a test subject to assist in confirming his theories about human behaviour, asking her if she would leave her curtains open when it began to get dark. When Esther answers in the affirmative, he asks her if she would close them before she turned the light on, and Esther states that she would not. The questions prove that Grad suspected early on that the MP witnessed the murder, a theory that is supported by forensics, which reveal that the murderer only pulled the curtains closed after the killing. Grad also catches the MP looking out his window and into the flat in which the murder took place, and connects the MP's obvious interest in the crime with other evidence – including the MP's request that Grad look into the background of the owner of the flat, the fact that the owner of the flat was dating the MP's daughter, and the MP's hostility toward the owner of the flat and opposition to his daughter marrying the owner – to conclude that the MP recognised the murderer as his daughter's beau. The only part of the story he fails to work out is the reason for the MP's reticence in reporting the crime, a mystery Esther solves by deducing that the MP had his mistress with him. However, given that Grad had already interviewed a witness who reported hearing the voices of the MP and a woman on the night in question, he likely would have eventually come to the same conclusion on his own.

Grad also deftly handles the people involved in his cases, as demonstrated in *The Cool Aquarian*, in which he endears himself to a retired policeman named Sutton by recalling a significant criminal that Sutton arrested. He is equally good with Sutton's wife, who fears for her missing niece. Sutton, who investigated countless cases in which young women disappeared, only to return home a few days later safe and sound, dismisses her fears as nothing more than female hysteria, and tells Grad that he only reported his niece as missing to placate his wife. Grad, however, does not patronise Sutton's wife, instead taking the case at face value and gathering details about the niece's appearance, movements, and life. This proves to be a difficult task, as Sutton and his wife have difficulty agreeing on how best to describe their niece's appearance, but

Grad takes the particulars down with as much patience as he can muster. He pairs these people skills with extreme diligence when he seriously considers the most significant piece of evidence that Mrs. Sutton offers as proof that her niece was taken against her will. Showing Grad a book that was her niece's most prized possession, Mrs. Sutton argues that her niece would have taken it with her if her departure was voluntary. Sutton dismisses his wife's theory as nonsense, but Grad does not, telling Mrs. Sutton that he believes her theory has merit and treating her with respect, kindness, and humanity. Grad's interactions with the MP in *Saturn's Rewards* also reveal his people skills and the humanity with which he conducts his work. He opts not to tell the MP's family about the affair the MP has been having, or to arrest him for severely injuring a murderer. This allows the MP to come out of the investigation with his family, career and reputation intact, and continue the work he is doing in government, while also sparing Esther's friend – the MP's daughter – considerable distress. Such gestures of goodwill should not, however, be taken as evidence that Grad cannot act authoritatively toward others when the job requires it. In the same episode, he takes charge of a crime scene, examines important evidence, and warns Esther that he is allowing her to be there "under sufferance".

Collectively, these moments reveal that Grad possesses excellent observation and deductive skills; is detail oriented, logical, diligent, authoritative, and a quick thinker; has a good understanding of human behaviour; and has good people skills, all qualities that contradict his own pronouncement that he is not a particularly valuable asset to the force. The lesson that Grad offers in this instance is that one should look at the facts in order to determine if one has a distorted view about one's abilities that does not reflect reality. People are often harder on themselves than they are on others, and this penchant for self-criticism can be extremely detrimental if unwarranted. Perhaps Grad's often-sour disposition would be sweetened if he took time to reassess his policeman's skill set and held it in higher regard.

Unhappy in your job? Reflect on whether it is the work itself that you dislike, or the circumstances surrounding it.

Along with his proclamation that he is not a good policeman, Grad also claims that he is not happy to be one, either, and only chose it as a career because working on the force was a condition that he was required to meet in order to receive funds from his grandfather's trust. However, when Esther expresses mock sympathy for his plight, Grad blithely replies, "Could be worse. Plenty of variety. I get the odd phone call. Could be anything from lending my flat to the assistant commissioner or coming out to meet intriguing people like you" (*Death of a Crab*). This comment suggests that Grad enjoys his work more than he lets on. His professed dislike for his reluctantly chosen profession is also blatantly contradicted by his actions. Rather than do the bare minimum required to maintain his position, Grad takes his duties very seriously and puts a lot of effort into performing them. In *The Cool Aquarian*, Grad's efforts to locate a missing woman include asking Esther to provide both astrological and psychic assistance, interviewing the businessman who received a ransom demand for the woman, questioning all of the woman's known contacts, putting a tail on the woman's employer, running surveillance on the woman's aunt and uncle to see if they are in contact with her, coordinating house-to-house inquiries, investigating known extortionists, having a policewoman walk the same route as the woman did on the day of her disappearance while wearing an identical dress, and running the woman's photo in newspapers and on television and posting it in shops. In *Saturn's Rewards*, his tenacity comes to the fore once again while investigating a woman's murder, during which he interviews an MP so many times that the man comments on Grad's efforts, to which Grad responds that good policework requires "perspiration and shoe leather".

One could argue that Grad's hard work is solely motivated by a desire to keep his position on the force. After all, if he was sacked for incompetence or laziness, he would be cut off from his trust.

However, Grad does not indicate that the trust requires him to attain any particular position on the force. If that is the case, why does he not opt for some dull, undemanding post, a desk job where he could wile away the hours doing paperwork without exerting himself? Of course, one could argue that Grad works hard in the hope that his efforts will elevate him to a cushy senior position, with all of its attendant perks. His constant attempts to get in his superiors' good books would seem to support this theory. However, if Grad is merely attempting to secure himself a promotion, he is going about it the hard way. He does not cut corners. He is not brusque or inhumane with the people involved in his cases for the sake of expediency. He is so diligent that he holds off on kissing Esther for fear that he will catch her cold and be unable to report for duty, rather than relishing the idea of taking a sick day (*Sting, Sting, Scorpio!*). Most notably, he chooses not to work with a lower-ranked partner with whom he could split the work and save himself a great deal of time and effort. Esther comments on Grad's lack of a partner in *Death of a Crab*, "How is it that you always come alone? I thought policemen worked in pairs?". Grad simply acknowledges that that is the typical ways of doing things – "You're right. It is usual." – without offering any explanation for his choice to go against the grain. Indeed, Esther appears to be the first and only person he has ever gone to for help on a regular basis, and he even opts to do without her assistance in *Saturn's Rewards*. Since Grad does not even want to be in charge of one person, it seems unlikely that he is motivated to attain a senior position that would put him in charge of many people. However, one might instead interpret Grad's proclivity for solo work as an indication that he does not like to share credit for good results, lest it hamper his ability to climb the ranks. It is likely the case that Grad does not always inform his superiors about the role Esther plays in solving his cases, as the show offers examples of him being willing to take sole credit for a good result, in spite of Esther's assistance (e.g., in *The Cool Aquarian*). However, if Grad is telling his superiors that all of his cases are solo efforts, why should he care if he solves a case on his own, as he does in *Saturn's Rewards*, when only he and Esther will ever know of his triumph?

The answer is that Grad takes more pride and enjoyment in doing his job, and doing it well, than he admits. As the grandson of a police commissioner, one wonders if policing is in his blood, and his grandfather, after noting that his grandson possessed the qualities needed for policing, created the trust to push him into a job that he knew he would be perfect for, but would never choose himself. Whatever the reason, Grad's claim that he does not like his job is not backed up by his behaviour. If Grad were to acknowledge to himself that he, in fact, enjoys the challenge of doing his work, and doing it well, it would provide a prime opportunity for him to reassess his career and his perception of, and relationship with, it. If he did, he might come to realise that it is not the job itself that he resents or dislikes, but rather the fact that he was 'forced' into it by his grandfather via the trust. Conducting a similar analysis may benefit anyone who feels dissatisfied with their work by allowing them to pinpoint the exact cause of their unhappiness.

If you find that you possess certain skills in some situations, but lack them in others, try to determine the reason for the discrepancy. You are often more competent than you think!

Though Grad displays good people skills in some situations, in others he is socially awkward, clumsy, and the antithesis of suave. He is often flustered when dealing with his overbearing, critical superiors, and is less-than-smooth when making an arrest after Esther glares at him for attempting to take full credit for solving the case (*The Cool Aquarian*). While distracted in *Strength of the Gemini*, he accidentally puts salt in his coffee instead of sugar. In *Saturn's Rewards*, his momentary smugness at having solved a case single-handed dissipates when an irate Esther discovers that he has lied to her. In *The Horns of the Moon*, he feels foolish when Esther claims that everybody but him knows that merchant banks do not hold money, and is awkward when interacting with a crying woman who hands him a sodden hanky – which he had to borrow from Esther in another socially awkward moment – and then asks him to stay close by while she changes. Later, he chastises Esther for questioning a suspect, then proceeds to self-consciously repeat her question, tacitly admitting that it was a good one. He also fails to retie his bowtie and has to ask Esther for help, scolds Esther without realising that a suspect is in the room, falls asleep on Esther's shoulder, fails to crack a safe, is 'bested' by Esther in both Monopoly and mathematics, and struggles to turn Esther's television off.

One wonders how Grad, who is capable of being so logical, authoritative, and composed in some situations, can become so flustered and awkward in others. *The Horns of the Moon* provides a possible explanation for this contradiction, as Grad seems to relate to his murder suspect Tony Weston's comments about his overbearing father, who acted more like a superior officer than a parent. When those implications about Grad's father are coupled with the overbearing actions of his grandfather in bestowing the trust, and Grad's less-than-complimentary comments about his brother (Grad remarks that his brother's eyes are too close together in *Saturn's Rewards*), one can conclude that it is the male members of Grad's family who have perhaps undermined Grad's confidence and made him prone to social awkwardness in certain situations, particularly when he feels self-conscious or is under pressure. Regardless of the reason for the discrepancy, if Grad called to mind situations in which he was competent and confident, perhaps he could work out how those situations differ from those in which he is not, and determine what he needs to do in the latter to overcome his discomfort. Grad therefore illustrates that people are perfectly capable of exhibiting contradictory traits depending on the situation, and his experiences encourage viewers to seek out and examine their own situation-specific traits. As Esther says in *Death of a Crab*, "the better you understand your own faculties, the better you can apply them."

People often put up fronts to hide their feelings; therefore, be aware that their behaviour toward you might not always reflect how they truly feel.

A recurring theme in the series is Grad's seeming lack of romantic interest in Esther, and apparent obliviousness to Esther's interest in him. This theme is evident from the beginning of the pair's acquaintance in *Death of Crab*, in which Grad charms Esther with a flattering palmistry reading, then tells her about a "gorgeous girl, long blonde hair, green eyes" that he hopes to ask out. Esther is intrigued at the prospect of a date with Grad, and is disappointed – and disgusted – when Grad reveals that he is talking about the assistant commissioner's secretary. Her hopes are raised and dashed once again in *The Cool Aquarian*. Grad, expressing his discomfort at the presence of Esther's borrowed butler, complains that they have no privacy. Esther suggestively asks him what he wants to do that he does not want to be "snooped on" by the butler, and clearly has several ideas of her own in mind. Grad, however, does not seem to register her amorous thoughts, and disappoints her by replying that he wants to indulge in impolite table manners. In *The Horns of the Moon*, Esther gets excited when Grad tells her he is taking her home. Back at her flat, the pair exchange suggestive dialogue that has Esther's hopes rising by the second:

Grad: Hope it doesn't take 'til morning.
Esther: Do you think it might?
...
Grad: It might, yeah. Do you mind?

Esther definitely does not mind, and smiles as Grad seems about to embrace her. The spell is broken, however, when it becomes apparent that Grad was stretching his arms out so he could pick up his coat, which was draped on the couch behind her. Esther then realises that he is only at her flat because he expects a murder suspect to drop by and confess everything he knows about the murder to Esther. Esther is angry at Grad for getting her hopes up, but Grad, seemingly oblivious to Esther's plans for the evening, merely complains that Esther has not put sugar in his coffee. In *Saturn's Rewards*, Grad bursts Esther's bubble once again when he fails to react to her glamorous appearance when he arrives to take her out for dinner. When Esther prods him to comment on how she looks, he responds with a distracted, "Fine." Her disappointment at his reaction carries over into the meal itself, during which Esther protests when Grad expresses his intention to interrupt another couple's romantic evening. Grad responds to Esther's concerns with a yawn, conveying that he believes them to be trivial, to which a sullen Esther replies, "I wouldn't expect you to understand," implying that she has concluded that Grad does not have a romantic bone in his body.

On other occasions, Grad's seeming lack of interest in Esther is conveyed by his decision to refrain from sexualising her in intimate or sexually charged situations. Their first meeting in *Death of a Crab* occurs while Esther is dressed in a short robe, a fact that Grad barely seems to register and makes no move to take advantage of, behaviour he replicates later in the story when Esther dons the robe again. In the same episode, he also regards her quite frankly despite her skimpy bikini. In *The Strength of the Gemini*, he looks her over when she is lounging on her balcony in a bathing suit, but it is a subtle glance rather than a leer and is not accompanied by any other action or comment. In the same story, he is too surprised to reciprocate in any way when Esther greets him with a kiss on the lips. In *The Cool Aquarian*, he massages Esther's sore shoulders, but does not sexualise the act, even though Esther is seated between his legs. In *Sting, Sting, Scorpio!*, he rebuffs her attempt to kiss him because he does not want to catch her cold.

Grad's seeming immunity or unwillingness to respond to Esther's charms is puzzling, as he expresses interest in other women over the course of the series, including the assistant commissioner's secretary (*Death of a Crab*) and the woman in the flat opposite

Esther's, who is not averse to changing with the curtains open (*Death of a Crab*, *The Cool Aquarian*, *The Strength of the Gemini*). He surreptitiously admires the assets of a woman working at a flower shop (*The Strength of the Gemini*), and has an active dating life, seeing a philosophy lecturer (*Sting, Sting, Scorpio!*) and a debutante (*The Horns of the Moon*) over the course of the series. He also enjoys the attentions of Julie Prentiss (*The Horns of the Moon*), and harbours lusty thoughts about Elizabeth Taylor (*Saturn's Rewards*). In *The Strength of the Gemini*, he answers the telephone with, "Hello, darling", to which Esther replies, "How did you know it was me?". Grad coyly responds, "How do you know which darling I was referring to?", implying that he has other female acquaintances. Given that the women who interest him seem to have nothing in common, Grad also does not appear to have a 'type' that would rule Esther out as a suitable partner for him, and even if he did, the fact that he spends so much time with Esther both socially and professionally indicates that he enjoys her company regardless. Why, then, does Grad not seem to reciprocate Esther's interest in him, and even appears to be oblivious to it?

The explanations that Esther offers for Grad's failure to react to her sexually forward behaviour include an inherent naivety and conservatism on Grad's part when it comes to sex and romance – implied in an exchange in which Grad expresses incredulity at the suggestion that an MP is having an affair ("He's an MP! He wouldn't take the risk."), and Esther responds by labelling him a "sweet, old-fashioned thing" – and his possession of an unromantic nature. While both of these explanations likely have some merit, the more probable answer is that there is another contradiction at work in Grad's character, as evidenced by many signs, subtle and otherwise, that Grad is anything but indifferent to Esther's charms, despite his outwardly cool behaviour toward her. First of all, there are hints that Grad has previously loved and lost, and that the experience has made him reluctant to get too deeply involved with anyone. In *Death of a Crab*, Esther intuits that Grad was disappointed in love in his early twenties. Grad does not confirm or deny this. If Esther is wrong, why does Grad not rub in that she is mistaken, as he usually does? The fact that he simply brushes past the topic without acknowledging it suggests that Esther is correct. Furthermore, in *Saturn's Rewards*, Grad responds to the question of whether he is married by saying that he believes in "travelling hopefully rather than arriving." This suggests that Grad was so badly burnt by the unhappy love affair in his twenties that he swore off commitment forever after, opting for fleeting relationships instead – the one with the philosophy lecturer in *Sting, Sting, Scorpio!* is very brief, while an evening at a charity dinner with the debutante ends when he is dragged away by a case in *The Horns of the Moon*. Indeed, Grad's relationships are so fleeting that Esther does not even bother to be jealous of his paramours, responding to the news that he is dating the philosophy lecturer in *Sting, Sting, Scorpio!* with nothing more than mild annoyance, while his revelation that he is seeing a debutante amuses her in *The Horns of the Moon*.

Grad's general resistance to commitment therefore makes his relationship with Esther an exceptional one, as it outlasts all of his flash-in-the-pan romances by a wide margin and is characterised by him spending a great deal of time with her at her home. Over the course of the series, Grad comes to Esther's to ask her for help with a case (*The Cool Aquarian*), share a meal (*The Cool Aquarian*, *The Strength of the Gemini*, *The Horns of the Moon*), lounge on her balcony (*The Strength of the Gemini*, *Saturn's Rewards*), cook her breakfast (*The Strength of the Gemini*), watch television (*The Strength of the Gemini*), take her out for the evening (*Saturn's Rewards*, *Sting, Sting, Scorpio!*), and play Monopoly (*The Horns of the Moon*). Aside from socialising with her on a regular basis, Grad's affinity for Esther is also signified by his willingness to assist her in personal matters. He tags along to Brighton to act as a sounding board while Esther investigates her mentor's murder, and helps her to catch a conman who is exploiting her abilities for financial gain. He also endeavours to stay in her good books, seemingly unable to bear the idea of her being angry with him. *Saturn's Rewards* ends with him desperately trying to explain to an irate Esther why it was necessary to lie to her for the sake of his case, while *Sting, Sting, Scorpio!* finds him defending his decision not to investigate her mentor's murder in the face of her obvious annoyance.

While Grad's close friendship with Esther is not in itself irreconcilable with his unwillingness to get involved in a serious romance or his seeming obliviousness to Esther's interest in him, there are other signs that indicate that his feelings for her run far deeper than he cares to admit. In *The Strength of the Gemini*, Esther pretends to romance a charming con artist as part of a plot to send him to jail. Though she is well-aware that the con artist is putting on an act, Esther hints to Grad that she is not completely immune to his charms. A jealous Grad's aloofness slips in response, and he takes great pleasure in arresting the man at the episode's end. In *Sting, Sting, Scorpio!*, he is jealous when a man who has taken a shine to Esther serenades her with a song he has written about her. Esther watches the performance while smiling and shooting smug looks at Grad, who responds to the performance with sour annoyance. In *The Horns of the Moon*, the stakes are upped from jealousy to peril when Grad realises that Esther is in danger of being killed and rushes to save her, his frantic, panicked concern for her well-being evidence of how much he cares for her. However, the most significant sign of his affection comes in the final moments of *Sting, Sting, Scorpio!*, in which Grad rescues Esther from a murderer. Lying in wait with the local police, he grabs Esther as she exits a door at knifepoint and pulls her to safety. While the police arrest the murderer, Grad holds Esther tight, one hand protectively cupping the back of her head, his face pressed into her hair in relief. Once the danger has passed, a visibly affected Grad strokes Esther's hair back from her eyes and frames her face with his hands as he asks her to promise to refrain from engaging in crime-solving on her own in the future, his chastisement laced with relief rather than unrelentingly stern. Just as revealing is the unchecked praise Grad offers in the next breath for her stunningly accurate astrological predictions. An elated Esther recognises that this is the grandest display of affection that she has ever received from Grad, and throws her arms around his neck and leans in to kiss him. An incredibly relieved Grad nearly reciprocates, only stopping short when he remembers that she has a cold. Abortive ending aside, it is an extremely intimate moment that leaves no doubt as to the sincerity and depth of Grad's feelings for Esther, his affection (and, one senses, love) shining through his concern. A moment in *The Strength of the Gemini* also suggests, albeit more subtly, that Grad harbours deep feelings for Esther. While sitting on the couch watching television together, Grad suddenly seems to notice how close he is to Esther and looks at her as if taking her in for the first time. He sighs heavily, as if with longing, then recovers himself when Esther looks his way. Moments such as these suggest that Grad's feelings for Esther are deeper than she realises, but only surface in moments of crisis or when Grad feels he can indulge in them unobserved. Grad therefore rebuffs Esther's advances, not because he is not attracted to her or does not notice them, but because his feelings for her run so deep that he knows that a relationship with her would be a serious one. Unfortunately, the lingering heartbreak of his first love has left Grad afraid of making himself vulnerable in such a romance, and possibly also scared of losing Esther's friendship should the romance go sour. Grad therefore offers a prime example of how people erect facades that conceal their true feelings, and how the reasons for those facades are not always what one may believe they are, providing an impetus for viewers to dig a little deeper into their own relationship dynamics.

Lessons from Esther Jones

Do not be fanatical about your deeply held beliefs.

Esther's most notable lesson comes courtesy of the mixed signals she sends regarding the faith she puts in astrology. On the one hand, Esther is a firm, sincere believer in astrology and the truths that it reveals. Indeed, Esther's faith in astrology is so strong that she uses it to draw conclusions about Grad's investigations that she is absolutely certain are true, and, to her credit, she is unerringly proven to be right. For example, in *Death of a Crab*, she looks at her husband's chart and correctly determines that he was drunk or drugged when he died, and that his killer was a Capricorn. Esther also refutes the idea that astrology is a pseudoscience, arguing that it has a scientific basis (*The Horns of the Moon*), and describing the calculations involved in casting a person's horoscope as a science and the act of interpreting the horoscope as an art (*Saturn's Rewards*). Her genuine faith in her trade also comes through in her rigorous defences of astrology to Grad and other detractors, such as Martin Secombe in *Saturn's Rewards*, who derisively uses the word "concoct" when describing how she puts together her charts, a term Esther finds offensive. She also adheres to astrology's dictates, believing that the full moon has the power to make things "tricky" (*Sting, Sting, Scorpio!*), and that the reason that her estranged husband would not grant her a divorce, even though the pair were no longer in regular contact, was because he was a Cancerian, i.e., a crab who "hung on" (*Death of a Crab*). When Grad queries why Esther married her husband, even though he was astrologically unsuitable for her, she explains that she did not know much about astrology at the time, suggesting that if she had, she would have ruled him out as a potential suitor on an astrological basis alone. Esther's belief in astrology also comes through in her defence of her astrological mentor, whom she states was not a fake and whose stunningly accurate predictions fired Esther's enthusiasm for astrology to such an extent that she was driven to change her career overnight (*Sting, Sting, Scorpio!*).

At the same time, Esther's belief in astrology does not tip over into the fanatical. She does not hold it up as a belief system into which people should place all of their faith or that they should use as the basis for all of their decisions. Indeed, for someone who makes her living from astrology, she is remarkably willing to tell her clients not to put too much stock in it! For example, in *The Cool Aquarian*, she casts the horoscope of a client's newborn son, but cautions him to let the child be himself and make his own way, and not let the horoscope become a blueprint for the child's life. In place of fanaticism, she offers a measured, pragmatic take on the supernatural, akin to a doctor prescribing medicine – it is good for what ails you, but you must be careful not to overdose and cause more harm than what you sought to cure. She is also quick to debunk any misconceptions about what astrology is and its capabilities. When Grad asks her to use astrology to pin down the details of a planned crime, Esther ruefully replies, "You really do have some strange ideas about astrology", implying that it is not a font of wisdom that will provide exact answers to all of life's problems on demand (*The Cool Aquarian*). Instead, for Esther, astrology is a deeply held belief that she subscribes to in a measured, non-fanatical way. Esther therefore serves as a model for how to treat one's own convictions – we can believe things fervently, but in doing so should not travel so far down the rabbit hole that we become blind to the limitations of those beliefs and the opportunities other ways of thinking offer to improve our lives.

Even confident people sometimes feel unsure of themselves. Do not be afraid to admit to your mistakes, but also trust your instincts and do not always assume you are the one in the wrong.

As noted above, Esther is typically confident about her astrological abilities and puts great faith in the conclusions she draws. In *Death of a Crab*, she confidently rattles off an assessment of Grad mere minutes after meeting him, one that accurately describes the date of his birth, his personality traits, and his health issues. Esther's confidence in her abilities is also implied when she guesses the star sign of Martin Secombe, a deceptive individual, and is told that she is incorrect, a pronouncement that Esther reacts to with disbelief: "I can be wrong, but not that wrong" (*Saturn's Rewards*). This quotation also demonstrates that Esther's faith in her abilities does not tip over into arrogance. She does not claim that she is never wrong about anything where her astrological predictions are concerned, but she is sure enough of herself that she believes that her errors will typically be near-misses rather than complete misfires. This is also evidenced by a conversation she has with Grad in the same episode, in which it is revealed that she lost a bet with him that she could determine Grad's brother's astrological sign by looking at his eyes alone. Her estimate of the brother's birthdate was off by four days, which happened to be a margin of error that was just enough to push Grad's brother into the next astrological sign. Though she defends her error by characterising it as a near-miss, when coupled with Secombe's denials, it is enough to rattle her confidence, and she tells Grad that she is "thinking of giving …up" guessing people's signs as "[i]t doesn't seem to work as well as it used to." Adding to her self-doubt is Grad's later claim that an MP murdered Secombe, which contradicts the chart that Esther prepared for the MP that indicated that he was incapable of killing. In the end, it transpires that her prediction of Secombe's sign was, in fact, accurate, as he was lying about his birthdate, and Grad also reveals that the MP did not kill Secombe, but only injured him. Esther is relieved to find that her abilities were not steering her wrong, and in *Sting, Sting, Scorpio!*, she is back to playing her 'guess the sign' game with stunning accuracy, divining that a woman is a Libra just by looking at her, before identifying the woman's boyfriend as a Scorpio, sight unseen. The fact that she struggled with self-doubt, however, demonstrates that her characteristic overriding confidence in her abilities is not unshakeable. Esther therefore demonstrates that being a confident person does not mean refusing to admit one's mistakes or entertain the possibility that one is wrong, but that doing so should not drive one to be plagued with self-doubt, either. Instead, engaging in a measured, ego-free assessment of the situation that takes into account all of the facts is the best course of action.

Err on the side of caution when describing your abilities, rather than over-promise on what you can deliver.

Throughout the series, Esther does not oversell her mystical abilities. In *The Cool Aquarian*, she states, "I'm an astrologer, not a spiritualist or a medium", and claims that she cannot go into a trance. In *Saturn's Rewards*, she says that she is "not a crystal gazer, any more than I'm a palmist". Perhaps these statements are true, and Esther does not want people to think that she can provide accurate readings or advice in an area in which she feels she does not possess the requisite expertise. Nevertheless, Esther's abilities do not seem to be limited to casting horoscopes and divining people's personalities from their astrological signs. In *Death of a Crab*, she calls at her client's flat and senses that someone is inside, even though no one answers the door. That someone is her estranged husband, Harry, and her connection to him seems to alert her to his presence, even though she does not have any reason to believe he is there. Back at her flat, she pauses and says Harry's name just as he collapses, as though she can sense his impending death, even though they are far apart. In the same episode, she states that she believes herself to be a bit psychic:

Esther: If you're the least bit psychic.
Grad: Which you, of course, are.
Esther: Well, I like to think I am. Anyway, people seem to think I am.

She bolsters this conviction in the same story by correctly predicting when Grad is about to telephone her. She also implies that she has psychic powers in *The Cool Aquarian*, in which she attempts to get a reading from a missing person's locket. When she fails to sense anything, she tells Grad, "It's not something you can just turn on to order." This somewhat tenuous grasp that Esther seems to have on her powers is reinforced later in the episode, when Grad reads out place names and water synonyms in the hope that Esther will be able to sense which one reveals the location of a kidnapped woman. "I've never felt less psychic in my life," an exhausted Esther groans, but still manages to get enough of a feeling about the word "mill" to allow the pair to work out where the woman has been taken. In *Strength of the Gemini*, her powers seem to be firing on all cylinders, as she correctly picks a racehorse with terrible odds as a winner. In *Saturn's Rewards*, she gets a psychic reading from Martin Secombe's lighter that makes her feel uneasy. The fact that the lighter is given to her by her friend, rather than Secombe himself, and she only asks who owns it after she has taken her reading, demonstrates that it is not merely Esther's dislike of the man that is the source of her ill feeling. Esther later reaffirms that she had an intangible psychic feeling after holding the object, revealing that "ever since I held his lighter...I've been feeling uneasy [about Martin]". The most stunning demonstration of her powers, however, unquestionably comes in *Sting, Sting, Scorpio!*. While having dinner with Grad, Esther suddenly smells the sea, while Grad cannot. Esther instantly intuits that something is wrong, and tells Grad that Peggy, a young woman who came to her for a tarot card reading, has just drowned. A concerned Grad asks Esther if Peggy fell or was pushed. Esther firmly states that Peggy was pushed. As the episode unfolds, it becomes apparent that Esther's psychic predictions about Peggy's fate were completely correct. She shows surprising prescience again later in the episode when confronted by Brian, Peggy's killer. Expertly reading his tarot cards, in a demonstration of another of her abilities, she correctly predicts Brian's defeat – which materialises in the form of his arrest – and describes his difficult upbringing. She follows the reading with an interpretation of his chart, which she had prepared in advance, feeling certain that Brian was her mentor's killer even before she met him. She tells the surprised Brian that he had a tough childhood, that his parents divorced when he was under two years old, and that he was brought up by his aunt alongside his three cousins. Brian confirms that all of her 'predictions' are correct.

Though Esther's abilities appear to reach far beyond being the slightly psychic astrologer that she claims to be, her decision to not oversell her abilities is a wise one. It protects her from accusations of chicanery and prevents her from getting people's hopes up when she feels that she cannot help them. It also gives her the element of surprise when facing off against those who would do her harm. The lesson to take away from Esther's description of her powers is therefore that it is better to be modest than to brag about one's abilities.

Temper mysticism and superstition with logic.

Throughout the series, Esther, rather surprisingly, makes a habit of undercutting the power of astrology and her 'mystical' abilities by attributing her conclusions and hypotheses to common sense, logic, and intuition. In *Death of a Crab*, Esther hypothesises that Grad found her missing bracelet by the sink in her client's bathroom. Grad queries whether she used astrology to determine the bracelet's location, but Esther replies that it was "grey matter", revealing that she used logic to deduce that she had lost the bracelet when she took it off to wash her hands. In the same episode, she uses logic to prove that she cannot be her husband's killer. When it is discovered that the killer lifted her husband's legs in the air in order to submerge him in a bathtub, she points out that, if the killer had long nails, there would be scratches on her husband's legs. Esther then brandishes her long-nailed manicure, proving that she could not be the killer. She also undercuts what could have been perceived as a demonstration of her psychic abilities by explaining the reasoning behind her prediction that the person calling her on the telephone is her friend, Sally. She tells Grad that Sally is due to call again, and that she will be particularly motivated to call that day because she will have heard about the death of Esther's husband. In *The Strength of the Gemini*, Esther uses logic once again to work out the link between a florist and a con artist, pointing out that florists would learn women's birthdates, and that a florist that catered to an aristocratic clientele would know the birthdates of aristocratic women and be able to pass the information on to the con artist for use in his scams. In *Sting, Sting, Scorpio!*, Esther notices that a woman named Peggy, who came to her for a tarot card reading, knows how to handle the tarot cards, and deduces that she has had a reading before. She then infers that the source of Peggy's unhappiness is her boyfriend, and Peggy asks how she could know that the person making her unhappy is a man. Esther does not attribute this insight to anything mystical, but "pure deduction. If you get a worried girl, it's often because of a boy." On other occasions, Esther uses her remarkable intuition and understanding of human behaviour to draw conclusions. In *Saturn's Rewards*, she expresses surprise when Martin Secombe claims to have no desire to see his horoscope chart. She explains that this is odd because even people who are not interested or do not believe in astrology typically want to see their chart, if only because they are curious or want to use it to poke fun at astrology. As a result, she (rightly) views Secombe as not being 'on the up and up'.

Therefore, while Esther takes great pains to advocate for astrology, she seems to be keen to stress that, in many instances, she has no need for it. Esther's willingness to attribute her insights to logic, deduction, intuition, her observational skills, and her intelligence teaches viewers a valuable survival skill, demonstrating that, rather than mysticism, facts, logic, and common sense are the best and most reliable tools for navigating and making sense of the world.

Seek out new challenges and ways to use your skills if you feel unfulfilled.

Esther's interest in the field of crime-solving, as evidenced by her engagement in Grad's cases and pursuit of her own investigations, demonstrates that even someone who is very happy with their identity and career can be driven to seek out new challenges. Grad's entry into Esther's life provides her with a new arena in which to apply her talents and prove her mettle as an intelligent woman with something of value to offer, and the enthusiasm with which she embraces this new challenge suggests she may have subconsciously craved it. Esther's example therefore encourages us to determine if we, too, feel as though we are not living up to our full potential, and to take action to rectify the situation.

The Grad/Esther Relationship

Opposites can attract – and help each other.

The nature of Grad and Esther's relationship provides us with some food for thought. Indeed, the fact that the pair have any kind of relationship at all is thought-provoking, as, on the surface, it is difficult to conceive of them engaging in a civil conversation, let alone becoming friends or, potentially, lovers. Grad is an upright sort who uses legwork, evidence, and deduction to solve crimes; follows laws and rules to the letter; and becomes flustered when others fail to follow suit. As Esther says, he is also forthright, resolute, and egotistical, meaning his pride is easily hurt and, consequently, he has a stubborn tendency to cling to the conviction that he is right even when doubt worms its way into his mind. Conversely, his ego can be inflated to the point of smugness when things go his way. He also has no difficulty telling people what he thinks of them, and is prone to mocking or dismissing them if he does not believe they have anything of value or interest to offer. He is also deeply practical and not given to grand romantic gestures. In short, he is often a difficult person for anyone to get along with, let alone the romantic, free-spirited Esther, who flouts rules, is generally composed, and has no interest in massaging Grad's ego – unless there is something in it for her!

However, rather than being problematic, Grad and Esther's differences have unexpected benefits for them both. Grad feels more able to be himself around Esther than with his fellow police, who seem to judge him solely on the basis of his professional performance rather than who he is as a person. Esther has also added spice and colour to both his professional and personal life. Her astrological predictions and unconventional ways of assessing suspects, gathering evidence, and putting together theories not only bolster his career by helping him to solve crimes, but also increase his engagement with the job. While he previously hovered between ennui and active dislike when it came to his profession, once Esther begins to involve herself in his cases, his passion for his work is ignited. Grad is not only stimulated by their lively, no-holds-barred debates about whose method of solving crimes is better, but is also driven to prove himself as a detective, actively choosing to solve cases without Esther's assistance in order to prove to her, and himself, that he is capable of doing so. Esther also challenges him on a personal level. She is his equal or superior when it comes to everything from general knowledge to witty repartee, which makes her stimulating company. When coupled with her quasi-bohemian lifestyle and unorthodox array of beliefs, Esther cannot help but make Grad's life more interesting. Perhaps most importantly, Esther draws Grad out of himself by challenging his, at times, stubbornly held preconceptions and beliefs. As Grad opens himself to Esther, he also opens himself up to new ideas and ways of thinking that he had previously not considered. While Grad does not (and should not) completely accept or agree with everything Esther puts forward, the very act of engaging with Esther acts as an antidote to his somewhat conservative tendencies. Esther's dynamism is therefore the proverbial shot in the arm for Grad, injecting excitement, variety, and challenge into his life.

Esther, in turn, would undoubtedly not have anticipated forming a strong bond with a sceptic of her profession. However, from Esther's standpoint, after contending with a husband who lost money and descended into alcoholism, Grad is a gem because he is reliable, loyal, treats her well, takes pride in his work, and is someone with whom she can freely speak her mind and engage in evenly matched debates. Grad also looks out for Esther's well-being in situations where she is in peril, but not to the point of being overbearing or infantilising in his treatment of her. Indeed, while Grad brings Esther back down to earth when the stars in her eyes prevent her from registering some very real dangers, he generally allows Esther to pursue courses of action that he believes to be folly, allowing her to reassess the wisdom of her ways rather than expecting her to take his word for it. Even Grad's seeming reluctance to take Esther up on her romantic overtures may, counterintuitively, be comforting for Esther, as it signals that Grad will not take advantage of her physically or emotionally. This means that their relationship is a safe space for Esther, in which she can be as free and open as she wants without having to worry if she is potentially making herself vulnerable to someone who will abuse her trust, as her husband did. Subtle jealousy aside, Grad is also not possessive of Esther, whereas her husband 'hung on' and refused to grant her a divorce. Unlike her husband, Grad is also financially solvent, drawing regular incomes from both his work as a policeman and his trust, but while he dresses well and enjoys a good meal, there is no indication that he is a spendthrift – he does not even seem to own a car – who would impose on her financially. At the same time, Grad is also happy to let Esther pay for a meal, instead of always taking care of the bill himself, making them equals when it comes to finances. Overall, therefore, Grad is a safe, stabilising force in Esther's life, as well as a stimulating companion.

The pair's willingness to give someone who is very different from themselves a chance, and the subsequent rewards that they reap from their relationship, encapsulate the series' recurring message of the importance of opening oneself up to new possibilities. We should therefore not assume that we cannot form meaningful relationships with those who are very different than us, or dismiss such people because of our own biases.

Conflict is not always a bad thing in a relationship.

Unsurprisingly, Grad and Esther's differing personalities give rise to petty irritations and conflicts. In *The Strength of the Gemini*, Esther attempts to check Grad's pride at having taken surreptitious surveillance pictures by telling him, "You're not James Bond." In the same story, Esther offers Grad some of her alfalfa tea, which he does not enjoy, to Esther's mild annoyance. She gets back at him later by pronouncing him "an awful judge of character." In *Saturn's Rewards*, Grad's fastidiousness proves irritating to Esther when he discovers blackfly on her plants and offers to lend her some spray, then later complains when he finds a fly in his drink – "I really must lend you that spray."

The pair's differing personalities also cause them to butt heads when it comes to solving crimes. They regularly argue about the best way to approach a mystery, compete about whose theory of the case is better, and indulge in one-upmanship. Adding fuel to the fire are Grad's mocking comments about astrology and other spiritual practices, which irk Esther, while Grad, in turn, is annoyed by Esther's smug self-satisfaction when her predictions are proven to be correct, as well her habit of taking liberties during cases despite not being a police officer. *Saturn's Rewards* provides many examples of their case-based squabbling:

Grad: There are certain cases that I can actually solve alone, unaided, and by myself.
Esther: Really?
Grad: Yes, really.
Esther: It must be straightforward. What happened, did you find the killer drunk on the floor, prints all over the murder weapon and a signed confession in his top pocket?
Grad: You do know that sarcasm is the lowest form of wit, don't you? You stick to crystals and I'll stick to crime, all right?

Later in the story, the same themes emerge:

Grad: I told you before. I can handle this on my own, right? I don't need any rabbit's feet or goat's entrails or anything like that.
Esther: Oh, you arrogant man!
Grad: Arrogant? Me? Rubbish.
Esther: Yes, you're like most men.
Grad: How's that?
Esther: Terrified to ask for help.
Grad: I don't need help, particularly the kind of help you can offer. Bed, book, and candle.
Esther: Bell, book, and candle, please!

Grad also asserts his authority in this episode, telling Esther she is allowed at his crime scene "on sufferance only", an instruction that

Esther, surprisingly, abides by. However, that goodwill inevitably dissipates when Grad solves the case without Esther's assistance and goes too far in celebrating his triumph, rubbing in that Esther's chart, which predicted that an MP was incapable of committing murder, led her astray. This comes back to bite him when he is forced to admit that the MP did not, in fact, commit murder, and that he told others, including Esther, otherwise in order to force a confession from the MP. An irate Esther labels him a "lying, deceitful bastard" and the episode closes with her ranting angrily at Grad.

The pair clash repeatedly, and even more violently, over a case in *Sting, Sting, Scorpio!*. The animosity surfaces early on, with Esther annoyed at Grad for refusing to investigate the death of her mentor. In retaliation, she refuses to give Grad a ride home before she departs for Brighton, instead telling him she will drop him at the bus stop. Esther's mood does not improve when Grad later appears in Brighton, where she is attempting to find her mentor's killer, but only offers to act as a sounding board rather than do any actual investigating, as Brighton is outside of his jurisdiction. Later, Esther admits that she feels guilty for pressuring a young woman named Peggy to give her information about her mentor's death, as she believes that Peggy may have been killed for talking to her. Despite expressing said guilt, she is outraged when Grad agrees that her amateur sleuthing contributed to Peggy's demise. It is at this point that Grad gets his own back, hammering home that crime-solving is a serious undertaking, not the amusing diversion that Esther sometimes treats it as. Grad emphasises the responsibility that comes with his work as a detective, which includes the duty to consider the well-being of the people he interviews in the course of his investigation, who may face retaliation for cooperating with the police. Esther, in contrast, had not been called on to shoulder such responsibility in their previous investigations, cosseted as she was by the protection offered by Grad and his authority. Outside of Grad's jurisdiction, she has no such protection, but still chooses to investigate on her own rather than leave the matter to the local police. Esther's failure to give any credence to Grad's assertions that policework is a serious business means that Grad has no mercy for her when her methods come at the expense of the life of another:

Esther: You see, it's all my fault.
Grad: Right.
Esther: If I hadn't have pressured her, it wouldn't have happened.
Grad: It wouldn't.
Esther: She'd still be alive.
Grad: Alive and well.
Esther: I beg your pardon?
Grad: I was agreeing with you.
Esther: You're supposed to be helping.
Grad: A sounding board, that was the offer. Not a long round of applause or a curtain call.
Esther: And what does that mean?
Grad: It means don't squeal if you get burned...Look, if you want to play policeman, fine, but there's more to it than size 10 boots and a helmet. It's no good crying if you goof and other people get hurt.
Esther: So you're saying I shouldn't interfere?
Grad: That's up to you, but if you are going to, you must learn to lose occasionally, particularly if you play it as irresponsibly as you do.
Esther: That's beastly. That's the cruellest thing you've ever said to me...Bastard.
Grad: Not a bit.
...
Esther: What happened to gallant men?
Grad: It was decided at the last male chauvinists' convention that doors would no longer be opened, seats given up, and there'd be no more squeezing out of tear-soaked hankies, right?
Esther: If you say so.

Grad remains unmoved even as Esther spits insults at him, determined that Esther learn her lesson and feel the full consequences of her choices in the hope that she will understand just how dangerous the business of crime-solving can be. It is their most hostile clash, rising above their usual petty squabbling to visceral anger on Esther's part and firm reprisal on Grad's. It is also arguably Grad's most successful entry in their ongoing debate about whose crime-solving methods are better. While in the rest of the series Esther's intuitions and predictions give her the upper hand, here Grad is the more knowledgeable one, and uses Esther's mistakes to lay down some hard truths about the life and death realities of his job. Esther, for her part, takes her medicine with little grace, and, even after her theory of the case receives a poor reception from the local police force, she spurns Grad when he attempts to protect her from the danger her investigations have put her in, instead choosing to take a petty shot at his masculinity:

Grad: Shall I walk you [to the library]?
Esther: Oh, I shouldn't bother. I should think I'll be safe unless there's been a mass breakout from Roedean.

A similar scenario appears in *The Horns of the Moon*, in which Grad calls Esther to the carpet for interfering with his investigation, then scolds her for being in unlawful possession of keys to a bank and warns her that she will be committing a crime if she uses them. Esther, however, is convinced that she is in the right, having one-upped him throughout the case with correct predictions regarding everything from a son's innocence in the death of his banker father (Grad thought he was guilty), to the banker's consumption and replacement of the bank's wine, which was purchased as an investment, and so she chooses to act against his advice. However, this case, like that in *Sting, Sting, Scorpio!*, demonstrates that Esther does not take Grad as seriously as she should when he dispenses his policeman's wisdom, as her entry of the bank using the purloined keys results in her nearly being killed by the murderer.

Grad also attempts to make Esther take the business of crime-solving more seriously in *Death of a Crab*, in which Esther treats

Grad's investigation of her in relation to the death of her husband as an amusing diversion. As the evidence begins to point toward Esther as the prime suspect, however, Grad provides a very sobering warning that cuts through Esther's flippancy and brings her crashing back to Earth:

Esther: I'm going to be nicked?
Grad: The very word. May only be circumstantial, but the evidence is piling up like drifting snow.
…
Esther: Suddenly doesn't seem funny anymore.

Grad's dire warnings push Esther to stop treating the situation as a game in which she can have fun applying her astrological talents and trying to 'better' Grad, and to instead collaborate with him to bring the killer to justice. These situations therefore demonstrate that Esther's free-wheeling approach and desire to come out on top fuel their squabbles as much as Grad's conventionality and egotism.

However, despite the pair's petty squabbles and serious arguments, they, rather counterintuitively, share a very close, comfortable, trusting friendship that develops surprisingly quickly. In *Death of a Crab*, shortly after they become acquainted, Esther trusts Grad enough to agree to act as bait in a trap he has set for a murderer. It is a huge vote of confidence on Esther's part to put her life in the hands of a virtual stranger, even one who is a policeman, but Esther appears to have no qualms about doing so. By the episode's close, the pair's comfort level has already been established, with Grad dropping by Esther's flat for a visit after the case is closed. Both treat Grad's visit as natural and not unexpected, a sign that the pair have already developed an, possibly unspoken, accord and affinity that causes them to welcome one another into their lives almost without having to think about it. That comfort level is also evident in other ways. Esther gifts Grad with a key to her flat (*The Cool Aquarian*), and Grad has no qualms about making Esther pay for dinner after she loses a bet with him, suggesting that he feels they know each other well enough for this to not cause long-standing offence (*Saturn's Rewards*). Esther, in turn, is supremely casual around Grad in *The Strength of the Gemini* – in one scene, she drinks his wine, then puts pâté on a cracker, eats some of it, and stuffs the rest in Grad's mouth. In *The Cool Aquarian*, they have settled into borderline domesticity, with Grad complaining about his boss to Esther in much the same way that husbands regularly do to their wives:

Grad: The commander's gone back to calling me "Inspector".
Esther: Is that bad?
Grad: Yeah, well, last weekend it was "Gradley".
Esther: What's the next rung down?
Grad: Here, you!...you're only as good as your last arrest.

Grad also tells her that he took the lid off the commander's humidifier to ruin his expensive cigars in retaliation. In return, Esther occasionally plays the stereotypical wife, albeit for her own ends. In *The Horns of the Moon*, Esther smiles sweetly and expresses enthusiasm when Grad tells her that his superior is happy with his work and wants to play golf with him, while secretly setting him up to prove a point about her own theory of the case. More domestic meal-taking comes in *The Strength of the Gemini*, with Grad cooking breakfast for them both and the pair pushing Esther's plate back and forth when Esther rejects it. *The Horns of the Moon* finds Esther making her feelings known about the case over another dinner, and later the pair watch television in another domestic and cozy scene. They share another meal, this time at a restaurant, in *Sting, Sting, Scorpio!*, during which Grad makes a comment to Esther – "One thing I like about you – you don't smoke between courses. Actually, there are two things...You don't have funny pictures hanging in the loo." – that one can only make to someone one knows well, and who can be relied on not to take offence. The pair's comfort level with one another also creates a certain intimacy between them, with Grad calling Esther at the office of one of her clients, demonstrating that he knows her schedule for the day, and rubbing a tired Esther's stiff shoulders after she has slaved away casting a horoscope for his case (*The Cool Aquarian*).

How can a pair who spend so much of their time arguing form such a comfortable friendship? The answer is that one dynamic leads to the other – it is the pair's conflict that allows them to be so close and comfortable with each other. Esther may be irritated or angered by Grad's warnings that she is not taking crime-solving seriously, his opinion of astrology, and his attempts to prove that his ways of solving crimes and theories of the case are superior, but no matter the situation, she can always be certain that Grad is being honest with her about what he thinks. Esther is, of course, equally honest with Grad, speaking her mind and regularly voicing her disagreement with his conclusions. The fact that the pair have realised that they can be completely honest with each other – to the point that they can ardently disagree with each other about any topic under the sun without the other party retaliating with anything more than words (which they are prepared and willing to handle), holding grudges, or severing their friendship – has resulted in them being tremendously comfortable with one another. The pair's mutual honesty is a valuable quality to have in a friendship, or indeed any relationship. Grad and Esther's dynamic therefore teaches us that we should not forgo relationships with individuals just because they might involve an element of conflict, as long as that conflict unfolds in a way in which the people involved feel safe and are not being abused or browbeaten.

A Lesson from All of *Zodiac*'s Characters

Do not judge people based on appearances or one's own prejudices and biases.

Throughout, the show is keen to frame Grad as, in creator Roger Marshall's own words, "a snob" [1] who believes "interesting crime is the prerogative of the rich and the articulate; as a boy his hero was Nick Charles, the 'Thin Man' and Gradley is quite at home arresting murderous butlers". [2] Grad initially seems to adhere to this description. Our introduction to him in *Death of a Crab* finds him ordering room service at the expensive penthouse where he is investigating a murder, and the order, his clothes, and the confident, proprietorial way he moves around the space initially suggest that he is the penthouse's well-to-do occupant rather than a police inspector, the illusion only shattered when he begins questioning people and making observations. Esther, like the audience, is equally surprised to discover that Grad is a detective, taking in his well-tailored cream suit, way of speaking ("You didn't learn to talk like that giving evidence in Bow Street."), and general air, and concluding that he is an unlikely policeman. Grad replies that he is asked "three times a day, at least" how he came to be a copper, but seems to enjoy subverting people's expectations with his manner and wardrobe, telling Esther, "We no longer sport blue serge and silver buttons." The series maintains Grad's clotheshorse status throughout, putting him in a number of well-tailored suits, often in light, airy colours. References to his grandfather's trust reinforce his snobbish image, as does his penchant for adopting an aristocratic identity when conducting undercover work. In *The Strength of the Gemini*, he plays the role of the aristocratic twit to a tee, adopting the requisite mannerisms, way of speaking, and general air of cheerfully eccentric denseness. While the case required Grad to adopt an aristocratic cover, it is clear from his performance that he relishes the opportunity to play an upper-crust character. He seizes on the opportunity to do the same in *Saturn's Rewards* by specifically asking Esther to introduce him as "the Honourable". He is also status conscious, hoping to borrow Esther's temporary butler for an event with his superior in *The Cool Aquarian*. Other signs that he is concerned about his status come in the form of his disappointment when a newspaper article about a crime he is investigating fails to mention him (*Saturn's Rewards*), and his attempt to impress Esther by feigning that he has taken surveillance photos with a high-tech camera watch, when he actually used a small camera (*The Strength of the Gemini*).

However, Grad does not always behave snobbishly. While he generally dresses well, in *The Strength of the Gemini* he turns up at Esther's for what he believes will be a casual meal in double denim and a black t-shirt, and re-wears said denim while on a semi-holiday in *Sting, Sting, Scorpio!*, demonstrating that, while he likes to dress up, he only does so when in professional mode or if the occasion warrants it. A truly vain, dandy snob would not dream of being less than perfectly turned out at all times. Grad's willingness to let his hair down in his downtime and opt for comfort over style therefore proves that he is not as worried about appearing suave and sophisticated as one might believe. We also discover that he is not a strict gourmand. He orders and eats chips, a staple of the ordinary man, in *Death of a Crab*, and rolls his eyes when the person taking his order insists on referring to them as "French fries". He also cooks Esther and himself a hearty breakfast of eggs and sausage in *The Strength of the Gemini*, a meal that is the antithesis of the pâté she serves him in the same episode; of the two dishes, Grad appears happier with the breakfast. Most importantly, Grad does not respond to the snobbery of others with obsequiousness or a sense of camaraderie. He mocks the snobbish hotel manager in *Death of a Crab*, who, in response to Grad's complaint that his chips are not accompanied by salt, vinegar, and newspaper, suggests that he should have asked for them. Grad responds by asking whether the manager would expect someone to ask for a glass if they ordered beer. He is also unimpressed when the manager insists on taking a dead body out through the service entrance, sarcastically commenting that it would not do to disrupt the lunch trade and that it is a pity the body is not small enough to smuggle out in a beer crate. "You joke," replies the manager, taken aback at Grad's comment. "You noticed," retorts Grad, without any humour, clearly taking the manager's attitude toward the dead as an insult to humanity. Grad's various encounters with an MP in *Saturn's Rewards* are more respectful than those he has with the manager, in keeping with the MP's position relative to Grad, but Grad does not treat the MP in a way that could be described as overly deferential. Most notably, when Esther temporarily acquires a butler in *The Cool Aquarian*, Grad regards the man as an affront to his privacy, rather than a perk to be coveted, griping that the butler is preventing him from indulging in some decidedly unsnobbish behaviour – "I want to eat the fish with my fingers. I want to paddle in my wine!" In the end, Grad warms to the butler and asks him to perform a few small tasks, but is far more interested in the butler's knack for handwriting analysis, which provides crucial leads in Grad's case. This demonstrates that Grad values the butler as a person rather than as a servant, as does the fact that Grad winds up donning an apron to help the butler polish the silver while the pair chat and sip drinks. In the end, Grad does most of the work, while the butler supervises and critiques his efforts. In the course of their conversation, it emerges that the butler knew the butler who served Grad's grandfather, but Grad does not take this as a cue to adopt an air of authority. He is far more interested in 'chewing the fat' with a man whom his grandfather would likely have barely given the time of day, the ultimate proof that this man who revels in pretending to be an aristocrat is remarkably unpretentious in private.

While Grad is less concerned with being judged based on his image than one would think, Esther appears to be actively combatting prejudicial judgments made about her. Her habit of attributing her conclusions to logic and reason, rather than astrology, may be an attempt to bolster her credibility with people who do not believe in astrology, so that they do not dismiss her as a starry-eyed, New Age type. Esther may also wish to attribute the conclusions she draws to logic in order to demonstrate her intellect. As an attractive blonde woman, she is probably regularly dismissed as an 'airhead' with nothing of substance to offer. This may explain why Esther's confidence can occasionally be rattled, as she is used to being undermined and condescended to. Esther asserting that she uses good old-fashioned grey matter to solve puzzles and draw conclusions is therefore a way for her to dispel negative stereotypes prompted by her looks and area of expertise.

Some incidental characters in the series are similarly the victims of prejudiced assessments of their character. Julie Prentiss, the lover of a murdered banker, is misjudged by both Grad and Esther in *The Horns of the Moon*. Grad is taken in by Julie's feminine charms, believing her to be nothing more than a sobbing damsel in distress, and enjoys having her hang off of him as he comforts her. However, when Julie's tearful, feminine image gives way to reveal a boldly sensual woman who asks Grad to stay in the next room while she changes, Grad is disconcerted and struggles to make sense of the lack of correspondence between this new behaviour and the image she put forward seconds earlier. He then makes new assumptions about Julie based on her sexual forwardness, which, in turn, cause him to misinterpret Julie's meaning when she tells him that she played "games" with her lover every other night. He is therefore surprised when he removes a drop cloth from a table and finds an elaborate wargame underneath. An earlier scene in which Julie is shown beating her lover at said wargame demonstrates that Julie is not a brainless sexpot, but is actually quite clever. The wargame in question requires strategic and creative thinking, both of which Julie possesses in spades, to the point that she is able to out-strategize her ex-military lover. Julie proves her intelligence again, as well as her resilience, when she assists Esther in capturing her lover's murderer, preventing Esther from becoming the murderer's next victim in the process. The capture of the murderer also proves that Julie played no part in her lover's demise, and undercuts yet another incorrect assumption made about her. Julie tearfully throwing herself at Grad invites Esther's derision, and likely leads her to peg Julie as a manipulative individual who uses any means available, from feminine wiles to murder, to get what she wants. Grad also toys with this reading of Julie as the episode goes on, expressing surprise when he discovers that Julie was not in her lover's will, implying that he assumed that Julie was only with her lover for his money, and was willing to kill for it. In fact, Julie was well aware that she was not in the will, but did not care and planned to leave the country to live with her lover, suggesting that she genuinely cared about, and enjoyed spending time with, him, irrespective of his wealth.

This misjudgment of Julie makes her the counterpoint to many of the series' villains, and also highlights a certain double-standard at work between the sexes. Julie has done nothing wrong, but is judged harshly and suspected of devious motives simply because she is a glamorous, sexually bold woman, while the series' male villains put on a good face to cover up their misdeeds, and their surface image often goes unchallenged. Examples of such deceptive men include *Saturn's Rewards*' ruthlessly handsome Martin Secombe, who cultivates the image of a well-to-do man about town to conceal his sexual exploitation of women for his own financial gain, and a broke conman in *The Strength of the Gemini*, who lives in a rundown flat while pretending to be a wealthy sophisticate in order to charm rich women out of their money. Brian in *Sting, Sting, Scorpio!* is a heartless, self-centred villain, only concerned with protecting his spoils from a robbery and keeping himself out of jail, to the point that he is willing to murder his girlfriend. His girlfriend's willingness to stay with him in spite of his threatening behaviour can be explained by his acting ability. He feigns being concerned, sensible, forceful, and soothing when he is seeking to persuade his girlfriend and others to do as he says, and convincingly conveys grief and shock when his girlfriend's body is discovered. Only when he drops his mask is he revealed to be who he truly is – cold, calculating, and psychopathic, with no regard for others.

Other characters initially invite straightforward readings with their image and behaviour, but are subsequently revealed to be much more complex. In *Saturn's Rewards*, an MP who witnesses a murder while spending the night with his mistress is, unsurprisingly, reluctant to report what he has seen, fearing the damage the revelation of his infidelity would do to his family and political career. Even when he learns that his daughter is dating the murderer, he opts to have the man investigated rather than tell the police what he knows. This suggests that, while he is concerned for his daughter, he values his political career and personal pleasure over his family's happiness and well-being. However, the selfish streak that prevents him from taking relatively easy actions – talking to the police, telling his daughter what he saw, remaining faithful to his wife – does not stop him from taking far more drastic ones to protect those he loves. The MP eventually confronts the murderer about his actions and warns him to stay away from his daughter, then violently strikes the murderer when he tauntingly tells the MP what he plans to do to his daughter once they are married. The seemingly self-centred MP therefore reveals himself to be willing to nearly commit murder to protect his daughter. This selfish man's surprisingly altruistic streak resurfaces later in the story when, having finally confessed his misdeeds to Grad, he asks if he may vote in the House before Grad arrests him. It is a small but unexpectedly selfless gesture made by a character who spent the majority of the episode trying to save his own skin.

Elsewhere, *The Cool Aquarian* gives us two businessmen, Mark Braun and Reuben Keiser, who both prove to be more complicated than their surface images would have us assume. Braun and Keiser are asked to pay the ransom for a kidnapped young woman. Braun expresses horror at the young woman's plight and is in favour of paying the ransom out of company funds. Keiser – who operates the company with a cold, clinical shrewdness that leads him to buy a very rare and expensive stamp and then burn it to increase the value of another stamp of the same type that he has in his possession – is unmoved by Braun and Grad's pleas to aid in the rescue of the young woman. Eventually, Keiser changes his mind and agrees to pay the ransom, but only because not paying the ransom would make him look cruel and heartless, hurting the company's reputation and bottom line. However, it is later revealed that the supposedly kind-hearted Braun is, in fact, the kidnapper. Disgusted with the way Keiser operated and having learned that Keiser was about to dismiss him, Braun decided to emulate Keiser by doing one sharp deal before he left, just for his own satisfaction. Braun therefore reveals himself to be far worse than the man he sought to teach a lesson. Keiser may sacrifice inanimate objects in the name of business, but there is no indication that he would go so far as to use a human being to gain leverage over a business rival. Furthermore, while Keiser's decision to pay the ransom because it will benefit him is not an admirable one, it cannot be denied that the kidnapping is not a problem of his own making and, consequently, is not one that he is obliged to resolve. Therefore, despite engaging in cutthroat business dealings, Keiser reveals himself to be, counterintuitively, the better man of the two. He is at least open about his actions and motives and does not care what anyone thinks of him. Braun, in contrast, seeks to present himself as a humanitarian while filling his own pockets at Keiser's expense. Like many of the characters in *Zodiac*, Braun and Keiser warn us to not let ourselves be taken in by surface images or to let our biases and prejudices get the better of us.

A Final Lesson from *Zodiac*

Do not fear uncertainty. Accept it. It may have unexpected benefits.

Does astrology have any merit, or is it simply bunk? The series does not come down on one side or the other. On the one hand, there is plenty of evidence that Esther is simply an extremely intuitive individual who is very insightful about human behaviour and blessed with exceptional logic, observation, and deduction skills, and that these combined attributes create the illusion of a woman possessed with supernatural 'gifts'. However, the series muddies the waters with Esther's most inexplicable predictions, such as pinpointing the exact time and means of Peggy's murder by drowning. In that instance, Esther has no evidence to which to apply her logic, intuition, and insightfulness, as she is nowhere near the location where Peggy meets her end.

Grad's, and our, inability to decide whether Esther's abilities and the predictive power of astrology are genuine is symbolic of the uncertainty that all of us have to deal with in our lives. We cannot explain every occurrence, strange or otherwise, to our satisfaction, nor can we anticipate every event in our lives and how it will unfold. Rather than be anxious about this state of affairs, or attempt to find certainty where we cannot, reconciling ourselves to the fact that an element of the unknown will always exist can, paradoxically, provide comfort by giving us licence to not worry about what might happen, and simply take things as they come.

Conclusion

The 1970s was a decade in which social, economic, and political realities weighed heavily on many, making it the cynical tonic to the more optimistic 60s. The decade's *zeitgeist* was reflected in the television of the period, which often swapped the 60s' penchant for light-hearted adventure for gritty tales of survival. *Zodiac*, however, was an unusual entry in the middle of this cynical decade, straddling as it did the gulf between late-60s and early-70s television. Esther's astrological/psychic powers, fashions, and décor channel a late-60s hippie-esque mysticism that lends the series a tele-fantasy bent akin to the likes of *Randall and Hopkirk (Deceased)*, *The Champions*, and the later incarnations of *The Avengers*. On the other hand, Esther's admitted use of deduction and logic, coupled with Grad's scepticism about her powers and emphasis on the value of using hard work and evidence to crack cases, ground the series in the more reality-based 70s. This mixture of reason and mysticism allowed the series to push back against 70s television's bid for gritty, sometimes bitter, realism, to make room for other ideas and themes. On the face of it, those ideas and themes centred on the role that 'mystical' powers, such as astrology, play in our lives. As producer Jacqui Davis put it, "I think we're catering in this series for people who...wouldn't admit to taking [astrology] seriously, but secretly wonder whether there is anything in it." [3] However, the show's use of astrology is merely a pretext, a catalyst for a variety of situations and character moments from which we can draw a number of 'existential survival skills' that have the potential to help us not only survive, but thrive. These 'survival skills' — these lessons from the stars — are applicable to astrological devotees and non-believers alike, and are as valuable today as they were during Grad and Esther's 70s adventures, when they worked together with the series' warmth and humour to provide a flicker of light in the pervasive televisual darkness.

© JZ Ferguson

1. Ken Irwin, 'Anouska cops a real star part', *Daily Mirror*, February 25, 1974, p. 19.
2. Albert Watson, 'ITV unveil their new star-struck snob cop', *Evening Express*, October 13, 1973, p. 2.
3. Ibid.

TWO VISIONS OF SUBURBIA: *THE FALL AND RISE OF REGINALD PERRIN* AND *TERRY AND JUNE*

In 1909, the Liberal politician C.F.G. Masterman described the suburban middle classes in his polemic *The Condition of England* as:

'...easily forgotten for they do not strive or cry; and for the most part only ask to be left alone. They have none of those channels of communication in their possession by which the rich and the poor are able to express their hostility to any political or social change.' [1]

Furthermore, Masterman viewed a suburban existence as 'a life of Security; a life of Sedentary occupation; a life of Respectability'. Worse, 'No one fears the Middle Classes, the suburbans; and perhaps for that reason, no one respects them. They only appear articulate in comedy' [2]. Of the two BBC sitcoms in this chapter, *Terry and June* (1979-1987) and *The Fall and Rise of Reginald Perrin* (1976-79), Terry and June would have probably heartily agreed with the idea of a life of respectability. Meanwhile, Reginald Iolanthe Perrin did not merely strive for change; he aimed at escape via complete reinvention.

These very different situation comedies' suburban backgrounds are essentially a 19th-century development. Dr. Matthew Taunton notes how public transport in the form of omnibuses and the railway network allowed the lower-middle and middle classes to live miles from their offices, separating work and domestic life. [3] To quote Charles Pooter in *The Diary of a Nobody*, 'After my work in the City, I like to be at home. What's the good of a home if you are never in it? "Home, Sweet Home," that's my motto'. For the hero of George and Weedon's comic novel, which commenced as a *Punch* magazine series in 1888, his castle is The Laurels. It is more than 'a nice six-roomed residence, not counting basement, with a front-breakfast parlour' [4] in Brickfield Terrace, Holloway, for it is his bastion against the trials of everyday life. Terry and June followed in the tradition of *The Diary of a Nobody*'s gentle domesticity; indeed, Terry Scott and June Whitfield would have made an excellent Charles and Carrie Pooter.

Terry and June is also one of the most famous examples of that much-derided sub-genre, the domestic sitcom. To cite but a few examples, BBC Radio's *Ray's a Laugh* (1949-1961) contained husband-and-wife sketches between Ted Ray and Kitty Bluett, and *Life With The Lyons* (1950-1961 on radio and a 1955-1960 television adaptation), starring the expatriate American couple Bill Lyons and Bebe Daniels. Ten days after the launch of commercial television on 22nd September 1955, ATV screened *Joan and Leslie*, starring the husband-and-wife team Joan and Leslie Randall, which lasted until 1958. Two years later, Associated-Rediffusion commenced a five-year run of *The Dickie Henderson Show*. To look at the limited amount of surviving black and white footage is to marvel at a realm where if the characters do not say 'Hello darling - I'm home!', they look as though they are on the verge of doing so.

Such fascinatingly twee domesticity was evident in certain British film comedies of that era, such as *Upstairs and Downstairs* (Ralph Thomas 1959), which required little more of Michael Craig than wearing a tweed jacket with verve and aplomb and saying 'gosh!' on a regular basis. In 1954 Kenneth Tynan described much of West End theatre as 'Loamshire' where 'joys and sorrows are giggles and whimpers: the crash of denunciation dwindles into "Oh stuff, Mummy!" and "Oh really, Daddy!" In his view, this was a 'glibly codified fairy-tale world of no more use to the student of life than a dolls' house would be to a student of town-planning'. [5]

However, Tynan perceptively noted that theatrical works 'could still tickle the palate' and on television suburbia as a fantasy realm continued on the BBC and ITV throughout the 1960s and 1970s. Andrew Tudor argued that 'Genre notions – except in the case of arbitrary definition – are not critics' classifications made for special purposes; they are sets of cultural conventions. Genre is what we collectively believe it to be' [6]. The 'we' of that period could reasonably expect a jolly theme tune, some exterior filmed sequences of suburban villas close to the studio and some 'hilarious' misunderstandings. Many such programmes are 'Missing, Believed Wiped', leaving behind tantalising descriptions in the *Radio* or *TV Times*. The sole surviving edition of *Just Jimmy* (1964-1968) starring Jimmy Clitheroe now appears less sitcom and more Czech New Wave cinema transposed to Lancashire and co-starring Mollie Sugden. By 1969, the plot of Thames TV's *A Present for Dickie*, in which Mr. Henderson received an elephant (with hilarious consequences), now reads like a Jean-Luc Godard-inspired deconstruction of the art of comedy.

Even in the 1980s, many British sitcoms seemed to form a composite fantasy of humorous misunderstandings. The parody *Oh Crikey!* in *The Young Ones* (1982-1984) was not entirely removed from the programmes this writer viewed with (over) avid interest. The realm of *Pig in The Middle* (1980-1983), with a jovial announcer referring to one character as 'the scourge of suburbia', was so far removed from rural Hampshire as to be surreal. No milkmen with Sidney James cockney accents ever seemed to call at the 1960s 'executive housing' developments where once stood strawberry fields. Similarly, if any of my neighbours ever held a dinner party with hilarious consequences, I was unaware of these social events. A few miles away, the outskirts of Southampton appeared to be endless rows of grey pre-war semi-detached villas, leavened by the occasional grim post-war housing estate. There seemed little prospects of any of the inhabitants saying 'Oh crikey' or, in December, The Boss/The Vicar/The Mother-In-Law/The 32-Year-Old-Kings Road Punk Son arriving at the scene of a plum pudding disaster. With even more hilarious consequences. [7]

What differentiated *Terry and June* from *My Wife Next Door* and other such forgotten shows was Terry Scott and June Whitfield. Owen John Scott was born in Watford in 1927 and abandoned a suitably Pooterish career in accountancy for repertory theatre. By 1951 *The Stage* praised 'the frantic efforts of Terry Scott who vainly endeavours to enact a one-man drama that demands a change of costume at every other line' [8] at Collins's Music Hall, and four years later he co-starred with Bill Maynard in the BBC's *Great Scott – It's Maynard!*. By 1962, Scott's comic partner was the character actor Hugh Lloyd, with *Hugh and I* lasting for 71 editions and five years. Tony Hancock apparently berated the result as stealing his mannerisms, but the Scott of 33 Lobelia Avenue in Tooting is more overbearing and pompous than the master of 23 Railway Cuttings. Looking at the surviving *Hugh and I* stories, it is evident that Scott needed a partner who would stand up to him on screen.

In 1968 June Whitfield guest-starred in an edition of Scott's BBC sketch show *Scott On…*, following in her tradition of enhancing the careers of post-war British male comics. Her 1961 observation, 'I am quite good at creeping out of other people's shows. I am the girl who says loudly and clearly the unfunny line before the comedian's funny line. I prefer to leave it at that' [9] has to be one of the greatest understatements in the history of British entertainment. Frank Muir was somewhat more accurate when he said, 'June always understands what we are getting at and gets more out of it than we put in. She is the answer to a scriptwriter's prayer. She is phenomenal'. [10]

June Rosemary Whitfield was born in South London in 1925 and graduated from RADA in 1944. Nine years later, Muir and Denis Norden were so impressed by her performance in the West End musical *Love From Judy* that they invited her to join the BBC Light Programme's *Take It From Here* (1948-1960) as the new female lead. By the time Whitfield first worked with Scott, she had already appeared alongside Arthur Askey, Stanley Baxter, Richard Briers, Jimmy Edwards, Tony Hancock, Benny Hill, Frankie Howerd, and Leslie Phillips. The surviving footage of *Scott On…Marriage* features the pair in a 'hippy sketch', [11] and, despite the cliché-ridden script, the pair's chemistry is palpable. Four years later, they appeared in the cinematic version of *Bless This House* (Gerald Thomas), filmed in Windsor and Burnham. The result was the *Citizen Kane* of British sitcom spin-off films, but Scott's 'Ronald Baines' is not yet the 'Terry' character; he is pompous, officious and professional. The middle manager as an overgrown schoolboy persona [12] did not reach fruition until the first edition of *Happy Ever After* on 7th May 1974. Over the next five years, John Chapman, Eric Merriman, Christopher Bond, John Kane and Jon Watkins created 41 tales of misunderstandings that did not always delight the critics. Peter Fiddick of *The Guardian* ranted about 'middle-class pretensions', how Scott 'could not resist signposting the jokes' and how HEA was 'the sort of blunt, nudging joke-show that tends to get blamed on ITV' [13]. However, such reviews did not prevent strong viewing figures. With a change of principal scriptwriter to Kane, the show was reformatted as *Terry and June* in October 1979, running for another nine seasons. [14]

Throughout 65 episodes, Terry and June Medford resided in a world almost as self-contained as The Village in *The Prisoner* (1967-1968), with none of the seething lower-middle-class rage of Tony Hancock, Captain Mainwaring or Basil Fawlty. Earlier in the chapter, I mentioned *The Diary of a Nobody*, but Terry and June's materially comfortable and safe existence is far removed from Charles and Carrie Pooter. The household at The Laurels depends on the paterfamilias' clerical job lest they descend into genteel poverty. Meanwhile, the Medfords' BBC sitcom contemporary, Martin Bryce of *Ever Decreasing Circles* (1984-1989), attempts to stave off loneliness and even despair with frantic involvement with local clubs and societies. Terry Medford's dilemmas tend to revolve around the purchase of a new video recorder and 'The Boss' coming for dinner. Yet, to criticise *Terry and June* for not evoking the unhappiness behind the suburban dream would be to complain that Turkish Delight is overly sweet. One storyline had Terry involved with a children's fancy dress party while June was missing her new colander. With most sitcoms, the consequences would probably be as 'hilarious' as Peter Watkins' *The War Game* (1966) but Scott and

Whitfield could make virtually any stock scenario funny. The film and television historian Andy Medhurst accurately observed of the last season: 'Perhaps one of the keys to the series' longevity rests precisely with the performers and the generic types they so skilfully embody. *Terry and June* is a warm bath of a programme, soothingly anachronistic and reassuringly repetitive' [15]. This view was more accurate and tolerant than Q.D. Leavis's opinion of suburban culture, which apparently had 'no fine rhythms to draw on and is not serious...it is not only formed to convey merely crude states of mind but is destructive of any fineness' [16]. But then, the great academic probably never witnessed the Medfords' am-dram performances in *The King & I*.

Meanwhile, elsewhere in South London suburbia, Reggie is probably contemplating the prospect of the daily commute with feelings oscillating between dread and despair. For *Terry and June*, Purley's well-kept avenues are a virtual playground, while for Perrin, a mortgaged villa is a form of prison. The idea of middle-class respectively as a straitjacket to creativity has a long tradition in English literature. The hero of H.G. Wells' *The History of Mr. Polly* viewed himself as 'A weakly wilful being struggling to get obdurate things round impossible corners' [17]. By 1935, when Reginald Perrin was at school, Anthony Bertram fulminated:

'The man who builds a bogus Tudoresque villa or castellates his suburban home is committing a crime against truth and tradition. He is denying the history of progress, denying his own age and insulting the very thing he pretends to imitate by misusing it'. [18].

In 1955 Iain Nairn's famous essay *Subtopia* argued:

'Places are different: Subtopia is the annihilation of the difference by attempting to make one type of scenery standard for town, suburb, countryside and wild. So what has to be done is to maintain and intensify the difference between places' [19]

By then, our hero was on the verge of a management career in 'Sunshine Desserts', selling confections made from the finest artificial ingredients. In his words, during his conference speech, "Are We Getting Our Just Desserts?", he rants that on his gravestone will be the inscription, 'Here lies Reginald Iolanthe Perrin. He didn't know the names of the trees and the flowers, but he knew the rhubarb crumble sales figures for Schleswig-Holstein'. This lament was the creation of David Nobbs, who, as Jonathan Coe points out, had virtually a double career by 1975. 'There is no other example, as far as I know, of a writer achieving such success in the mainstream of popular entertainment while also writing serious literary novels' [20]. The result of the BBC's suggestion to Nobbs that he adapt *The Death of Reginald Perrin* (1975) for television was unlikely to be straightforward. The Cambridge graduate who wrote comedy routines for *That Was The Week That Was* (1962-1963) and Les Dawson was also the creator of a story whose protagonist wrote a suicide letter to a wife who believed it genuine. Nobbs wrote in his memoirs how the screenplay of *Some Like It Hot* (Billy Wilder 1959) carefully established that the Tony Curtis and Jack Lemmon characters are in genuine danger [21]. The same applied to the retitled *The Fall and Rise of Reginald Perrin* aired on 8th September 1976.

On the surface, the series followed in the decade's tradition of suburban sitcoms: 'tinged with an aura of failed ambition... disenchantment with suburbia had become the conventional wisdom in both the popular and the academic press'. [22] Outside of the situation comedy genre, the sadistic mental games played by the various members of Yorkshire Television's *The Organization* (1972) would have been all too familiar to Reggie. The Public Relations department of Greatrick never seems to assist in producing any goods, just as the confections marketed by Perrin for Sunshine Desserts appear largely inedible. By the end of the decade, Dave Allen's estate agent in Alan Bennett's LWT play *One Fine Day* rejects his everyday existence by hiding in the empty office block his employers have tasked him with selling. The image of George Phillips sitting in a deckchair, listening to opera and isolated from his work colleagues and family could have been Perrin at bay.

Possibly the ultimate representation of such a character is Paul Rogers' Raymond Clemens in the 1972 episode of *Public Eye* (1965-1975) *The Man Who Said Sorry* – self-pitying, raging and subsumed by his mental pain. Nobbs's achievement was to frame similar and equally devasting angst within an ostensibly conventional sitcom setting, complete with studio laughter. Clive James's faint dismissal of 'there is nothing fresh in the idea of a harried mediocrity seeing his wishes fulfilled in fantasy: from Walter Mitty through to Billy Liar and beyond, the line stretches on' [23] was slightly misplaced. Perrin was not a middle-aged William Fisher, nor was he the figure of W H Auden's *Letter to Lord Byron*:

'The bowler hat who strap-hangs in the Tube,
And kicks the tyrant only in his dreams,
Trading on pathos,
Dreading all extremes'. [24]

If Reggie had a template in British television, it was probably Gurney Slade, the 1960 Anthony Newley creation, who retreated into his mind to escape deadening conformity.

The Strange World of Gurney Slade achieved audience confusion, rapidly diminishing viewing figures for ATV and a small group of devoted followers, including the future David Bowie. It took decades for Newley's masterpiece to gain its proper appreciation, while the BBC intended *The Fall and Rise of Reginald Perrin* to have mass appeal. Nobbs envisaged Ronnie Barker in the title role. However, the Corporation opted for Leonard Rossiter, the character actor with eyes ever alert for signs of mendacity, betrayal, or weakness in his opponents. Nobbs later wrote, 'Leonard did teeter on the edge of over-acting, and that was what was glorious about him. He didn't play safe; he took the risks; he really went for it. But he just, always, allowed the truth to win, and never allowed the scene to become unreal'. [25]

Rossiter, then almost 50, became a professional actor at 27 after spending six years with the Commercial Union Insurance Company. Between 1959 and 1961, he appeared at the Bristol Old Vic and, in

1962, played the leading role of Fred Midway, an obsessive social climber in David Turner's *Semi-Detached* at Coventry's Belgrade Theatre. One critic observed, 'Mr. Rossiter speaks at such speed that the part appears to be longer than it is'. [26]

This sensation of speed would be a key to many of Rossiter's characterisations. Even when he speaks deliberately and slowly, as with the social services investigator in *The Whisperers* (Bryan Forbes 1966), there is often the impression of barely suppressed frustration. Such an approach might have seen Rossiter typecast as a CID officer, but he declined the chance to make his Detective-Inspector Bamber a regular on *Z-Cars* (1962-1978). In 1963 he told *The Stage*, 'The really frightening thing about television is the way you can get identified with a character if you play it regularly. People forget your name'. [27] Near the end of the 1960s Ronald Bryden described Rossiter's performance in the title role of Brecht's *The Resistible Rise of Arturo Ui* as: 'The power he displays in it has always been there, but never before has it found such an opportunity'. [28] At that time, he had starred in several major television plays, but it would not be until 1973 that the actor achieved mass fame with his Rupert Rigsby in Yorkshire Television's *Rising Damp* (1974-1978).

The BBC naturally wished to capitalise on Rossiter's stardom when casting *The Fall and Rise* but the character trait that Rigsby and Perrin had in common was their vulnerability. Reginald is well-groomed, well-spoken and increasingly erratic. As David Quantick so perceptively described the series, it 'rode on the wheels of the sitcom', with the central character faking his own death in the opening credits. 'And he did so not because of his wife or the funny neighbours, but because he was enduring an existential crisis – not a situation ever faced by Stan from *On the Buses*'. [29] This is illustrated as early as the second episode of the first series, where the Perrins, with their daughter, son-in-law and grandchildren in tow, are having an outing at a safari park. The entire family is trapped in the confines of a Ford Cortina Mk. III Estate, an archetypal company car of that era, and the shots of it crawling through the reconstituted wilderness perfectly capture the glorious passage in the original novel:

'It seemed as if the whole world was on safari in Surrey. Behind them, hidden by a discreet ridge, was the stately home itself. On their left were the toilets and a souvenir stall. On their right was the Tasteebite Cafeteria'. [30]

The artifice that bedevils Reggie at the office as he is obliged to promote 'the inedible to the unthinking' pervades his escape attempts. This is nature contained by suburbia, and Perrin's reaction takes the form of a near breakdown. The response of the audience watching the filmed sequence seems almost as uneasy as the reaction to Harold Steptoe's collapse at the end of the 1962 *Comedy Playhouse* story *The Offer*. The reaction of Pauline Yates as Mrs. Perrin is perfectly judged; compassion and fear that she cannot help, as her husband rants that he is a failure. June can always control Terry, but Reggie is now slipping away from her guidance.

There is no subtext of such angst in Terry and June Medford's suburbia, but nor was there ever meant to be. A further difference is that of the setting. *Perrin* exists firmly within the late 1970s, with Reggie spurning his brother-in-law Major Jimmy Anderson's quasi-Imperial quasi-fascistic delusions. [31]. The past is no solution to his dilemmas, but Scott and Whitfield reside in a Home Counties combining trace elements of the 1950s, with modern trappings. When re-watching *Terry and June*, the viewer often experiences confusion about the setting. In 1983's *The Artistic Touch*, Brian Hall's cockney burglar appears to have emerged from a 1954 *Scotland Yard* B-film and references Pablo Picasso in a joke probably last heard on the BBC Home Service during the premiership of Anthony Eden. Penelope Gilliatt's description of the *Carry On* films as 'strangely timeless, a dream-mixture of periods' [32] is equally applicable to *Terry and June* and it is when the Medfords attempt to engage with the outside world that they appear charmingly dated.

By series six, *A Day in Boulogne* has the couple on location in France, looking bizarrely out of place among the Renault 20s and the Peugeot 305s. Plus, of course, the final series plot of *Age Before Beauty*, which has June dressing, rather fetchingly, it must be said, as a 'punk rocker'. There is an entire thesis to be written on 1980s sitcoms' obsessions with out-of-date punks, just as British cinema persisted in referring to 'The Teds' into the 1960s. Sadly, the scriptwriter missed a trick by not having Terry don a green wig, only for Reginald Marsh as The Boss to arrive for dinner suddenly.

The other significant difference is in the depiction of the marriage. The Perrins are a believable married couple, whereas the Medfords' last martial relations attempts seem to have occurred during the Festival of Britain. It is a virtual mother-son relationship, with Terry regularly embarking on his latest great adventure. In the driveway is a Leyland Princess or an Austin Ambassador, but Terry does not take advantage of their (admittedly modest) capacity for speed. While various dramas and *Plays for Today* feature apparent escapees from John Betjeman's *Meditation on the A30,* Medford's main concerns involve the office drama society more than 'Who dares to come hooting at me? I only give way to a Jag'. At almost all times he appears to be a middle-aged schoolboy who appears to have emerged from *Just William*. In addition, what truly dates both series is that neither Elizabeth Perrin nor June Medford works outside of the house; as late as 1971, only 47% of married women had jobs. [33]. Eleven years earlier, Maureen Nichol established the National Housewives' Register, a support network for bored *hausfraus*, which organised talks and coffee mornings through local newsletters to break up the daily routine. By 1970 it had 5,000 members. [34]. Nor was Elizabeth or June arranging dinners for their husband's work colleagues entirely implausible. The 1978 book *Executive Stress* observed:

'The two most important dimensions as far as the manager in his work role is concerned appear to be those of time management and social support. Factors such as the wife's "occupation", her satisfaction with this, the part the manager's job plays in their joint life, the extent to which he is required, and wants, to participate in activities outside work, all have significant bearing on these, and ultimately the manager's "performance" in his job.' [35]

Fortunately, neither did *The Fall and Rise of Reginald Perrin* followed the primrose path of *Suburban Wives* (Derek Ford 1971) nor any other 1970s British cinematic 'sex comedy'. In such non-epics, semi-detached ladies tend to be unaccountably attracted to flared trousered lotharios with Jason King sideburns. Instead, June Whitfield and especially Pauline Yates subtly hint at their characters' inner lives. Nobbs later reflected on Elizabeth's 'peculiarly bland and servile attitude, just being there to cook meals and never complaining about anything: that struck one as much more extraordinary now than it would've done in 1976'. [36]. But Yates's performance is anything but bland – a subtle blend of strength and sexuality. With both Elizabeth Perrin and June Medford, one thinks of Jake Thackray's *Castleford Ladies' Magic Circle*. Reggie might have been impressed but had Terry found out, he would probably have fainted. [37]

Finally, with two genuinely seminal domestic situation comedies, there is the temptation to play the intriguing, if futile, game of 'Alternative Casting'. Had Tony Hancock lived, he would almost certainly have been a natural for Reggie, while the role of Terry Medford was structured around Terry Scott's long-established persona. It is impossible to envisage Rossiter in the role; his final sitcom, Thames TV's dire 1984 *Tripper's Day*, demonstrated his uneasiness in broad farce. But the idea of Scott as Perrin is more plausible. In 1976 he modestly told one reporter: 'I'm a nice, steady type of chap, who has been fortunate enough to be in work for ten years without a break'. [38]. Yet ten years earlier, John Neville wanted him to join the Nottingham Playhouse – 'Because he is such a good actor. I have admired him for a long time'. [39]. When Scott portrayed Arnolphe in Moliere's *School For Wives*, The Guardian noted: 'Terry Scott is nearly always Terry playing Arnolphe, so well'. [40]. As with Robert Morley, Scott appeared an actor by force of personality, and could have been equally suited to tragedy. The moment Reggie arrives at the Dorset coast and contemplates committing suicide is a testament to Rossiter's power as an actor. It truly is a dark night of the soul, and all the genre conventions of the 1970s sitcom have entirely vanished. Nobbs reflected of the earlier drunken conference speech: 'Reggie means all this seriously. I mean all this seriously. How do you incorporate that into a sitcom? You make him drunk. The audience doesn't listen'. [41]. Now Perrin is isolated from his family and facing the demons he has attempted to keep at bay. It is impossible to imagine anyone else but Rossiter at that moment. Yet, Scott's often-underused gift for pathos, [42] with that malleable, expressive face, might have produced a different but equally affecting moment.

As it was to Terry Medford, suburbia is a realm of endlessly exciting adventures screened every week. To paraphrase George Orwell's description of Frank Richards's stories, 'Everything will be the same for ever and ever' – including Terry exclaiming 'Cor!' at the latest catastrophe. He would probably have agreed with Charles Pooter's philosophy, 'I always feel people are happier who live a simple, unsophisticated life'. But for Reggie, such routine is his prison and a reflection of his pain, with his domestic environment resembling Nairn's *Subtopia*:

'Is the open heath or down being rapidly enclosed by wire fences? Are there notice boards and red flags to warn you off? Are the rights of way kept open? Do you ever feel civilisation is a long way off? Is it being 'opened up' for the tourists or are they coming on the landscape's own terms? Is everything made easy for the tepid majority – motels, cafés, motorways – or are the facilities kept simple for those prepared to walk their way around?' [43]

As it is, Perrin will continue to flee an artificial world for the South Coast, faking his death even after he comes to realise, 'We can never escape our destiny...because whatever happens to us becomes our destiny'. And Terry will continue to burst through the door of his villa with the clarion cry of "June!" [44]

© Andrew Roberts

1. C.F.G Masterman, *The Condition of England* (London: Methuen, 1960), p. 56.
2. Masterman passim.
3. Matthew Taunton, *Suburbia*, The British Library.
4. George and Weedon Grossmith, *The Diary of a Nobody* (London: Arrowsmith, 1892), p. 1.
5. Kenneth Tynan, 'At The Theatre: Apathy', *The Observer*, 31st October 1954, p. 6.
6. Andrew Tudor, *Genre and Critical Methodology in Movies and Methods* - Volume One, An Anthology by Bill Nichols (ed.) (Berkeley: University of California Press, 1976), pp. 118-125 (p. 122).
7. When I briefly lived in such a street during the 1990s, I found my predictions to be very accurate.
8. 'Round The Halls', *The Stage*, 8th February 1951, p. 5.
9. Quoted in Ramsden Greig, 'June is Happy Feeding Comics', The Aberdeen Evening Express, 27th December 1961, p. 2.
10. Greig passim.
11. A typical scenario for a British comedy of the late 1960s; see also the unconvincing 'Flower Power' dancers of *Carry On Camping* (Gerald Thomas 1969).
12. Such a character had long been an aspect of Scott's comic armoury; readers with long memoires may recall his 1962 record *My Brother* constantly played on Junior Choice.
13. Peter Fiddick, 'Happy Ever After on television', *The Guardian*, 15th August 1974, p. 10.
14. 'The BBC wanted to continue with the show, and to avoid legal complications were forced to change any details on which Chapman could claim copyright. Since the characters shared their first names with the performers, it was decided that the surnames only needed changing' – Matthew Coniam, BFI Screenonline.
15. Andy Medhurst, 'Terry and June' in *The Listener*, Vol. 118 (p. 32).

16. Q.D. Leavis 1965, quoted in Roger Webster, 'Suburbia Inside Out' in *Expanding Suburbia: Reviewing Suburban Narratives* by R. Webster (ed.) (New York: Berghahn Books, 2001), p. 4.
17. H. G. Wells, *The History of Mr. Polly* (London: Grosset and Dunlap, 1909), p. 68.
18. Anthony Bertram, *The House: A Machine for Living In; a Summary of the Art and Science of Homemaking Considered Functionally* (London: A. & C. Black Limited, 1935), p. 21.
19. Ian Nairn, 'Subtopia', *The Architectural Review*, June 1955.
20. Jonathan Coe, *On David Nobbs*.
21. David Nobbs, *I Didn't Get Where I Am Today* (London: Penguin Random House, 2004) p. 159.
22. Paul L. Knox, *Better by Design? Architecture, Urban Planning, and the Good City* (Blacksburg VA: Virginia Tech Publishing, 2020), p. 205.
23. Clive James, 'Wet Lips: Television', *The Observer* 19th September 1976, p. 26.
24. W.H. Auden and Edward Mendelson (ed.), 'Letter to Lord Byron', *The Complete Works of W. H. Auden: Poems*, Volume I (Princeton: Princeton University Press, 2022), p. 239.
25. David Nobbs, www.leonardrossiter.com.
26. J.C. Trewin, 'Semi-Detached' Belgrade, *Birmingham Daily Post*, 9th June 1962, p. 21.
27. Marjorie Bilbow, 'Meeting The Demands of an Exciting But Challenging Medium; People and their work – Leonard Rossiter', *The Stage*, 22nd August 1963, p. 10.
28. Ronald Bryden, 'Heroic Acting in Gangsterland', *The Observer*, 13th April 1969, p. 24.
29. David Quantick, 'David Nobbs's Reginald Perrin: "a stealth drama riding on the wheels of a sitcom"', *The Guardian*, 10th August 2015.
30. David Nobbs, *The Fall and Rise of Reginald Perrin* (London: Random House, 2013), e-book.

31. 'You realise the sort of people you're going to attract, don't you, Jimmy? Thugs, bully-boys, psychopaths, sacked policemen, security guards, sacked security guards, racialists, Paki-bashers, queer-bashers, Chink-bashers, anybody-bashers, rear Admirals, queer admirals, Vice Admirals, fascists, neo-fascists, crypto-fascists, loyalists, neo-loyalists, crypto-loyalists'.
32. Penelope Gilliatt, *Unholy fools; wits, comics, disturbers of the peace: film & theatre* (New York: Viking Press, 1973), p. 285.
33. Dominic Sandbrook, *State of Emergency: The Way We Were: Britain 1970–1974* (Allen Lane 2010), pp. 392-3.
34. Sally Waller, *A Sixties Social Revolution? British Society 1959–1975* (Nelson Thornes, 2008), p. 85.
35. Judi Marshall and Cary L. Cooper, *Understanding Executive Stress* (London: Palgrave Macmillan, 1978), p. 120.
36. Jonathan Coe, www.leonardrossiter.com.
37. After exclaiming 'Cor!' very loudly.
38. Quoted in Val Marriott, 'No ups and downs for Terry Scott – "a steady type of chap"', *The Leicester Chronicle*, 16th July 1976, p. 2.
39. Quoted in 'TV star Terry heads for city', *The Guardian Journal*, 21st November 1966, p. 1.
40. Desmond Christy, 'Bromley – School for Wives', *The Guardian* 15th March 1984, p. 20.
41. Nobbs, p. 303.
42. Think of Scott's beautifully timed reaction to the death of Private Hale (Peter Gilmore) in *Carry On Up The Khyber* (Gerald Thomas 1968).
43. Subtopia passim.
44. Editor: This reminds me of what writer Andy Hutchcraft said to me recently: "Catchphrases are the glue that holds great comedy together. They make us feel comfortable with our comedy. We wait for and expect those familiar lines, like the warmth from being with a family member."

TRAPPED IN A DOLL'S HOUSE: *BUTTERFLIES*

"I'm not one of your butterflies. You can't scoop me up into your net and stick a pin through my navel."
(Ria Parkinson, *He'll Have to Go, Butterflies*)

The 1970s has been described by some historians and critics as a 'Golden Age' of British television. Certainly, it was a vintage decade for the sitcom, [1] thanks in no small measure to the fecund talents of a generation of predominantly male writers, including Ian La Frenais, Dick Clement, Eric Chappell, Brian Cooke, John Mortimer, Roy Clarke, John Esmonde and Bob Larbey. A list of memorable situation comedies would probably include the following: *The Liver Birds* (1969-79), *Whatever Happened to the Likely Lads?* (1973-74), *Porridge* (1974-77), *Rising Damp* (1974-78), *The Fall and Rise of Reginald Perrin* (1976-79), *The Good Life* (1975-78), *Fawlty Towers* (1975 and 1979), and *To the Manor Born* (1979-81) among many others. I would add Carla Lane's subversive *Butterflies* (1978-83) to the list of the classic 70s sitcoms even if, arguably, it fits uncomfortably within the genre. For the purpose of this essay, I will be concentrating on the first two series, the ones which appeared in the 1970s.

Lane set about writing a sitcom series with a difference – a bittersweet 'situation tragedy' – when she created *Butterflies*. In 2002 she commented: 'I wanted to write a comedy about a woman seriously contemplating adultery.' [2] That juxtaposition of 'comedy' with 'seriously' is a telling one. Over the course of its twenty-eight-episode, four series run, there is a delicate, unsettling balance, with much of the dialogue offering both humour and satirical, social commentary. It is, perhaps, unsurprising that it took Lane three years to convince the BBC that her daring concept would work as a 'sitcom'.

The opening episode – *When Ria Met Leonard* – offers us plenty of back story to middle-aged housewife Ria Parkinson (Wendy Craig) and her family. Lane finds inventive ways to drip-feed us the background while introducing the over-arching narrative:

"Once upon a time there was a handsome young dentist, with a sense of humour...What happened?"

Intriguingly, Ria describes her suburban home, husband and children as "pleasant". She tells stranger Leonard (Bruce Montague) that she is "happily" but not "excitingly" married. Even in this introductory episode, we can see how Lane daringly subverts the conventional formula of the middle-class sitcom. As Michael Hogan observes:

'For every conventional comic scene – Ria's calamitous cookery, a car prang, keep-fit class, nosy neighbour or family squabble – there was an internal Ria monologue or dream sequence.' [3]

Those monologues not only allow us access to her thoughts, but they also reinforce the sense of Ria being trapped. The playful use of dream sequences allows us to share her fears or desires. (As the series develops, we will also gain access to her husband's thoughts.) If Lane is subverting the conventional structure and realism of the sitcom, Ria herself is a subversive character from some respects. In contrast to the stereotypical housewife, she cannot cook, openly berates her family for taking her for granted and often speaks in (unrealistic) literary metaphors, such as the butterfly one she offers in the initial episode:

"We're all kids chasing butterflies. You see it, you want it, you grab it, and there it is, all squashed in your hand."

The symbolic significance of the butterfly does not simply apply to people's dashed aspirations, it also refers to Ria as a trapped creature, something which is illustrated when we first see that her husband, Ben, is a collector of butterflies, pinning them under glass. Already, in this first episode, we are left to wonder whether Ria will choose at some point to flap her wings and fly off.

Lane acknowledged that *Butterflies* was semi-autobiographical, reflecting the double life she was living at the time. [4] She was writing the series in a social context where an increasing number of journalists and social commentators were examining the role of the housewife/mother, either as undervalued, unpaid 'worker', or as a restricted, 'invisible' human being. Dominic Sandbrook sees *Butterflies* as part of the mid-70s sitcom's 'sustained and popular indictment of suburbia' with 'their portrait of a monotonous world of lonely, frustrated housewives'. [5] However, as he acknowledges, suburbia was an aspiration for millions, despite being ridiculed by some intellectuals as banal. It now had an important place 'at the centre of Britain's physical and imaginative landscape'. Another source of inspiration may well have been Jenny Joseph's poem *Warning* (1961) in which a respectable, middle-aged housewife and mother contemplates breaking free of convention, both in her clothing and behaviour. Just as Joseph's narrator considers wearing nothing but purple with a mismatching red hat, sitting on pavements, setting off alarms and learning to spit, Ria fantasises about painting the house purple and even adding a rude door knocker. There is also more than a touch of Ibsen's *A Doll's House* here, the play which had shocked European theatre audiences in 1879 when Nora Helmer eventually walks out on her husband and children. It says a lot about conventional society that, a century later, the theme of a married mother contemplating flight (or infidelity here) could still represent a controversial topic.

The opening episode sets up a nice contrast between the straitlaced Ben who confesses to finding the modern world of 1978 – where people talk openly about sex, where teenagers push the boundaries – confusing and unsettling, and Ria, who senses that it is a changing society in which she might be able to break free or rebel. This, after all, is the decade of *Spare Rib* and Virago, a time when the idealised image of the 'little angel in the house' was being challenged by feminists. The fact that Ria decides not to meet Leonard in a café at the end of the initial episode feels like a postponement of 'illicit' opportunity, rather than an abandonment of it.

'Television makes no guarantees. Each episode is an adventure. Even 'series television', defined by repetition, forever plays havoc with our expectations.' [6]

Literary critic Christopher Anderson is referring here to action-adventure shows, but his comments can be used in relation to a series such as *Butterflies*. Anderson argues that a television series episode is made up of both 'similarity' and 'difference'. Similarity being how it identifies with previous instalments; difference being its disruption of those preceding ones. In a sense, as viewers, we seek both; we crave the familiarity, but we also want an element of the new. This first outing of *Butterflies* leaves the viewer wondering how Lane will be able to offer us 'difference' in subsequent episodes, inventively drawing on her formula, rather than simply offering us formulaic repetition.

The subsequent episodes in the first series continue to draw upon familiar aspects of the traditional domestic sitcom, in particular what we might term the 'normal dysfunctionality' of the suburban couple or family, a staple ingredient of the genre. These elements are firmly placed in their late-70s context, such as Ria excusing her sons' inability to find a job when she observes that there are "millions of unemployed" people. The culture drain is also explored as she joins elder son Russell (Andrew Hall) in a naked protest about a significant public work of art being sold off to the United States, in *The Lovers*. The conservatism of traditional gender politics is examined, as when she comments that married women cannot have male friends, or when she is turned down for an interview for a chauffeuring job because the boss (Leonard) insists on a male driver. While Ben confesses that, "I'm living in a world I don't understand", his argument that he wants to be the sole "provider" or breadwinner cannot simply be dismissed as that of a man who is not up with the times; his fixed beliefs reflected many (middle-class) men's ideologies: "Why can't you just be a wife?"

The sense of being trapped in the suburban home is reinforced each week, with the house variously described as a "brick prison", "a cage", and "a hut in a suburban jungle". Where *Butterflies* stands out is its sometimes surreal – and even shocking – use of Ria's monologues. In *Breaking the Silence*, she creates a Ben figure out of a sofa cushion with his green butterfly-catching hat and begins with the casual comment, "I might kill myself today." Initially we are unsure whether to take this remark at face value. Her speech then takes us into Jenny Joseph territory as she adds a list of things that she would like to do first: shoplifting, writing poetry, wandering naked through Harrods, adding graffiti to a work of art in the Louvre.

The off-beat nature of the humour equally applies to her interactions with Ben, a man who alternates between offering staid views – about marriage, neighbours, teenagers, busking, fashion, female campaigners etc. – and heartfelt attempts to meet Ria halfway. When she expresses her desire for "illegal" sexual activity – "rape" – or at the very least unconventional sex, on the sofa or even in the potting shed, rather than being shocked, he surprises us with his measured reaction. Carla Lane is not offering a simplistic scenario of a woman stuck in a loveless marriage, but one where Ria Parkinson is "frustratedly bored". The humour stems partly from her flights of fancy and oddball behaviour, but also from Ben's witty retorts. Geoffrey Palmer is a master at dry comedy, as in the delivery of his remark that a potting shed encounter will require "a month's notice and central heating".

The butterfly leitmotif and analogies, introduced in *When Ria Met Leonard*, continue to run, from her sense that she is "a bottle of butterflies but I can't take the top off", to the moment when she releases Ben's captured butterfly in the meadows, in *Thinking*

About A Job. Her philosophical remark that "we're here for five minutes, that's all" reinforces her sense of time passing, the theme of *carpe diem*, of wanting to experience new sensations, rather than simply living in a hermitically sealed suburban box with a metaphorical seat belt attached. In *The Lovers*, Ria expresses a dislike of mirrors and clocks, both of which she sees in symbolic terms. For her, they represent constant reminders of Andrew Marvell's 'time's winged chariot hurrying near'.

Bruce Montague's Leonard is an interesting character. From some respects he is not only Ria's admirer but also her secret sharer, happy to indulge her idiosyncrasies and equally aware as she is of time passing. However, as demonstrated by his purchase of The Lovers statue, he is also a predator, a businessman who thinks that love – or sex – can be bought. Unlike Russell or Ria, he has no appreciation of it as a work of art; it is simply an (expensive) object which he hopes will earn him her attention or gratitude. In Series 2, chauffeur Thomas (Michael Ripper) – as much Leonard's conscience as his confidant – will voice a question we have already asked ourselves: "Is that love I see...or something less commendable?"

The first series of *Butterflies* concludes with *He'll Have to Go*. The running theme of *carpe diem* is taken to its extreme as Ria's walk through a churchyard brings her to a *memento mori* headstone poem:

'Remember me as you pass by
As you are now so once was I
As I am now so you will be
Prepare thyself to follow me'

The visual and literary reminder of the inevitability of death leads to an amusing address to God in the church: "You're depressing me... Couldn't you think of something less final?" It also acts as a reminder of the need to 'seize the day', and with it a re-evaluation of what really matters in her life. Rather than tackle this soberly,

Lane uses it to great comic effect, including Ria's comment to Ben: "I was in a graveyard this morning. Everybody was dead!" It is an example of her charming naivety, as if she has been walking around in a daze and has only just grasped the harshness of reality. In many respects Ria Parkinson is as childlike as Ben, with his tantrums over the bath, a damaged golf club or screwdriver, or a missing hose. There is a delightful sense of the absurd at the heart of Lane's humour, illustrated by a bizarre, offbeat speech offered by one of Ben's patients, Mr Worth, played with aplomb by Robert Gillespie:

"I was brought up to believe that carrots are good for your eyes, based on the theory that you never see rabbits wearing glasses. So I ate lots of carrots, and now I wear glasses."

It is a perfect illustration of how *Butterflies* frequently provides humour through non sequiturs, Ria's stream-of-consciousness, characters' thoughts and the foibles of human eccentricity, a reminder perhaps that neither the series nor life should be taken completely seriously.

Leaving sees Adam (Nicholas Lyndhurst) as the main focal point after his girlfriend dumps him. We are taken into the late-1970s bedroom of a teenager with its dark walls, nude pin-ups and provocative or subversive door message: 'If you can't solve it – run away from it'. Ben attempts to dismiss "the young today" as a lost generation of promiscuous kids, before confessing that he too had several pre-marital sexual experiences, including one with an older woman who introduced him to "the forbidden wall" before taking the proverbial "ladder" away. Adam's self-assessment – that he is 'undesirable' – is seen as a timeless one which afflicts people regardless of their age or experience. (After all, part of Leonard's attraction for Ria is that he clearly finds her desirable.) The enigmatic note Adam leaves – "I've gone" – and the description of his empty bedroom being like the Marie Celeste offers a foretaste of what life will be like for a stay-at-home mother once her children have flown the family nest, a theme briefly explored in Series 3's opening episode, *An Empty Cage*. Does she then somehow lose her sense of purpose and identity?

Worrying is a stand-out episode where Lane demonstrates the series' ability to provide us with surprising narrative and character twists. Initially, we are offered a familiar contrast between a hyperactive Ria and a hypochondriac Ben, daydreaming about his demise:

"You imagine that everything is going to be beautiful, until you get there and find out that it isn't. Whereas I knew it wasn't going to be beautiful before I went. What you suffer from is optimism."

That contrast between a beaming Ria exercising in the living room and a sullen Ben sat contemplating (imaginary) heart disease and death – "I'm laughing all the time; my face just refuses to co-operate" – is wonderfully reversed as Ben decides to take a new, positive approach to life, including increasing his sons' allowances and praising his wife's cooking. Meanwhile, Ria's chat in the park with a philosophical tramp (Patrick McAlinney) has her wondering whether extramarital sex/love is something to be avoided, rather than embraced. Her two potential paths are nicely mirrored by the sight of both Ben and Leonard jogging in the park and passing each other, an image which is both humorous and touchingly symbolic. Naturally, we know that Ben will be back to his dry, sardonic best in time for the next episode, a reminder that this is still a sitcom, not a realistic drama serial.

Carla Lane frequently draws on sitcom clichés, only to subvert them. In *A Dog's Life* we are introduced to the stereotype unfriendly, fussy neighbour. Mrs Conrad (Wendy Williams) appears to be a bitter killjoy with her complaints about the boys' errant Frisbee, yet after a series of chance encounters – in the church, doctor's surgery and park – the park bench confrontation between her and a depressed Ria leads to the reveal that she is childless and deeply scarred, putting Ria's own "nervous exhaustion" about her "carefree, lazy" teenagers into context. Rather than Lane offering a moral judgement about Ria's self-pity, it is another example of the way the series explores a wide variety of characters and their "multi-coloured moods".

Putting the Christmas Special to one side, *Lunch With Leonard* brings the second series of *Butterflies* to a satisfying, cyclical conclusion, with Ria and Leonard reflecting on "a very long brief encounter", and the two couples heading out separately – and inevitably – to the same restaurant for romantic dinners. Perhaps most memorable is the surreal scene where she watches women with "worn faces" struggling out of a supermarket, with "oven timers ringing in their heads" and decides to go on strike from the drudgery of housework.

Butterflies, in many respects, revolves around Ria Parkinson's need to carve out an identity for herself, other than those of 'wife' and 'mother'. Despite Carla Lane's statement that this is a comedy about a woman contemplating adultery, to me it is a far wider canvas. Whether it is public demonstrations – about national works of art being sold off, or fox hunting as a "merciless massacre" – meeting new people, applying for a job, contemplating having an affair, it is essentially about expanding horizons and adding spontaneity to her life. Nor is it necessarily solely gender specific. As the generally unimaginative Ben confesses in *Fox Hunting*, he too sometimes feels "trapped" in the routine of "teeth-lunch-teeth", a predictable cycle with "open wide, please" at its core. While Ria and Ben may disagree about numerous things, from pornography to collecting butterflies – "murder" or "preservation" – they are far from being polar opposites. If Russell and Adam are young people trying to make sense of and find their place in a "hostile world" – of high unemployment and complex (or casual) sexual relationships – so too are their parents. Perhaps the main difference between Ria and the others is that she feels the need to analyse everything, from signs of ageing in the mirror, questioning whether she still fancies her husband, to wondering if the teapot is the reason her tea-making is so poor. Ria also surprises us sometimes with a wicked, biting sense of humour. On one occasion, as she watches an attractive, confident younger female in the hairdressers openly flirting with the stylist, she comments that the woman is so precocious that she was probably taking the Pill with her school milk. In contrast, she remembers her own youth as one where females were "imprisoned by modesty". She confesses that her comparison between the late-1950s and late-1970s is borne out of jealousy, not moral outrage.

Dolly Parton's 1974 song *Love is Like a Butterfly* – sung by Clare Torry for the television series – is self-evidently a romantic love song:

'Love is like a butterfly
As soft and gentle as a sigh
The multi-coloured moods of love are like its satin wings
Love makes your heart feel strange inside
It flutters like soft wings in flight
Love is like a butterfly
A rare and gentle thing'

In the context of the series, the simile of the butterfly works in a more general sense, referring to a multitude of things: the ephemeral nature of life, the beauty of everyday things such as a walk in the park or a picnic in the meadows, the fragility of relationships, the complexity of the human mind and the constant fluctuation of our moods. *Butterflies* veers between realism and surrealism, between almost slapstick comedy, light humour, social satire and darker elements. This daring blend of ingredients is part of the secret to its success. Even today, Ria's admission that, for example, she enjoys looking at her sons' porn magazines, carries a *frisson* of shock in its conservative, suburban sitcom context.

Lane's creation of Ria Parkinson represents a landmark moment in the British sitcom. Her impulsive, frustrated, quirky character was one that many women could relate to and who was instantly likeable, for all her eccentricities. Indeed, those foibles and imperfections arguably add to her charm. The series has its roots in its late-70s context, yet it retains an almost timeless appeal, where some other domestic sitcoms have simply dated. Ultimately, it is both a product of its time and a winning combination of imaginatively crafted scripts and magnificent performances, from Wendy Craig and Geoffrey Palmer in particular.

© Rodney Marshall

1. In the introduction to his book *Raising Laughter*, Robert Sellers suggests that 'in the 1970s the sitcom was seen as the main ingredient of the television week…the general population needed cheering up'. This can no doubt also be applied to the comedy sketch shows of *The Two Ronnies* (1971-87)and *The Morecambe & Wise Show* (1968-77).
2. Lane's own term, cited by Michael Hogan, *Carla Lane's Midlife-crisis Masterpiece*, The Guardian, 02/06/2016.
3. Michael Hogan, *Carla Lane's Midlife-crisis Masterpiece*, The Guardian, 02/06/2016.
4. Hogan comments: 'It all rang so true, partly because it was. At the time, Lane was commuting between Liverpool and London – married with children back home, but having secret liaisons in the capital with a TV producer she called "Him".'
5. Dominic Sandbrook, 'Metro-Land', *State of Emergency*, p. 331. It is worth observing that *Butterflies* was filmed in Cheltenham, so not strictly speaking in Metro-land.
6. Christopher Anderson, 'Reflections on *Magnum PI*', *TV: The Critical View*, OUP, 1987.

CONTRIBUTORS

JZ Ferguson is a British popular culture enthusiast with a particular affinity for television series of the 60s and 70s. She contributed chapters to all five volumes in *The Avengers on film* series: *Bright Horizons, Mrs. Peel, We're Needed, Anticlockwise, Avengerland Regained* and *Avengerland Revisited*. She was joint-editor of *The New Avengers* and Definitive Guide volumes. She has also written for the *Classic British Television Drama* book series, penning chapters on shows including *The Saint, Man in a Suitcase, Danger Man, The Persuaders!*, and *Gideon's Way*. She wrote a guest essay for *Man in a Suitcase: A Critical Guide* and contributed chapters to *Tis Magic! Our Memories of Catweazle* and *Swinging TV*. She has also written for the website *The Avengers Declassified*. She lives in Canada.

Darren Flower After graduating from Imperial College (BSc, ARCS) and the University of Leeds (PhD), he worked first in the pharmaceutical industry (Fisons, Astra) and then academia (Oxford, Aston), helping to discover drugs and developing methods for vaccine design. A lifelong devotee of what was once called British Telefantasy, he now devotes his time to working from home. He contributed a chapter on science and technology in *Swinging TV*.

Michael Herbert lives in Greater Manchester and is a freelance historian. He watched the first episode of *Doctor Who* on 23rd November 1963, aged 8, and has been watching it ever since. His favourite eras are the William Hartnell and Patrick Troughton years. He is currently working on a full-length biography of Malcolm Hulke, including his contributions to *Pathfinders in Space, The Avengers* and *Doctor Who*. His published work includes *Never Counted Out! The Story of Len Johnson, Manchester's Boxing Hero and Communist*; *'Up Then Brave Women!': Manchester's Radical Women, 1819 to 1918*; and *'For the sake of the women who are to* *come after': Manchester's Radical Women; 1914-194*5. He writes about history and about classic science fiction.

Trevor Knight stumbled into a career as a senior manager at Staffordshire and Aston Universities but has always wanted to be a writer. He has a lifelong love of 'classic' television, films and popular culture especially from the 1950s (though he is not *that* old) to the end of the 20th century after which it all went a bit blank, as well as music of various genres including film and TV scores. He lives in Worcestershire with his wife, son and an excitable Jack Russell.

Rodney Marshall is a former tutor at the Universities of Exeter and Plymouth. The son of prolific television and film script-writer Roger Marshall, he writes and edits guides to classic British and American television series. He is a co-host of the *ITC Entertained the World* podcast. He contributed chapters on *Callan*, railways, Harry Pottle, and *Danger Man* in *Swinging TV*. He lives in Suffolk, UK.

Mike Pegler is an occasional writer and blogger on subjects including TV, music, film, cooking, gardening, astronomy and the exploration of the natural world. In his spare time, he enjoys actively participating in the last four of these activities and also drawing. He has read and owns enough books and records to stock a library, is a country boy at heart and was probably a shepherd or a sailor in a past life. He contributed a chapter about the Establishment in *Swinging TV*.

Andrew Roberts is the author of *Idols of the Odeons: Post-war British film stardom*, published by the Manchester University Press in 2020. He is a film and television historian who vividly recalls viewing *Terry and June* and *Reginald Perrin* during his youth. His corner of Hampshire seemed less 'hilarious consequences' and more 'Inside No. 9', so he is grateful to both. The Medfords offered respite and Reggie Perrin showed him the delicate balance between comedy and tragedy.

Al Samujh is a co-host of the *ITC Entertained the World* podcasts and an occasional essayist, having written studies on both *Man in a Suitcase* and *Catweazle*. A lifelong cinephile, TV addict and researcher, you will find his name peppered amongst several volumes of film and television studies, sometimes as a complete surprise to him. He contributes to books and magazines on classic horror films and, back in the days of old technology, wrote Teletext notes on vintage television for a satellite TV company. He contributed a chapter about cars in *Swinging TV*.

Stu Sterling is a civil servant who escapes Whitehall mainly through archive TV, which is a passion that was passed to him by his dad. He believes that there is nothing better for keeping memories of lost loved ones alive than re-watching or reading those series and books that were a shared passion. He misses being able to start a quote from a series or book and it being finished for him, before it then moving into a full rehearsal of a much-loved TV script, much to the annoyance of all those around.

Cailin Thomas runs the popular and humorous *Sweeney Archive* Twitter feed and is a "major car buff", with a passion for restoring old classics.

SELECT BIBLIOGRAPHY

Archer, Simon and Stan Nicholls, *Gerry Anderson, The Authorised Biography* (Legend Books, 1996)

Auden, W. H, and Edward Mendelson, Edward (ed.), 'Letter to Lord Byron', *The Complete Works of W. H. Auden: Poems, Volume I* (Princeton: Princeton University Press, 2022)

Bertram, Anthony, *The House: A Machine for Living In; a Summary of the Art and Science of Homemaking Considered Functionally* (London: A. & C. Black Limited, 1935)

Bilbow, Marjorie, 'Meeting The Demands of an Exciting But Challenging Medium; People and their work – Leonard Rossiter', *The Stage*, 22nd August 1963

Bingham, A, '*An era of domesticity?' Histories of women and gender in interwar Britain*, (Cultural and Social History, Vol. 1, 2004)

Britton, Piers D and Simon J Barker, *Reading Between Designs: Visual Imagery and the Generation of Meanings in The Avengers, The Prisoner, and Doctor Who* (University of Texas Press, 2003)

Brotherstone, Stephen and Dave Lawrence, *Scarred for Life Volume One: The 1970s* (Lonely Water Books, 2017)

Bryden, Ronald, 'Heroic Acting in Gangsterland', *The Observer*, 13th April 1969

Chapman, Giles, *TV Cars: Star cars from the world of television* (2006, Haynes, 2011)

Christy, Desmond, 'Bromley – School for Wives', *The Guardian* 15th March 1984

Drake, Chris, *UFO and Space 1999* (Boxtree Limited, 1994)

Fairclough, Robert and Mike Kenwood, *Sweeney! The Official Companion* (Reynolds & Hearn, 2002)

Fane-Saunders, Kilmeny (ed), *Radio Times Guide to Science Fiction* (BBC Worldwide Ltd, 2001)

Fiddick, Peter, 'Happy Ever After on television', *The Guardian*, 15th August 1974

Fulton, Roger, *The Encyclopedia of TV Science Fiction,* New Edition (Boxtree Limited, 1997)

Garland, Patrick, *The Incomparable Rex: A Memoir of Rex Harrison in the 1980s* (London: Macmillan, 1998)

Gilliatt, Penelope, *Unholy fools; wits, comics, disturbers of the peace: film & theatre* (New York: Viking Press,1973)

Greig, Ramsden, 'June is Happy Feeding Comics', *The Aberdeen Evening Express*, 27th December 1961

Grossmith, George and Weedon, *The Diary of a Nobody* (London: Arrowsmith, 1892)

Hirsch, David and Robert E Wood, with Christopher Penfold *To Everything that Might Have Been: The Lost Universe of Space 1999* (Telos Publishing, 2022)

Howe, David J, Mark Stammers, Stephen James Walker, *Doctor Who: The Sixties* (Virgin Publishing Ltd, 1993)

Howe, David J, Mark Stammers, Stephen James Walker, *Doctor Who: The Seventies* (Virgin Publishing Ltd, 1994)

Howe, David J, Stephen James Walker, *Doctor Who: The Television Companion* (BBC Worldwide Ltd, 1999)

James, Clive, 'Wet Lips: Television', *The Observer* 19th September 1976

Knox, Paul L., *Better by Design? Architecture, Urban Planning, and the Good City* (Blacksburg VA: Virginia Tech Publishing, 2020)

La Riviere, Stephen, *Filmed in Supermarionation* (Network Distribution Ltd – new edition – 2014)

Lewis, Richard, *The Encyclopedia of Cult Children's TV* (Allison & Busby Ltd, 2001)

Marriott, Val, 'No ups and downs for Terry Scott – "a steady type of chap"', *The Leicester Chronicle*, 16th July 1976

Marshall, Judi, and Cooper, Cary L., Understanding Executive Stress (London: Palgrave Macmillan, 1978)

Marshall, Rodney, *Blake's 7, A critical guide to Series 1-4* (Out There Publications, 2015)

Masterman, C.F.G, *The Condition of England* (London: Methuen, 1960)

Medhurst, Andy, 'Terry and June' in *The Listener*, Vol. 118

Moore, Roger, *My Word is My Bond* (O'Mara, 2008)

Muir, John Kenneth, *A History and Critical Analysis of Blake's 7, the 1978-1981 British Television Space Adventure* (McFarland & Company, 2006)

Nation, Terry, *Survivors*, (Futura Publications Limited, 1976)

Newcomb, Horace (editor), *TV: The Critical View* (Oxford University Press, 1987)

Nobbs, David, *The Fall and Rise of Reginald Perrin* (London: Random House, 2013), e-book

Nobbs, David, *I Didn't Get Where I Am Today* (London: Penguin Random House, 2004)

O'Flaherty, Terrence, *Masterpiece Theatre, A Celebration of 25 Years of Outstanding Television* (KQED inc., 1996)

Quantik, David, *David Nobbs's Reginald Perrin: 'a stealth drama riding on the wheels of a sitcom'*, The Guardian, 10th August 2015

Rivière, Jean-François, *Voitures de Rêve: Des Séries Britanniques* (Yris, 2011)

Rogers, Dave, *The ITV Encyclopaedia of Adventure* (Boxtree Limited, 1988)

Rogers, Dave, *The Complete Avengers* (St. Martin's Press, 1989)

Rogers, Dave, *The Ultimate Avengers* (Boxtree, 1995)

Sandbrook, Dominic, *State of Emergency: The Way We Were: Britain, 1970-1974* (2010, Penguin, 2011)

Sandbrook, Dominic, *Seasons in the Sun: The Battle for Britain, 1974-1979* (2012, Penguin, 2013)

Sangster, Jim and Paul Condon, *TV Heaven* (HarperCollins, 2005)

Sellers, Robert, *Raising Laughter: How the Sitcom Kept Britain Smiling in the 70s* (The History Press, 2021)

Shearman, Robert and Toby Hadoke, *Running Through Corridors, Rob and Toby's Marathon Watch of Doctor Who, Volume 2: The 1970s* (Mad Norwegian Press, 2016)

Trewin, J. C., 'Semi-Detached' Belgrade, *Birmingham Daily Post*, 9th June 1962

Tudor, Andrew, 'Genre and Critical Methodology in *Movies and Methods - Volume One, An Anthology* by Bill Nichols (ed.) (Berkeley: University of California Press, 1976)

Turner, Alwyn W, *The Man who Invented the Daleks, The Strange Worlds of Terry Nation* (Aurum Press Limited, 2011)

Tynan, Kenneth, 'At The Theatre: Apathy', *The Observer*, 31st October 1954

Waller, Sally, *A Sixties Social Revolution? British Society 1959–1975* (Nelson Thornes, 2008)

Webster, Roger, 'Suburbia Inside Out' in *Expanding Suburbia: Reviewing Suburban Narratives* by R. Webster (ed.) (New York: Berghahn Books, 2001)

Wells, H, G., *The History of Mr. Polly* (London: Grosset and Dunlap, 1909)

Wyndham, John, *The Day of The Triffids* (Michael Joseph, 1951)

Young, Rob, *The Magic Box: Viewing Britain Through the Rectangular Window* (Faber & Faber, 2022)

NEW WAVES TV

1980s Britain & the television series

edited by Rodney Marshall

To be published in January 2024

Printed in Great Britain
by Amazon